Lecture Notes in Computer Science 15916

Founding Editors

Gerhard Goos
Juris Hartmanis

Editorial Board Members

The series Lecture Notes in Computer Science (LNCS), including its subseries Lecture Notes in Artificial Intelligence (LNAI) and Lecture Notes in Bioinformatics (LNBI), has established itself as a medium for the publication of new developments in computer science and information technology research, teaching, and education.

LNCS enjoys close cooperation with the computer science R & D community, the series counts many renowned academics among its volume editors and paper authors, and collaborates with prestigious societies. Its mission is to serve this international community by providing an invaluable service, mainly focused on the publication of conference and workshop proceedings and postproceedings. LNCS commenced publication in 1973.

Sharib Ali · David C. Hogg · Michelle Peckham
Editors

Medical Image Understanding and Analysis

29th Annual Conference, MIUA 2025
Leeds, UK, July 15–17, 2025
Proceedings, Part I

Springer

Editors
Sharib Ali ⓘ
University of Leeds
Leeds, UK

David C. Hogg ⓘ
University of Leeds
Leeds, UK

Michelle Peckham ⓘ
University of Leeds
Leeds, UK

ISSN 0302-9743   ISSN 1611-3349 (electronic)
Lecture Notes in Computer Science
ISBN 978-3-031-98687-1   ISBN 978-3-031-98688-8 (eBook)
https://doi.org/10.1007/978-3-031-98688-8

Preface

The 29th Conference on Medical Image Understanding and Analysis (MIUA 2025) was held at the University of Leeds, UK, during July 15–17, 2025. The MIUA 2025 proceedings feature presentations from the authors of all accepted papers. MIUA is a UK-based international conference for the communication of image processing and analysis research and its application to medical and biomedical imaging and analysis. This year's edition was co-chaired by Sharib Ali (Lecturer/researcher in Medical and Biomedical Image Analysis, University of Leeds), David Hogg (Professor of Artificial Intelligence, University of Leeds), and Michelle Peckham (Professor of Cell Biology, University of Leeds). The conference was organized with sponsorship received from Frontiers in Medical Technology (Gold), AI-Medical (Silver) and Springer (Best Paper Award). The conference proceedings were published in partnership with Springer. The diverse range of topics covered in these proceedings reflects the growth in the development and application of medical and biomedical imaging including surgical data science. The conference proceedings feature the most recent work in the fields of (1) Image synthesis and generative AI; (2) Image-guided diagnosis; (3) Image-guided intervention; (4) Medical image segmentation; (5) Retinal and vascular image analysis; and (6) Frontiers in Computational Pathology.

The number of submissions to MIUA 2025 continued the growth trend that begun with MIUA 2024. In total, 99 submissions were submitted to the Conference Management Toolkit (CMT), and after an initial quality check, the papers were sent out for the peer-review process completed by the Program Committee and 134 volunteer reviewers. To keep the quality of the reviews consistent with the previous editions of MIUA, the majority of the reviewers were invited from (i) a pool of previous MIUA conference reviewers, (ii) a call for reviewers form, and (iii) authors and co-authors of papers presented at the past and current MIUA conferences. All submissions were subject to double-blind review by at least two reviewers and meta-reviewed by at least one of the Program Committee members. Based on their recommendations, 54 papers were among early accept papers, 25 papers were among early rejected and 20 papers proceeded into the rebuttal stage. The final outcome of the review decisions results in a total of 67 full paper accepted (68%). Out of these, 45 papers had an oral presentation (67%) and 22 papers were presented as posters (33%). These papers comprise three volumes of Lecture Notes in Computer Science (LNCS) proceedings.

Submissions were received from authors at different institutes from 23 countries, including Australia (6), Austria (3), Denmark (3), Finland (1), Germany (5), India (10), Republic of Ireland (2), Mexico (4), Nepal (2), Netherlands (1), Norway (2), Pakistan (2), Poland (1), Portugal (1), Russia (1), Singapore (1), Spain (4), Switzerland (1), T'urkiye (2), the UK (36), the UAE (2), and the USA (5). We thank all members of the MIUA 2025 Organizing, Steering, Program, Publicity, Social Media, Special Session, Sponsorship, and Doctoral Community Committees. In particular, we sincerely thank all who contributed greatly to the success of MIUA 2025: the authors for submitting their work, the reviewers for insightful comments improving the quality of the proceedings, the sponsors for financial support, and all participants in this year's in-person MIUA conference.

We thank our keynote speakers Andrew King (School of Biomedical Engineering and Imaging Sciences, King's College London) and Susan Astley Theodossiadis (University of Manchester) for sharing their success, knowledge, and experiences. The conference also hosted a panel discussion on "Transforming Medical Imaging with AI: Challenges, Data & Infrastructure, Advancing Research, and Translating Innovations", chaired by Susan Astley Theodossiadis and Bogdan Matuszewski. Our thanks to the session chairs and all the other people who made this event possible.

July 2025

Sharib Ali
David C. Hogg
Michelle Peckham

Organization

General Chairs

Sharib Ali   University of Leeds, UK
David C. Hogg   University of Leeds, UK
Michelle Peckham   University of Leeds, UK

Program Chairs

Nashid Alam   Aberystwyth University, UK
Binod Bhattarai   University of Aberdeen, UK
Luisa Cutillo   University of Leeds, UK
Ping Lu   University of Leeds, UK
Bartlomiej Papiez   University of Oxford, UK
Arash Rabbani   University of Leeds, UK
Nishant Ravikumar   University of Leeds, UK
Duygu Sarikaya   University of Leeds, UK

Special Session Chairs

Derek Magee   University of Leeds, UK
Anh Nguyen   University of Liverpool, UK
Pietro Valdastri   University of Leeds, UK

Sponsor and Publicity Chairs

Owen A. Johnson   University of Leeds, UK
Gilberto Ochoa-Ruiz   Monterrey Institute of Technology and Higher
                          Education, Mexico
Mohammad Yaqub   Mohamed bin Zayed University of Artificial
                          Intelligence, UAE

Doctoral Community

Pedro Chavarrias	University of Leeds, UK
Edward Ellis	University of Leeds, UK
Francisco Lopez-Tiro	Monterrey Institute of Technology and Higher Education, Mexico
Raneem Toman	University of Leeds, UK

Proceeding Chairs

Toni Lassila	University of Leeds, UK
Christian Mata	Polytechnic University of Catalonia, Spain

Local Organising Committee

Pedro Chavarrias	University of Leeds, UK
Alison Whiteley	University of Leeds, UK

Reviewers

Abdul Karim Abbas
Bashayer Abdallah
Asfak Ali
Mansoor Ali
Mohsin Ali
Omar Al-Kadi
Anissa Alloula
Ahmed Alshenoudy
Mohammed Yusuf Ansari
Connor Atkins
Akoramurthy Balasubramaniam
Shashvat Bargale
Subrata Bhattacharjee
Binod Bhattarai
Zhiyan Bo
James Borgars

William Cancino
Jacob Carse
Volodymyr Chapman
Nilanjan Chattopadhyay
Veronika Cheplygina
Wing Keung Cheung
Omar Choudhry
Allison Clement
Rhys Compton
Timothy Cootes
Fredrik Dahl
Theo Dapamede
Noémie Debroux
Rocio del Amor
Nanyu Dong
Daniel Dorda

Ant Duru
Mohamed Elawady
Di Fan
Xinqi Fan
Umar Farooq
Jamil Fayyad
Jiling Feng
Mona Furukawa
Carles Garcia Cabrera
Guillaume Garret
Elham Ghelichkhan
Sushobhan Ghosh
Deep Gupta
Gourav Gupta
Gousia Habib
Palak Handa
Mohammad Mehedi Hassain
Mansoor Hayat
Angie Hernandez
Rahmat Heroza
Mohammad Mithun Hossain
Raza Imam
Mostafa Jahanifar
Bushra Jalil
Syed Javed
Muhammad Jawaid
Xi Jia
Benjamin Jin
Robert John
Dmitrii Kaplun
Tushar Kataria
Benjamin Keel
Ayse Keles
Charan Kodi
Adrian Krenzer
Lalit Kumar
Marie-Ange Lebre
Duway Lesmes Leon
Zhibin Liao
Derek Magee
Anish Mahishi
Stephen J. McKenna
Oliver Mills
Nandini Modi
Carmel Moran

Souradeep Mukhopadhyay
Muhammad Amin Nadim
Sabrina Nefoussi
Fnu Neha
Mark Nixon
Varun Ojha
Pedro Osorio
Alessandro Perelli
Michalis Pistos
Sandesh Pokhrel
Nakul Poudel
Pranav Poudel
Payel Pramanik
Muhammad Qadir
Mohammad Areeb Qazi
Lavdie Rada
Aimon Rahman
Mohammad Masudur Rahman
Kashif Rajpoot
Shan Raza
Zia Rehman
Samuel D. Relton
Dewinda Rumala
Bertram Sabrowsky-Hirsch
Shaheer Ullah Saeed
Nematollah Saeidi
Johannes Schuiki
Mehwish Shaikh
Mohd Faraz Shaikh
Fahad Shamshad
Bheeshm Sharma
Tahira Shehzadi
MohammadJavad Shokri
Zuzanna Skórniewska
Ikboljon Sobirov
Yang Sun
Arvapalli Susmitha
Maciej Szymkowski
Aashay Tinaikar
Raneem Toman
Emanuele Trucco
María del C. Valdés Hernández
Maria Vasconcelos
Irina Voiculescu
Juan Wachs

Contents – Part I

Image Synthesis and Generative Artificial Intelligence

Contents – Part II

Image-Guided Intervention

Contents – Part III

Medical Image Segmentation

Retinal and Vascular Image Analysis

Frontiers in Computational Pathology

Transductive Survival Ranking for Pan-Cancer Automatic Risk Stratification Using Whole Slide Images

Ethar Alzaid[1,2]([✉]) [iD] and Fayyaz Minhas[1] [iD]

[1] Tissue Image Analytics (TIA) Centre, Department of Computer Science,
University of Warwick, Coventry, UK
ethar.alzaid@warwick.ac.uk.com
[2] Department of Computer Science and Artificial Intelligence, University of Jeddah, Jeddah,
Kingdom of Saudi Arabia

Abstract. *Using histological whole slide images (WSIs), how can we stratify patients into meaningful risk groups by leveraging data from both patients with known survival times and event indicators and those without, while requiring no manual post-hoc thresholding of predicted risk scores?* Existing survival stratification methods in computational pathology train a supervised model on patients with known survival times and event indicators, then apply it to a test set to generate risk scores. These scores are typically thresholded, often at the median, to assign patients to high- or low-risk groups. Such inductive pipelines overlook the large pool of unlabelled patients even though number of cases with known survival times are typically limited and observed events are even rarer. As a result, existing methods often fail to uncover meaningful risk groups. In this work, we introduce the first Transductive Survival Ranking (TSR) model for WSIs, designed to leverage both labelled and unlabelled data for improved survival prediction. Given a dataset where only a subset of WSIs have associated survival time and event information, our approach (1) ranks patients by predicted survival times, (2) automatically discovers risk groups without requiring manual thresholding, and (3) transduces differential survival patterns from patients with observed events to those without events. We evaluate the proposed approach on multiple pan-cancer datasets, demonstrating that it achieves statistically significant risk sub-grouping in cases where classical approaches fail while producing high concordance indices. Unlike traditional survival models that rely solely on labelled data for training and manual cutoffs, this work leverages transductive learning to make data-driven, threshold-free risk stratification possible, offering a more reliable and data-efficient framework for survival analysis in computational pathology.

Keywords: Transductive learning · Survival Ranking · Risk Stratification · WSI

1 Introduction

Whole Slide Images (WSIs) are valuable sources of information in computational pathology, offering detailed insights into tissue morphology and disease characteristics [1]. Advancements in digital pathology have made the acquisition of WSIs more accessible.

S. Ali et al. (Eds.): MIUA 2025, LNCS 15916, pp. 3–15, 2026.
https://doi.org/10.1007/978-3-031-98688-8_1

However, a significant challenge for survival analysis lies in the scarcity of WSIs with survival outcome data. Additionally, even when survival data is available, it is frequently subject to high censoring rates [2]. Censoring occurs when the event of interest (e.g., death or relapse) has not occurred by the end of the study or is unobserved for some patients, complicating the analysis and potentially leading to biased estimates if not properly addressed.

While survival prediction models, including those based on numerical clinical data [3–7] and WSI-based approaches [8–11], are designed to handle censored data, they do not utilise unlabelled samples. Such samples may contain useful information that can aid in both ranking and stratification of the patient without being explicitly annotated with survival duration and outcomes. Additionally, risk stratification in survival analysis often depends on arbitrary thresholding techniques, such as setting the median risk score as the cutoff [12]. While such heuristic might provide a simple way to separate high- and low-risk groups, they are highly dataset-dependent and may not align with underlying pathobiological patterns that influence survival. This reliance on post-hoc thresholding can lead to insignificant group formation. A more meaningful solution would involve identifying risk groups through a principled method that reflects underlying survival patterns, rather than relying on heuristic thresholds.

These limitations highlight the need for a generalisable survival ranking framework that can scale across datasets and support automatic, threshold-free risk stratification. A key question arises: Can we leverage the abundance of unlabelled WSIs to enhance survival analysis and address these challenges? In this work, we propose a WSI-based Transductive Survival Ranking (TSR) model to address this question. Using Transductive learning, the model can:

1- Improve ranking performance by incorporating additional, unlabelled patient data to refine survival predictions.
2- Provide automatic risk stratification without relying on heuristic thresholding.
3- Transduce survival knowledge from patients with observed survival outcomes to those with censored outcomes to handle highly censored datasets.

To the best of our knowledge, this work is the first application of transductive learning for survival analysis using WSIs. Unlike traditional survival models that require manual or post-hoc thresholding, our method employs a fixed threshold of 0, ensuring a consistent and interpretable stratification criterion that generalises across diverse datasets. To achieve this, we incorporate a transductive loss [13] that leverages unlabelled test samples, maximising the margin between survival distributions for more reliable risk stratification. To validate our approach, we evaluate TSR on multiple WSI datasets from The Cancer Genome Atlas (TCGA) [14], demonstrating its ability to improve survival ranking and risk stratification across diverse cancer types.

2 Methods

The proposed pipeline aims to perform survival ranking and automatic risk stratification from WSIs. An overview of the pipeline is illustrated in Fig. 1. The model leverages both labelled and unlabelled WSI samples to improve ranking performance and facilitate automatic risk stratification. First, WSIs are processed to extract fixed-size slide

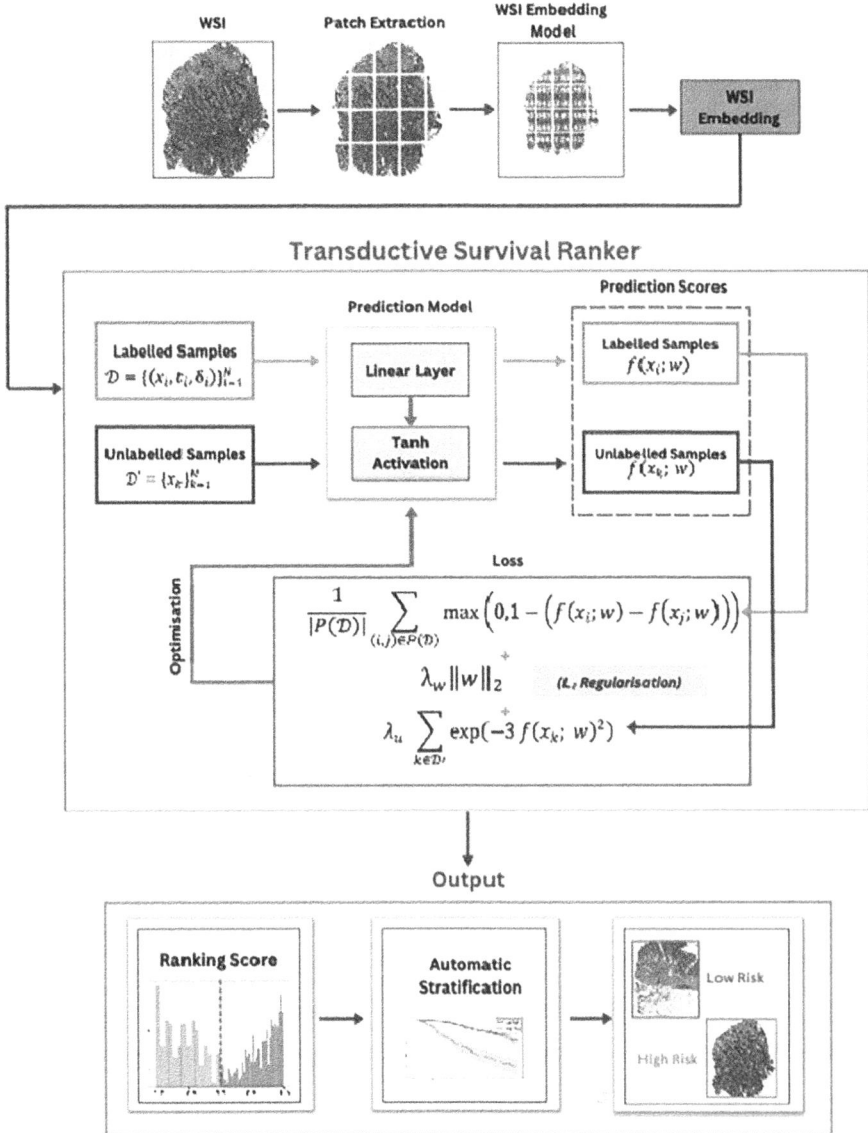

Fig. 1. Overview of the proposed Transductive Survival Ranking (TSR) model. WSIs are first processed using WSI-level feature extraction model to extract fixed-size slide embeddings. The prediction model takes both labelled and unlabelled WSI embeddings to generate prediction scores. The labelled predictions are used to optimise the model for ranking using ranking loss, while the unlabelled predictions are used in the transductive loss to enable automatic stratification. The output of the model is a ranking score used to rank samples and stratify them into high-risk and low-risk groups.

embeddings to capture high-dimensional histopathological data. These embeddings are

then fed into TSR Model, which optimises a ranking function using ranking and transductive losses, allowing the model to leverage both labelled and unlabelled samples to
enhance risk separation. The model generates a ranking score, and patients are stratified
into high- and low-risk groups based on a fixed threshold of 0, ensuring consistent and
interpretable stratification.

2.1 WSI Encoding

Traditionally, WSI analysis has been performed using patch-based methods, where large
WSIs are segmented into smaller regions for feature extraction in order to overcome
memory constraints associated with processing entire slides at once [9, 10, 15]. However,
an emerging alternative focuses on single-slide representations, which encode the entire
WSI into a compact and informative embedding vector. These representations facilitate
efficient downstream analysis while significantly reducing computational complexity
[16]. In this work, we employed TITAN foundation model [17] (vision-only pretrained)
to encode WSIs into fixed-size 768-dimensional embedding vectors. These embeddings
serve as the input features for the survival ranking and risk stratification model. However,
in principle, any other approach for WSI embedding can be used.

2.2 Survival Ranking Preliminaries

Consider a labelled dataset $\mathcal{D} = \{(x_i, t_i, \delta_i)\}_{i=1}^{N}$ of N samples, where each sample i
consists of a feature vector $x_i \in \mathbb{R}^d$ of d features or covariates from a WSI embeddings.
The observed time t_i denotes either the time of event occurrence or the last follow-up if
the event has not yet occurred. The censoring indicator δ_i is defined as $\delta_i = 1$ if the event
is observed at time t_i, and $\delta_i = 0$ if the event is censored, meaning it was not observed by
t_i. In addition, assume we have a set of unlabelled samples $\mathcal{D}' = \{x_k\}_{k=1}^{M}$ with samples
containing WSI embeddings only without true survival times or event indicators. The
objective of survival analysis is to learn a ranking function $f(x; w)$ with trainable weights
or parameters w that maps each feature vector x to a prediction score.

In this work, we use a simple linear model with a hyperbolic tangent activation,
$f(x; w) = tanh(w^T x)$ with an optional bias term. While more complex neural architectures can be used in principle, we constrain the output using a tanh activation to
ensure that prediction scores lie within the range $[-1, +1]$. As explained in the following section, this bounded output range plays a crucial role in our transductive prediction
framework by encouraging confident risk group assignments for unlabelled patients.

2.3 Transductive Prediction

The TSR model used in this work is built on the concept of transductive learning [13]
and was originally introduced in our previous work [18]. This form of transductive
training has been shown to enhance model generalisation [19, 20]. The model takes in
a dataset with two sets of samples, labelled and unlabelled $(\mathcal{D}, \mathcal{D}')$ to rank and stratify
the unlabelled set. Unlike conventional survival models that rely solely on labelled data,
TSR incorporates unlabelled samples during training via a transductive loss term. This

term penalises prediction scores that are close to zero, effectively pushing unlabelled predictions away from the stratification decision boundary. Similar to how a Support Vector Machine (SVM) [21] maximises the margin between classes, TSR encourages the decision function $f(x; w) = 0$ to pass through regions of low data density. This results in a clearer separation between risk groups, enabling more robust and automatic stratification.

TSR loss learning objective is formulated as follows:

$$\mathcal{L}(w; \mathcal{D}, \mathcal{D}') = \lambda_w \|w\|_2 + \frac{1}{|P(\mathcal{D})|} \sum_{(i,j) \in P(\mathcal{D})} \max\left(0, 1 - \left(f(x_i; w) - f(x_j; w)\right)\right) \\ + \lambda_u \sum_{k \in \mathcal{D}'} \exp\left(-3f(x_k; w)^2\right) \tag{1}$$

The first term represents L_2 (Ridge) [22] regularisation, with λ_w as a hyperparameter controlling its strength. This regularisation ensures that small variations in input covariates do not lead to large fluctuations in the prediction scores to improve the model's ability to generalise to unseen test samples especially in the light of the fact that WSI embeddings can be very high dimensional while the amount of available data can be small. The second term corresponds to the survival ranking loss, computed using a pairwise ranking loss across all comparable labelled pairs $P(\mathcal{D}) = \{(i,j) | t_i > t_j, \delta_j = 1, and i, j = 1, \ldots, N\}$ averaged over the labelled set. This term enforces the correct ranking of survival times based on observed outcomes [23]. The third term is the transductive loss, where λ_u controls the strength of the penalty applied to predictions close to zero. This discourages the model from producing scores near zero and extends the margin between risk groups. As a result, patient stratification is achieved automatically with a threshold of zero without the need for additional post-processing. This threshold is fixed and applied consistently across all datasets, regardless of their WSI embedding distribution. To ensure that this transductive mechanism functions as intended, a bounded activation function such as tanh is required to constrain the output scores and make the margin-based penalty effective and stable.

2.4 Evaluation Datasets

We conducted experiments on the proposed framework using WSI stained with haematoxylin and Eosin (H&E) from TCGA, including five distinct cancer types: Breast Carcinoma (BRCA), Kidney Renal Colorectal Adenocarcinoma (COAD), Clear Cell Carcinoma (KIRC), Liver Hepatocellular Carcinoma (LIHC), and Lung Adenocarcinoma (LUAD), with an endpoint of Disease Specific Survival (DSS). The WSIs in these subsets exhibit substantial variability in tissue morphology, tumour microenvironment, and staining artifacts, reflecting the heterogeneity inherent in real-world pathology and are collected across multiple centres [14]. For example, BRCA slides contain dense glandular structures [24], KIRC slides display clear cytoplasm and distinct nuclei [25], while COAD WSIs often present irregular gland formation. This variability poses a challenge for survival prediction models, as different cancer types require distinct morphological cues for prognostication. However, it also serves as a rigorous testbed to assess the robustness and generalisability of the proposed automatic risk stratification pipeline in handling the heterogeneity present in WSIs across multiple cancer types.

2.5 Performance Evaluation

We performed a out of sample bootstrap analysis with 1,000 iterations to evaluate the model's ranking performance. In each iteration, we resampled the dataset with replacement, trained the model on the resampled data, and tested it on out-of-sample data. Concordance Index (c-index) [26] was used as the primary metric, measuring the model's ability to correctly rank survival times. Given two samples (x_i, t_i) and (x_j, t_j) where $t_i > t_j$, the c-index computes the proportion of correctly ranked pairs, i.e., $f(x_i) > f(x_j)$. A c-index of 1.0 indicates perfect ranking, while 0.5 suggests random performance.

We assessed the statistical significance of the stratification using the log-rank test [27] to compute the p-value, measuring how distinct the two risk groups are. Stratification was based on a fixed threshold of 0, assigning samples with $f(x) \leq 0$ to the high-risk group and $f(x) > 0$ to the low-risk group. A lower p-value indicates stronger evidence that the model effectively differentiates risk groups. To summarise significance results across bootstrap runs, we computed a combined p-value by taking the median of individual p-values, multiplied by 2 [28]. Kaplan-Meier (KM) curves [29] were used to visualise differences in survival probabilities over time. Importantly, both the concordance index and log-rank p-values are computed solely on the unlabelled set, without using any information from labelled patients during evaluation.

3 Results

3.1 Ranking and Stratification Performance

We evaluated the performance of the proposed model across multiple WSI cancer subsets. The mean c-index, standard deviation, and combined p-value for risk stratification across cancer subsets are reported in Table 1. Existing survival models are inductive and rely on post-hoc thresholding for stratification. However, to ensure that the model's ranking performance is in line with established methods, we compared it against CoxPH [3] model, using the median of training predictions as the stratification threshold which is a common practice in survival analysis [30].

While WSI embeddings reduce the dimensionality of the data, the model effectively leverages these representations to capture meaningful prognostic signals that are indicative of patients' risk. To visually highlight the effect of the transductive loss, Fig. 2 (A) presents the distribution of the model's predicted scores. A low-density region is notable around 0, forming an optimal cutoff point for risk stratification. Across all subsets, the combined p-values for risk stratification are significant ($p < 0.05$), while in most cases the classical approach CoxPH with the median cutoff failed to obtain a statistically significant risk stratification. This statistical significance proves the effectiveness of the automatic threshold of 0 in distinguishing high- and low-risk groups. It is important to note that this significant stratification is still observed even when the mean c-index is relatively low, as seen in LUAD subset. The strength of this automatic stratification is further evident in the KM curves in Fig. 2 (B), where the survival curves of the low- and high-risk groups show clear separation. In contrast, Fig. 2 (C) shows CoxPH collapsing risk groups in a single trajectory (as seen with BRCA and LIHC), or overlapping curves with low-risk group eventually getting lower survival time.

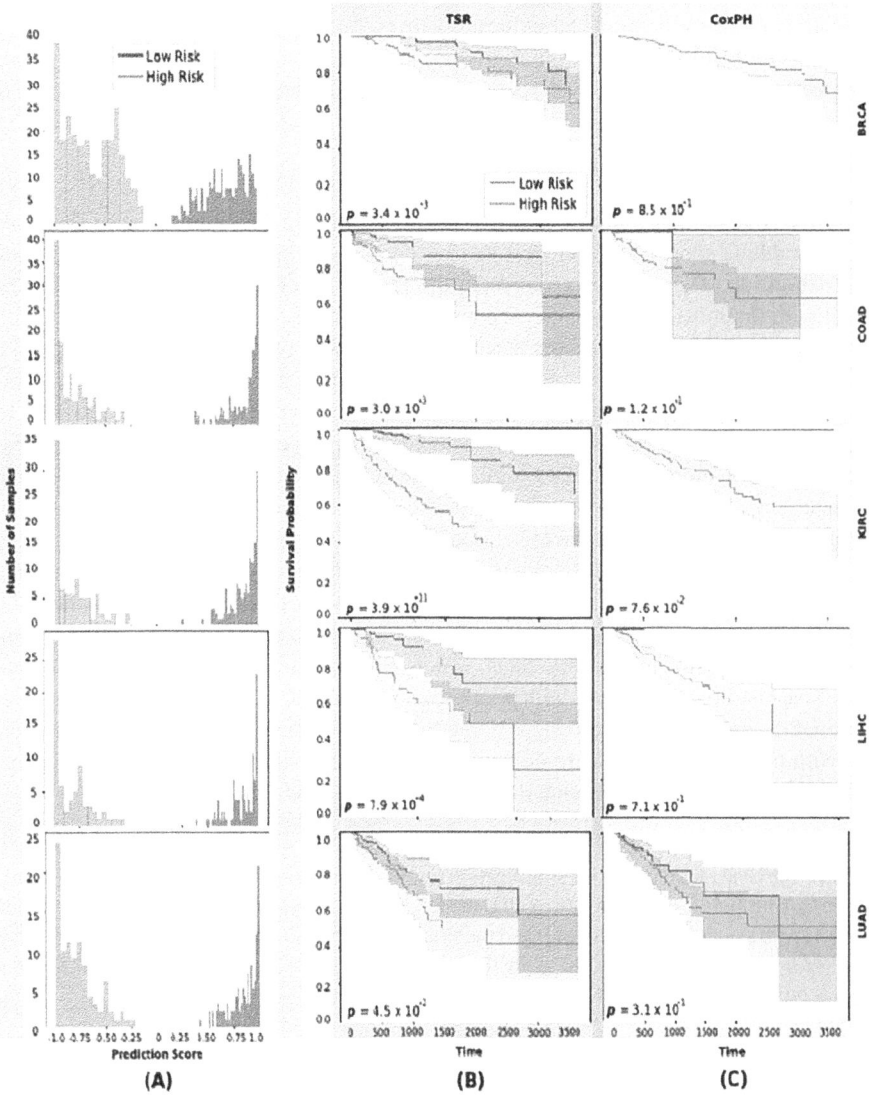

Fig. 2. Survival ranking and risk stratification results for all subsets. (A) Distribution of prediction scores where clear separation of the two risk groups can be observed. Kaplan Meier Curves with p-values for low and high-risk groups after the risk stratification (B) using TSR and (C) using CoxPH.

For ranking performance, the proposed model consistently outperforms CoxPH across all subsets. The highest performance was for KIRC subset with a c-index of 0.78, demonstrating the model's strong predictive ability despite the compressed feature space. The decline in both ranking and stratification performance for CoxPH can be attributed to its assumption of a linear relationship, which may not hold for the complex, high-dimensional features encoded in WSI embeddings.

While other stratification techniques rely on post-processing and do not consistently produce significant group separation, the proposed method eliminates the need for this extra step and achieves statistically significant stratification across all datasets.

3.2 Ranking Scores as Subgroup Identifiers

To further analyse the model's predictions, we examined the patients with the most extreme ranking scores, those closest to 1 in the low-risk group and closest to -1 in the high-risk group. These patients represent the most confidently classified cases by the model with the most distinct survival characteristics of each risk subgroup. WSIs with the highest and lowest risk scores across all five cancer types are shown in Fig. 3. If we take COAD as an example, we observed that the lowest risk WSI samples are predominantly colon polyp (benign formation in the colon that can potentially progress to malignant tumour in a later stage [31]). The nuclei in these samples are uniformly distributed, with an elongated morphology. In contrast, high-risk samples display invasive characteristics, including disorganised nuclear architecture, irregular gland formation [32] and the presence of prominent heterochromatin, visible as white nuclear inclusions [33]. All these visual cues are characteristics of high-grade colon adenocarcinoma, hence the patient is at higher risk and is predicted correctly by the model. For instance, the first COAD sample shown in Fig. 3 has a very low prediction score of -0.99 and an observed survival time of just 496 days, which supports the model's ability to associate aggressive histological features with poor prognosis. In BRCA, high-risk samples exhibit prominent necrotic regions known as comedonecrosis [34], which is commonly associated with high-grade ductal carcinoma. This feature is visually identifiable in WSIs as central areas of necrosis surrounded by dense tumour cells.

Table 1. Survival ranking and risk stratification results for all subsets for both the proposed model and the Cox Proportional Hazards (Cox PH) model. Metrics include the mean Concordance Index (c-index) with standard deviation (Std) and the stratification p-value. Proposed model stratification threshold is fixed to 0 in all subsets, while the threshold used for CoxPH is the median of training samples predictions computed for each subset.

Cancer Type	Proposed Model		CoxPH	
	c-index (Mean ± Std)	p-value	c-index (Mean ± Std)	p-value
BRCA	**0.75 ± 0.04**	**6.4 × 10–4**	0.71 ± 0.05	0.9
COAD	**0.68 ± 0.05**	**1.9 × 10⁻³**	0.67 ± 0.05	5.0×10^{-2}
KIRC	**0.78 ± 0.04**	**2.7 × 10⁻⁹**	0.69 ± 0.03	0.1
LIHC	**0.70 ± 0.04**	**1.2 × 10⁻²**	0.66 ± 0.04	0.3
LUAD	**0.60 ± 0.05**	**5.0 × 10⁻²**	0.57 ± 0.04	0.6

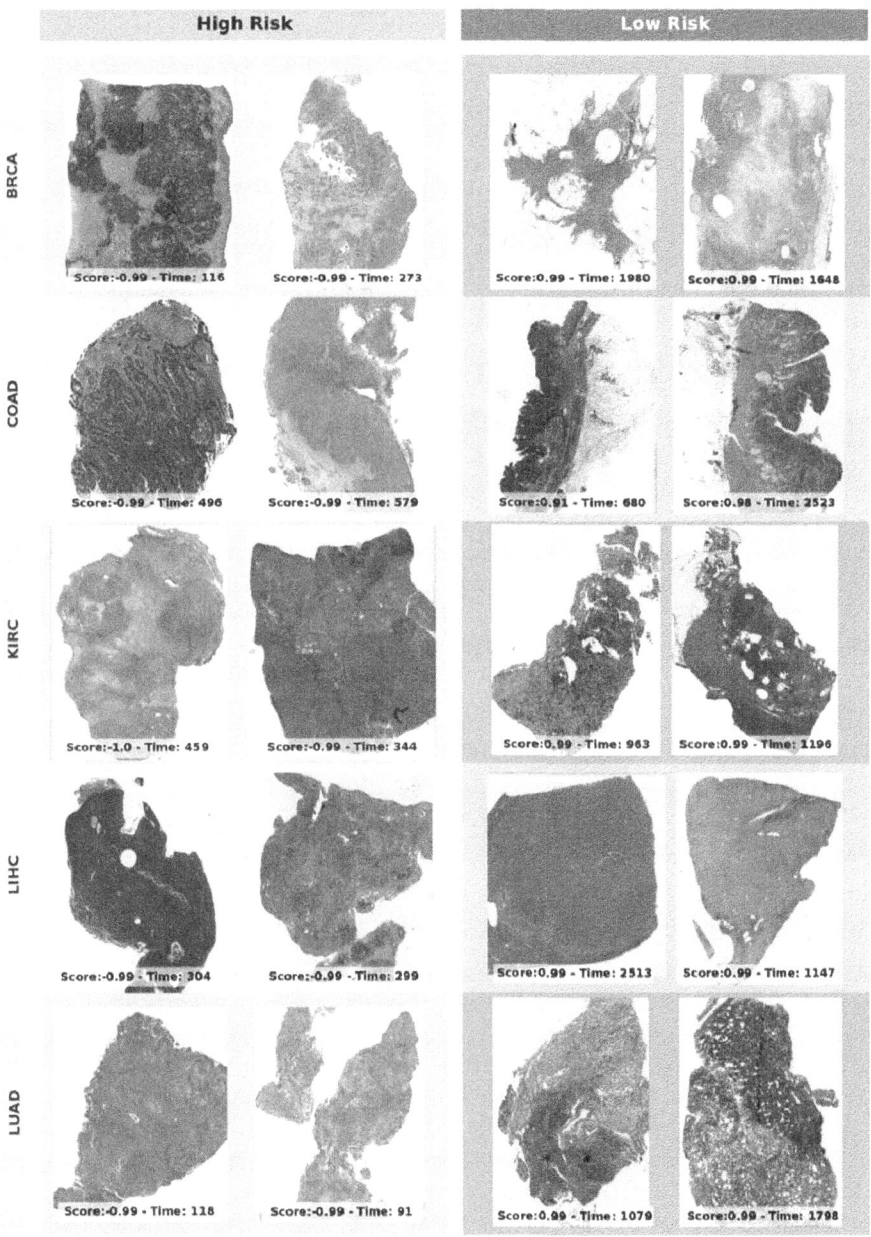

Fig. 3. Highest and lowest risk WSI predicted by the model for all cancer types. Each sample is annotated with the predicted score (negative scores are high risk, positive scores are low risk) and the true survival time.

3.3 Ablation Study

We compared the TSR model against a variant trained without the transductive loss (baseline model) to examine the specific impact this term has on both survival ranking and automatic risk stratification. The mean c-index, standard deviation, and combined p-value for risk stratification across cancer subsets are reported in Table 2.

The baseline model uses the median of the training set as a threshold for risk stratification. However, this heuristic approach only yields meaningful group separation when the underlying ranking is already strong. In contrast, TSR consistently achieved statistically significant stratification across all cancer subsets using a fixed threshold of zero. This improvement is attributed to the use of unlabelled samples during training, which guided the model to learn a decision boundary that better reflects the underlying data distribution. As a result, even in challenging cases such as COAD and LUAD where the baseline model failed or produced weak stratification, TSR maintained robust group separation with lower p-values.

Table 2. Survival ranking and risk stratification results for all subsets for both the proposed model (TSR) and the same model without transductive loss (Baseline Model). Metrics include the mean Concordance Index (c-index) with standard deviation (Std) and the stratification p-value. Proposed model stratification threshold is fixed to 0 in all subsets, while the threshold used for the model without transductive loss is the median of training samples predictions computed for each subset.

Cancer Type	TSR		Baseline Model	
	c-index (Mean ± Std)	p-value	c-index (Mean ± Std)	p-value
BRCA	**0.75 ± 0.04**	**6.4 × 10–4**	0.74 ± 0.04	6.1×10^{-3}
COAD	**0.68 ± 0.05**	**1.9 × 10^{-3}**	0.66 ± 0.05	0.1
KIRC	**0.78 ± 0.04**	**2.7 × 10^{-9}**	0.77 ± 0.03	8.0×10^{-6}
LIHC	0.72 ± 0.04	**0.8 × 10^{-3}**	0.72 ± 0.04	3.0×10^{-2}
LUAD	**0.60 ± 0.05**	**5.0 × 10^{-2}**	0.57 ± 0.04	0.6

In terms of ranking performance, TSR showed either matching or better performance across all subsets. Among the evaluated cancer types, LUAD remains one of the most challenging for survival prediction [35]. TSR achieved significant stratification with a c-index of 0.60, compared to 0.57 for the baseline model with no significant grouping. While the numerical difference in c-index may appear small and stratification significance is marginal ($p \approx 0.05$), it is noteworthy given the difficulty of the task and the limited discriminative cues available in the WSIs.

4 Discussions

This study introduced a WSI-based transductive learning approach for survival ranking to facilitate automatic stratification of cancer patients into risk groups without post-processing. It leverages unlabelled samples in the training process to enable stratification with a fixed threshold of 0. The method was evaluated on WSI of five cancer datasets from TCGA and showed significant stratification of patients based on predicted survival scores.

Beyond methodological advancements, the proposed approach has potential implications for clinical decision-making. By providing an automated and interpretable risk stratification method, it could assist oncologists in identifying high-risk patients more effectively, potentially guiding personalised treatment strategies. Unlike conventional risk stratification approaches that require manual cutoff selection, this method establishes a data-driven threshold, improving consistency and reliability in patient classification.

WSIs are routinely acquired and widely available, however, relying solely on annotated slides to train high-performing models places a significant burden on expert pathologists, whose time and availability are limited within the field. This approach addresses this limitation by leveraging unlabelled WSIs during training, reducing dependence on exhaustive manual annotations while still achieving robust survival ranking and reliable risk stratification.

While the proposed method demonstrates strong performance in survival ranking and automatic risk stratification, there remain opportunities for further improvement. The current model uses a simple neural architecture with tanh activation, which promotes interpretability and efficiency, but more complex architectures [36] may better capture non-linear patterns in WSI embeddings. Additionally, although the method currently uses a pretrained encoder, it can be extended to support end-to-end training, an area we are actively exploring to improve adaptability and representation learning.

Acknowledgments. EA is supported by the Saudi Cultural Bureau in London, UK. The authors acknowledge support from the Tissue Image Analysis Centre at the University of Warwick, Coventry, UK.

Disclosure of Interests. EA and FM have no competing interests to declare that are relevant to the content of this article.

References

1. Kumar, N., Gupta, R., Gupta, S.: Whole slide imaging (WSI) in pathology: current perspectives and future directions. J. Digit. Imaging **33**(4), 1034 (2020). https://doi.org/10.1007/s10278-020-00351-z
2. Yu, M., Zhao, W., Zhou, Y., Wu, C.: Robust online detection on highly censored data using a semi-parametric EWMA chart. J. Stat. Comput. Simul. **93**(9), 1403–1419 (2023). https://doi.org/10.1080/00949655.2022.2139379
3. Cox, D.R.: Regression models and life-tables. J. R. Stat. Soc. Ser. B Methodol. **34**(2), 187–202 (1972). https://doi.org/10.1111/j.2517-6161.1972.tb00899.x
4. Katzman, J.L., Shaham, U., Cloninger, A., Bates, J., Jiang, T., Kluger, Y.: DeepSurv: personalized treatment recommender system using a Cox proportional hazards deep neural network. BMC Med. Res. Methodol. **18**(1), 24 (2018). https://doi.org/10.1186/s12874-018-0482-1
5. Chen, Y., Jia, Z., Mercola, D., Xie, X.: A gradient boosting algorithm for survival analysis via direct optimization of concordance index. Comput. Math. Methods Med. **2013**, e873595 (2013). https://doi.org/10.1155/2013/873595

6. Pickett, K.L., Suresh, K., Campbell, K.R., Davis, S., Juarez-Colunga, E.: Random survival forests for dynamic predictions of a time-to-event outcome using a longitudinal biomarker. BMC Med. Res. Methodol. **21**(1), 216 (2021). https://doi.org/10.1186/s12874-021-01375-x

7. Ching, T., Zhu, X., Garmire, L.X.: Cox-nnet: An artificial neural network method for prognosis prediction of high-throughput omics data. PLOS Comput. Biol. **14**(4), e1006076 (2018). https://doi.org/10.1371/journal.pcbi.1006076

8. Zhu, X., Yao, J., Zhu, F., Huang, J.: WSISA: making survival prediction from whole slide histopathological images. In: 2017 IEEE Conference on Computer Vision and Pattern Recognition (CVPR) , pp. 6855–6863. IEEE, Honolulu (2017). https://doi.org/10.1109/CVPR.2017.725

9. Wang, Z., et al.: Dual-stream multi-dependency graph neural network enables precise cancer survival analysis. Med. Image Anal. **97**, 103252 (2024). https://doi.org/10.1016/j.media.2024.103252

10. Yan, R., Lv, Z., Yang, Z., Lin, S., Zheng, C., Zhang, F.: Sparse and hierarchical transformer for survival analysis on whole slide images. IEEE J. Biomed. Health Inform. **28**(1), 7–18 (2024)

11. Wang, Z., et al.: Surformer: an interpretable pattern-perceptive survival transformer for cancer survival prediction from histopathology whole slide images. Comput. Methods Programs Biomed. **241**, 107733 (2023). https://doi.org/10.1016/j.cmpb.2023.107733

12. Chen, H.-C., Kodell, R.L., Cheng, K.F., Chen, J.J.: Assessment of performance of survival prediction models for cancer prognosis. BMC Med. Res. Methodol. **12**(1), 102 (2012). https://doi.org/10.1186/1471-2288-12-102

13. Collobert, R., Sinz, F., Weston, J., Bottou, L.: Large scale transductive SVMs. J. Mach. Learn. Res. **7**(62), 1687–1712 (2006)

14. Liu, J., et al.: An integrated TCGA pan-cancer clinical data resource to drive high-quality survival outcome analytics. Cell **173**(2), 400-416.e11 (2018). https://doi.org/10.1016/j.cell.2018.02.052

15. Tang, Z., et al.: Explainable survival analysis with uncertainty using convolution-involved vision transformer. Comput. Med. Imaging Graph. **110**, 102302 (2023). https://doi.org/10.1016/j.compmedimag.2023.102302

16. Shaikovski, G., et al.: PRISM: a multi-modal generative foundation model for slide-level histopathology (2024). arXiv: arXiv:2405.10254. https://doi.org/10.48550/arXiv.2405.10254

17. Ding, T., et al.: Multimodal whole slide foundation model for pathology (2024). arXiv: arXiv:2411.19666. https://doi.org/10.48550/arXiv.2411.19666

18. Alzaid, E., Dawood, M., Minhas, F.: A transductive approach to survival ranking for cancer risk stratification. In: Proceedings of the 18th Machine Learning in Computational Biology meeting, pp. 101–109. PMLR (2024). https://proceedings.mlr.press/v240/alzaid24a.html. Accessed 27 Mar 2024

19. Huang, J.: Transductive transfer learning for visual recognition (2023), https://doi.org/10.32657/10356/164573

20. Shu, L., Latecki, L.J.: Transductive domain adaptation with affinity learning. In: Proceedings of the 24th ACM International on Conference on Information and Knowledge Management, CIKM '15, pp. 1903–1906. Association for Computing Machinery, New York (2015). https://doi.org/10.1145/2806416.2806643

21. Vapnik, V.N.: The vicinal risk minimization principle and the SVMs. In: Vapnik, V.N. (ed.) The Nature of Statistical Learning Theory. Statistics for Engineering and Information Science, pp. 267–290. Springer, New York (2000). https://doi.org/10.1007/978-1-4757-3264-1_9

22. Ng, A.Y.: Feature selection, L1 vs. L2 regularization, and rotational invariance. In: Proceedings of the Twenty-First International Conference on Machine Learning, ICML '04 , p. 78. Association for Computing Machinery, New York (2004). https://doi.org/10.1145/1015330.1015435

23. Minhas, F., Toss, M.S., ul Wahab, N., Rakha, E., Rajpoot, N.M.: L1-regularized neural ranking for risk stratification and its application to prediction of time to distant metastasis in luminal node negative chemotherapy naïve breast cancer patients. In: Kamp, M., et al. (eds.) Machine Learning and Principles and Practice of Knowledge Discovery in Databases, pp. 390–400. Springer, Cham (2021)

24. Makki, J.: Diversity of breast carcinoma: histological subtypes and clinical relevance. Clin. Med. Insights Pathol. **8**, 23 (2015). https://doi.org/10.4137/CPath.S31563

25. Sanchez, D.J., Simon, M.C.: Genetic and metabolic hallmarks of clear cell renal cell carcinoma. Biochim. Biophys. Acta Rev. Cancer **1870**(1), 23 (2018). https://doi.org/10.1016/j.bbcan.2018.06.003

26. Harrell, F.E., Lee, K.L., Califf, R.M., Pryor, D.B., Rosati, R.A.: Regression modelling strategies for improved prognostic prediction. Stat. Med. **3**(2), 143–152 (1984). https://doi.org/10.1002/sim.4780030207

27. Bland, J.M., Altman, D.G.: The logrank test. BMJ **328**(7447), 1073 (2004). https://doi.org/10.1136/bmj.328.7447.1073

28. DiCiccio, C.J., DiCiccio, T.J., Romano, J.P.: Exact tests via multiple data splitting. Stat. Probab. Lett. **166**, 108865 (2020). https://doi.org/10.1016/j.spl.2020.108865

29. Kaplan, E.L., Meier, P.: Nonparametric estimation from incomplete observations. J. Am. Stat. Assoc. **53**(282), 457–481 (1958). https://doi.org/10.1080/01621459.1958.10501452

30. Chen, H.-C., Kodell, R.L., Cheng, K.F., Chen, J.J.: Assessment of performance of survival prediction models for cancer prognosis. BMC Med. Res. Methodol. **12**, 102 (2012). https://doi.org/10.1186/1471-2288-12-102

31. Meseeha, M., Attia, M.: Colon polyps. In: StatPearls. StatPearls Publishing, Treasure Island (2025). http://www.ncbi.nlm.nih.gov/books/NBK430761/. Accessed 26 Mar 2025

32. Adenocarcinoma. https://www.pathologyoutlines.com/topic/colontumoradenocarcinoma.html. Accessed 26 Mar 2025

33. Bell, O., Burton, A., Dean, C., Gasser, S.M., Torres-Padilla, M.-E.: Heterochromatin definition and function. Nat. Rev. Mol. Cell Biol. **24**(10), 691–694 (2023). https://doi.org/10.1038/s41580-023-00599-7

34. Yagata, H., et al.: Comedonecrosis is an unfavorable marker in node-negative invasive breast carcinoma. Pathol. Int. **53**(8), 501–506 (2003). https://doi.org/10.1046/j.1440-1827.2003.01514.x

35. Wen, Z., et al.: Risk factors analysis and survival prediction model establishment of patients with lung adenocarcinoma based on different pyroptosis-related gene subtypes. Eur. J. Med. Res. **28**, 601 (2023). https://doi.org/10.1186/s40001-023-01581-x

36. Wiegrebe, S., Kopper, P., Sonabend, R., Bischl, B., Bender, A.: Deep learning for survival analysis: a review. Artif. Intell. Rev. **57**(3), 65 (2024). https://doi.org/10.1007/s10462-023-10681-3

Benchmarking Histopathology Foundation Models in a Multi-center Dataset for Skin Cancer Subtyping

Pablo Meseguer[1]([✉])[iD], Rocío del Amor[1,2][iD], and Valery Naranjo[1,2][iD]

[1] Universitat Politècnica de València (UPV), Valencia, Spain
pabmees@upv.es
[2] Artikode Intelligence S.L., Valencia, Spain

Abstract. Pretraining on large-scale, in-domain datasets grants histopathology foundation models (FM) the ability to learn task-agnostic data representations, enhancing transfer learning on downstream tasks. In computational pathology, automated whole slide image analysis requires multiple instance learning (MIL) frameworks due to the gigapixel scale of the slides. The diversity among histopathology FMs has highlighted the need to design real-world challenges for evaluating their effectiveness. To bridge this gap, our work presents a novel benchmark for evaluating histopathology FMs as patch-level feature extractors within a MIL classification framework. For that purpose, we leverage the AI4SkIN dataset, a multi-center cohort encompassing slides with challenging cutaneous spindle cell neoplasm subtypes. We also define the Foundation Model - Silhouette Index (FM-SI), a novel metric to measure model consistency against distribution shifts. Our experimentation shows that extracting less biased features enhances classification performance, especially in similarity-based MIL classifiers.

Keywords: Skin cancer subtyping · histopathology foundation models · multiple instance learning · distribution shifts

1 Introduction

Computational pathology (CPath) has recently experienced an overwhelming transformation due to foundation model (FM) development. The emergence of self-supervised pretraining strategies and high-capacity neural networks has permitted training general-purpose models with enhanced representation learning [4,11]. These breakthroughs in artificial intelligence, coupled with the availability of multiple large-scale datasets of histopathological imaging, have driven the development of a remarkable collection of state-of-the-art histopathology FMs. These models promise to effectively tackle diverse downstream CPath tasks ranging from visual applications such as patch-level classification to multi-modal challenges like tissue captioning.

Supplementary Information The online version contains supplementary material available at https://doi.org/10.1007/978-3-031-98688-8_2.

Histopathology FMs are characterized through a combination of the pretraining paradigm, the assembled dataset, and the model architecture. The need for massive datasets to train large models has turned the focus to less restrictive forms of supervision. In particular, we differentiate between vision-only self-supervised strategies based on masked image modeling [11] and vision-language supervision [12] to learn visual features from text supervision. Although each model uses slightly different configurations for model scale, vision transformers (ViT) [4] have emerged as the most popular choice for model architecture. Histopathology FMs primarily differ in the size, diversity, and quality of their pretraining corpora, which collection is conditioned by the pretraining strategy. While self-supervised pretraining relies on millions of patches extracted from massive collections of slides, vision-language supervision requires histopathology images paired with their textual description.

Automated whole slide imaging (WSI) analysis is the most promising challenge in CPath, as it mimics the diagnostic process of pathologists. Specialized scanners digitize tissue samples into WSI, enabling their incorporation into computer vision applications. However, the gigapixel scale of the slides makes them unmanageable by current hardware and leads to the incorporation of multiple instance learning (MIL) paradigms, a particular form of weakly-supervised learning. In MIL paradigms for CPath, a bag (slide) comprises multiple instances (patches), and the model aims to predict the bag-level label.

The diversity among pretraining strategies and evaluated downstream tasks has resulted in a heterogeneous comparison of histopathology FMs. Despite initial efforts on benchmarking, authors in [1] solely focused on self-supervised models and relied on single-center cohorts, which hinders insights about model consistency when facing distribution shifts. To solve this gap, this work comprehensively evaluates histopathology FMs pretrained under different forms of supervision in a skin cancer subtyping task. In particular, we refer to the AI4SkIN dataset [3], which encompasses WSIs of six cutaneous spindle cell (CSC) neoplasms, to evaluate the downstream performance in a MIL-based slide-level classification task. Additionally, we present the Foundation Model - Silhouette Index (FM-SI) to measure model robustness against scanner shifts and how it can limit the proficiency of the models in real-world scenarios. Overall, the proposed benchmark provides a robust assessment of model generalization and reliability in a challenging clinical task. The main contributions of our work can be summarized as follows:

- We conduct a comprehensive evaluation of histopathology foundation models, benchmarking their performance on a challenging, multi-center whole slide image dataset.
- We assess the effectiveness of each foundation model using two distinct MIL strategies, offering insights into their adaptability performance.
- We introduce the FM-SI metric to quantify the center-related information leakage in the extracted feature representations extracted, enabling the assessment of model consistency against distribution shifts.

2   Methodology

This section includes a description of the methodology used for the evaluation of histopathology FMs including the problem formulation, a description of the models and details on the MIL settings for slide classification. A graphical framework is provided in Fig. 1.

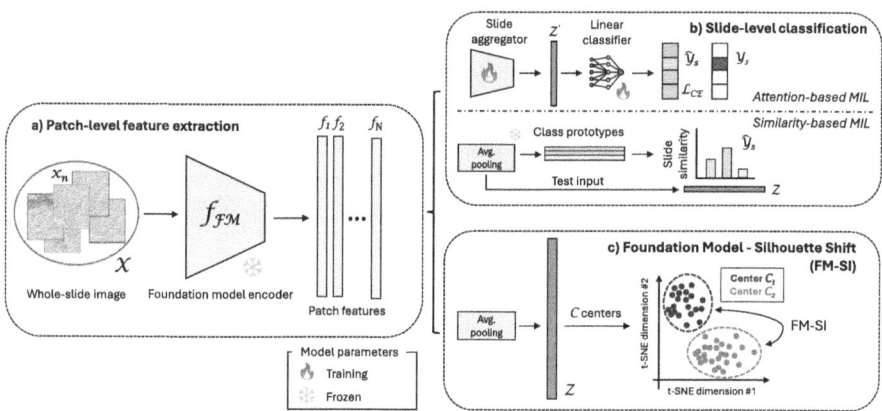

Fig. 1. *Histopathology foundation model evaluation framework*: Given a whole slide image (X), the feature extraction stage uses a foundation model encoder (f_{FM}) to extract patch representations (f_n). To address the slide-level downstream classification task, we rely on attention-based MIL (ABMIL) [6] including a slide aggregator and linear classifier optimized through the categorical cross-entropy loss $(\mathcal{L}_{CE})$ and a similarity-based MIL classifier (MI-SimpleShot) [2] which relies on class prototypes to compute the slide-level prediction $(\hat{Y}_s)$. Finally, the Foundation Model - Silhouette Shift (FM-SI) for the C available centers in the dataset is measured on top of the slide embeddings (Z) to evaluate the presence of scanner-related information in the extracted features.

2.1   Foundation Model Evaluation Framework

Problem Formulation: Computational pathology challenges manage the gigapixel scale of WSI by dividing whole slides into patches such as $X = \{x_n\}_{n=1}^{N}$, where N denotes the number of instances in a bag. In the multi-class scenario, each WSI is a member of one of S mutually exclusive classes, being $Y_s \in \{0, 1\}$ the slide-level ground truth. In a multi-center dataset, each WSI is associated with the pathology department of a particular hospital (C) from which it was acquired and digitized. In a slide classification task under the MIL paradigm, we aim to train a model capable of predicting bag-level labels using a combination of features extracted at the instance level by a histopathology FM. Let us denote a histopathology FM encoder (f_{FM}) which projects patches to a lower dimensional manifold $f \in \mathcal{F} \subset \mathbb{R}^d$, where d refers to the embedding dimension.

Histopathology Foundation Models: Large-scale screening programs and the expansion of digital pathology have permitted the collection of massive datasets of histopathological imaging, thus accelerating the development of foundation models for this particular medical imaging modality. This work considers up to 8 histopathology FM trained under different forms of supervision to operate as patch-level feature extractors in a MIL-based classification framework, as shown in Fig. 1 a). Table 1 summarizes each histopathology FM regarding its pretraining strategy, the embedding dimension, the number of model parameters, and the size of the pretraining dataset. Our comparison covers from vision-only models pre-trained with self-supervised strategies like UNI [2], VIRCHOW-2 [17], GPFM [9], and CHIEF [14] to multimodal vision-language models such as CONCH [8], MUSK [15], KEEP [16], and PLIP [5].

It is important to highlight the unique configuration of each model. Notably, the length of the latent space (d) varies between more condensed vectors for CONCH and PLIP ($d = 512$) and larger feature representations like MUSK ($d = 2048$). This configuration is critical as it will condition the models' size for a particular downstream task. Although ViTs are transversal to all FMs, we also note that ViT-Large with a patch size equal to 16 (ViT-L/16, 303 million parameters) is the most popular encoder as selected by UNI, MUSK and GPFM models.

Regarding dataset size, vision-language models are generally trained with fewer histopathology images, as language-image pretraining supposes a more restrictive form of supervision. As an exception, MUSK [16] was trained with 50 million (M) images with masked image modeling and later used one million text reports for multimodal alignment. VIRCHOW-2 was pre-trained on tiles extracted from 3.1 million slides, making it the largest training corpus among all models, marking a notable leap to the next largest dataset.

Table 1. A summary of the selected histopathology foundation models

Model	Pretraining strategy	Feature length (d)	Params. (M)	Tiles (M)
UNI [2]	Self supervision	1024	303	100
VIRCHOW-2 [17]		1280	632	3.1*
GPFM [9]		1024	303	190
CHIEF [14]		768	28	15
CONCH [8]	Vision-language supervision	512	90	1.7
MUSK [15]		2048	303	50
KEEP [16]		768	414	1
PLIP [5]		512	87	0.21

Note: * denotes number of slides

Multiple Instance Learning (MIL) Classifiers: As presented in Fig. 1 b), we used two MIL approaches to assess the performance of each foundation model in a slide classification task.

Attention-Based Multiple Instance Learning (ABMIL) [6]*:* We utilized the attention-based MIL to train a slide aggregator on top of the features extracted by the foundation model. ABMIL processes patch features through a learnable attention layer, which assigns attention weights to each patch reflecting its significance in the classification. Finally, a weighted average of instance features based on the learned scores outputs a slide-level representation (Z') of the slide, which is forwarded to a linear classifier to compute the bag-level predicted probabilities ($\hat{Y}_s$). Model parameters of the slide aggregator and the classification layer are updated by gradient descent using the categorical cross-entropy ($\mathcal{L}_{C\mathcal{E}}$) between the slide ground truths (Y_s) and predictions ($\hat{Y}_s$) as the cost function.

Similarity-Based Classifier (MI-SimpleShot) [2]*:* Multiple Instance (MI) - SimpleShot is a non-parametric approach for slide-level classification in CPath. Given a set of training data in the form of mean pooled feature embeddings (Z) representing the S classes in the task at hand, MI-SimpleShot constructs the s-th class prototype as the centroid of the feature representations for the data points of the s-th class within the training subset. For classification, it computes the slide-level cosine similarity between the constructed prototypes and the test input query to determine the slide's prediction ($\hat{Y}_s$). This approach is advantageous for evaluating the ability of pretrained feature extractors to generate robust feature representation without requiring additional training.

2.2   Center Shift Measurement

Various sources of distribution shift, such as differences in demographics, acquisition centers, staining protocols, and digital scanners, can significantly impact CPath tasks, potentially limiting model performance in real-world applications. Despite the large-scale pretraining stage of histopathology foundation models promising to obtain robust representation independent of these noise sources, careful evaluation of model consistency against domain shifts is required. This work focuses on measuring center-related scanner shifts as two scanners were used to digitize the tissue samples on the benchmarking dataset.

Inspired by intuitive data visualizations of high-dimensional feature and clustering analysis, we propose **F**oundation **M**odel **S**ilhouette **I**ndex (FM-SI) (see Algorithm 1), a novel metric to measure the center-related shift of histopathology FM. Given the dataset (D) of a downstream task composed of a set of patches for each slide (X), we initially extract the patch-level features using a particular foundation model (f_{FM}) and compute the slide embedding (Z) by mean pooling all instance features. In the following, we reduce the feature dimensionality of Z to two components using t-Distributed Stochastic Neighbor Embedding (t-SNE) [10] by minimizing the Kullback-Leibler divergence between the similarities of the high- and low-dimensional data. Finally, the silhouette coefficient [13] is calculated on top of the 2D slide representation by measuring the mean intra-cluster distance and the mean nearest-cluster distance, considering as clusters the different centers (C) in the dataset. An FM-SI score closer to 0 means overlapping clusters, while a higher values closer to 1 translates in better clustered data points according to the center label, thus denoting more center-biased features.

Algorithm 1. Foundation Model - Silhouette Index (FM-SI)

1: **Inputs:** Dataset $D = \{X_i\}$, center labels (C_i) and a foundation model (f_{FM})
2: **Output:** FM-SI score (σ)
3: **Step 1**: Obtain the slide representation (Z)
4: **for** each slide $i \in D$ **do**
5:     $f_n = f_{FM}(x_n)$ {Extract patch features}
6:     $Z = \frac{1}{N} \sum_{n=1}^{N} f_n$ {Compute slide embedding}
7: **end for**
8: **Step 2**: 2D t-SNE dimensionality reduction on Z
9:     $Z_{2D} = \text{t-SNE}(Z)$ {following [10]}
10: **Step 3**: Compute silhouette score σ
11:     $\sigma = \text{SilhouetteScore}(Z_{2D}, C)$ {following [13]}
12: **Return** σ as the FM-SI score

---

3   Experimental Configuration

In this section, we provide a summary of the experimental settings and present the multi-center dataset to define the benchmark of the downstream task.

3.1   Experimental Settings

We follow a 5-fold stratified cross-validation partition to validate both MIL approaches. We measure the balanced accuracy (BACC) score as the average of recall scores (sensitivity) across all classes, which is particularly useful for class-imbalanced datasets. Regarding the MIL approaches, attention MIL models were trained for 20 epochs with an AdamW, a cosine learning rate scheduler, and a peak learning rate of 10^{-4}. Weighted cross-entropy loss was used to consider less-represented classes fairly. We set the size of the intermediate layer in the attention network in ABMIL to a quarter of the input size of the feature to handle the different sizes of the latent space. Note that the similarity-based classifier does not require parameter updates. MI-SimpleShot constructs the prototypes directly from the training samples and computes the slide-level cosine similarity for a given test query without requiring parameter update.

3.2   AI4SkIN Dataset

The AI4SkIN dataset [3] encompasses WSIs from six subtypes of CSC neoplasms: leiomyomas (lm), leiomyosarcomas (lms), dermatofibromas (df), dermatofibrosarcomas (dfs), spindle cell melanomas (scm), atypical fibroxanthomas (afx). CSC neoplasms are skin lesions ranging from benign to malign tumors with notable morphological overlaps that are supposed to be a diagnostic challenge even for experienced pathologists. The subtle differences make it challenging for computer vision systems to discover hidden patterns for subtype identification. The emergence of histopathology FMs promises to extract discriminative features that may enhance the performance of computer-aided diagnosis systems for skin cancer subtyping.

The dataset is constituted of whole-slide images obtained by digitizing tissue sections of biopsies resected from patients with a skin cancer diagnosis. In particular, WSIs were digitized at two different centers in Spain: Hospital Clínico Universitario de Valencia (HCUV) and Hospital Universitario San Secilio (HUSC) in Granada. The digitization process was done at 40× equivalent magnification with Roche's scanner (Ventana iScan HT) at HCUV and Philips Ultra Fast Scanner at HUSC. The different scanners used for data acquisition generate distribution shifts that require careful consideration given its potential impact in real-world clinical applications, potentially leading to a decline in model performance. For that purpose, we propose a novel metric for distribution shift measurement and analyze its effect in the classification task.

We present an overview of AI4SkIN dataset in Table 2, including the counts of WSI for each center and skin cancer subtype. The proposed benchmark dataset consists of 621 slides, with 42.8% coming from the hospital in Valencia (HCUV) and 58.2% from the hospital in Granada (HUSC). It is worth mentioning that malignant subtypes (leiomyosarcoma and dermatofibrosarcoma) are underrepresented compared to its benign forms (leiomyoma and dermatofibroma) containing at least 2× more data samples.

Table 2. Counts of slides the AI4SkIN dataset per subtype and center

Skin cancer subtype	HCUV	HUSC	Overall
Leiomyoma	31	73	104
Leiomyosarcoma	21	23	44
Dermatofibroma	101	93	194
Dermatofibrosarcoma	21	34	55
Spindle cell melanoma	48	74	122
Atypical fibroxanthoma	44	58	102
Overall	**266**	**355**	**621**

4   Results

This section evaluates the presence of center-related information in the representations extracted by the foundation models and examines its impact on the performance of downstream MIL models.

4.1   Center Shift Measurement

Careful evaluation of model consistency against distribution shifts is fundamental for the integration of CPath applications in clinical practice. Recently, [7] proposed the Robustness Index (RI), a new metric to measure how much biological features dominate over confounding factors in pathology FM. The RI computes a ratio based on the proportion that belongs to the same biological class versus those that belong to the same medical center. In contrast, FM-SI provides a measurement of center shift without requiring class labels that intuitively correlates with the representation of the slide-level latent space.

Initially, we show in Fig. 2 how the Foundation Model - Silhouette Index correlates with the Robustness Index [7]. Our metric assesses how closely data points from each center cluster together, with higher values suggesting that the data representations extracted by a histopathological FM capture significant center-related information. Therefore, lower FM-SI values mean higher preponderance of pathological features and correspond with higher values of the robustness score for a particular model. Overall, FM-SI shows a strong correlation with the RI with a correlation coefficient of $|\rho| = 0.890$.

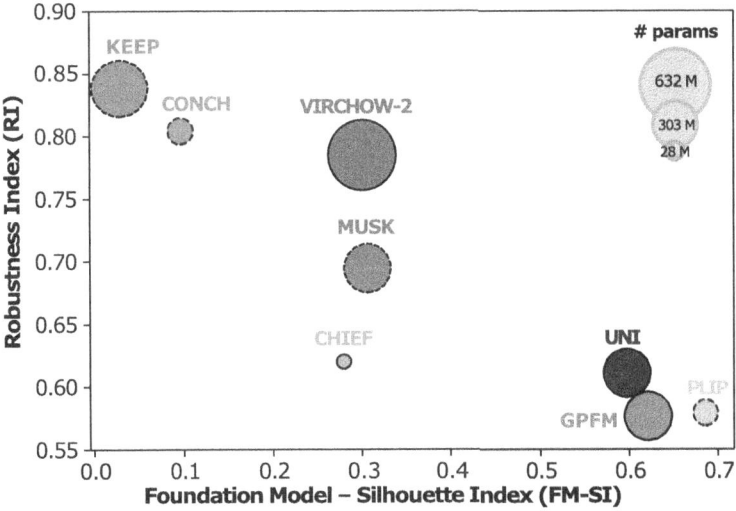

Fig. 2. Measurement of center shift consistency of histopathology foundation models in terms of Robustness Index (RI) [7] and Foundation Model - Silhouette Index (FM-SI).

Additionally, Fig. 3 includes the 2D t-SNE [10] scatter plots where each point corresponds to the slide-level features (Z) extracted either by the PLIP or KEEP models and the color indicates the center where the sample was acquired. These models were selected as they return the highest (PLIP with $\sigma = 0.686$) and the lowest (KEEP with $\sigma = 0.028$) values for the FM-SI metric. The analysis of the latent space shows that the PLIP encoder strongly clusters the samples according to each center, while data points are more sparse in terms of acquisition center for the KEEP model. This illustration is a clear example of how the proposed metric intuitively correlates with dimensionality reduction techniques commonly used for exploratory data analysis of deep features.

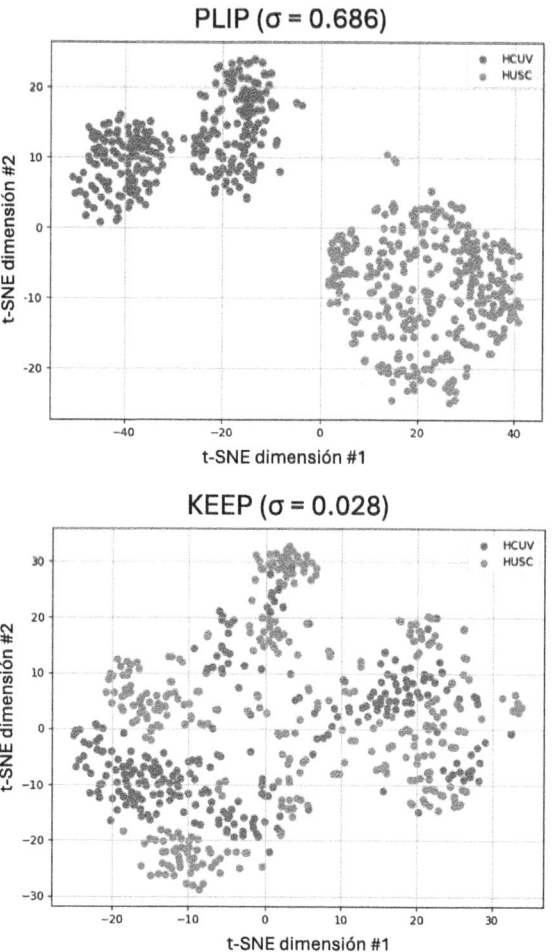

Fig. 3. Latent space visualization at the slide-level of two histopathology foundation models: PLIP [5] and KEEP [16].

4.2   Classification Performance

As previously stated, we investigate two different MIL approaches to address the slide-level classification task. We compare a MIL model relying on attention weights to obtain the slide representation embedding (ABMIL) and a non-parametric method (MI-SimpleShot) that computes similarities between constructed class prototypes and test input queries. To assess the potential impact of inter-center variability in the proposed benchmark, we analyze how the Foundation Model - Silhouette Index affects the downstream proficiency of FM for each MIL approach. For that purpose, we show in Fig. 4 a scatter chart where we plot the performance of each MIL approach and the FM-SI of the model.

It is worth noting than MI-SimpleShot performance presents a higher dependence on the center-biased representations as the trend shows a correlation between lower performance and higher values of the FM-SI metric ($R^2 = 0.428$). ABMIL improved and less-dependent effectiveness ($R^2 = 0.346$) indicates that learning phase enables to discover the relevant features and instances to enhance the subtyping classification compared to the non-parametric approach of MI-SimpleShot. Overall, attention-based MIL outperforms the MI-SimpleShot classifier by an average of 11.88% across all evaluated encoders. This decrease is particularly critical in GPFM, which outputs 80.88% balanced accuracy with ABMIL, but just 62.13% with MI-SimpleShot.

We find that VIRCHOW-2 excels in both similarity- and attention-based MIL classifiers reaching 77.75% and 86.81% balanced accuracy, respectively. Despite VIRCHOW-2 outputs the fourth lowest FM-SI value, it surpasses the next performing model by 4.92% on MI-SimpleShot and 3.81% in ABMIL. Since VIRCHOW-2 is pre-trained on the largest dataset and uses the most complex model, these findings emphasize the impact of scaling laws on corpus size and model weights in histopathology FM. However, the VIRCHOW-2 pretraining dataset was assembled with 85% of the slides from the same medical institution [17] highlighting that dataset diversity is crucial to obtain robust center-independent data representations.

Furthermore, PLIP gets the lower proficiency for both MIL methods with a notable reduction in attention-based classification (67.53%), more than ten points lower than the second-bottom performer (CHIEF). The fact that PLIP collected pathology image-text pairs from Twitter raises critical questions about the quality and source knowledge of the data for pretraining FM. It is also worth highlighting that CONCH (90M params.) promotes models efficiency and reduces computational costs as it obtains comparable performance to MUSK and KEEP (303M params) which require model architectures with a notably higher number of parameters. Moreover, CONCH and KEEP encoders extract the few center-biased features suggesting that the incorporation of vision-language supervision to the pretraining stage provides them a higher focus on biological features self-supervised strategies relying solely on visual information.

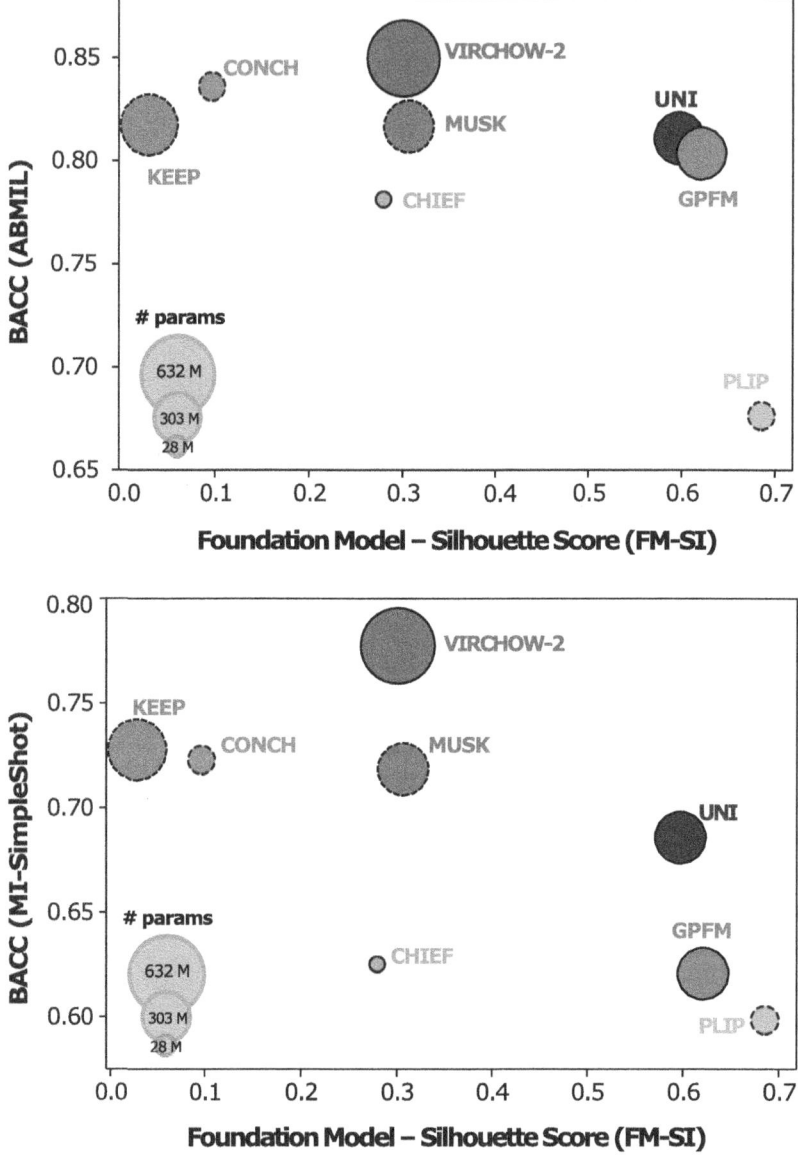

Fig. 4. Downstream performance in terms of balanced accuracy (BACC) for skin cancer subtyping on the AI4SkIN dataset with ABMIL (top) and MI-SimpleShot (bottom) correlated with the Foundation Model - Silhouette Index (FM-SI) metric. Solid and dotted lines represent self-supervised and vision-language models, respectively.

5   Conclusions

The continuous development of histopathology foundation models remarks the need for defining benchmarks to validate the performance of these models. This work presents a novel benchmark through the AI4SkIN dataset to compare self-supervised and vision-language histopathology foundation models in a challenging skin cancer subtyping task. Through two different multiple instance learning approaches, we evaluated the ability of FMs to extract discriminative features for addressing the downstream task while measuring the impact of center bias in the extracted features. Our findings show that the CONCH [8] and KEEP [16] vision-language models can extract features with fewer center bias. Meanwhile, VIRCHOW-2 [17] achieves the highest performance despite confounding features, suggesting that the scaling laws regarding dataset and model size promise foundation models obtaining a better understanding of the data. The comparison of the performance of both MIL settings highlights that attention-based MIL approaches are more robust against distribution shifts than prototype-based classifiers, which depend on the raw extracted features.

Although our work covers an extensive range of histopathology FM, it is still limited to patch-level encoders. Future work could focus on benchmarking weakly supervised foundation models proposed to learn slide feature representations in an unsupervised fashion. Our benchmark relies on a multi-center dataset, which allows us to evaluate the presence of scanner-related information in the features extracted by a foundation model. Our proposed FM-SI score provides a quantitative and intuitive measurement of center-shift in the aggregated latent space of each encoder without requiring class labels. The insights about consistency to scanner shift presented in this work highlight the need for rigorous assessment of other distribution shifts, such as demographics-related ones, and their potential impact in real-world CPath applications.

Acknowledgments. We gratefully acknowledge the support from the Generalitat Valenciana (GVA) with the donation of the DGX A100 used for this work, an action co-financed by the European Union through the Operational Program of the European Regional Development Fund of the Comunitat Valenciana 2014-2020 (IDIFEDER/2020/030). This work has received funding from the Spanish Ministry of Economy and Competitiveness through the projects PID2022-140189OB-C21 (ASSIST) and CIPROM/2022/20 (COMTACTS2).

References

1. Campanella, G., et al.: A clinical benchmark of public self-supervised pathology foundation models. arXiv preprint arXiv:2407.06508 (2024)
2. Chen, R.J., et al.: Towards a general-purpose foundation model for computational pathology. Nat. Med. **30**(3), 850–862 (2024)
3. Del Amor, R., et al.: A fusocelular skin dataset with whole slide images for deep learning models. Sci. Data **12**(1), 1–7 (2025)

4. Dosovitskiy, A., et al.: An image is worth 16x16 words: transformers for image recognition at scale. In: International Conference on Learning Representations (2020)
5. Huang, Z., Bianchi, F., Yuksekgonul, M., Montine, T.J., Zou, J.: A visual-language foundation model for pathology image analysis using medical twitter. Nat. Med. **29**(9), 2307–2316 (2023)
6. Ilse, M., Tomczak, J., Welling, M.: Attention-based deep multiple instance learning. In: International Conference on Machine Learning, pp. 2127–2136. PMLR (2018)
7. de Jong, E.D., Marcus, E., Teuwen, J.: Current pathology foundation models are unrobust to medical center differences. arXiv preprint arXiv:2501.18055 (2025)
8. Lu, M.Y., et al.: A visual-language foundation model for computational pathology. Nat. Med. **30**(3), 863–874 (2024)
9. Ma, J., et al.: Towards a generalizable pathology foundation model via unified knowledge distillation. arXiv preprint arXiv:2407.18449 (2024)
10. Van der Maaten, L., Hinton, G.: Visualizing data using t-sne. J. Mach. Learn. Res. **9**(11) (2008)
11. Oquab, M., et al.: Dinov2: learning robust visual features without supervision. Trans. Mach. Learn. Res. J., 1–31 (2024)
12. Radford, A., et al.: Learning transferable visual models from natural language supervision. In: International Conference on Machine Learning, pp. 8748–8763. PmLR (2021)
13. Rousseeuw, P.J.: Silhouettes: a graphical aid to the interpretation and validation of cluster analysis. J. Comput. Appl. Math. **20**, 53–65 (1987)
14. Wang, X., et al.: A pathology foundation model for cancer diagnosis and prognosis prediction. Nature **634**(8035), 970–978 (2024)
15. Xiang, J., et al.: A vision–language foundation model for precision oncology. Nature, 1–10 (2025)
16. Zhou, X., et al.: A knowledge-enhanced pathology vision-language foundation model for cancer diagnosis. arXiv preprint arXiv:2412.13126 (2024)
17. Zimmermann, E., et al.: Virchow2: scaling self-supervised mixed magnification models in pathology. arXiv preprint arXiv:2408.00738 (2024)

MitoNet: Efficient Ki-67 Detection in H&E-Stained Images

Celia Benitez Camacho$^{(\boxtimes)}$ (ID), Esha Sadia Nasir(ID), and Shan E. Ahmed Raza(ID)

Tissue Image Analytics (TIA) Centre, Department of Computer Science, University of Warwick, Coventry, UK
{celia.benitez-camacho,esha.nasir,shan.raza}@warwick.ac.uk

Abstract. We present a deep learning approach for nuclear-level prediction of Ki-67 expression directly from H&E-stained breast cancer images, potentially eliminating the need for costly and time-consuming immunohistochemistry (IHC). Our two-phase pipeline integrates HoVerNet for precise nuclei segmentation with a specialized ResNet-style classifier (MitoNet) optimized for small patch classification. Our model, trained on 215,825 annotated nuclei, achieves 82.4% accuracy, with high sensitivity (recall: 0.925) in detecting proliferating cells. Comparative analysis demonstrates MitoNet's superior generalization on external validation data (91.5% accuracy), while maintaining computational efficiency (2.1M parameters). Unlike previous approaches focusing on region-based predictions, our approach enables cell-level identification of Ki-67 positive nuclei, providing pathologists with granular proliferation assessment comparable to IHC staining.

Keywords: Ki-67 · H&E Stain · Breast Cancer · Computer Vision

1 Introduction

The rapid advancement of artificial intelligence (AI) is revolutionizing digital pathology. Computational models can now perform quantitative analyses with accuracy that rivals human expertise in critical diagnostic tasks [3,5,6]. This is particularly relevant in oncology, where these models assess tumor proliferation. This critical parameter quantifies the rate of cancer cell division and is strongly associated with tumor aggressiveness, prognosis, and response to therapy [35].

Among primary proliferation markers, Ki-67 stands out as a well-established and clinically significant biomarker. This nuclear protein is expressed during the active phases of the cell cycle (G1, S, G2, M) and absent in quiescent cells (G0) [11,21,23]. In breast cancer, the Ki-67 labeling index (LI), i.e., the percentage of Ki-67 positive tumor cells, is critical for molecular subtyping, prognosis, and therapeutic decisions [8,12]. High Ki-67 expression is associated with aggressive tumor phenotypes, higher histological grades, and poorer clinical outcomes [33, 40]. In hormone receptor-positive breast cancer, Ki-67 assessment is essential for

S. Ali et al. (Eds.): MIUA 2025, LNCS 15916, pp. 29–42, 2026.
https://doi.org/10.1007/978-3-031-98688-8_3

distinguishing between luminal A and luminal B subtypes, directly influencing decisions regarding chemotherapy versus endocrine therapy [8,32,33].

Current detection methods for Ki-67 rely primarily on immunohistochemistry (IHC), a widely used technique that employs antibodies to visualize specific proteins in tissue samples. While effective for Ki-67 quantification and clinical decision-making in breast cancer management, IHC presents several significant challenges in clinical practice [7,30].

The cost of IHC staining is substantially higher compared to standard hematoxylin and eosin (H&E) staining, making H&E a more economical alternative in resource-limited settings [10,24]. Additionally, the processing time for IHC results is considerably longer, requiring additional processing beyond standard histopathology protocols. This delay can affect timely diagnosis and treatment decisions, especially in time-sensitive clinical scenarios [7].

Access to IHC remains limited in healthcare settings with resource constraints, particularly in low-income regions where a comprehensive cancer diagnostics infrastructure is not available [30,39].

Furthermore, IHC results can demonstrate significant variability due to differences in antibody selection, tissue fixation protocols, and interpretation methodologies, raising concerns regarding standardization and reproducibility [10,15]. This variability is particularly problematic in the Ki-67 assessment, where interobserver inconsistencies can affect treatment decisions in breast cancer management [30].

These limitations underscore the need for alternative Ki-67 assessment approaches that are more accessible, efficient and cost-effective while maintaining diagnostic accuracy. In this paper, we present a deep learning-based approach to predict Ki-67 status directly from H&E-stained images, bypassing the need for IHC while maintaining diagnostic accuracy. The main contributions of this work are summarised as follows:

- Developed a two-phase pipeline with a segmentation model followed by a specialized classifier (MitoNet) for identifying Ki-67 positive nuclei in H&E images at the cell level.
- Utilized a comprehensive dataset of 215,825 annotated nuclei from paired H&E and IHC images, much larger than previous datasets used in similar studies.
- Validated the approach through ablation studies, external dataset validation, and comparisons with state-of-the-art architectures, demonstrating the robustness and clinical applicability of our model.

The remainder of this paper is organized as follows. Section 2 reviews related work in biomarker prediction from H&E images. Section 3 describes the methodology, including dataset preparation, ground truth generation, and model architecture development. Section 4 presents experimental results and discusses their clinical significance. Finally, Sect. 5 concludes with the broader implications of this work and directions for future research.

2   Related Work

Recent advances in computational pathology have demonstrated that the state of IHC biomarkers can be predicted directly from images stained with hematoxylin and eosin (H&E) stained images. For instance, Naik et al. (2020) demonstrated the feasibility of this approach by predicting estrogen receptor (ER) status in breast cancer using H&E whole slide images (WSIs), showcasing the potential of convolutional neural networks (CNNs) to analyze histological features associated with biomarker expression [31].

Another approach, SlideGraph+, utilized a graph neural network to predict human epidermal growth factor receptor 2 (HER2) status from H&E images by modeling cellular architecture as a graph [27]. Beyond breast cancer, Jiao et al. (2024) applied a weakly supervised CLAM framework to predict HER2 status from H&E slides in bladder cancer, achieving AUCs of 0.92 (validation) and 0.88 (test), demonstrating the broader applicability of computational pathology [22].

In the domain of Ki-67 prediction from H&E images, various approaches have been explored. Martino et al. (2023) used generative adversarial networks to generate virtual Ki-67 stains, but this method encountered challenges with interpretability and lacked sufficient clinical validation [29]. Similarly, Liu et al. (2020) applied convolutional neural networks (CNNs) to a relatively small dataset of 18,000 patches, raising concerns about the generalizability of their findings [25]. More recently, Akbarnejad et al. (2025) applied Vision Transformers to identify Ki-67 hotspot regions in breast cancer, though their region-level approach limited the cell-specific granularity needed for accurate Ki-67 labeling index calculation [2].

Several researchers have explored integrated approaches combining H&E and IHC data for Ki-67 assessment. Swiderska-Chadaj et al. (2020) developed a CNN-based approach that utilized mutual information from paired H&E and Ki-67 IHC whole slide images to detect proliferation hotspots [36]. Similarly, Duanmu et al. (2022) incorporated spatial attention mechanisms to identify regions of interest for proliferation assessment [13]. While these integrated approaches showed promise for enhancing Ki-67 assessment, they still relied on IHC for definitive evaluation, limiting the potential cost and time savings of a purely H&E-based approach.

Unlike prior methods, the proposed approach emphasizes the analysis of individual nuclei, providing granular information comparable to IHC. By accurately delineating nuclear boundaries, this study has the potential to enable a quantitative assessment of cell proliferation comparable to traditional IHC methods.

3   Materials and Methods

This section details our methodological approach, highlighting the key decisions that enabled accurate nuclear-level classification.

3.1 Dataset Selection and Preparation

We selected two datasets to ensure both comprehensive training and robust external validation. The primary dataset, IHC4BC, provided the foundation for model development with its extensive collection of 30,000 high-resolution images (300×300 pixels) derived from 90 whole slide images (WSIs) [1]. This dataset's unique strength lies in its near-perfect cell-level correspondence between H&E and IHC stains, achieved through precise image registration techniques.

As discussed in Sect. 2, the IHC4BC dataset [1] allowed us to establish a robust ground truth by mapping Ki-67-positive nuclei in IHC images to their corresponding H&E counterparts. From these images, we extracted 215,825 nuclei patches (32×32 pixels), creating a substantial corpus for deep learning model training. The class distribution in the processed dataset was relatively balanced, consisting of 121,478 (56.3%) positive samples and 94,347 (43.7%) negative samples. It was divided into training (70%), validation (15%), and test (15%) sets using a patch-level separation strategy.

To assess model generalizability, we incorporated a secondary dataset from Liu et al. (2020) [25], containing approximately 20,000 patches (64×64 pixels) from 12 WSIs. Although its small size made it suboptimal for primary training, it served as an excellent external validation resource to evaluate performance across varied data sources and acquisition protocols.

3.2 Ground Truth Generation

The lack of cell-level Ki-67 status labels in the original datasets posed a significant challenge in developing an accurate ground truth for our study. To address this, we designed a comprehensive ground truth generation pipeline that combined established tools with custom algorithms to create precise nuclear-level annotations.

Initially, we implemented a custom MATLAB-based registration pipeline to align hematoxylin and eosin (H&E) and immunohistochemistry (IHC) stained serial sections at the nuclear level. This critical alignment step utilized initially rigid registration via estimating phase correlation between fixed and moving image followed by Demons based non-rigid registration, accommodating the tissue deformations between serial sections. The goal was to achieve precise spatial alignment of nuclei across the differently stained tissues. The non-rigid registration algorithm [37] can be described mathematically as follows:

$$v(x) = \frac{(I_m(x) - I_f(x))\nabla I_f(x)}{\|\nabla I_f(x)\|^2 + (I_m(x) - I_f(x))^2} \tag{1}$$

where $I_m(x)$ and $I_f(x)$ represent the moving and fixed images, respectively, at location x, and $\nabla I_f(x)$ denotes the gradient of the fixed image.

For the detection of Ki-67 positive nuclei in the IHC images, we employed QuPath [4], customizing its functionality with Groovy scripts. Importantly, the DAB staining threshold of 0.12 used for identifying Ki-67 positive nuclei was explicitly recommended and verified by an expert pathologist associated with the primary dataset [1]. This pathologist-validated threshold ensures that our ground truth generation is aligned with clinical standards for Ki-67 assessment, mitigating potential algorithmic biases.

The core of the ground truth mapping process involved transferring the Ki-67 status from IHC images to corresponding nuclei in the H&E images, relying on spatial coordinates established through the registration process. To minimize mapping errors due to minor misalignments, we utilized a nearest-neighbor algorithm with a defined distance threshold, ensuring reliable label assignment even in cases of slight registration discrepancies.

As shown in Fig. 1, this approach effectively maps the ground truth coordinates onto the H&E images, providing a reliable reference for Ki-67 detection.

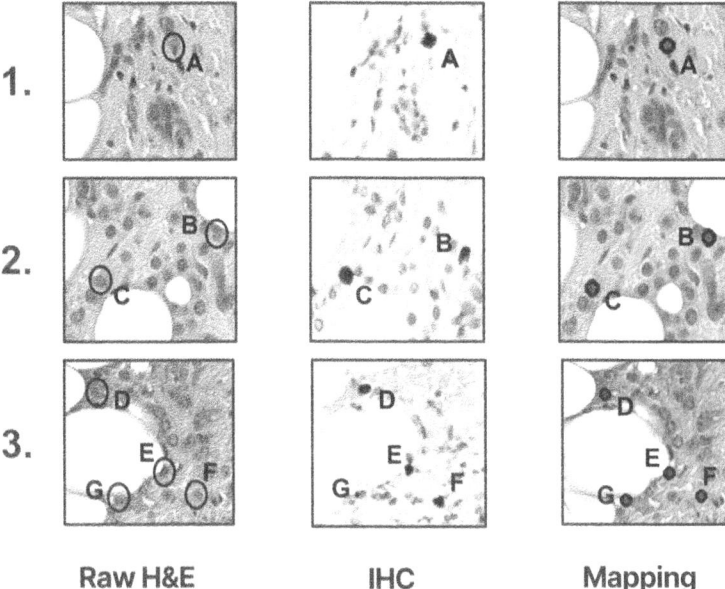

Raw H&E   **IHC**   **Mapping**

Fig. 1. Nuclear-level Correspondence Between H&E and IHC Images for Ki-67 Detection. Left column: Raw H&E-stained tissue sections with added red circles highlighting nuclei of interest (labeled A-G). Middle column: Corresponding IHC-stained serial sections showing Ki-67 expression, with brown-stained nuclei indicating positivity. Right column: Mapping visualization in H&E with blue circles representing the ground truth coordinates taken from the IHC image. (Color figure online)

Next, we extracted 32 × 32 pixel patches centered on each identified nucleus from the H&E images, assigning the corresponding Ki-67 status label based on the IHC mapping. This patch size was chosen through empirical testing to balance the need for sufficient contextual information with a focused representation of nuclear features.

To mitigate staining variability and enhance the generalization ability of our model, we employed Lanczos resampling [14], which was preferred over bilinear interpolation due to its superior ability to preserve fine details and reduce aliasing. This high-quality interpolation ensured consistent patch sizes and minimized artifacts, thereby improving the robustness of the ground truth generation process.

3.3   Model Architecture and Development

In our initial experiments, we observed challenges while inferring directly full image for both segmentation and classification tasks simultaneously. Key issues included overlapping nuclei and class imbalance, which hindered effective model performance. To overcome these challenges, we devised a modular two-phase pipeline that separates the tasks into manageable components: first, nuclei segmentation, followed by classification.

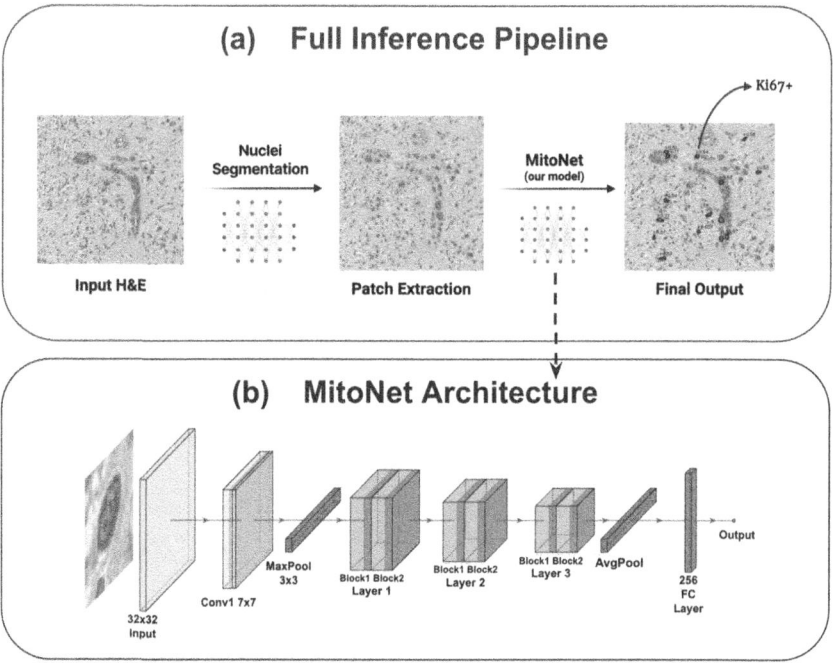

Fig. 2. Two-phase approach for Ki-67 prediction from H&E images. Panel (a) shows the complete workflow of the proposed inference pipeline from input H&E image through nuclei segmentation, patch extraction, and classification to final output with highlighted Ki-67+ nuclei. Panel (b) depicts the architecture of the proposed MitoNet classifier designed specifically for Ki-67 status prediction in H&E-stained nuclei patches.

For the segmentation phase, we leveraged HoVerNet [17] from the TIAToolbox library, selecting it for its dual capabilities in instance segmentation and cell-type classification. This allowed us to specifically target neoplastic cells (the primary cells of interest for Ki-67 assessment) while filtering out non-relevant cell types. The pre-trained model on PanNuke dataset [16] proved particularly effective for this task, providing accurate delineation of individual nuclei even in densely packed tumor regions.

In the classification phase, we evaluated several architectural approaches, including Vision Transformers (ViT). However, we found ViT models unsuitable for small 32×32 patches due to their tokenization approach, which further divided already limited spatial information, leading to a loss of critical features. After thorough experimentation, we found that a ResNet-style CNN architecture, optimized for small patch classification, provided superior performance.

This architecture, named MitoNet, is shown in Panel (b) of Fig. 2. Each stage contains two residual blocks with 3×3 convolutions, batch normalization, and ReLU activation functions, tailored to efficiently extract nuclear morphological features. Early downsampling layers efficiently process small patches, while residual connections and batch normalization help mitigate staining effects. To avoid overfitting, a crucial concern due to the heterogeneous nature of breast cancer tissue morphology, dropout layers and a limited number of fully connected layers were incorporated.

In addition, we performed extensive ablation studies to assess the impact of various design decisions. These included variations in input patch size (16×16, 32×32, 64×64), model depth (number of residual blocks), network width (base channel count), segmentation quality (comparison of different nuclei segmentation approaches), and training strategies. These experiments provided valuable insights into the relative importance of each component of our pipeline and informed our final model configuration.

3.4 Training and Optimization

The training process for the model was carried out using binary cross-entropy loss $\mathcal{L}_{\mathrm{BCE}}$ defined as:

$$\mathcal{L}_{\mathrm{BCE}} = -\frac{1}{N}\sum_{i=1}^{N}[y_i\log(\hat{y}_i) + (1 - y_i)\log(1 - \hat{y}_i)] \qquad (2)$$

where $y_i \in \{0,1\}$ represents the ground truth Ki-67 status for the i-th nucleus, $\hat{y}_i \in [0,1]$ is the model's predicted probability of Ki-67 positivity, and N is the batch size.

For optimization, we used the AdamW optimizer [26], a variant of the Adam optimizer that includes weight decay for better regularization. This helps in controlling the model's complexity and prevents overfitting, especially in cases with high-dimensional data. The initial learning rate was set to 1×10^{-4}, and the batch size was set to 64. The learning rate was adjusted dynamically during training using a learning rate scheduler based on the validation loss. Specifically, we employed ReduceLROnPlateau with a factor of 0.5 to reduce the learning rate when the validation loss plateaued for more than three epochs, aiding in better convergence.

To avoid overfitting, we employed early stopping. The training process was monitored, and if the validation loss did not improve for 7 consecutive epochs (with a minimum change in the validation loss of 0.001), training was stopped early. This strategy helps prevent the model from continuing to train on noisy or less informative data, thereby improving generalization.

Given the inherent variability in histopathology images, data augmentation was essential for model robustness. During training, we applied random transformations including horizontal/vertical flips, rotations (up to 30°C), and color jittering (brightness, contrast, and saturation adjustments). These augmentations simulated real-world variations, enhancing generalization. For validation, we used only normalization without augmentation to ensure fair evaluation on unseen data.

4   Results

4.1   Qualitative Evaluation

The qualitative evaluation demonstrates a high degree of concordance between the model's predictions and the ground truth IHC staining patterns. As illustrated in Fig. 3, visual inspection of the predicted maps confirms precise identification of Ki-67 positive nuclei across various tissue architectures and staining conditions. Notably, the model successfully detects proliferating nuclei in challenging scenarios, including those with heterogeneous staining intensities, overlapping cells, and complex tissue microenvironments.

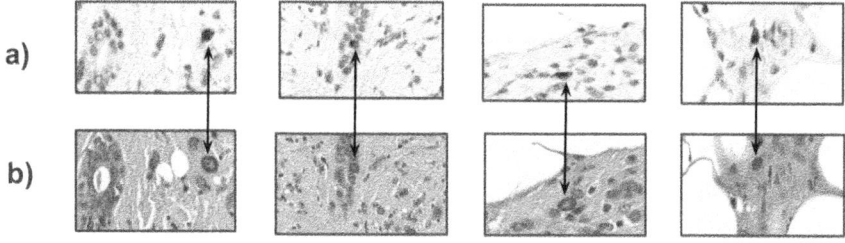

Fig. 3. Ground truth and model detection comparison of Ki-67 expression. The top row (a) shows IHC-stained sections displaying brown-stained nuclei representing Ki-67 positive expression (ground truth). The bottom row (b) presents corresponding H&E-stained sections with red circles marking nuclei identified as Ki-67 positive by the proposed approach. (Color figure online)

4.2   Quantitative Evaluation

This section presents the quantitative performance results of the MitoNet model on both the primary IHC4BC dataset [1] and an external validation dataset. The model addresses class imbalance effectively, as shown by the ROC and Precision-Recall curves in Fig. 4.

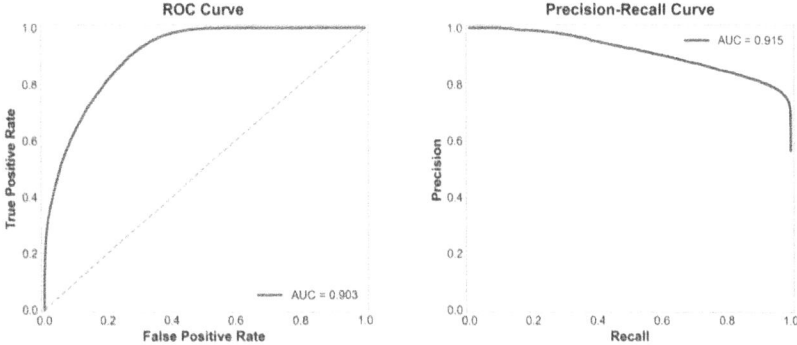

Fig. 4. MitoNet performance on the IHC4BC test set. Left: The ROC curve shows strong discriminative ability with an AUC of 0.903 for Ki-67 status prediction. Right: The Precision-Recall curve, with an AUC of 0.915, highlights the model's high precision across recall thresholds.

MitoNet demonstrated superior performance on both primary and external validation datasets while maintaining computational efficiency. As shown in Table 1, it achieved 82.4% accuracy on the IHC4BC dataset [1] with fast inference time, outperforming lightweight models like ShuffleNetv2 [28] and MobileNetv3 [19], as well as deeper architectures such as DenseNet169 [20], ResNet101 [18] and MLP-Mixer [38].

Table 1. Performance comparison across models on the IHC4BC primary dataset [1].

Model	Accuracy (%)	F1 (Pos)	F1 (Neg)	Inference Time[a] (s)
MitoNet	**82.4**	**0.857**	**0.772**	**20.26**
ShuffleNetv2	81.3	0.844	0.764	19.34
MobileNetv3	80.3	0.846	0.728	19.67
DenseNet169	81.8	0.848	0.763	63.41
ResNet101	80.1	0.829	0.762	72.24
MLP-Mixer	76.2	0.792	0.715	117.96
Full Inference Models[b]				
EfficientUNet	78.1	0.837	0.667	—
TransUNet [9]	81.3	0.864	0.700	—

[a] Measured on Nvidia RTX 2080Ti GPU with a batch size of 32
[b] Architectures performing end-to-end segmentation and classification

The performance gap widened further on the external Liu et al. dataset [25], as demonstrated in Table 2, where MitoNet demonstrated exceptional generalizability with 91.5% accuracy and balanced F1 scores for both classes (0.914 and 0.916). This substantial improvement over the second-best performer (DenseNet169 [20] at 89.7%) validates our architectural design choices. The evaluation code of MitoNet on the Liu et al. test set is publicly available on GitHub[1].

Table 2. Performance comparison across models on the external Liu et al. dataset [25]. Results for Liu et al. model are taken directly from their original study, using the same testing split.

Model	Accuracy (%)	F1 (Pos)	F1 (Neg)	Inference Time[a] (s)
MitoNet	**91.5**	**0.914**	**0.916**	**1.42**
ShuffleNetv2	87.2	0.876	0.868	1.31
MobileNetv3	88.6	0.887	0.885	1.29
DenseNet169	89.7	0.897	0.897	3.65
ResNet101	84.4	0.831	0.855	4.25
MLP-Mixer	77.5	0.781	0.768	6.82
Liu et al.	—	0.909	0.913	—

[a]Measured on Nvidia RTX 2080Ti GPU with a batch size of 32

In addition to its superior accuracy, MitoNet excels in computational efficiency, requiring only 2.1M parameters while maintaining competitive training and inference times. This efficiency is particularly advantageous for potential clinical deployment, where limitations on processing time and hardware resources often present significant barriers to implementation.

Furthermore, the external testing of MitoNet on Liu's dataset [25] consisting of neuroendocrine tissue further demonstrates its strong generalization capabilities. Although the model was primarily trained on breast cancer tissue samples, it also exhibited robust performance when evaluated on the neuroendocrine dataset, highlighting its ability to effectively learn and adapt to different tissue types during training.

It is worth noting that the Liu et al. dataset [25], with a much smaller size (approximately 20K patches) compared to our dataset (which contains nearly 200K patches), is considerably cleaner, potentially influencing the observed difference in accuracy.

4.3   Limitations

While our approach shows promise, the inherent challenge of correspondence between serial H&E and IHC sections introduces some limitations on achievable accuracy. In most cases, although we were able to perform near perfect nucleus-to-nucleus alignment between adjacent tissue sections, for some cases it remained

---

[1] https://github.com/celiabenitez/mitonet-evaluation.

difficult to attain due to unavoidable physical deformations during slide preparation. This can be rectified by using consecutive H&E and IHC re-stained sections rather than serial sections.

Regarding the validation strategy, we deliberately prioritized robust external validation across different institutions and cancer types over traditional cross-validation. This decision was driven by the recognition that generalizability across diverse clinical settings represents a more significant challenge in computational pathology than performance variations within a single dataset. Our use of an independent external test set from Liu et al. (2020) [25] with different acquisition parameters and tissue types provides a more stringent and clinically relevant assessment than would be achieved through cross-validation.

5   Conclusion

Nuclear-level prediction of Ki-67 status from H&E images is both feasible and approaches the diagnostic accuracy of traditional IHC assessment. By eliminating reliance on costly and time-intensive IHC staining, our approach democratizes access to critical prognostic information, particularly in resource-limited settings. Our method provides a pathway for extracting key diagnostic information from standard histology, facilitating the retrieval of varied biomarkers from H&E images. Rather than replacing traditional workflows, this technology complements them by enabling rapid, cost-effective preliminary assessments to guide selective IHC use. Future work directions could include enhance model explainability with Grad-CAM [34] to validate H&E features linked to Ki-67, expand to multi-biomarker predictions (ER, PR, HER2) to reduce IHC reliance, and correlate Ki-67 predictions with survival outcomes for prognostic insights in clinical decision-making.

Acknowledgments. SEAR reports financial support by the MRC (MR/X011585/1) and the BigPicture project, which has received funding from the Innovative Medicines Initiative 2 Joint Undertaking under grant agreement No 945358.

Disclosure of Interests. The authors have no competing interests.

References

1. Akbarnejad, A., Ray, N., Barnes, P., Bigras, G.: Predicting Ki67, ER, PR, and HER2 Statuses from H&E-stained Breast Cancer Images (2023). arXiv preprint arXiv:2308.01982. https://doi.org/10.48550/arXiv.2308.01982
2. Akbarnejad, A., Ray, N., Barnes, P., Bigras, G.: Toward accurate deep learning based prediction of Ki67, ER, PR, and HER2 status from H&E-stained breast cancer images. Appl. Immunohistochem. Molec. Morphol. **33**(3), 131–141 (2025). https://doi.org/10.1097/PAI.0000000000001258
3. Asif, A., Rajpoot, K., Graham, S., Snead, D., Minhas, F., Rajpoot, N.: Unleashing the potential of AI for pathology: challenges and recommendations. J. Pathol. **260**(5), 564–577 (2023). https://doi.org/10.1002/path.6168

4. Bankhead, P., et al.: QuPath: open source software for digital pathology image analysis. Sci. Rep. (2017). https://doi.org/10.1038/s41598-017-17204-5

5. Bilal, M., et al.: An aggregation of aggregation methods in computational pathology. Med. Image Anal. **88**, 102885 (2023). https://doi.org/10.1016/j.media.2023.102885

6. von Chamier, L., Laine, R., Henriques, R.: Artificial intelligence for microscopy: what you should know. Biochem. Soc. Trans. **47**(4), 1029–1040 (2019). https://doi.org/10.1042/BST20180391

7. Chatrian, A., Colling, R., Browning, L., Snead, D., Rittscher, J., Verrill, C.: Artificial intelligence for advance requesting of immunohistochemistry in diagnostically uncertain prostate biopsies. Mod. Pathol. **34**(9), 1780–1794 (2021). https://doi.org/10.1038/s41379-021-00826-6

8. Cheang, M., et al.: Ki67 Index, HER2 status, and prognosis of patients with luminal B breast cancer. JNCI: J. Natl. Cancer Inst. **101**(10), 736–750 (2009). https://doi.org/10.1093/jnci/djp082

9. Chen, J., et al.: TransUNet: rethinking the U-Net architecture design for medical image segmentation through the lens of transformers. Med. Image Anal. **97**, 103280 (2024). https://doi.org/10.1016/j.media.2024.103280

10. Deng, X., et al.: MCRANet: MTSL-based connectivity region attention network for PD-L1 status segmentation in H&E stained images. Comput. Biol. Med. **184**(C) (2025). https://doi.org/10.1016/j.compbiomed.2024.109357

11. Đokić, S., et al.: Clinical and analytical validation of two methods for Ki-67 scoring in formalin fixed and paraffin embedded tissue sections of early breast cancer. Cancers **16**(7), 1405 (2024). https://doi.org/10.3390/cancers16071405

12. Dowsett, M., et al.: Assessment of Ki67 in breast cancer: recommendations from the international Ki67 in breast cancer working group. JNCI: J. Natl. Cancer Inst. **103**(22), 1656–1664 (2011). https://doi.org/10.1093/jnci/djr393

13. Duanmu, H., et al.: A spatial attention guided deep learning system for prediction of pathological complete response using breast cancer histopathology images. Bioinformatics **38**(19), 4605–4612 (2022). https://doi.org/10.1093/bioinformatics/btac558

14. Duchon, C.: Lanczos filtering in one and two dimensions. J. Appl. Meteorol. **18**, 1016–1022 (1979). https://doi.org/10.1175/1520-0450(1979)018<1016>2.0.CO;2

15. van Eekelen, L., Spronck, J., Looijen-Salamon, M., et al.: Comparing deep learning and pathologist quantification of cell-level PD-L1 expression in non-small cell lung cancer whole-slide images. Sci. Rep. **14**, 7136 (2024). https://doi.org/10.1038/s41598-024-57067-1

16. Gamper, J., Alemi Koohbanani, N., Benet, K., Khuram, A., Rajpoot, N.: PanNuke: an open pan-cancer histology dataset for nuclei instance segmentation and classification. In: Reyes-Aldasoro, C.C., Janowczyk, A., Veta, M., Bankhead, P., Sirinukunwattana, K. (eds.) ECDP 2019. LNCS, vol. 11435, pp. 11–19. Springer, Cham (2019). https://doi.org/10.1007/978-3-030-23937-4_2

17. Graham, S., et al.: Hover-net: simultaneous segmentation and classification of nuclei in multi-tissue histology images. Med. Image Anal. **58**, 101563 (2019). https://doi.org/10.1016/j.media.2019.101563

18. He, K., Zhang, X., Ren, S., Sun, J.: Deep residual learning for image recognition. arXiv preprint arXiv:1512.03385 (2015). https://doi.org/10.48550/arXiv.1512.03385

19. Howard, A., et al.: Searching for MobileNetV3. In: International Conference on Computer Vision (ICCV) (2019). https://doi.org/10.48550/arXiv.1905.02244

20. Huang, G., Liu, Z., van der Maaten, L., Weinberger, K.: Densely connected convolutional networks. In: IEEE Conference on Computer Vision and Pattern Recognition (CVPR) (2017). https://doi.org/10.48550/arXiv.1608.06993

21. Jakobsen, J., Sørensen, J.: Clinical impact of ki-67 labeling index in non-small cell lung cancer. Lung Cancer **79**(1), 1–7 (2013). https://doi.org/10.1016/j.lungcan.2012.10.008

22. Jiao, P., et al.: Prediction of HER2 status based on deep learning in H&E-stained histopathology images of bladder cancer. Biomedicines **12**(7), 1583 (2024). https://doi.org/10.3390/biomedicines12071583

23. Li, L., Jiang, G., Chen, Q., Zheng, J.: Ki67 is a promising molecular target in the diagnosis of cancer (Review). Mol. Med. Rep. **11**, 1566–1572 (2015). https://doi.org/10.3892/mmr.2014.2914

24. Liu, S., et al.: Unpaired stain transfer using pathology-consistent constrained generative adversarial networks. IEEE Trans. Med. Imaging **40**(8), 1977–1989 (2021). https://doi.org/10.1109/TMI.2021.3069874

25. Liu, Y., et al.: Predict Ki-67 positive cells in H&E-stained images using deep learning independently from IHC-stained images. Front. Mol. Biosci. **7**, 183 (2020). https://doi.org/10.3389/fmolb.2020.00183

26. Loshchilov, I., Hutter, F.: Decoupled weight decay regularization. In: International Conference on Learning Representations (ICLR) (2019). https://doi.org/10.48550/arXiv.1711.05101

27. Lu, W., Toss, M., Dawood, M., Rakha, E., Rajpoot, N., Minhas, F.: SlideGraph+: whole slide image level graphs to predict HER2 status in breast cancer. Med. Image Anal. **80**, 102486 (2022). https://doi.org/10.1016/j.media.2022.102486

28. Ma, N., Zhang, X., Zheng, H.T., Sun, J.: ShuffleNet V2: practical guidelines for efficient CNN architecture design. arXiv preprint arXiv:1807.11164 (2018). https://doi.org/10.48550/arXiv.1807.11164

29. Martino, F., et al.: A deep learning model to predict Ki-67 positivity in oral squamous cell carcinoma. J. Pathology Inf. **15**, 100354 (2023). https://doi.org/10.1016/j.jpi.2023.100354

30. Molnar, C., Tavolara, T., Garcia, C., McClintock, D., Zarella, M., Han, W.: IHC-ScoreGAN: an unsupervised generative adversarial network for end-to-end ki67 scoring for clinical breast cancer diagnosis. In: Proceedings of the 7nd International Conference on Medical Imaging with Deep Learning. Proceedings of Machine Learning Research, vol. 250, pp. 1011–1025 (2024)

31. Naik, N., Madani, A., Esteva, A., et al.: Deep learning-enabled breast cancer hormonal receptor status determination from base-level H&E stains. Nat. Commun. **11**, 5727 (2020). https://doi.org/10.1038/s41467-020-19334-3

32. Nielsen, T., et al.: Assessment of Ki67 in breast cancer: updated recommendations from the international Ki67 in breast cancer working group. JNCI: J. Natl. Cancer Inst. **113**(7), 808–819 (2021). https://doi.org/10.1093/jnci/djaa201

33. Nishimura, R., Osako, T., Okumura, Y., Hayashi, M., Arima, N.: Clinical significance of Ki-67 in neoadjuvant chemotherapy for primary breast cancer as a predictor for chemosensitivity and for prognosis. Breast Cancer **17**(4), 269–275 (2010). https://doi.org/10.1007/s12282-009-0161-5

34. Selvaraju, R.R., Cogswell, M., Das, A., Vedantam, R., Parikh, D., Batra, D.: Grad-CAM: visual explanations from deep networks via gradient-based localization. Int. J. Comput. Vision **128**(2), 336–359 (2019). https://doi.org/10.1007/s11263-019-01228-7

35. Swanson, K., Wu, E., Zhang, A., Alizadeh, A., Zou, J.: From patterns to patients: advances in clinical machine learning for cancer diagnosis, prognosis, and treatment. Cell **186**(8), 1772–1791 (2023). https://doi.org/10.1016/j.cell.2023.01.035

36. Swiderska-Chadaj, Z., Gallego, J., Gonzalez-Lopez, L., Bueno, G.: Detection of Ki67 hot-spots of invasive breast cancer based on convolutional neural networks applied to mutual information of H&E and Ki67 whole slide images. J. Appl. Sci. **10**(21), 7761 (2020). https://doi.org/10.3390/app10217761

37. Thirion, J.P.: Image matching as a diffusion process: an analogy with Maxwell's demons. Med. Image Anal. **2**(3), 243–260 (1998). https://doi.org/10.1016/S1361-8415(98)80022-4

38. Tolstikhin, I., et al.: MLP-mixer: an all-MLP architecture for vision. arXiv preprint arXiv:2105.01601 (2021). https://doi.org/10.48550/arXiv.2105.01601

39. Wang, S., Zhang, Z., Yan, H., Xu, M., Wang, G.: Mix-domain contrastive learning for unpaired H&E-to-IHC stain translation. arXiv preprint arXiv:2406.11799 (2024). https://doi.org/10.48550/arXiv.2406.11799

40. Yerushalmi, R., Woods, R., Ravdin, P., Hayes, M., Gelmon, K.: Ki67 in breast cancer: prognostic and predictive potential. Lancet Oncol. **11**(2), 174–183 (2010). https://doi.org/10.1016/S1470-2045(09)70262-1

ASTER: Automated Segmentation of Endometrial Histology Images for Reproductive Health Assessment

George Wright[1]([✉])[iD], Paul Brighton[2][iD], Hiroyuki Yoshihara[2], Joe Thornton[2], Joanne Muter[2][iD], Jan Brosens[2,3][iD], and Fayyaz Minhas[1][iD]

[1] Department of Computer Science, University of Warwick, Coventry, UK
{george.wright.1,fayyaz.minhas}@warwick.ac.uk
[2] Warwick Medical School, Division of Biomedical Sciences, University of Warwick, Coventry, UK
{p.j.brighton,hiroyuki.yoshihara,j.muter,j.muter,
j.j.brosens}@warwick.ac.uk
[3] Tommy's National Centre for Miscarriage Research, University Hospitals Coventry and Warwickshire National Health Service Trust, Coventry, UK

Abstract. The endometrium undergoes rapid cycles of menstrual breakdown and repair. In each cycle, oestrogen-dependent proliferation followed by progesterone-dependent differentiation of the endometrium culminates in a sterile inflammatory tissue response, termed the decidual reaction, at the start of the embryo implantation window. Analysis of timed endometrial biopsies is widely used to investigate a spectrum of reproductive disorders, including recurrent implantation failure in IVF and recurrent miscarriage. Deep profiling of whole slide images (WSIs), capturing the spatial and functional organization of key histological structures, such as nuclei, glandular and luminal epithelium, subluminal stroma and spiral arterioles, holds significant promise for automated endometrial assessment. To address the lack of such methodologies, we developed ASTER, a multi-task deep learning model for simultaneous segmentation of multiple histological structures in immunostained endometrial WSIs. ASTER has been developed and validated over a large dataset of 2,652 endometrial whole slide images, including 35,135 annotated objects obtained using a pathologist-in-the-loop methodology. The model demonstrates strong performance across all segmentation tasks. Further, analysis of an independent set of 2,082 unseen WSIs showed that ASTER-derived features correlate with cycle-dependent endometrial gene expression. This represents the first systematic study linking segmented morphological characteristics to molecular and temporal markers of endometrial function, demonstrating its effectiveness in enabling comprehensive and automated profiling. This highlights the potential of ASTER to support personalized management of women experiencing reproductive failure. Segmentation results are available for interactive exploration at https://tiademos.dcs.warwick.ac.uk/bokeh_app?demo=ASTER.

Keywords: Segmentation · Histology · Machine Learning · CNN · Endometrium · Reproductive health

S. Ali et al. (Eds.): MIUA 2025, LNCS 15916, pp. 43–57, 2026.
https://doi.org/10.1007/978-3-031-98688-8_4

1   Introduction

The female reproductive system is a complex network of organs designed to support pregnancy. Central to this system is the uterine mucosa, or endometrium, which undergoes cyclical changes during reproductive years to prepare for embryo implantation [2,3]. Each cycle begins with the breakdown of the superficial (functional) endometrial layer, leading to menstrual bleeding, followed by rapid repair of the surface (luminal) epithelium. This is succeeded by proliferation of stromal and glandular epithelial cells and active angiogenesis in response to rising ovarian oestradiol production. Post-ovulation, progesterone interacts with the primed endometrium to initiate a sequence of events culminating in a decidual reaction—an inflammatory response that marks the opening of the midluteum implantation window [21]. At this stage, the endometrial system enters a bistable state: it either transitions to menstrual breakdown in non-conception cycles or evolves into a robust immune-tolerant matrix (decidua) capable of supporting the invasive placenta throughout pregnancy [12]. Histologically, the decidual reaction coincides with the onset of glandular secretion, vascular permeability, and proliferative expansion and differentiation of CD56+ uterine natural killer (uNK) cells [14,18]. This intricate coordination of hormonal, cellular, and immune mechanisms underscores the endometrium's essential function as the foundation for successful reproduction [13].

Endometrial biopsies are widely used clinically for a variety of indications, including investigation of abnormal uterine bleeding and detection of subclinical endometritis. In the context of fertility, timing of the implantation window is critical as it aligns embryonic development with a maternal environment supportive of post-implantation development. Consequently, asynchronous embryo implantation is considered a major cause of infertility and early pregnancy loss [19]. Apart of molecular analyses, endometrial biopsies are commonly evaluated by expert pathologists using haematoxylin and eosin (H&E) or immunohistochemically (IHC) stained slides to assess features such as gland morphology, stromal oedema, inflammatory cell infiltration, and vascular structures. In addition to being time consuming and error prone [20], the conventional assessments are limited by subjectivity, inter-observer variability, and an inability to fully capture spatial tissue complexity. With the adoption of high-resolution whole slide images (WSIs), there is a pressing need for automated, objective methods that can perform deep profiling of endometrial tissue. Accurate segmentation of key histological structures across thousands of WSIs can provide scalable and reproducible insights into endometrial function and dysfunction, ultimately enhancing both research and clinical decision-making.

While significant progress has been made in segmenting histological structures in other tissue types, the endometrium received comparatively little attention, with no existing method capable of generating deeply profiled histological maps through automated segmentation. Efforts to date have been limited to structures like epithelium and stroma to distinguish between receptive and non-receptive states [15]. Other studies used CNNs to quantify CD138-positive cells or epithelial-to-stromal area ratios [5,7]. However, these approaches remain

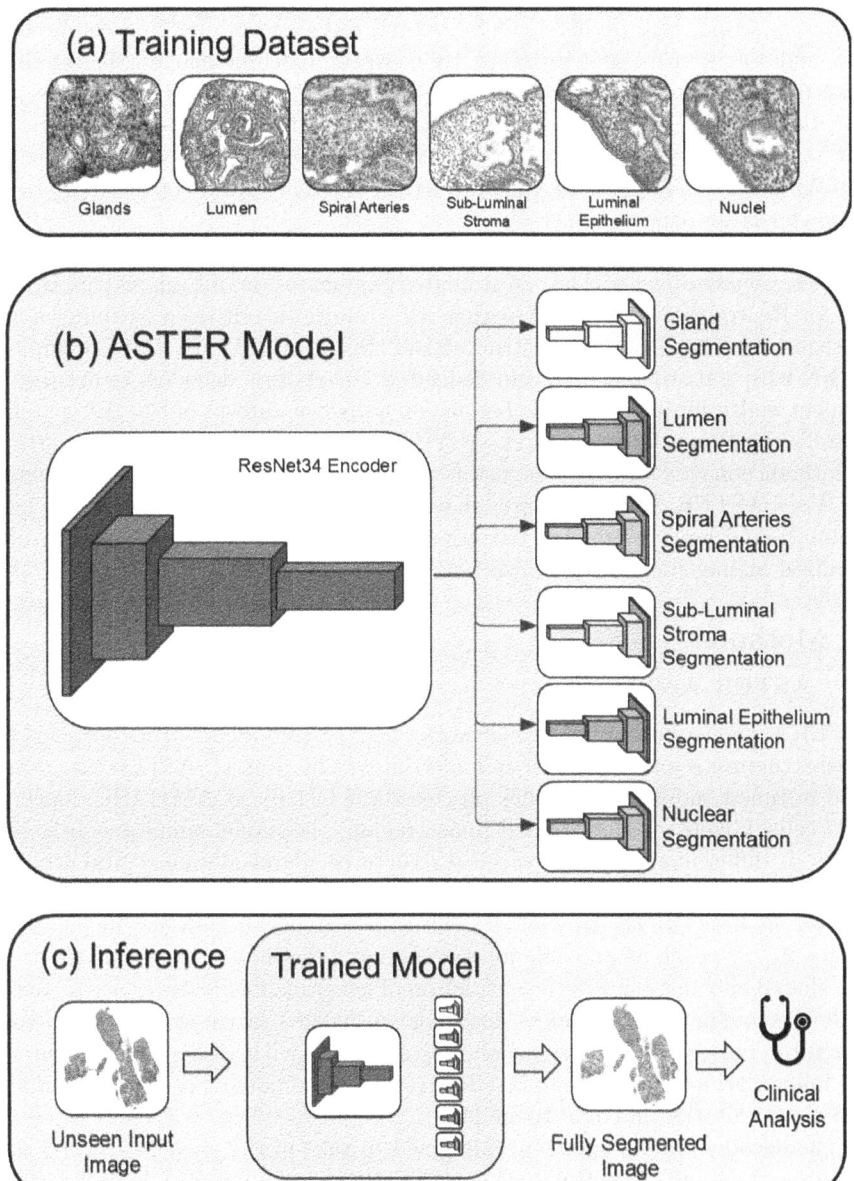

Fig. 1. A high level overview of the proposed CNN-based machine learning framework for segmenting endometrial whole slide images (WSIs). (A) A large training dataset of patches for each annotation class is collected and used to train the model. (b) The model is trained using a shared ResNet34 encoder and has a separate head for each target. (c) The trained model can then be used to fully segment unseen images.

narrow in scope, lack public availability, and fall short of enabling comprehensive, multi-structure tissue profiling. By contrast, machine learning has enabled powerful image analysis tools - such as segmentation, classification, and object detection [9,17] - across a range of other tissues. For example, a CNN-based method for colorectal cancer achieved state-of-the-art gland segmentation on 599 WSIs from The Cancer Genome Atlas, releasing over 900,000 annotated glands for large-scale analysis [4]

To address the lack of comprehensive segmentation methods for endometrial biopsies, we introduce ASTER (Automated Segmentation of Endometrial Histology for Reproductive Health Assessment), a multi-output deep learning model for segmenting key histological structures in IHC-stained WSIs. ASTER employs a CNN with a shared encoder and dedicated U-Net-style decoders to accurately segment multiple tissue regions. Trained on a diverse dataset of 570 IHC patches with 35,135 annotated structures, ASTER is the first model to achieve strong performance across all major segmentation tasks. When applied to 2,048 external WSIs, ASTER-derived features showed correlations with known luteal phase dynamics and gene expression patterns, supporting its potential to aid in personalized management to optimize fertility.

2   Methods

2.1   ASTER Architecture

ASTER is a convolutional neural network (CNN)-based architecture designed for multi-structure segmentation of endometrial tissues (Fig. 1). ASTER was developed in timed endometrial tissues processed for CD56 (NCAM1) IHC, marking uNK cells. Given a CD56-stained image region, the model simultaneously segments six different types of histological structures: glands, lumen, spiral arteries, sub-luminal stroma, luminal epithelium, and nuclei. ASTER employs a shared encoder, Φ, based on the ResNet34 architecture, alongside task-specific decoders Ψ_t, $t = 1 \ldots T$, each responsible for segmenting a distinct histological structure. The shared encoder enables the extraction of generalizable features across tasks, while the independent decoders allow for specialized learning tailored to each structure. This modular design balances efficiency with task-specific accuracy, and follows principles shown to be effective in related domains such as gland and nuclei segmentation in colon tissue [4].

The decoders in our model are designed to take in the encoder features and upsample them by a factor of 2 using a U-Net style architecture. At each level of the decoder hierarchy, each decoder includes skip connections from corresponding layers in the encoder and two 3×3 kernel convolutions with batch normalization. The upsampling process is repeated until the output size matches the input image, resulting in a fully segmented binary output for each task.

2.2   Data Collection of Annotations

For the development of ASTER, we used a dataset comprising 2,652 formalin-fixed paraffin-embedded (FFPE) brightfield images of endometrial biopsy

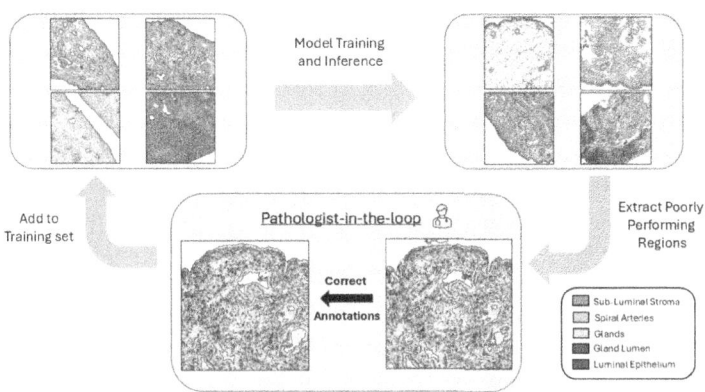

Fig. 2. Pathologist-in-the-loop pipeline for the collection of annotations and creation of the dataset.

Table 1. Summary of data generated in the pathologist-in-the-loop pipeline for model training and testing.

	Glands	Lumen	Epithelium	Sub-Luminal Stromal	Spiral Arteries	Nuclei
Initial Data	2496	2311	273	206	180	–
Corrected data	10368	14497	1032	545	3290	–
Total	12864	16808	1305	751	3470	1559722

samples, read at a spatial resolution of 0.50 microns per pixel (MPP). The whole slide images (WSIs), stained with CD56 and counter-stained with hematoxylin to visualize cell nuclei, were obtained from University Hospital Coventry & Warwickshire (UHCW) National Health Service (NHS) Trust.

We employ a pathologist-in-the-loop annotation collection pipeline to create a large dataset of accurately labelled patches from the WSIs. This approach follows a three-step process: (i) train the model on an initial dataset of labelled images; (ii) refine the model's predictions by experts review and correction; and (iii) input of corrected patches to the training set for further model improvement. Steps 2 and 3 were repeated until the model's performance metrics stop improving. An overview of the iterative labeling strategy is shown in Fig. 2.

We started with manually annotated 3000×3000 patches obtained from WSIs. The initial images were taken from a random selection of WSIs of endometrial biopsies obtained 4 to 12 days after the pre-ovulatory luteinizing hormone surge (LH+days). We then trained a model on this initial set and processed a selection of WSIs. Poorly performing regions were located with patches reviewed by the three pathologists, corrected, and added to the training set before repeating the process. This iterative refinement continued until the model's performance metrics plateaued across all annotation types, resulting in 570 fully labelled patches. Table 1 provides a summary of the number of annotations for each class.

For nuclei segmentation, the StarDist algorithm [22], a deep learning-based approach specifically designed for the segmentation of star-convex shapes, was used to create ground truth masks due to the impracticality of manually creating annotations. The patches from the dataset were input into the pretrained StarDist model, with detections filtered at a probability threshold of 0.5, generating a large, labelled dataset. We implemented a quality control assessment with domain experts confirming that the segmentations accurately represented the underlying cellular structures.

2.3   Multi-task Training

Since annotated image patches typically contain only a subset of the object types, we adopt a multi-task training strategy. During training, 448×448 pixel image patches are sampled independently for each task. All input images are normalized to the [0, 1] range in the RGB color space before being passed into the network. Each training batch corresponds to a single task and is forwarded through the shared encoder Φ and the associated task-specific decoder Ψ_t to generate segmentation predictions.

We use the standard cross-entropy loss to measure the discrepancy between the predicted and ground truth segmentation masks. To ensure that only the relevant components of the model are updated during backpropagation, we apply task-specific masking: only the shared encoder Φ and the active decoder Ψ_t receive gradient updates, while the losses for all other decoders are masked to zero. The loss function $\mathcal{L}$ for a sample y_i and task $t \in T$ is thus defined as:

$$\mathcal{L}(\{\phi, \Psi_t\}, y_i, \hat{y}_i) = -y_i \log(\hat{y}_i) \tag{1}$$

We hold out 10% of patients for testing, 10% for validation, and the remaining 80% of the data is used to train the model. This is done at a patient level to ensure that multiple patches from a WSI stay in the same split. The training process uses the Adam optimizer, with a learning rate of 1e-4 and a batch size of 6. Data augmentation techniques, including random flipping, rotation, Gaussian blur, median blur, and colour perturbation were applied prior to input enabling the model to learn more invariant representations. The framework was developed using PyTorch version 1.13 and employed an NVIDIA RTX A5500 GPU with 24 GB of RAM.

2.4   Post Processing

All binary prediction maps were amalgamated to generate a comprehensive segmented image. Any segmented lumen regions detected outside of the glands are implausible and therefore are removed. To mitigate potential anomalous predictions, we implemented a stringent size thresholds for glandular structures. The upper and lower bounds were established at 2,000,000 pixels and 50 pixels, respectively.

Table 2. Results of our proposed method on the external test set, evaluated using DICE for segmentation quality, and precision and recall for instance-level accuracy across various annotation types.

Annotation Class	DICE	Precision	Recall
Gland	0.938 ± 0.041	0.88 ± 0.097	0.88 ± 0.117
Glandular Lumen	0.831 ± 0.092	0.722 ± 0.161	0.83 ± 0.119
Luminal Epithelium	0.614 ± 0.288	0.675 ± 0.352	0.773 ± 0.309
Sub-Luminal Stroma	0.528 ± 0.304	0.685 ± 0.392	0.681 ± 0.384
Spiral Arteries	0.381 ± 0.233	0.44 ± 0.263	0.749 ± 0.329
Nuclei	0.744 ± 0.017	0.989 ± 0.015	0.940 ± 0.036

2.5   Evaluation Metrics

To assess the segmentation performance of our model, we use the Dice score to evaluate the similarity between the ground truth mask and the prediction mask by calculating the ratio of their Intersection over Union (IoU). To assess whether instances were located correctly, precision and recall were calculated. An object is considered as correctly predicted if the IoU between the predicted and ground truth bounding boxes exceeds a threshold of 0.1. The mean and standard deviation of each metric were calculated independently for each input image and for each class.

2.6   Analysis of Cycle-Dependent Endometrial Gene Expression

To investigate the association between gland morphology and gene expression, we analyzed a large independent dataset comprising 2,082 WSIs also from UHCW. For 628 out 2,082 WSIs, quantitative reverse transcription polymerase chain reaction (RT-qPCR) gene expression data were available [8]. This analysis enabled us to explore potential relationships between histological gland features and cycle-dependent molecular indicators of endometrial function. For each detected gland, we extracted a set of morphological features, including solidity, eccentricity, area, and major and minor axis lengths. Additionally, we computed colour features such as the mean and standard deviation of pixel intensities in the haematoxylin (H) and CD56 channels. These features were aggregated across all glands within a slide to generate a WSI-level descriptor used for subsequent analysis.

3   Results

3.1   Quantitative Segmentation Performance

The segmentation performance of our machine learning model was rigorously evaluated across all annotation types in held out test patches. These results are

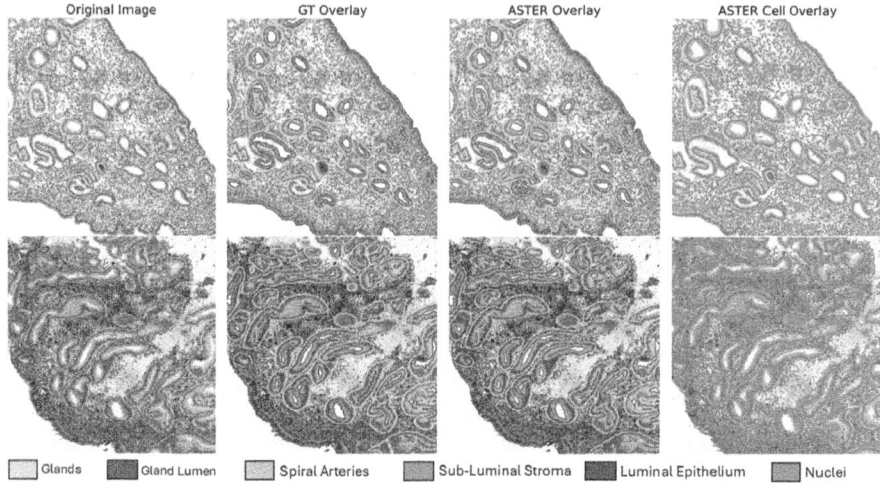

Original Image   GT Overlay   ASTER Overlay   ASTER Cell Overlay

☐ Glands   ■ Gland Lumen   ☐ Spiral Arteries   ☐ Sub-Luminal Stroma   ■ Luminal Epithelium   ☐ Nuclei

Fig. 3. Performance of Segmentation Model. From left to right: Original test image; Ground truth prediction mask; Model's predicted mask; Model's predicted nuclei mask. The comparison demonstrates the accuracy of our model in identifying and segmenting different endometrial structures.

summarized in Table 2. The model achieved high scores across all recorded metrics for glands. This performance is particularly significant given the complex morphology of glands in endometrial histological images, which presents a challenge for automated segmentation methods. Similarly, gland lumen segmentation showed strong performance. Nuclei segmentation achieved very high precision and recall indicating that it can effectively mimic the output of StarDist.

In contrast, luminal epithelium and the corresponding sub-luminal stromal regions achieved a lower set of performance metrics. While the model achieved a high precision and recall, the Dice score is weaker. Spiral arteries proved to be the most challenging annotation type to segment, exhibiting the lowest dice score. This outcome is not unexpected, given the inherent uncertainty in the exact outline, with even inter-annotator disagreements common. However, the segmentation results for spiral arteries demonstrated a notably high recall. This suggests that the model successfully identified spiral arteries, while also detecting numerous additional structures classified as false positives. These apparent false positives may, in fact, represent legitimate spiral arteries that were inadvertently omitted during the manual annotation process due to their elusive nature.

3.2   Qualitative Evaluation of Model Performance

To complement our quantitative analysis, we conducted a comprehensive qualitative evaluation of the ASTER model's segmentation performance. This assessment aimed to visually demonstrate the model's capabilities and evaluate its generalization to unseen WSIs. Figure 3 illustrates examples of the segmenta-

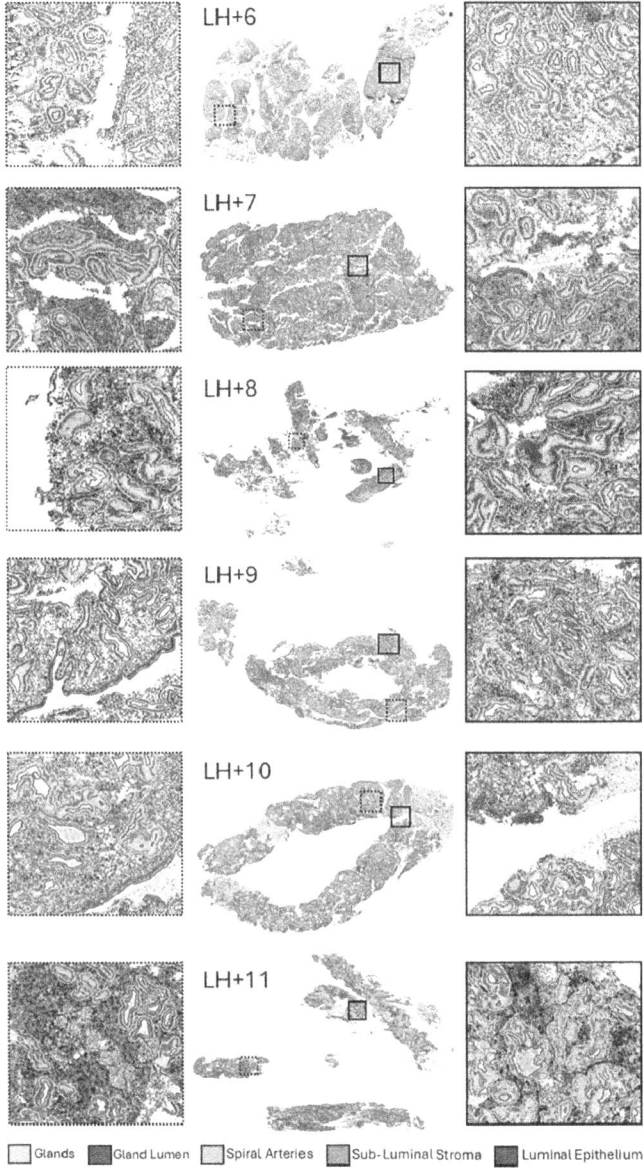

LH+6 LH+7 LH+8 LH+9 LH+10 LH+11

Glands Gland Lumen Spiral Arteries Sub-Luminal Stroma Luminal Epithelium

Fig. 4. Segmentation results of the proposed model on whole slide images (WSIs) from different days. Each row represents a different day, showing representative patches extracted from the corresponding WSI. These results demonstrate the model's consistent performance across temporal variations in WSIs, effectively segmenting key features.

tion results juxtaposed with ground truth annotations. These visual comparisons reveal that while the model effectively segments the regions of interest, there remains an inherent subjectivity in the precise delineation of boundaries. To further assess the model's robustness across varying glandular morphologies, Fig. 4 demonstrates accurate gland instance segmentation with precisely delineated boundaries across different days of the luteal phase. This consistency suggests that our model effectively handles the variability and complexity inherent in glandular histology throughout the luteal phase.

To visually assess the generalization capabilities of the ASTER model, we conducted an extensive qualitative assessment on a diverse set of tissue samples external to the training set. The segmentation results obtained from the ASTER model on these unseen WSIs were reviewed by experts. Challenges were encountered in specific cases. Tissue artifacts, such as folds, and areas where the tissue was severely degraded or disrupted, potentially due to sub-optimal fixation or processing, showed a decline in the model's performance.

3.3   Model Efficiency

The multi-task segmentation model ASTER demonstrates significant advancements in computational efficiency and versatility compared to the established StarDist algorithm. ASTER exhibits markedly reduced inference processing times, completing the analysis of a representative $100k \times 250k$ px WSI containing approximately 300,000 cells in 29 min on average, compared to StarDist which required over 2 h for the same task. Despite this substantial reduction in computational time, ASTER maintains high segmentation accuracy, achieving 0.989 ± 0.015 precision. In addition to nuclei, the model also accurately segments five additional annotation types within the same processing pipeline. This capability contrasts with StarDist, which is only designed for cell segmentation and would require additional models and processing time for other structures.

3.4   Cycle-Dependent Temporal Variations in Gland Morphology

We analysed an additional 2,082 WSIs not included in the training or test data. We measured morphological features of the endometrial glands to investigate changes across the mid-luteal phase of the menstrual cycle. For each WSI, the mean values of glandular solidity and eccentricity were calculated. Our analysis revealed a statistically significant decrease in mean glandular solidity (Spearman's correlation coefficient = -0.403, $p < 10^3$.) and an increase in median glandular eccentricity (Spearman's correlation coefficient = 0.223, $p < 10^{-26}$). This is consistent with the Noyes criteria, which describe the morphological transformation of endometrial glands from regular, rounded shapes to irregular, elongated forms during the luteal phase [14]. Figure 5 illustrates these trends with boxplots, while Fig. 4 provides visual examples of glandular changes across different days of the luteal phase.

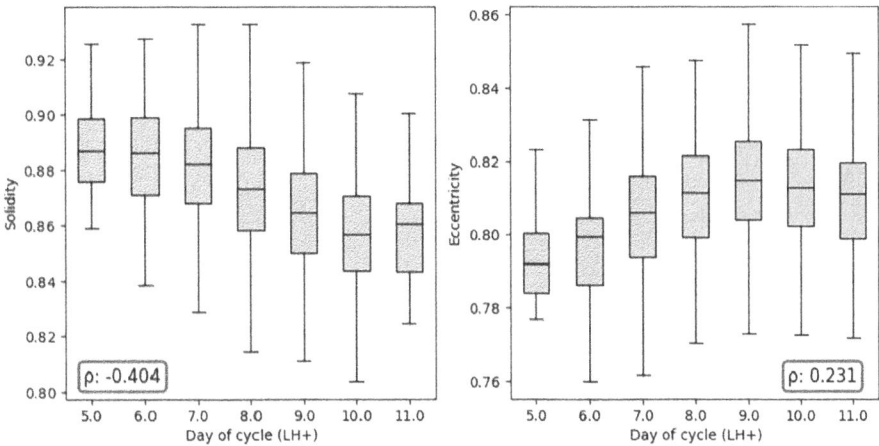

Fig. 5. Boxplots illustrating the distribution of gland solidity and eccentricity across days following a self-reported positive luteinizing hormone (LH) test. Each box represents the median and interquartile range, while whiskers indicate the smallest and largest values within 1.5 times the interquartile range. This visualization highlights changes in gland morphology over time relative to the LH surge.

3.5   Gland Features and Cycle-Dependent Gene Expression

We conducted an analysis of 628 WSIs that included RT-qPCR data for 13 endometrial genes [8]. Our investigation revealed statistically significant correlations ($p < 10^{-3}$) between WSI mean gland solidity and the expression of three gland-specific genes: *GPX3*, *CXCL14*, and *DPP4*. These findings indicate a moderate negative correlation between the expression of these genes and gland solidity, which decreases as glands become more irregular as the menstrual cycle unfolds. This observation aligns with the change in glandular morphology upon onset of apocrine secretions, coinciding with increased gene expression. Figure 7 presents hexbin scatter plots illustrating these negative correlations with a clear trend visible across the range of expression values. While our focus was on these three genes due to their strong correlations and biological relevance, we also observed relationships between other genes and glandular features. Figure 6 provides a comprehensive heatmap overview of the correlations between all 13 analysed genes and various glandular morphology features.

3.6   Spiral Arterioles

To investigate the temporal patterns of spiral arteries, we analysed the density across the luteal phase by normalizing the number of detected spiral arteries relative to the tissue size. Our study revealed a consistent increase in spiral artery density as the luteal phase progressed. This observed trend aligns with the emergence of decidual cells surrounding spiral arterioles, reinforcing the

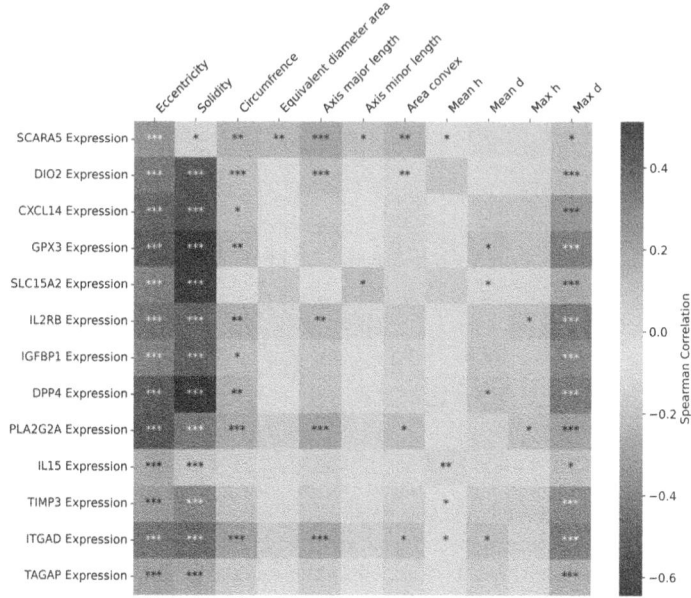

Fig. 6. Heatmap showing Spearman's correlation coefficients between various gland features and gene expression levels. Asterisks denote statistical significance levels of correlation p-values: $* : p < 0.05, ** : p < 0.01, *** : p < 0.001$. This analysis reveals the strength and direction of relationships between glandular morphology and the expression of genes potentially involved in tissue structure and function.

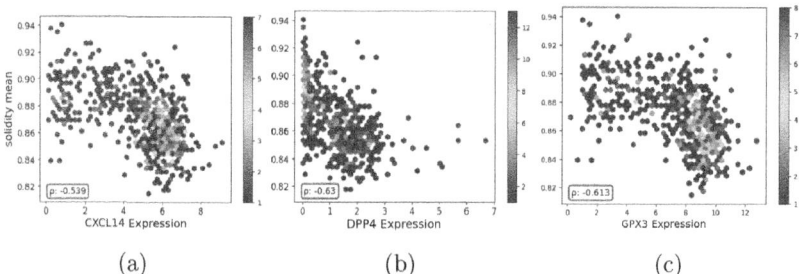

Fig. 7. Correlation between mean glandular solidity and gene expression in whole slide images (WSIs). Hexbin scatter plots depicting the relationship between the mean solidity of all glands within a WSI and gene expression values for (a) *CXCL14*, (b) *DPP4*, and (c) *GPX3*. Colour intensity indicates the density of data points. The y-axis represents mean glandular solidity, while the x-axis shows gene expression levels. This shows the associations between glandular morphology and the expression of genes implicated in tissue architecture and function.

detection capabilities of the model. To quantify this relationship, we conducted a Spearman's correlation analysis between spiral artery density and luteal phase progression. This result yielded a statistically significant correlation $(p < 10^{-3})$

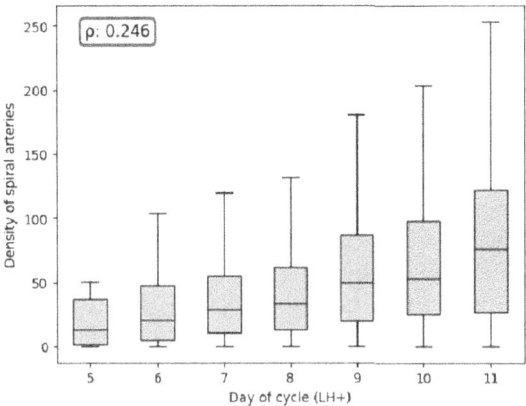

Fig. 8. Boxplot illustrating the density of spiral arteries in whole slide images (WSIs) relative to the time in luteal phase. The y-axis quantifies spiral artery density as the count per megapixel of tissue, while the x-axis represents days post-positive urinary ovulation test (LH+). This visualization demonstrates that the number of detected spiral arteries aligns with known patterns of endometrial vascular development throughout the menstrual cycle.

with a coefficient of 0.246 validating the trend in the models' predictions as visualised in Fig. 8.

3.7   Interactive Visualisation

We provide an interactive demo showcasing the system's capabilities in segmenting and visualizing key structures in WSIs available at https://tiademos.dcs. warwick.ac.uk/bokeh_app?demo=ASTER. The demo allows users to explore sample WSI results at a range of levels, with the full output of ASTER's deep learning model displayed to explore the quality of detections.

4   Discussion and Conclusion

The establishment of an optimal environment for embryo implantation is a complex process characterized by coordinated and time-sensitive cellular and structural changes. While accurate delineation of endometrial structures is essential for both computational analysis and clinical assessment, manual methods are impractical for large-scale applications due to their time-intensive nature. To address these unique challenges posed by the dynamic nature of the cycling endometrium, we introduce ASTER, a novel multi-task machine learning model for endometrial tissue analysis. This advanced computational approach simultaneously segments several endometrial structures directly from images, offering a scalable and comprehensive solution for tissue analysis. ASTER's efficiency is crucial in clinical settings where rapid analysis of whole slide images is essential.

The model's strong performance across independent test images, coupled with its ability to capture features that align with known biological trends in large-scale analysis, demonstrates its reliability and potential to significantly impact reproductive health management.

ASTER's capabilities have significant clinical implications. Spatio-temporal perturbation in endometrial organisation, is a major driver of reproductive failure [1,6,11]. By providing accurate segmentation, ASTER facilitates quantitative analysis of features associated with aberrant endometrial tissue including conditions such as Polycystic Ovary Syndrome (PCOS) and endometriosis. Notably, glandular features such as solidity and eccentricity show high Spearman's correlation with gene expression ($DPP4$: $\rho = 0.644, p < 0.001$), yielding results comparable to specialized machine learning methods designed specifically for gene expression prediction [10,16]. These applications emphasize ASTER's potential to enhance diagnostic workflows and provide actionable insights in clinical settings.

While ASTER demonstrates robust performance, certain limitations warrant further investigation. The model's performance on segmentation of endometrial vasculature could be improved, potentially requiring IHC of endothelial or pericyte markers. Additionally, validation across a diverse range of staining protocols and sample preparations is necessary to ensure broad applicability. Future work will focus on developing specialized interpretable AI models for predicting clinical variables from features derived from segmented structures. This could provide additional insights into the underlying biological processes governing endometrial function.

In conclusion, ASTER represents a significant advancement in computational endometrial analysis, offering the first model capable of concurrent quantification of multiple key biomarkers directly from whole slide images. By bridging the gap between computational pathology and reproductive health, ASTER has the potential to accelerate research into endometrial dysfunction and improve clinical decision-making in fertility management. As we continue to refine and expand ASTER's capabilities, its impact on reproductive health research and clinical practice is poised to grow, ultimately contributing to improved outcomes for patients experiencing reproductive failure.

Disclosure of Interests. The University of Warwick is seeking patent protection on the use of machine learning to predict endometrial biomarkers (Application number: GB2416405.5)

References

1. Ball, E., et al.: Late sporadic miscarriage is associated with abnormalities in spiral artery transformation and trophoblast invasion. J. Pathol. J. Pathol. Soc. Great Britain Ireland **208** (2006)
2. Boyd, J.D., Hamilton, W.J.: The Human Placenta. Heffer, Cambridge (1970)
3. Critchley, H.O., Maybin, J.A., Armstrong, G.M., Williams, A.R.: Physiology of the endometrium and regulation of menstruation. Physiol. Rev. (2020)

4. Graham, S., et al.: One model is all you need: multi-task learning enables simultaneous histology image segmentation and classification. Med. Image Anal. **83**, 102685 (2023)
5. Kangasniemi, M.H., et al.: Artificial intelligence deep learning model assessment of leukocyte counts and proliferation in endometrium from women with and without polycystic ovary syndrome. F&S Sci. **3**(2), 174–186 (2022)
6. Kelleher, A.M., DeMayo, F.J., Spencer, T.E.: Uterine glands: developmental biology and functional roles in pregnancy. Endocr. Rev. **40**(5), 1424–1445 (2019)
7. Lee, S., et al.: Dynamic changes in ai-based analysis of endometrial cellular composition: analysis of pcos and rif endometrium. J. Pathol. Inf. **15**, 100364 (2024)
8. Lipecki, J., et al.: EndoTime: non-categorical timing estimates for luteal endometrium. Human Reprod. **37**(4), 747–761 (2022)
9. Litjens, G., et al.: A survey on deep learning in medical image analysis. Med. Image Anal. **42**, 60–88 (2017)
10. Mondol, R.K., et al.: hist2rna: an efficient deep learning architecture to predict gene expression from breast cancer histopathology images. Cancers **15**(9) (2023)
11. Muter, J., Kong, C.S., et al.: Stalling of the endometrial decidual reaction determines the recurrence risk of miscarriage. In: bioRxiv, pp. 2024–11 (2024)
12. Muter, J., Lynch, V.J., McCoy, R.C., Brosens, J.J.: Human embryo implantation. Development **150**(10), dev201507 (2023)
13. Neykova, K., Tosto, V., Giardina, I., Tsibizova, V., Vakrilov, G.: Endometrial receptivity and pregnancy outcome. J. Maternal-Fetal Neonatal Med. **35**(13), 2591–2605 (2022)
14. Noyes, R., Hertig, A., Rock, J.: Dating the endometrial biopsy. Obstet. Gynecol. Surv. **5**(4), 561–564 (1950)
15. Raudonis, V., et al.: Towards metric-driven difference detection between receptive and nonreceptive endometrial samples using automatic histology image analysis. Appl. Sci. **14**(13), 5715 (2024)
16. Schmauch, B., et al.: A deep learning model to predict rna-seq expression of tumours from whole slide images. Nat. Commun. **11**(1), 3877 (2020)
17. Song, A.H., et al.: Artificial intelligence for digital and computational pathology. Nat. Rev. Bioeng. **1**(12), 930–949 (2023)
18. Strunz, B., et al.: Continuous human uterine nk cell differentiation in response to endometrial regeneration and pregnancy. Sci. Immunol. **6**(56), eabb7800 (2021)
19. Sun, B., Yeh, J.: Non-invasive and mechanism-based molecular assessment of endometrial receptivity during the window of implantation: current concepts and future prospective testing directions. Front. Reprod. Health **4**, 863173 (2022)
20. Wahab, N., et al.: Semantic annotation for computational pathology: multidisciplinary experience and best practice recommendations. J. Pathol. Clin. Res. **8**(2), 116–128 (2022)
21. Wang, W., et al.: Single-cell transcriptomic atlas of the human endometrium during the menstrual cycle. Nat. Med. **26**(10), 1644–1653 (2020)
22. Weigert, M., Schmidt, U.: Nuclei instance segmentation and classification in histopathology images with stardist. In: 2022 IEEE International Symposium on Biomedical Imaging Challenges (ISBIC), pp. 1–4. IEEE (2022)

Leveraging Pathology Foundation Models for Panoptic Segmentation of Melanoma in H&E Images

Jiaqi Lv[1]([✉]), Yijie Zhu[1], Carmen Guadalupe Colin Tenorio[3,4], Brinder Singh Chohan[2], Mark Eastwood[1], and Shan E Ahmed Raza[1]

[1] Tissue Image Analytics Centre, Department of Computer Science, University of Warwick, Coventry, UK
tia@warwick.ac.uk
[2] University Hospitals of Derby and Burton NHS Foundation Trust, Derby, UK
[3] Department of Pathophysiology and Allergy Research, Center for Pathophysiology, Infectiology and Immunology, Medical University of Vienna, Vienna, Austria
[4] TissueGnostics GmbH, Vienna, Austria

Abstract. Melanoma is an aggressive form of skin cancer with rapid progression and high metastatic potential. Accurate characterisation of tissue morphology in melanoma is crucial for prognosis and treatment planning. However, manual segmentation of tissue regions from haematoxylin and eosin (H&E) stained whole-slide images (WSIs) is labour-intensive and prone to inter-observer variability, this motivates the need for reliable automated tissue segmentation methods. In this study, we propose a novel deep learning network for the segmentation of five tissue classes in melanoma H&E images. Our approach leverages Virchow2 [25], a pathology foundation model trained on 3.1 million histopathology images as a feature extractor. These features are fused with the original RGB images and subsequently processed by an encoder-decoder segmentation network (Efficient-UNet) to produce accurate segmentation maps. The proposed model achieved first place in the tissue segmentation task of the PUMA Grand Challenge [20], demonstrating robust performance and generalizability. Our results show the potential and efficacy of incorporating pathology foundation models into segmentation networks to accelerate computational pathology workflows.

Keywords: Deep Learning · Tissue Segmentation · Foundation Model · Melanoma · Whole-Slide Images

1 Introduction

Melanoma is an aggressive form of skin cancer with rapid progression, high metastatic potential, and poor prognosis, particularly at advanced stages [8]. Effective clinical management of melanoma relies on accurate diagnosis and precise characterization of tissue morphology from histopathology slides. Previous

studies have highlighted that tumour-infiltrating lymphocytes (TILs) can potentially serve as a strong prognostic biomarker [23,24]. Specifically, the density
and spatial organization of TILs can provide insights into tumour progression,
response to treatment, and patient survival [2,10,19]. However, manual assessment of TILs from haematoxylin and eosin (H&E)-stained whole-slide images
(WSIs) is labour-intensive, time-consuming, and susceptible to inter-observer
variability. This underscores the need for reliable automated methods for precise and reproducible tissue segmentation and cell detection in histopathological
images.

Automated computational approaches using deep learning have emerged as
promising solutions to address these challenges and have demonstrated strong
performance in various histopathology tasks, including nuclei detection, tissue
segmentation, and WSI-level classification [21]. Among these methods, U-Net
remains popular and continues to achieve state-of-the-art (SOTA) results in
many medical image segmentation tasks, primarily due to its ability to extract
multi-level features and the skip connections between its encoder and decoder
[17]. A more recent work, nnUNet, optimizes the U-Net architecture by automatically selecting dataset-specific hyperparameters, streamlining the segmentation pipeline and achieving consistently high performance in several biomedical
imaging benchmarks [13]. However, its fully automated pipeline reduces flexibility, restricting researchers from modifying the model architectures or employing
tailored training strategies.

Advancements in computer vision have shown that vision transformers (ViTs)
can surpass traditional convolutional neural networks (CNNs) on natural image
recognition benchmarks such as ImageNet [6]. Nevertheless, ViTs are inherently
data-hungry, they require large-scale annotated datasets for effective training,
which poses a significant challenge in computational pathology due to the costs
and labour involved in creating extensive, high-quality annotations, especially
for rare cancers or tissues. For example, prior to the recently released PUMA
Challenge dataset [20], there were no publicly available datasets specifically for
melanoma tissue segmentation, severely limiting research progress in this area.

Pathology foundation models have recently emerged as a promising solution to the challenges of computational pathology. Foundation models are typically based on ViTs, these models are trained on millions of unlabelled or
sparsely annotated histopathology images through self-supervised or weakly-
supervised learning, thereby circumventing the need for extensive manual annotations. Examples of such foundation models include UNI [3], Phikon-v2 [7],
TITAN [5], and Virchow2 [25]. These foundation models have demonstrated
exceptional generalization capabilities and strong performance in diverse downstream histopathology tasks, such as cancer classification, cancer grading, and
prognosis prediction. Nonetheless, most existing studies that utilise foundation
models have predominantly focused on classification tasks involving aggregation
of patch-level features from WSIs. To date, exploration of the use of foundation models for high-resolution pixel-level segmentation tasks remains limited.
Recently, CellViT++ [12] has emerged as one of the first approaches to utilise

foundation models for nuclei segmentation, achieving SOTA performance on multiple cell segmentation benchmarks. However, to our knowledge, currently there is no published study that directly investigates the effectiveness of pathology foundation models for tissue segmentation on a large scale.

1.1 Main Contributions

Our main contributions are summarised as follows:

- We propose a novel deep learning network that integrates the Virchow2 pathology foundation model with an EfficientNetV2 [22] based encoder-decoder architecture (Efficient-UNet) to segment five tissue classes in H&E-stained images of melanoma.
- We introduce a dual stage loss strategy that provides intermediate and final supervision, which encourages consistent feature learning throughout the network.
- We validate our method in the PUMA Challenge [20], where it achieved first place in the tissue segmentation task.

2 Method

2.1 PUMA Dataset

The dataset used in this study is sourced from the PUMA Challenge [20]. The organisers collected a total of 310 H&E-stained region-of-interest (ROI) images. These include 155 primary and 155 metastatic melanoma samples. All ROIs were scanned at 40× magnification (0.23 μm per pixel), with a spatial resolution of 1024 × 1024 pixels. Both tissue and nuclei annotations were initially created by a medical expert and subsequently reviewed and refined by a dermatopathologist. While all slides were digitised at a single melanoma referral centre, 76 cases were referral consultations from other hospitals, which may introduce variability in staining due to differing processing techniques.

Training Dataset. The released training set includes 103 primary and 102 metastatic melanoma ROIs (one image was removed because of missing annotations). We use this dataset to train our models using 5-fold cross-validation.

Test Dataset. Two separate test sets are used for evaluation: a preliminary test set consists of 10 ROIs: 5 primary and 5 metastatic melanomas for initial validation. A final test set consists of 94 ROIs: 47 primary and 47 metastatic ROIs for the final evaluation to determine the challenge winners.

Tissue Classes. The annotations include six tissue classes: tumour, stroma, epidermis, necrosis, blood vessels and background. Among these, tumour and stroma occupy the majority of tissue area, with epidermis, necrosis, and blood vessels being the minority classes.

In this paper, we report the performance of our proposed method, alongside our baseline models and top-performing models from other teams, on the preliminary and final test sets. Background class is excluded from evaluation.

2.2 Overview of the Proposed Framework

Our goal is to design a neural network capable of learning robust and generalisable features for accurate tissue segmentation in melanoma. To achieve this, we use Virchow2 [25], a 632-million-parameter ViT trained on 3.1 million histopathology WSIs, as a frozen feature extractor. Patch tokens from the pretrained Virchow2 provide guidance for segmentation, which we integrate into an EfficientNetV2 based encoder-decoder segmentation model (Efficient-UNet). Another motivation for selecting Virchow2 is its ability to produce patch tokens out-of-the-box.

1. **Input Image**: Given an input RGB image of shape $3 \times 1024 \times 1024$ ($C \times H \times W$) pixels at 40× magnification, it is downsampled to $3 \times 224 \times 224$ pixels using bilinear interpolation, we obtain X.
2. **Patch Token Extraction**: X is passed to Virchow2, which produces a sequence of patch tokens T of dimension 1280×256.
3. **Permutation**: We rearrange T into a multidimensional grid T' of shape $1280 \times 16 \times 16$ ($C \times H \times W$). This facilitates convolution operations.
4. **Progressive Transposed Convolution (PTC) Module**: T' is progressively upsampled by the PTC Module. The output is a $5 \times 224 \times 224$ ($C \times H \times W$) spatially resolved feature map, T''
5. **Feature Concatenation**: T'' is concatenated with the original image patch X, producing X', a tensor of dimension $8 \times 224 \times 224$ ($C \times H \times W$). This step preserves both token-based features from Virchow2 and raw context from the input image.
6. **EfficientUNet Segmentation**: X' is passed to EfficientUNet, an encoder-decoder network, with an EfficientNetV2-M backbone. It outputs a segmentation map of dimension $5 \times 224 \times 224$ ($C \times H \times W$), corresponding to five target tissue classes.
7. **Dual Stage Loss**: Loss is computed at two stages, after the PTC Module (L_{PTC}) and at the final output stage (L_{Output}). L_{PTC} and L_{Output} are combined using a weighted sum. Details about the loss functions are explained in Sect. 2.5.

A visualisation of these steps is shown in Fig. 1.

2.3 Progressive Transposed Convolution (PTC) Module

We propose a PTC module to restore spatial information from patch tokens. This module consists of three convolution layers with sigmoid activations, which

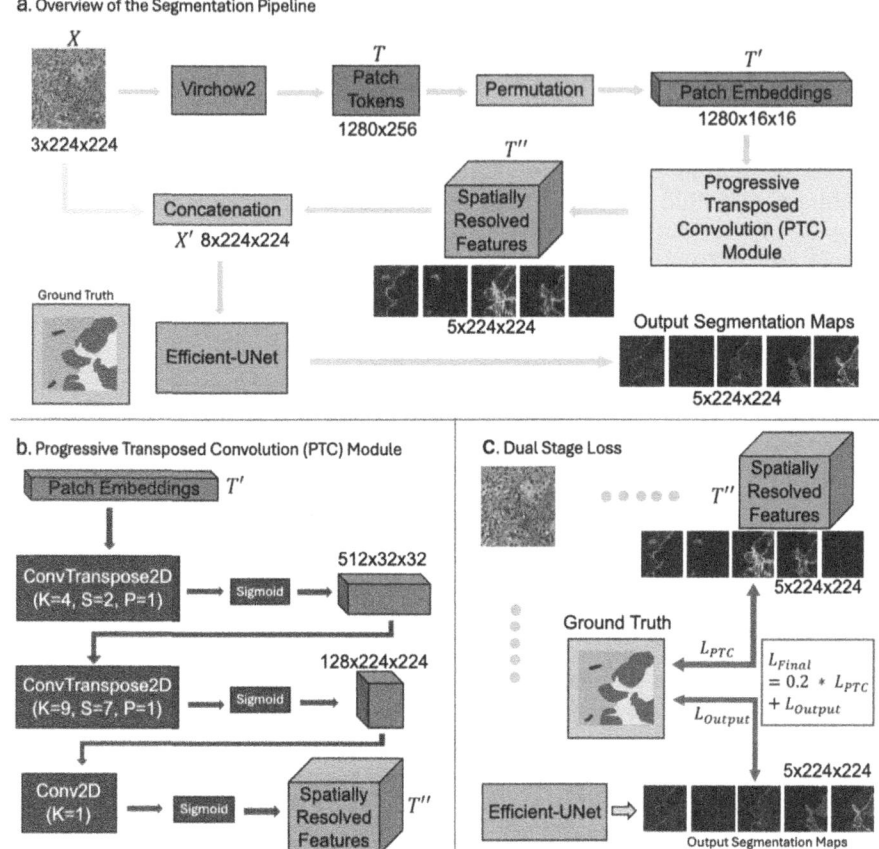

Fig. 1. Illustrations of our proposed method. **a.** The end-to-end segmentation pipeline: the input RGB image is passed through Virchow2 to extract patch embeddings. These embeddings are processed by the Progressive Transposed Convolution (PTC) module to generate spatially resolved feature maps. The resulting features are then concatenated with the original RGB image and passed to an Efficient-UNet for final segmentation. **b.** Architecture of the PTC module: patch embeddings are upsampled and reduced in dimensionality through two consecutive ConvTranspose2D layers, followed by a Conv2D layer to produce the final spatially resolved output with the desired number of channels. **c.** Illustration of the dual stage loss: losses are computed at both the intermediate stage after the PTC module (L_{PTC}) and the final output stage (L_{Output}). This encourages consistent feature learning throughout the network.

upsample patch tokens from 16×16 to 224×224 while reducing the channel dimension from 1280 to 5. We choose five output channels here because it matches the number of target tissue types, it provides a direct feature mapping to the segmentation network and it facilitates intermediate loss calculation (this is explained in Sect. 2.5).

As illustrated in Fig. 1b, the patch tokens extracted by Virchow2 from an input RGB image are passed through two ConvTranspose2D layers. A final 1×1 convolution is applied to generate the 5-channel output corresponding to the target tissue classes. We employ sigmoid activations following each convolution block; in our experiments, this significantly stabilizes training by constraining intermediate feature values within [0,1], which mitigates exploding gradients compared to ReLU activation.

We also considered fusing the spatially resolved features with Efficient-UNet at its bottleneck layer, but the network showed poor performance in our internal cross-validation.

2.4   Efficient-UNet

We constructed an encoder–decoder network with U-Net–style skip connections [17], replacing the encoder with an EfficientNetV2-M [22] backbone pre-trained on ImageNet, and added Spatial and Channel Squeeze & Excitation (SCSE) modules [18] into the decoder blocks. We refer to this segmentation model as Efficient-UNet. Similar approaches have been explored in other studies [9,11,15].

2.5   Dual Stage Loss

Loss Function. The loss function is a combination of Dice loss and Focal loss ($Dice_{FL}$), with a larger weighting on Dice loss. The weighting factor was chosen empirically based on internal cross-validation. The equation of $Dice_{FL}$ is shown in Eq. 1.

$$Dice_{FL} = 2 * Dice_{loss} + Focal_{loss} \tag{1}$$

The equation of Dice loss ($Dice_{loss}$) is shown in Eq. 2. It is calculated as one minus the Dice coefficient between the ground truth g and the predicted probability p for each pixel i, we set $\epsilon = 1e^{-6}$ to avoid division by zero.

$$Dice_{loss} = 1 - Dice = 1 - \frac{2 \sum_i p_i g_i}{\sum_i p_i + \sum_i g_i + \epsilon} \tag{2}$$

The equation of Focal loss ($Focal_{loss}$) is shown in Eq. 3. We set $\alpha = 0.3$ and $\gamma = 3.5$, based on our internal cross-validation experiments.

$$Focal_{loss} = \begin{cases} -\alpha(1 - p_i)^\gamma \log p_i & \text{if } g_i = 1 \\ -(1 - \alpha)p_i^\gamma \log 1 - p_i & \text{if } g_i = 0 \end{cases} \tag{3}$$

With a combination of Dice loss and Focal loss, we effectively optimise region-based overlap, while providing more emphasis on minority classes.

Loss Computation. We employ a dual stage loss strategy to reinforce robust feature learning throughout the pipeline, as illustrated in Fig. 1c. We introduce an intermediate loss after the PTC Module computed using $Dice_{FL}$ (L_{PTC}), which is combined with the output loss from the final segmentation layer computed using $Dice_{FL}$ (L_{Output}) through a weighted sum.

Following the PTC Module, we obtain spatially resolved features of dimension $5 \times 224 \times 224$. Supervising this initial output against the ground truth provides an explicit training signal that encourages the PTC Module to learn task-relevant features. Additionally, gradients can flow directly back to the PTC Module without being diluted through the full segmentation network.

$$L_{Final} = 0.2 * L_{PTC} + L_{Output} \tag{4}$$

We combine L_{PTC} and L_{Output} using a weighted sum, where a weight of 0.2 on L_{PTC} was selected empirically based on internal cross-validation. A larger weight on L_{PTC} was found to destabilize training and make it difficult to converge, it is likely because the PTC Module alone cannot be expected to generate accurate segmentation maps purely from patch tokens. By keeping this weight small, we ensure the intermediate stage remains guided by useful feedback while the Efficient-UNet is ultimately responsible for making the final predictions.

2.6 Implementation Details

Hardware: We trained our model on a high-performance compute node using two CPU cores (Intel(R) Xeon(R) Platinum 8168), 20 gigabytes (GBs) of RAM, and one Nvidia Tesla V100 GPU with 32 GBs of memory.

Data Pre-processing: Each image and its corresponding mask are resized to 224×224 pixels by interpolation.

Training: We implemented all models using PyTorch version 2.5 and trained them using the AdamW optimizer with an inital learning rate of 0.001 and a weight decay of 0.005, the batch size was set to 24. Early stopping was used to prevent overfitting. On average the models take 30 min to finish training.

Weighted Sampling: We implemented a pixel-level weighted sampling strategy. Patches containing more tissue of rare classes are assigned higher sampling probabilities, this ensures that images with necrosis, blood vessels or epidermis are more frequently included during training.

Data Augmentation: We apply a wide range of data augmentations during training, this includes random RGB shift, random hue saturation and value (HSV) shift, Gaussian blur and sharpening, image compression, random brightness and contrast adjustments, random shifts and scaling, random 90-degree rotations and horizontal/vertical flips.

Post-processing: We apply argmax on the output segmentation map to select the tissue class with the highest probability at each pixel. To remove small holes and spurious objects, we perform morphological opening followed by morphological closing using a circular kernel of size 13 pixels.

3   Results

We tested our proposed method on the PUMA Challenge dataset, we report performance on both the preliminary test set and the final test set. For comparison, we also include the results of the top performing segmentation models submitted by the top three teams in the challenge, Team LSM, Team rictoo, and Team Biototem. While their methods remain unpublished at the time of writing, their results serve as strong reference points for benchmarking performance across both evaluation phases.

3.1   Internal Cross-Validation

We conducted 5-fold cross validation on the training set to evaluate model performance and select the best configuration. Our method was compared against two baseline models: Efficient-UNet and a U-Net with a Swin Transformer encoder [14] (Swin-UNet).

Our method achieved the highest average Dice score (68.23%). We found that incorporating the dual-stage loss strategy led to an improvement in segmentation performance, from 66.84% to 68.23%. However, we also observed a large standard deviation in Dice scores for the rarer tissue classes, notably epidermis, blood vessels, and especially necrosis. This could be attributed to the class imbalance within the dataset. A summary of our internal cross validation results is presented in Table 1.

To further illustrate the performance differences between models, we present a visual comparison in Fig. 2, showing segmentation outputs from our proposed method, Efficient-UNet, and Swin-UNet on image samples from the validation set. Overall, our method consistently produces more accurate segmentations, it particularly excels at tumour, stroma and epidermis regions. In contrast, the baseline models often misclassify tissue boundaries or completely fail to detect under-represented classes.

3.2   Preliminary Test Phase

In the preliminary test phase, we compared our method against Efficient-UNet, Swin-UNet, and nnUNet [13] which was trained by the PUMA Challenge organizers. Our approach consistently outperformed these architectures, achieving a micro Dice score of 73.41%, with particularly strong performance in tumour, stroma, and necrosis segmentation. While our average score was slightly behind Team rictoo and Team LSM, this was primarily due to lower performance on the blood vessels class. However, it is important to note that the preliminary test set comprises only 10 images, therefore is not a representative indicator of large scale performance. A summary of these results is presented in Table 2.

Table 1. Summary of tissue segmentation results (Dice%) from our **internal 5-fold cross validation**. *Our method trained using only L_{output} loss rather than the proposed dual stage loss.

Method	Micro Average	Tumour	Stroma
Our Method	**68.23 ± 6.61**	**93.73 ± 1.44**	**83.60 ± 5.46**
Our Method(L_{output} only)*	66.84 ± 8.05	93.09 ± 1.42	82.72 ± 3.19
Efficient-UNet	45.99 ± 5.61	91.48 ± 2.41	78.65 ± 3.33
Swin-UNet	66.79 ± 9.86	92.77 ± 1.73	82.69 ± 5.13

Method	Nercosis	Blood Vessels	Epidermis
Our Method	33.86 ± 32.85	52.51 ± 6.84	**77.49 ± 3.78**
Our Method(L_{output} only)*	**39.11 ± 31.09**	**55.24 ± 6.02**	72.48 ± 8.51
Efficient-UNet	0.00 ± 0.00	11.34 ± 13.78	48.48 ± 16.23
Swin-UNet	32.11 ± 41.02	48.74 ± 10.85	68.73 ± 12.72

Table 2. Summary of tissue segmentation results (Dice%) on the PUMA Challenge **Preliminary Test Set**. *Methods have not been publicly released at the time of writing.

Method	Micro Average	Tumour	Stroma	Necrosis	Blood Vessels	Epidermis
Our Method	73.41	93.36	**86.41**	**64.97**	33.02	89.29
Team rictoo*	**75.83**	91.47	83.80	59.52	59.13	85.23
Team LSM*	75.53	90.62	82.69	47.63	**66.46**	90.22
Team Biototem*	69.22	88.21	77.78	37.82	51.35	90.03
Efficient-UNet	59.01	91.53	84.93	0.0	26.27	**92.32**
Swin-UNet	69.21	87.97	78.46	52.03	36.97	90.64
nnUnet (baseline)	62.88	**93.37**	84.92	0.0	50.83	85.30

Table 3. Summary of tissue segmentation results (Dice%) on the PUMA Challenge **Final Test Set**. *Methods have not been publicly released at the time of writing. **Results reported by the authors using two significant figures.

Method	Micro Average	Tumour	Stroma	Necrosis	Blood Vessels	Epidermis
Our Method	**78.23**	**93.58**	**83.59**	**82.04**	45.70	86.26
Team rictoo*	63.26	91.77	81.49	15.19	47.22	80.63
Team LSM*	77.98	92.46	81.28	74.49	**54.37**	**87.32**
Team Biototem*	72.69	91.43	81.29	57.18	47.35	86.17
nnUnet (baseline)	55.48	91.09	78.51	1.52	34.99	71.30
MaskFormer-UNI**	44.00	86.00	62.00	9.00	1.00	64.00

3.3   Final Test Phase

Our method ranked first in the final test phase of the PUMA Challenge, with a micro-average Dice score of 78.23%. It demonstrated strong segmentation performance across most tissue classes. This represents a substantial improvement over the nnUNet baseline (Dice = 55.48%) as well as team rictoo (Dice = 63.26%), both of which showed significant performance degradation on the final test set. Furthermore, the challenge organizers trained a MaskFormer [4] model using the UNI foundation model [3] as backbone, but it performed poorly (Dice = 44.00%)

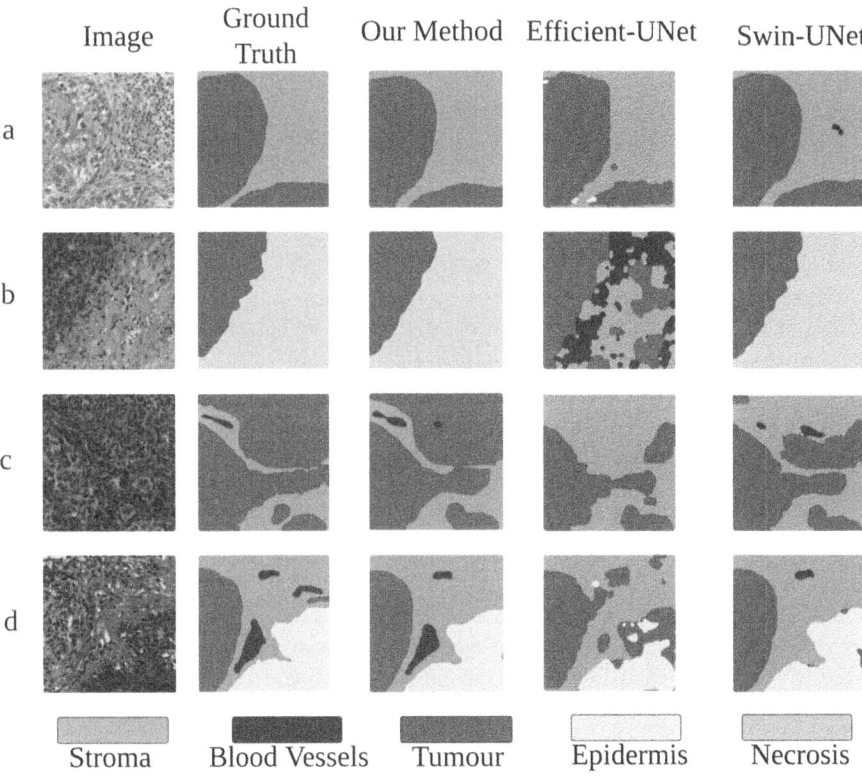

Fig. 2. Qualitative comparison of segmentation results between our proposed method, Efficient-UNet, and Swin-UNet on the internal 5-fold cross-validation set. **a**: Our method accurately segments tumour and stroma regions. Efficient-UNet introduces false positive epidermis, while Swin-UNet incorrectly predicts a blood vessel. **b**: Our method and Swin-UNet correctly segment tumour and necrosis regions. Efficient-UNet fails to detect necrosis and over-predicts multiple tissue types, especially blood vessels and stroma. **c**: Our method introduces a minor false positive blood vessel. Efficient-UNet and Swin-UNet misclassifies a large tumour region as stroma. **d**: Our method misses one blood vessel and a small tumour region. Efficient-UNet fails to detect blood vessels and confuses tumour with stroma and epidermis. Swin-UNet misses two blood vessels and partially misclassifies tissue boundaries.

Table 4. Average inference time per image (in seconds).

Method	Inference Time
Our Method	0.0774 ± 0.0009
Efficient-UNet	0.0103 ± 0.0007
Swin-UNet	0.0113 ± 0.0005

[20]. This highlights the challenge of effectively integrating pathology foundation models into segmentation networks. A summary of the final challenge leaderboard is provided in Table 3.

3.4   Visualisation

To further validate the effectiveness of the patch tokens from Virchow2 and the ability of our Progressive Transposed Convolution (PTC) module to generate meaningful spatially resolved features, we visualise the PTC output as probability heat maps, where each of the five output channels corresponds to a specific tissue class: stroma, blood vessels, tumour, epidermis, and necrosis (see Fig. 3).

We observe that these spatially resolved feature maps closely resemble the ground truth annotations, which indicates the PTC module, when supervised with our dual-stage loss, is able to capture semantically relevant tissue representations at high resolution.

However, as expected, these intermediate predictions are not always correct. For example, in Fig. 3a, the spatially resolved features contain a false positive blood vessel instance in the top right corner (circled in red); Similarly, in Fig. 3b, the spatially resolved features failed to separate instances of two blood vessels (circled in red). Since these features are fused with the original RGB image and passed through an Efficient-UNet, the network is able to use the PTC output as a guidance rather than as a hard constraint. This allows Efficient-UNet to correct errors, resulting in a final segmentation map that is both smooth and accurate, excluding the false positive blood vessel and separating instances of blood vessels in these examples.

4   Inference Time

We measured the inference time of our model and compared it against the baseline models Efficient-UNet and Swin-UNet. All models were evaluated on a workstation equipped with an NVIDIA RTX 3060 GPU. For each model, the forward pass was executed 100 times using the same image resolution (224×224), the average inference time per image along with the standard deviation are summarised in Table 4. As shown, our method incurs a higher inference cost compared to the baseline models, due to the overhead of incorporating Virchow2. Despite this, the inference time remains under 80 milliseconds per image, suggesting that the method is still practical for deployment.

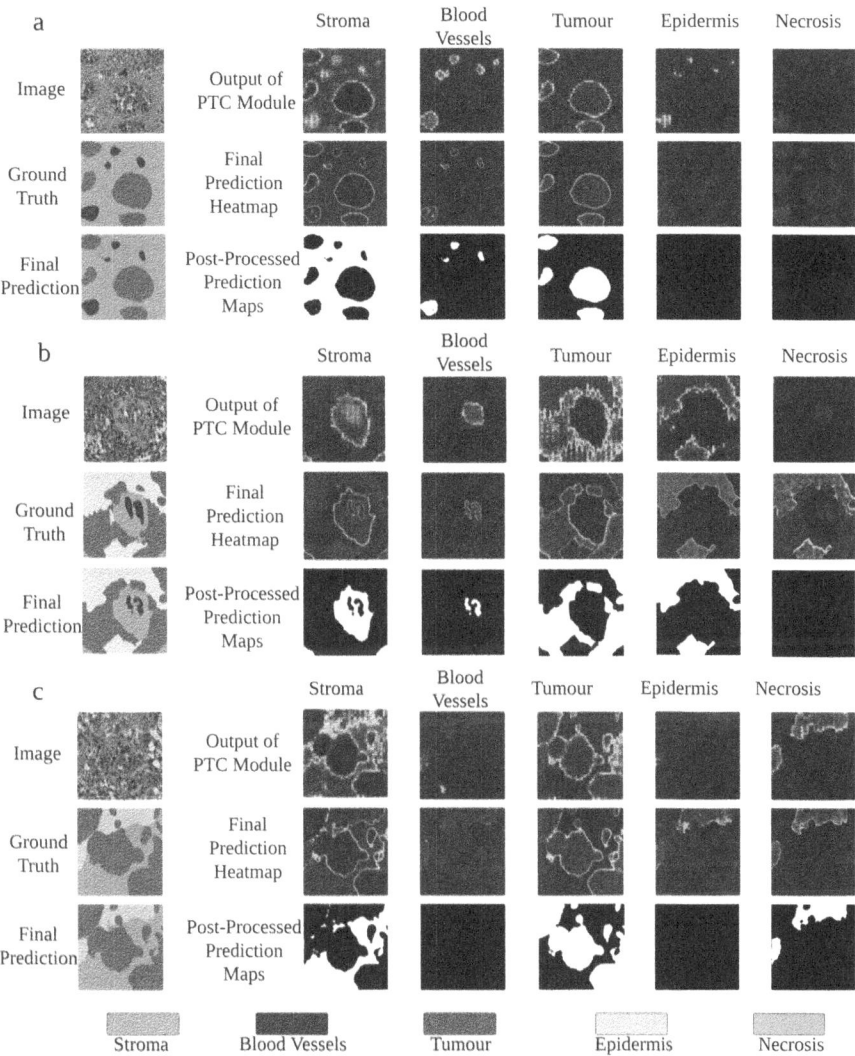

Fig. 3. a, b, c: Visualisation of example images predicted by our network. (**Top row**: Spatially resolved feature maps generated by the PTC Module from Virchow2 patch tokens, where each channel corresponds to one tissue class. **Middle row**: Probability maps produced by Efficient-UNet from the fusion of the spatially resolved feature maps and the RGB image. **Bottom row**: Final segmentation output after post-processing.) **a**: A false positive blood vessel instance (circled in red) can be seen in the output of the PTC Module, this is resolved by Efficient-UNet. **b**: Blood vessels prediction from the PTC Module falsely merged two instances into one (circled in red), this is resolved by Efficient-UNet. These show that the PTC output is used as a guidance rather than a hard constraint. **c**: Output from the PTC module is refined by Efficient-UNet. (Color figure online)

5   Conclusion

In this work, we proposed a novel segmentation network that effectively harnesses the power of Virchow2, a pathology foundation model, for the segmentation of five tissue classes in H&E-stained melanoma images. We introduce a Progressive Transposed Convolution (PTC) module to transform Virchow2 patch tokens into spatially resolved features. These features are then fused with the original RGB image and processed by an Efficient-UNet to produce precise segmentation maps. In addition, we employ a dual stage loss strategy that provides supervision at both the intermediate and the final stage of the network to encourage learning of consistent features throughout the pipeline.

Quantitative results demonstrate that our model delivers strong performance and generalises effectively to unseen data. It achieved first place in the PUMA Challenge for the tissue segmentation task, significantly outperforming several baseline models. Furthermore, by examining the spatially resolved features, we observe that while Virchow2 is a powerful foundation model, it could still produce false predictions in challenging melanoma tissue regions.

In future work, we aim to further validate our method on larger datasets such as the BCSS dataset [1], and conduct a detailed quantitative evaluation using only the spatially resolved features as the final output to better understand their predictive value. We also plan to perform an ablation study to assess the impact of different weighting configurations in the dual stage loss strategy, and to explore the use of alternative pathology foundation models, such as UNI [3], Phikon-v2 [7], and TITAN [5]. Additionally, we will investigate the effect of using different input image resolutions, as our current approach includes resizing input images from 1024×1024 to 224×224 which may distort smaller structures such as blood vessels. Using higher-resolution inputs or a multiscale approach may yield further performance gains.

The original source code will be made publicly available on GitHub, the link can be found from the PUMA Challenge [20] website (https://puma. grand-challenge.org/). Moreover, after conducting detailed ablation studies as a part of our future work, we will integrate the full inference pipeline of an extended version of our model into TIAToolbox [16] (https://github.com/ TissueImageAnalytics/tiatoolbox/tree/master/examples/inference-pipelines), a cross-platform Python library offering easy-to-use APIs for whole-slide image analysis in computational pathology. These future developments aim to create a robust and extensible tissue segmentation framework to support large-scale studies of the tumour micro-environment.

Acknowledgments. JL is supported by the UK Engineering and Physical Sciences Research Council (EPSRC). YZ is funded by China Scholarship Council - University of Warwick Scholarship. CGCT is supported by the European Union Grant agreement ID: 101119427. SEAR reports financial support by the MRC (MR/X011585/1) and the BigPicture project, which has received funding from the Innovative Medicines Initiative 2 Joint Undertaking under grant agreement No 945358.

Disclosure of Interests. The authors have no competing interests.

References

1. Amgad, M., et al.: Structured crowdsourcing enables convolutional segmentation of histology images. Bioinformatics **35**(18), 3461–3467 (2019)

2. Bruni, D., Angell, H.K., Galon, J.: The immune contexture and immunoscore in cancer prognosis and therapeutic efficacy. Nat. Rev. Cancer **20**, 662–680 (2020). https://doi.org/10.1038/s41568-020-0285-7

3. Chen, R., et al.: Towards a general-purpose foundation model for computational pathology. Nat. Med. **30**, 850–862 (2024). https://doi.org/10.1038/s41591-024-02857-3

4. Cheng, B., Misra, I., Schwing, A., Kirillov, A., Girdhar, R.: Masked-attention mask transformer for universal image segmentation (2021). https://doi.org/10.48550/arXiv.2112.01527

5. Ding, T., et al.: Multimodal whole slide foundation model for pathology (2024). https://arxiv.org/abs/2411.19666

6. Dosovitskiy, A., et al.: An image is worth 16x16 words: transformers for image recognition at scale. In: International Conference on Learning Representations (2021). https://openreview.net/forum?id=YicbFdNTTy

7. Filiot, A., Jacob, P., Kain, A.M., Saillard, C.: Phikon-v2, a large and public feature extractor for biomarker prediction (2024). https://arxiv.org/abs/2409.09173

8. Gershenwald, J., et al.: Melanoma staging: evidence-based changes in the American joint committee on cancer eighth edition cancer staging manual: melanoma staging: AJCC 8th edition. CA Cancer J. Clin. **67** (2017). https://doi.org/10.3322/caac.21409

9. Gomroki, M., Hasanlou, M., Reinartz, P.: Stcd-effv2t unet: semi transfer learning efficientnetv2 t-unet network for urban/land cover change detection using sentinel-2 satellite images. Remote Sens. **15**(5) (2023). https://doi.org/10.3390/rs15051232. https://www.mdpi.com/2072-4292/15/5/1232

10. Hendry, S., et al.: Assessing tumor-infiltrating lymphocytes in solid tumors: a practical review for pathologists and proposal for a standardized method from the international immunooncology biomarkers working group. Adv. Anat. Pathol. **24**, 1 (2017). https://doi.org/10.1097/PAP.0000000000000162

11. Huo, G., Lin, D., Yuan, M.: Iris segmentation method based on improved unet++. Multimedia Tools Appl. **81**(28), 41249–41269 (2022). https://doi.org/10.1007/s11042-022-13198-z

12. Hörst, F., Rempe, M., Becker, H., Heine, L., Keyl, J., Kleesiek, J.: Cellvit++: energy-efficient and adaptive cell segmentation and classification using foundation models (2025). https://arxiv.org/abs/2501.05269

13. Isensee, F., Jaeger, P., Kohl, S., Petersen, J., Maier-Hein, K.: nnu-net: a self-configuring method for deep learning-based biomedical image segmentation. Nat. Methods **18**, 1–9 (2021). https://doi.org/10.1038/s41592-020-01008-z

14. Liu, Z., et al.: Swin transformer: hierarchical vision transformer using shifted windows (2021). https://doi.org/10.48550/arXiv.2103.14030

15. Pillai, M.B., Nair, J.J.: Nuclei segmentation using unet with efficientnctv2 as encoder. In: Tuba, M., Akashe, S., Joshi, A. (eds.) ICT Systems and Sustainability, pp. 603–613. Springer, Singapore (2023)

16. Pocock, J., et al.: TIAToolbox as an end-to-end library for advanced tissue image analytics. Commun. Med. **2**(1), 120 (2022). https://doi.org/10.1038/s43856-022-00186-5. https://www.nature.com/articles/s43856-022-00186-5

17. Ronneberger, O., Fischer, P., Brox, T.: U-net: convolutional networks for biomedical image segmentation (2015)
18. Roy, A.G., Navab, N., Wachinger, C.: Concurrent spatial and channel 'squeeze & excitation' in fully convolutional networks. In: Frangi, A.F., Schnabel, J.A., Davatzikos, C., Alberola-López, C., Fichtinger, G. (eds.) Medical Image Computing and Computer Assisted Intervention - MICCAI 2018, pp. 421–429. Springer, Cham (2018)
19. Saltz, J., Gupta, R., et al.: Spatial organization and molecular correlation of tumor-infiltrating lymphocytes using deep learning on pathology images. Cell Rep. **23**(1), 181–193.e7 (2018). https://doi.org/10.1016/j.celrep.2018.03.086. https://www.sciencedirect.com/science/article/pii/S2211124718304479
20. Schuiveling, M., et al.: A novel dataset for nuclei and tissue segmentation in melanoma with baseline nuclei segmentation and tissue segmentation benchmarks. GigaScience **14** (2025). https://doi.org/10.1093/gigascience/giaf011
21. Srinidhi, C.L., Ciga, O., Martel, A.L.: Deep neural network models for computational histopathology: a survey. Med. Image Anal. **67**, 101813 (2021). https://doi.org/10.1016/j.media.2020.101813. https://www.sciencedirect.com/science/article/pii/S1361841520301778
22. Tan, M., Le, Q.: Efficientnetv2: smaller models and faster training (2021). https://doi.org/10.48550/arXiv.2104.00298
23. Taube, J., et al.: Implications of the tumor immune microenvironment for staging and therapeutics. Mod. Pathol. **31** (2017). https://doi.org/10.1038/modpathol.2017.156
24. Weiss, S., et al.: Immunologic heterogeneity of tumor infiltrating lymphocyte composition in primary melanoma. Hum. Pathol. **57** (2016). https://doi.org/10.1016/j.humpath.2016.07.008
25. Zimmermann, E., et al.: Virchow 2: scaling self-supervised mixed magnification models in pathology (2024). https://doi.org/10.48550/arXiv.2408.00738

SMatt-DINO: Spatially Aware Masked Attention Network for High Resolution Brain Image Classification

Moitreya Chaudhuri[1]([✉]), Ayantika Das[1], Keerthi Ram[2],
and Mohanasankar Sivaprakasam[1,2]

[1] Indian Institute of Technology, Madras, Chennai, India
moitreyachaudhuri95@gmail.com
[2] Healthcare Technology Innovation Centre, IIT Madras, Chennai, India

Abstract. Digital **histopathological** image analysis encounters processing level challenges due to the extremely **high resolution** of whole slide images (WSI), which requires resource-intensive annotations and extensive computational resources. Due to these limitations, histological processing is heavily reliant on **self-supervision** and **patch**-level processing. While there are multiple modelling approaches which consider the aspect of limited supervision and patch-level processing, most of the models are not capable of capturing spatial context while focusing into the local cellular-level details. This simultaneous processing of global **spatial context** along with cellular details at the patch-level again becomes computationally inefficient to handle. In order to circumvent these issues, we devise a **spatially** aware **masked attention** based DINO network (SMatt-DINO) that processes spatial neighbourhood in an efficient manner by selectively masking the attention layers within the network. This capacitates our model to generate robust representations that are capable of efficiently classifying brain regions in histological images in a self-supervised manner. We further incorporate **positional** information into the network to enhance classification in anatomical boundary regions. Through experimentation, we validate that our model has better performance in classification of regions in fetal brain, specifically reducing **misprediction** in the anatomical **boundary** regions. We have also validated the **generalization** capability of our model by testing it on a fetal brain from a completely different acquisition setup. This demonstrates the robustness and effectiveness of our model in histological tasks.

1   Introduction

Digital histopathological image analysis has witnessed significant advancements in recent years, driven by the increasing adoption of deep learning techniques [2]. These innovations have enabled automated analysis of whole slide images (WSI), facilitating improved disease diagnosis and semantic segmentation. However, deep learning-based analysis of WSIs remains **challenging** due to their

S. Ali et al. (Eds.): MIUA 2025, LNCS 15916, pp. 73–86, 2026.
https://doi.org/10.1007/978-3-031-98688-8_6

extremely high resolution. These high-resolution images pose a hindrance in their analysis due to (i) resource-intensive annotation requirements and (ii) extensive computational resource requirements. The processing of these images requires modelling approaches which can capture both local cellular details and global tissue context simultaneously in an efficient manner.

Unsupervised learning, particularly self-supervised approaches, is crucial in digital pathology due to the resource-intensive nature of data annotation. By leveraging large amounts of unlabelled pathology images, these methods extract meaningful features and patterns, enabling robust representation learning for downstream tasks. This reduces dependency on labelled datasets while enhancing generalization and scalability across diverse pathology applications [10,23]. ViTs, one such technique, enable a simple document-like treatment of images by decomposing them into sequences of visual tokens, much like words in a sentence [3,21]. Each patch acts as a token that carries localized visual meaning, analogous to a phrase in a paragraph. When these patches are arranged in spatial order, the model processes them as a sequence, allowing it to infer higher-level structure and semantic coherence, much like understanding the topic of a document from its sentences. This tokenized view transforms image understanding into a form of **sequence modelling**, where visual concepts are learned directly from relationship between the patch contents and their positioning within the broader context. An effective approach for the integration of unsupervision with sequence modelling is Distillation with No Labels (**DINO**) [4,17], which learns representations of images by modelling them sequentially with ViTs, without relying on label-based supervision.

Masked attention aggregation is a technique used to manage **long input sequences** by selectively limiting which tokens can attend to each other [8,9]. In the context of WSI images, where patch sequences can be very large, this approach helps in preserving meaningful spatial relationships. By designing masks that respect spatial proximity or anatomical relevance, the model focuses attention within localized neighbourhood regions or hierarchies, then progressively aggregates information across broader contexts. This structured aggregation enables effective long-sequence modelling without overwhelming the model, supporting scalable and spatially-aware representation learning. Incorporating **relative spatial priors**, such as distance or adjacency between patches enhances the model's understanding of spatial relationships beyond what pure attention can infer. These priors, when encoded directly into attention masks, can guide the model to infer better in anatomical boundaries of tissue regions.

Contributions: We present a spatially-aware masked attention-based DINO (**SMatt-DINO**) framework that selectively masks and aggregates the spatial neighbourhood of histological image patches (Nissl) to form an effective attention mechanism and learn efficient representations for the patches without relying on label-based supervision. We consider the spatial neighbourhood of a histological image patch as an ordered sequence, which is processed in an efficient and aggregative manner to achieve brain region classification. We specifically use masking within the attention layers of our model, which is extracted by aggregating the sequence of image patches. Additionally, we incorporate the spatial positions of the image patches to attain better anatomical understanding. Our **key contributions** are:

– We have devised a **spatially aware** masked attention-based network which can learn robust representations to classify regions in the fetal brain. Spatial awareness is incorporated through an efficient neighbourhood aggregation mechanism and position information incorporation.
– We demonstrate that spatial awareness has specifically enhanced performance in anatomical **boundary regions** of the brain, despite being deviated from the non-boundary regions seen during training.
– We validate the **generalizability** of our model on data acquired in a varied setup, specifically when the acquisition plane of brain images is different.

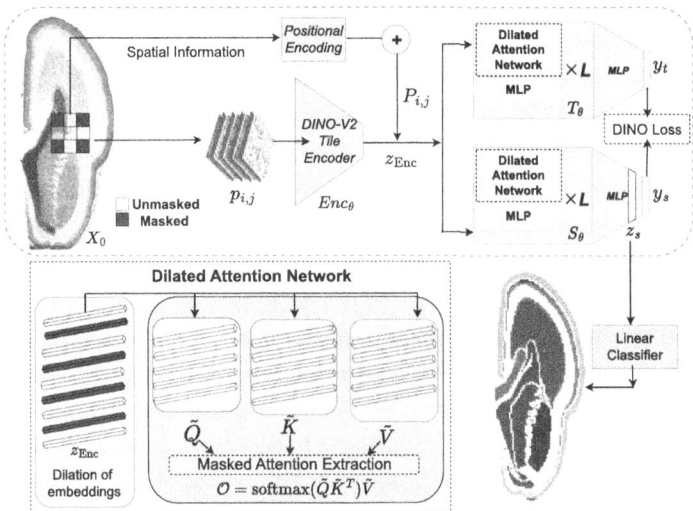

Fig. 1. In the top section (left to right), the patch and its neighbours $(p_{i,j})$ are extracted from a Nissl image (X_0) and passed through the Tile Encoder (Enc_θ) to obtain embeddings (z_{Enc}). These embeddings are input to the teacher (T_θ), and student (S_θ) masked aggregated attention networks, optimized using the DINO loss. In the bottom section (right to left), processing of trained embedding (z_s) for classification, and details of the Dilated Attention Network.

1.1 Related Works

This section discusses the recent progress in spatial integration, unsupervised learning, and aggregation methods in histopathology, positioning our approach as a spatially-aware, transformer-based framework for efficient and robust tissue classification.

Spatial Information Incorporation: Capturing spatial relationships in histopathology is essential for modelling both local cellular-level and global tissue-level information. Multi-resolution modelling enables the analysis of high-resolution WSI content while maintaining computational efficiency. Token merging approaches simplify visual content by collapsing similar patches into meta-tokens, thus reducing complexity. However, such techniques may compromise critical boundary details essential in histopathological contexts [13,24]. Similarly, pyramid-based architectures leverage hierarchical downsampling to aggregate local and global features across scales. These approaches have shown success in capturing structural variations but often struggle with irregular anatomical transitions due to their reliance on fixed-scale resolutions [12,19].

Unsupervised Learning Paradigms: CNN-based inter-domain transfer learning approaches like the Deep-Texture [11] have been adopted for histological image analysis by incorporating histology-specific constraints in a zero-shot manner. Contrastive Learning has been widely adopted for self-supervised learning in histopathology. This self-supervised paradigm has been translated to the recent advancements in vision language models and utilized in histology-based tasks by models like the CONCH [16].

Aggregation Techniques: Modelling long sequences of image patches from WSIs requires effective aggregation methods [6,7] that preserve spatial hierarchies and contextual relevance. Sliding window mechanisms, such as in Swin Transformers [15], allow local attention with controlled cross-window interactions. Grid-based sampling approaches [22] dynamically adjust receptive fields to capture spatial variation more flexibly. Graph-based aggregation [14] has also been explored for its ability to model irregular tissue structures, but GNN-based methods face key limitations in computer vision: over-squashing of distant node features, difficulty in handling variable patch densities, and costly graph construction. These drawbacks hinder scalability and limit multi-scale expressivity compared to hierarchical ViT designs. In order to address these, we propose a spatial aggregation-based technique that uses masking within the attention layers of the transformer to learn efficient histological representations.

2   Methodology

We propose a spatially aware network that processes patches from high-resolution Nissl brain images ($X_0 \in \mathbb{R}^{3 \times H \times W}$) to construct a representational space suitable for brain region classification. The schematic flow of our model is detailed in Fig. 1. We extract image patches ($p_{i,j} \in \mathbb{R}^{3 \times h \times w}$) within a spatial neighbourhood ($\mathcal{N}_{m,n}$) by tiling entire brain sections (X_0), which are then processed using a pre-trained Tile encoder (Enc_θ). The processed embeddings (z_{Enc}) from Enc_θ are combined with the positional encoding of the spatial location of the central patch and given as input to our SMatt-DINO network. Our model is a transformer-based architecture that leverages self-attention for feature extraction; the attention scores are computed using a set of queries (Q), keys (K), and values (V) [8]. As our module is spatially aware and processes the sequence of images along with their neighbouring patches, evaluating attention scores with the conventional transformer approach becomes computationally inefficient. To alleviate this, our model uses a masking approach by dilating selective neighbourhoods from the sequence of patches; this creates a dilated attention with $\tilde{Q}$, $\tilde{K}$ and $\tilde{V}$ [8]. Our network formulation incorporates a series (L) of cascaded dilated attention mechanisms and is trained in a DINO technique [17], as detailed below in Subsect. 2.1.

2.1 SMatt-DINO

Masked Attention Aggregation: We devise a mechanism to process Nissl image patches $(p_{i,j})$ within a spatial neighbourhood $(\mathcal{N}_{m,n})$ as an ordered sequence, adopting strategies analogous to language sequence handling technique in LongNet [8]. The neighbourhood can be represented as,
$\mathcal{N}_{m,n} = \{p_{i,j} \mid m-1 \leq i \leq m+1,\ n-1 \leq j \leq n+1\}$, where m and n are the columns and rows spanning the neighbourhood considering a certain patch size (h or w) between m and n. We generate embeddings $(z_{Enc} \in \mathbb{R}^d)$ from pre-trained Tile Encoder (Enc_θ), a DINO-V2 [17] based histopathological foundational model [20]. All the generated embeddings (z_{Enc}) from $\mathcal{N}_{m,n}$ are fed into our attention-based network module to generate dilated attention. The dilation is achieved by masking the sequences in desired intervals (r). The modified attention after dilation is given as:

$$\tilde{Q} = [Q_0, Q_r, Q_{2r}, \ldots, Q_{\lfloor \frac{m \cdot n}{r} \rfloor r}]$$
$$\tilde{K} = [K_0, K_r, K_{2r}, \ldots, K_{\lfloor \frac{m \cdot n}{r} \rfloor r}]$$
$$\tilde{V} = [V_0, V_r, V_{2r}, \ldots, V_{\lfloor \frac{m \cdot n}{r} \rfloor r}]$$

where $\lfloor \frac{m \cdot n}{r} \rfloor$ is the maximum integer such that $\lfloor \frac{m \cdot n}{r} \rfloor r \leq m \cdot n$. Utilizing this, the mask attention aggregation output is extracted and is given as:

$$\mathcal{O} = \text{softmax}(\tilde{Q}\tilde{K}^T)\tilde{V}.$$

Positional Encoding: We generate a positional encoding $(P_{i,j} \in \mathbb{R}^d)$ for the spatial location of the image patch $(p_{i,j})$ from the $\mathcal{N}_{m,n}$ we are processing [20]. The spatial locations (x_c, y_c) of the patch are extracted from the whole brain section (X_0) and further normalised with H and W. The positional embeddings for each of the patches are extracted using the following:

$$P_{i,j}^k = \begin{cases} \sin\left(\dfrac{pos}{10000^{\frac{2k}{d}}}\right), & \text{if } k \text{ is even} \\[3mm] \cos\left(\dfrac{pos}{10000^{\frac{2k}{d}}}\right), & \text{if } k \text{ is odd} \end{cases}$$

where $k \in \{0, 1, \ldots, d-1\}$ and $pos = x_c \cdot h + y_c$. These positional embeddings $(P_{i,j})$ are added to z_{Enc} for processing.

Objective Function: We process the position-integrated embeddings through a series of cascaded dilated attention block in an aggregative manner [8]. These aggregative features form a representational space which is spatially aware in terms of neighbourhood and positions [20]. We adopt a DINO-based self-supervised objective to train our network [17]. To align with the architectural requirements of the DINO framework, we process the embeddings from our dilated attention block through an MLP head that projects these embeddings into a space compatible with the required number of classes N (brain regions). This combined network is instantiated twice to form the teacher (T_θ) and the student (S_θ) component, which gives the student (y_s) and teacher (y_t) distribution. The objective function is given as $\mathcal{L} = \sum_{cl} -y_t^{cl} \log(y_s^{cl})$, where $cl \in \{1, \ldots, N\}$ [17]. To better stabilize the teacher network we use an adaptive centering mechanism given as, $y_t = \mathrm{softmax}\left(\frac{\hat{y}_t - c}{\tau_t}\right)$, where c is a learned parameter and τ_t is a hyperparameter denoting temperature of T_θ [17].

During inference, the representational space ($z_s \in \mathbb{R}^{256}$) of the student network is processed through a linear classifier to discriminate image patches into different brain regions. To ensure better consistency at the brain section level, we use an aggregation schema considering all the neighbourhood predictions for the final classification.

Table 1. Training parameters, model parameters and other details.

Parameter	Value	Parameter	Value
Momentum (α)	0.996	Dimension (d) of z_{Enc}	1536
Temperature (τ_t)	0.1	Dimension of y_t	9
Learning rate	0.0001	Dimension of y_s	9
Optimizer, Weight decay	AdamW, 0.0005	Dimension of z_s	256
Epoch	50	Classifier	SVM
Batch size	32	SVM Kernel	Linear
PyTorch version	2.6.0	SVM Regularization Parameter	1
H,W	order of 10^4	h,w	256,256
m,n	3,3	L,r	6,2
CUDA version	12.1	GPU memory	80 GB

3 Experimental Setup

3.1 Dataset

We utilized Nissl-stained data from the Allen BrainSpan repository[1] (Allen Brain) and our in-house data (DHARANI Brain) [18].

---

[1] http://brainspan.org.

Allen Brain: We have considered a fetal brain of 21 post-conceptual weeks (pcw), which was digitized at a resolution of $1\,\mu m$ per pixel, with thicknesses of $20\,\mu m$, and the plane of the acquisition was coronal. The regions considered for classification are (i) cortical plate (10515), (ii) subplate zone (10522), (iii) subventricular zone (10536) (iv) ventricular zone (10542), (v) caudal ganglionic eminence (10552), (vi) caudate nucleus (10334), (vii) putamen (10338), (viii) corpus callosum (10561), (ix) internal capsule (10581).

DHARANI Brain: We have considered a fetal brain of 23 pcw, which was digitized at a resolution of $0.5\,\mu m$ per pixel, with thicknesses of $20\,\mu m$, and the plane of the acquisition was sagittal. We selected nine regions similar to the Allen Brain and included the intermediate zone (10529) region, excluding the ventricular zone (10542).

3.2   Evaluation Metrics and Benchmarks

We have compared the representations of our model with histopathology specific (i) CNN-based approach Deep Texture [11], (ii) ViT-DINO based approach HIPT [5], histological foundational models (iii) CONCH [16], (iv) PathDino [1], and (v) GigaPath [20]. All the models were implemented using their official repository and their pretrained weights were used.

Evaluation Metrics: For classification analysis, we have used Accuracy to capture overall performance along with F1 score to capture the precision and recall of the model. For representational space analysis, we utilized t-SNE[2].

3.3   Implementation Details

The dataset details used for training and testing are as follows: For the *Train Set*, we have considered 6,298 image patches from alternate brain sections of Allen Brain, each of size 256×256. All training patches were non-boundary, ensuring each patch was fully annotated to one of nine regions. For the *Test Set*, we have considered total 1575 image patches comprising of (i) non-boundary and (ii) boundary patches (*Allen Boundary Set*) from the remaining alternate sections of Allen Brain, and (iii) non-boundary patches from the DHARANI Brain. DHARANI Brain patches, acquired at $0.5\,\mu m$, were patched at 512×512 and resized to 256×256 for compatibility with the training setup.

The model details and parameters used for training are shown in Table 1.

4   Results and Discussion

We analyze the quantitative and qualitative performance of our method in comparison with baselines, using fetal brain images from the *Test Set*.

---

[2] https://scikit-learn.org/stable/modules/generated/sklearn.manifold.TSNEl.

Table 2. The classification performance of our model and the baselines, reported in terms of Accuracy and F1-score.

Model	Pre-training Dataset	Allen Brain		DHARANI Brain	
		Accuracy	F1 Score	Accuracy	F1 Score
CONCH [16]	Histology Images & Text	0.80	0.80	0.82	0.82
Deep-Texture [11]	ImageNet Images	0.86	0.84	0.86	0.86
HIPT [5]	Histopathology Images	0.86	0.86	0.86	0.87
PathDino [1]	Histopathology Images	0.87	0.86	0.87	0.88
GigaPath [20]	Histopathology Images	0.88	0.89	0.87	0.87
SMatt-DINO	Histology Images	**0.90**	**0.91**	**0.89**	**0.88**

4.1   Quantitative Analysis

We quantify the classification performance of our model, along with the baselines in Table 2. Our model SMatt-DINO performs better, in terms of Accuracy and F1-score, than comparative baselines by leveraging spatial context-aware processing. This context awareness achieved through efficient incorporation of embeddings of neighbourhood patches and spatial locations, reduces misclassifications within brain regions. Among the comparative baselines in Table 2, Giga-Path [20] performs better than other models since it is based on a DINO-v2 backbone which enables the extraction of more robust features. The PathDino [1] and HIPT [5] models, built on conventional DINO-based architecture, perform better than Deep-Texture and CONCH by leveraging self-supervised training, enabling richer and more informative feature extraction. The Deep-Texture model [11] based on a convolution backbone and pre-trained on ImageNet is made adaptable to histology images by enforcing spatial invariance. The CONCH model [16], built on a ViT backbone with a semi-supervised contrastive loss for multimodal feature learning, performs relatively lower in classification tasks due to lesser class-wise separability in feature space.

Non-boundary Region Analysis: We report the class-wise classification performance of non-boundary patches from the Allen Brain in Fig. 2(a). It is evident from the figure that our model performs better than the baselines in high-cell-density regions (10515, 10542) by processing spatial location information and neighbouring patches simultaneously, reducing misprediction in heterogeneous non-boundary areas of the brain regions. Similarly, for the regions with very low cell densities (10581 and 10561), our model shows performance improvement. In medium-cell-density regions (10536 and 10522), classification improves away from boundaries due to neighbourhood aggregation. However, boundary-adjacent areas remain prone to misclassification, as their gradual cell density transitions offer less support from neighbouring patches, unlike the steep changes in high and low-density regions. Our model reduces the inter-class misclassification for regions (10338 and 10334) which are spatially co-located with similar cell densities.

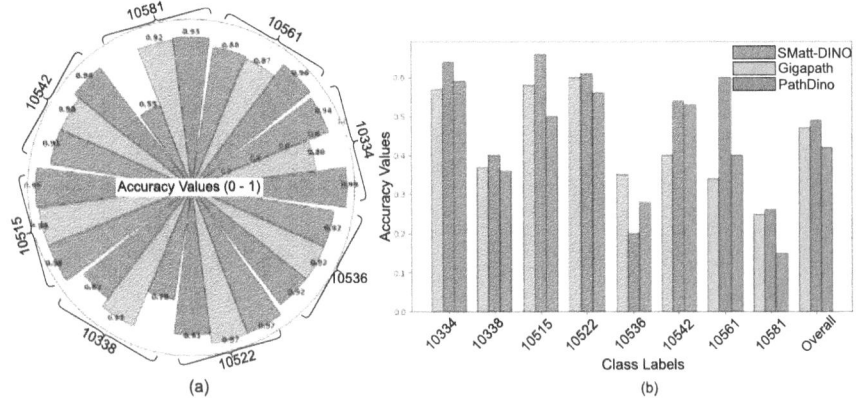

Fig. 2. From left to right, Class-wise classification performance of (a) non-boundary and (b) boundary patches from Allen Brain.

Boundary Region Analysis: We showcase the class-wise and overall classification performance of boundary patches from the Allen Brain (*Allen Boundary Set*) in Fig. 2(b). Our model has better accuracy averaged across all the classes for the *Allen Boundary Set*, despite having deviations from the non-boundary set seen during training. In boundary regions within a certain neighbourhood, patches belong to multiple regions, impacting classification based on neighbourhood aggregation. The high (10515 and 10542) and low (10581 and 10561) cell-density regions have steep changes in the boundary. Hence the neighbourhood patches are more discriminatory in nature, so our neighbourhood aggregation-based model, SMatt-DINO, performs better. Similarly, medium-cell-density regions (10338 and 10334) also perform better as compared to other models since they have relatively steep changes in the boundary. However, Giga-Path performs better in region 10536, as mispredictions in the gradual-transition boundary neighbourhood patches have propagated across the region.

Generalization: We present the Accuracy and F1 score of DHARANI Brain in Table 2. Our model SMatt-DINO exhibits better performance than the comparative baselines for both metrics. This shows that our model is generalizable across data settings and acquisition planes. This is primarily due to the training mechanism, which could effectively learn to extract robust features, enabling the model to generalize across sagittal-plane patches from the DHARANI Brain while being trained on Allen Brain patches from the coronal plane. Although the baseline models perform relatively lower than ours for the DHARANI Brain, their metrics remain comparable with the Allen Brain.

4.2   Qualitative Analysis

We present the qualitative performance of our model and the baselines in Fig. 3. From Fig. 3(d), it is evident that our model SMatt-DINO has lesser misclassi-

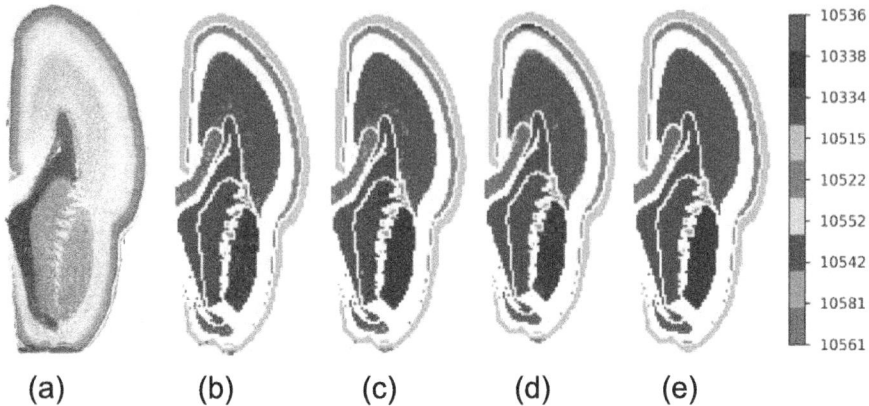

Fig. 3. (a) Nissl Image, Brain region classifications from (b) PathDino, (c) GigaPath, & (d) SMatt-DINO, and (e) Ground Truth Mask. In the represented brain section, our model (d) SMatt-DINO performs better, specifically (i) in the boundary-adjacent regions between 10536 (grey) and 10561 (red) and (ii) in non-boundary regions of 10334 (brown). (Color figure online)

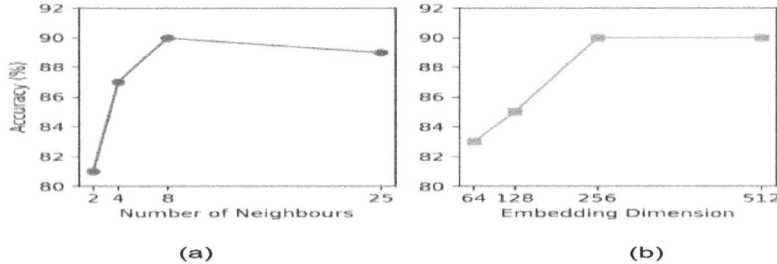

Fig. 4. From left to right, (a) Variation in classification accuracy with different numbers of neighbourhood patches, and (b) Accuracy variation with different embedding dimensions of z_s. Accuracy improves as the number of neighbouring patches increases up to 8, beyond which it gradually declines. Similarly, increasing the embedding dimension enhances performance up to 256, after which the accuracy saturates.

fication as compared to the baselines in several classes. For classes 10561 and 10581 (low cellular density, shown in red and green), our model performs better by effectively reducing false negatives within these regions and minimizing false positives in certain areas of class 10536. This is primarily due to the spatial awareness of the neighbourhood patches. The misclassification within regions 10338 and 10334 (indicated by black and brown) is reduced by our model as compared to the baseline. The regions with high cellular densities 10515 and 10542 (indicated by sky and dark blue) are consistently performing for all the models (PathDino and GigaPath in Fig. 3(b) and (c). However, boundary-adjacent areas of 10536 show better performance in the GigaPath model compared to ours, as the presence of less discriminative neighbouring patches has propagated mispredictions along the boundaries.

4.3   Ablation Study

Neighborhood Analysis: From Fig. 4(a), it is evident that classification accuracy increases (0.90) with the number of spatial neighbourhood patches, peaking at 8 patches ($m = 3$, $n = 3$). However, increasing the neighbourhood size to 24 patches ($m = 5$, $n = 5$) leads to a decline in accuracy (0.89). This suggests that while neighbourhood aggregation enhances contextual understanding, beyond a certain point, the inclusion of patches from other classes introduces interference, degrading the model's predictive performance.

Embedding Dimension Analysis: From Fig. 4(b) it is evident that increasing the embedding dimension of z_s from 64 to 256 enhances performance, with accuracy improving from 0.83 to 0.90. This indicates that larger embeddings capture richer feature representations. However, further increasing the dimension to 512 saturates the accuracy values, signifying that dimensions higher than 256 capture redundant information which does not add relevance to the classification task.

4.4   Analysis of Representational Space

In order to validate our choice of using the representational space (z_s) rather than choosing the final output (y_s) of the student network, we have projected these features into a two-dimensional space using t-SNE embeddings. Figure 5(a) and (b) represent the t-SNE of y_S and z_s, respectively. The t-SNE embeddings of z_s show better class-wise separability as compared to the embeddings of y_s. Specifically, classes 10522, 10536 and 10515 form compact and clearly delineable space in the t-SNE plot of z_s as shown in Fig. 5(b). However, these three classes share overlapping regions with multiple other classes in Fig. 5(a). The pair-wise classes (i) 10561 & 10581, (ii) 10542 & 10552, and (iii) 10334 & 10338, show better inter-pair separability in Fig. 5(a), but have lesser intra-pair separation in both the plots due to similar cellular density between the pairs.

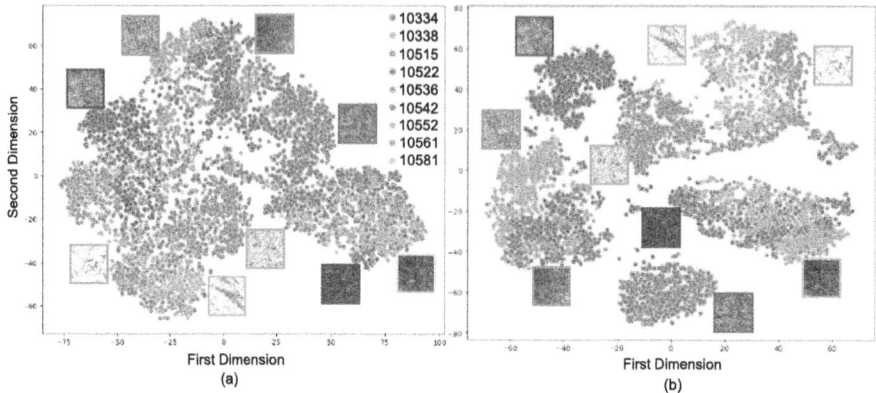

Fig. 5. From left to right, t-SNE plot of (a) the output (y_s) of the student network and (b) the representational space (z_s) of the student network. We have chosen z_s as a suitable feature for classification since the t-SNE plot of z_s shows better class-wise separation.

5 Conclusion

In this work, we introduced SMatt-DINO, a spatially aware, masked attention-based framework built on the DINO paradigm, designed to effectively aggregate and process spatial neighbourhood patches from high-resolution histology images. Our network incorporates positional embeddings into a masked attention mechanism that selectively dilates and efficiently aggregates spatial context across neighbouring patches. We demonstrate that SMatt-DINO learns robust histological representations, performing better than the comparative baselines in brain region classification. Notably, our model achieves better accuracy in anatomical boundary regions, despite not being trained on boundary-specific data—highlighting its capacity to resolve uncertainty through spatial context modelling. Furthermore, we establish the generalization ability of our approach by validating it on an unseen brain dataset acquired under a different imaging setup. *Future Work:* Potential directions include: (i) extending this approach to more downstream computational histopathology-based tasks such as tumour region delineation, (ii) integrating multimodal information (e.g., textual and visual features), and (iii) incorporating additional histology-specific priors alongside positional information to enhance performance.

References

1. Alfasly, S., et al.: Rotation-agnostic image representation learning for digital pathology. In: Proceedings of the IEEE/CVF Conference on Computer Vision and Pattern Recognition, pp. 11683–11693 (2024)
2. Asif, A., et al.: Unleashing the potential of AI for pathology: challenges and recommendations. J. Pathol. **260**(5), 564–577 (2023)

3. Baroni, G.L., et al.: Vision transformers for breast cancer histology image classification. In: International Conference on Image Analysis and Processing, pp. 15–26. Springer (2023)
4. Caron, M., et al.: Emerging properties in self-supervised vision transformers. In: Proceedings of the IEEE/CVF International Conference on Computer Vision, pp. 9650–9660 (2021)
5. Chen, R.J., et al.: Scaling vision transformers to gigapixel images via hierarchical self-supervised learning. In: Proceedings of the IEEE/CVF Conference on Computer Vision and Pattern Recognition, pp. 16144–16155 (2022)
6. Chen, S., et al.: Benchmarking embedding aggregation methods in computational pathology: a clinical data perspective. In: Ciompi, F., et al. (eds.) Proceedings of the MICCAI Workshop on Computational Pathology, vol. 254, pp. 38–50. Proceedings of Machine Learning Research. PMLR (2024). https://proceedings.mlr.press/v254/chen24a.html
7. Chen, S., et al.: Benchmarking embedding aggregation methods in computational pathology: a clinical data perspective. arXiv preprint arXiv:2407.07841 (2024)
8. Ding, J., et al.: Longnet: scaling transformers to 1,000,000,000 tokens. arXiv preprint arXiv:2307.02486 (2023)
9. Grisi, C., Litjens, G., van der Laak, J.: Masked Attention as a Mechanism for Improving Interpretability of Vision Transformers (2024). arXiv: 2404.18152. https://arxiv.org/abs/2404.18152
10. Huang, S.-C., et al.: Self-supervised learning for medical image classification: a systematic review and implementation guidelines. NPJ Digit. Med. **6**(1), 74 (2023)
11. Komura, D., et al.: Universal encoding of pan-cancer histology by deep texture representations. Cell Rep. **38**(9) (2022)
12. Li, H., et al.: Rethinking transformer for long contextual histopathology whole slide image analysis. In: Globerson, A., et al. (eds.) Advances in Neural Information Processing Systems, vol. 37, pp. 101498–101528. Curran Associates, Inc. (2024). https://proceedings.neurips.cc/paper_files/paper/2024/file/b7eecb72574b043ad0c69ea296212450-Paper-Conference.pdf
13. Liu, H., et al.: WSI-SAM: multi-resolution segment anything model (SAM) for histopathology whole-slide images. In: Ciompi, F., et al. (eds.) Proceedings of the MICCAI Workshop on Computational Pathology, vol. 254, pp. 25–37. Proceedings of Machine Learning Research. PMLR (2024). https://proceedings.mlr.press/v254/liu24a.html
14. Liu, J., et al.: Mgnni: multiscale graph neural networks with implicit layers. Adv. Neural. Inf. Process. Syst. **35**, 21358–21370 (2022)
15. Liu, Z., et al.: Swin transformer: hierarchical vision transformer using shifted windows. In: Proceedings of the IEEE/CVF International Conference on Computer Vision, pp. 10012–10022 (2021)
16. Lu, M.Y., et al.: A visual-language foundation model for computational pathology. Nat. Med. **30**(3), 863–874 (2024)
17. Oquab, M., et al.: Dinov2: learning robust visual features without supervision. arXiv preprint arXiv:2304.07193 (2023)
18. Verma, R., et al.: DHARANI: a 3D developing human-brain atlas resource to advance neuroscience internationally integrated multimodal imaging and high-resolution histology of the second trimester. J. Comp. Neurol. **533**(2), e70006 (2025)
19. Wang, J., et al.: Pyramid-based self-supervised learning for histopathological image classification. Comput. Biol. Med. **165**, 107336 (2023)

20. Xu, H., et al.: A whole-slide foundation model for digital pathology from real-world data. Nature **630**(8015), 181–188 (2024)
21. Hongming, X., et al.: Vision transformers for computational histopathology. IEEE Rev. Biomed. Eng. **17**, 63–79 (2023)
22. Yan, H., Wu, M., Zhang, C.: Multi-scale representations by varying window attention for semantic segmentation. arXiv preprint arXiv:2404.16573 (2024)
23. Yan, J., et al.: Deep contrastive learning based tissue clustering for annotation-free histopathology image analysis. Comput. Med. Imaging Graph. **97**, 102053 (2022)
24. Zhang, Z., et al.: Tmformer: token merging transformer for brain tumor segmentation with missing modalities. In: Proceedings of the AAAI Conference on Artificial Intelligence, vol. 38, no. 7, pp. 7414–7422 (2024)

Persistent Homology and Gabor Features Reveal Inconsistencies Between Widely Used Colorectal Cancer Training and Testing Datasets

Daniel Brito-Pacheco[1]([✉]) [iD], Riad Ibadulla[1] [iD], Ximena Fernández[1] [iD],
Panos Giannopoulos[1] [iD], and Constantino Carlos Reyes-Aldasoro[1,2] [iD]

[1] School of Science and Technology, City St. George's, University of London,
London EC1V 0HB, UK
daniel.brito@citystgeorges.ac.uk
[2] The Institute of Cancer Research, Integrated Pathology Unit, Division of Molecular
Pathology, Sutton, UK

Abstract. Recent work on computer vision and image processing has relied substantially on open datasets, which allow for an objective comparison of techniques and methodologies. In the area of computational pathology and, more specifically, on colorectal cancer, the dataset NCT-CRC-HE-100K, which consists of 100,000 patches of human tissue stained with Haematoxylin and Eosin has been widely used as a training set for deep learning studies. The patches are grouped into 9 classes of tissue (adipose, background, debris, lymphocytes, mucus, smooth muscle, normal colon mucosa, cancer-associated stroma, colorectal adenocarcinoma epithelium). The set is released with a separate set (CRC-VAL-HE-7K) of 7,180 patches that is commonly used for testing. In this work, features were extracted from both sets first with Persistent Homology, then, with Gabor filters to reveal that the training set presents a rather different distribution from the testing set. Namely, the distribution of features in the 7K-set presents a much higher class overlap than those in the 100K-set, which would imply a much higher separability in the testing set than in the training set.

Keywords: Persistent Homology · Gabor Features · Class separability

1 Introduction

The development and success of deep learning has relied on the existence of large sets of labelled data, in addition to high computational power provided by hardware like graphical processing units. Medical data usually requires labelling by experts, like radiologists, cytologists and pathologists, all of which have experienced shortages in recent years [1, 16, 18]. Thus, open datasets, such as those provided in *challenges* through websites such as Grand-Challenge (https://grand-challenge.org/), which, in some cases, are related to conferences like ISBI (IEEE International Symposium in Biomedical Imaging) or MICCAI (Medical Image Computing and Computer-Assisted Intervention) are welcome by the community. In many cases, the datasets are linked to a competition where algorithms or results are evaluated with certain criteria, e.g. accuracy or Jaccard index, and then ranked and placed in leaderboards. The reproducibility, interpretation and ranking aspects of some challenges have been scrutinised as rankings can vary depending on certain factors, e.g., rank and aggregate v. aggregate and rank, mean v. median, rank with Hausdorff distance (HD) v. rank with HD95, etc. [14]. Another important factor is the test data used for validation.

In this paper, a commonly used dataset (NCT-CRC-HE-100K [11,12]) is scrutinised. The dataset is commonly used to train deep learning architectures for the classification of histological images of colorectal cancer stained with Haematoxylin and Eosin (H&E). The dataset consists of 100,000 patches of human tissue stained with H&E of healthy and cancerous tissues grouped into 9 categories: adipose, background, debris, lymphocytes, mucus, smooth muscle, normal colon mucosa, cancer-associated stroma, colorectal adenocarcinoma epithelium, which are normally used for training, and a separate set (CRC-VAL-HE-7K) of 7,180 patches is commonly used for testing [13,19,21]. Concerns have already been raised about these datasets. In [9], the authors identified biases in the classes by performing classification experiments using simple models that focused solely on the colour of the images and obtaining satisfactory results. The authors also managed to identify compression artifacts that show up in different concentrations by class, leading to high classification accuracies.

This paper focuses on features of the patches that are not related to colour, namely texture and structure. By using Persistent Homology and Gabor filters it was observed that these two datasets were not equivalent in the separability of the classes, revealing further issues with the datasets. A visual analysis of the patches was also performed and the effects of normalisation on them was shown. Using these analyses, light is shed on the difference in qualities of the datasets, with CRC-VAL-HE-7K (7K-set) having a higher separability than NCT-CRC-HE-100K (100K-set). Additionally, an experiment was carried out in which a random forest was trained on the 100K-set and tested on the 7K-set before reversing the roles of the sets to train on 7K-set, and tested on 100K-set. This helped to confirm the differences between the sets and show the implications of training and testing on different-quality datasets.

2   Background: Persistent Homology

Persistent Homology (PH) is an important tool that belongs to the mathematical field of Topological Data Analysis (TDA), which allows to extract topological features from datasets and create statistical models. This tool has already seen applications in biomedical imaging [6]. Since PH and TDA are not commonly used in Computer Vision and Image Processing areas, a short review will be presented. For a comprehensive introduction to PH, the reader is referred to [8].

2.1   Components and Holes

PH analyses an image or a space to find its *components* and *holes*. A (connected) *component* is the set of a space where elements are connected to each other. In the case of an image, a component would correspond to a group of pixels that are adjacent to each other. A *hole* corresponds to a region that is completely surrounded by a single component and does not belong to that component. PH essentially tracks how the number of components and holes change as the conditions on the space or image change. Figure 1(a) illustrates six 2D spaces (binary images) with different numbers of components (1,2,3,3,2,1) and holes (0,0,0,1,1,0). These cases can also be understood as a process from left to right where components and holes are born (appear) and die (disappear). This is illustrated in Fig. 1(b), (c) where the birth of each is indicated with a vertical black line, and the death is indicated with a vertical grey line with a red cross.

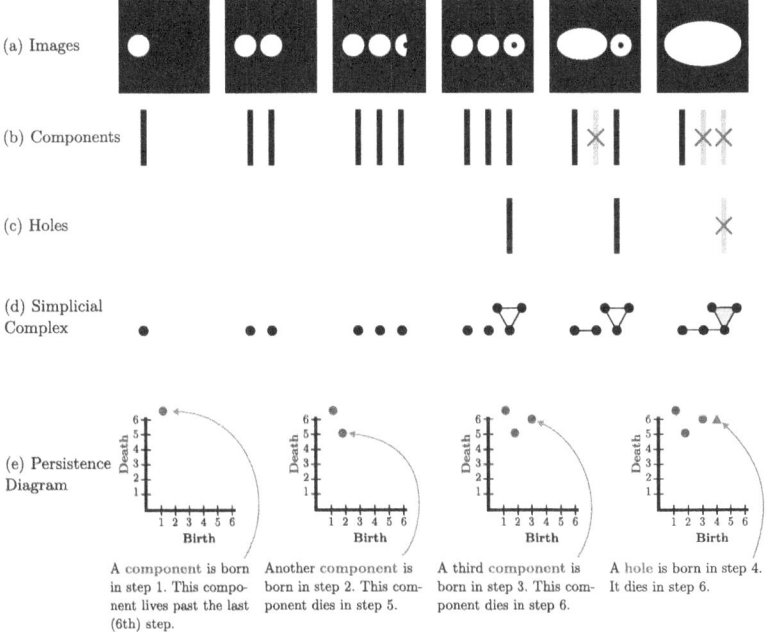

Fig. 1. Illustration of the main concepts of Persistence Homology: births, death, holes and components. (a) A sequence of six binary images (b) A black bar corresponds to the birth of a component and, a red cross and a grey bar indicates a death. (c) The birth and death of holes. (d) Representation of the components as a simplicial complex: A point corresponds to a component, except if there is a hole, in which case a cycle of 3 points and 3 edges are added. The cycle is filled with a triangle when the hole dies. (e) Step-by-step formation of the persistence diagram. (Color figure online)

2.2 Simplicial Complexes

Simplicial complexes are an abstraction from the components and holes previously described. Specifically, an *n-simplex* is an n-dimensional generalisation of a triangle. A 0-simplex is a point, a 1-simplex is an edge that connects 2 points, a 2-simplex is a triangle that connects 3 points, a 3-simplex is a tetrahedron, etc. A simplicial complex S is a collection of n-simplices such that their n-1-dimensional faces are also in S. This means, for example that if there is an edge e in S, then the two vertices at the ends of e also have to be present in S. In the context of PH, simplicial complexes are used as a way to represent a more complex object topologically as illustrated in Fig. 1(d). The topological information of the holes and components can be represented simply as a collection of vertices, edges and triangles. From left to right: A vertex appears when the first white component appears, a second vertex is added in the second column, a third vertex is added in the third column, a hole appears which is represented by a cycle of edges and their vertices, two components merge into one represented by an edge in row (d) (the component that was born last has died at this point), the hole is filled up; represented by adding a blue triangle in row (d) (the hole has died at this point).

It is important to highlight two points. First, a cycle of edges is different from a triangle. In the first case, the cycle has a hole, whereas a triangle has no hole. Second, a component in a simplicial complex is any union of vertices, edges, triangles, tetrahedron that are touching. A sequence of n simplicial complexes S_i is called a *filtration* if $S_1 \subset S_2 \subset S_3 \subset ... \subset S_n$. In Fig. 1 the sequence of simplicial complexes in row (d) makes a filtration. It is also worth mentioning that, in the literature on PH, the formal definition of filtrations applies to sequences of topological spaces, not just simplicial complexes.

2.3 Birth, Death, and Persistence Diagrams

Persistence Diagrams are a way to encode invariants about a filtration. Particularly, the points when a new topological feature appears, as well as when it disappears in the filtration. Alluded to before, at the step when a component or hole first appears, it is said to be "born". Analogously, at the step when a component or hole disappears from the filtration, it is said that it "dies". This information can be encoded in a scatter plot where the horizontal coordinate shows the birth of the component or hole, and the vertical coordinate shows the death of the component or hole as illustrated in Fig. 1(e).

It is important to note that holes die by being filled in, but components die by merging into each other. When two components merge, there is a choice to be made as to which component dies. Typically, the eldest component of the merger will survive.

2.4 Level-Set Filtration

A very common way to get a filtration from a greyscale image is through the level-set filtration, which is illustrated in Fig. 2. First, a greyscale image (Fig. 2(a))

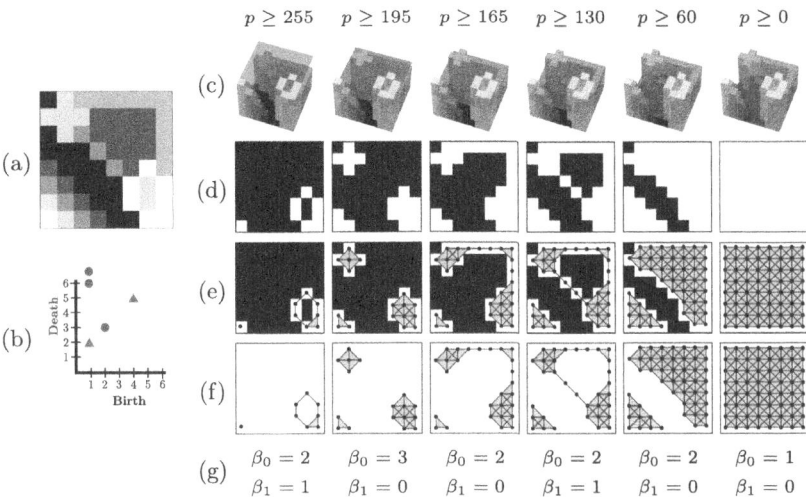

Fig. 2. Illustration of the filtration and PH calculation. (a) Original greyscale image in the range $[0, 255]$. (b) Persistence diagram. (c) 3D representation of the greyscale and a threshold. (d) Binary images of pixels above the threshold. (e) Filtration overlaid on the binary images. A vertex is placed at each white pixel. Edges are added between neighbouring pixels. A triangle is added when cycles of three edges are formed. (f) Filtration with pixels removed. (g) Betti numbers.

is thresholded at decreasing intensities to produce a series of binary images (Fig. 2(d)). Second, a vertex is added at every white pixel, an edge between the vertices if the corresponding pixels neighbour each other, and a triangle if three edges form a cycle (Fig. 2(e) and Fig. 2(f)). For completeness, Fig. 2(b) shows the persistence diagram computed from the filtration of simplicial complexes. There are other methodologies of filtration, which will not be covered in this paper and the reader is referred to [7].

3 Materials

In this work, two datasets of colorectal cancer slides stained with H&E were used: 100K-set and 7K-set, which contain 100,000 and 7180 images, respectively [11]. Both sets contain images of nine different classes: ADI: adipose tissue; BACK: background; CRC: colorectal cancer; DEB: debris; LYM: lymphocytes; MUC: mucus; MUS: smooth muscle; NORM: normal colon mucosa; STR: cancer-associated stroma; TUM: colorectal adenocarcinoma epithelium (Fig. 3). All details of the datasets are given in [11, 12]. The 100K-set's images were explicitly stated to be normalised using Macenko's method, but the 7K-set was not explicitly stated to be normalised. Upon closer inspection, it was found that the 7K-set had not been normalised. With the same reference image as the 100K-set, the 7K-set was normalised using Macenko's method on a per-patch basis before any further analysis was performed (Fig. 4).

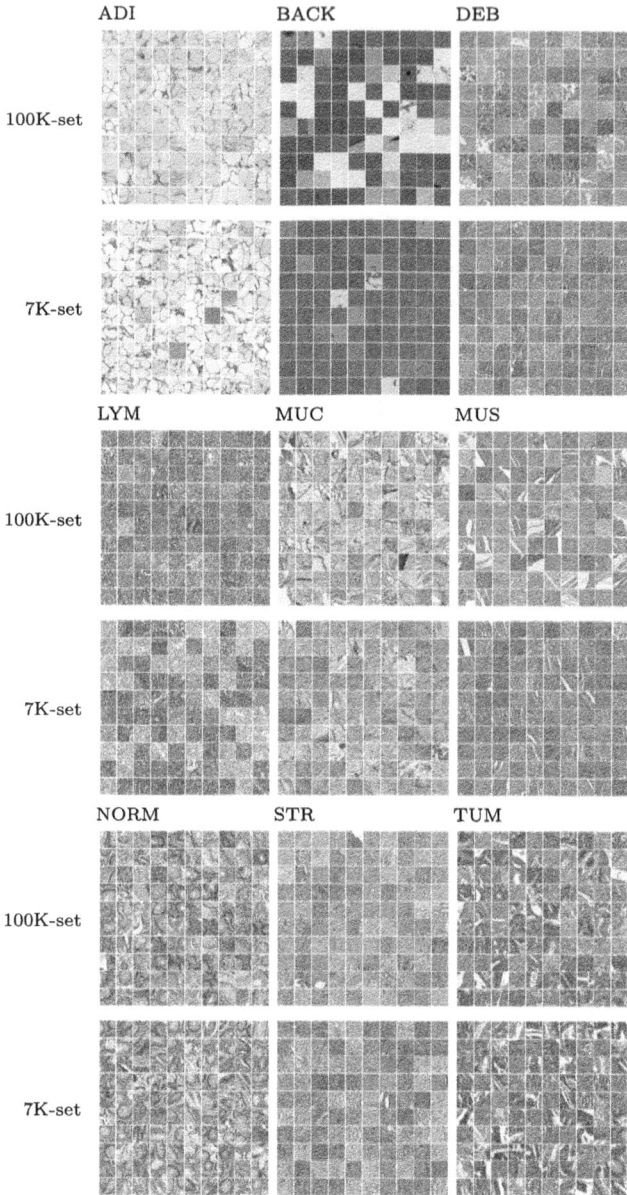

Fig. 3. Illustration of the datasets with 100 sample patches from each set. By class: NCT-CRC-HE-100K images are shown above, normalized CRC-VAL-HE-7K images are shown below. ADI: adipose tissue; BACK: background; CRC: colorectal cancer; DEB: debris; LYM: lymphocytes; MUC: mucus; MUS: smooth muscle; NORM: normal colon mucosa; STR: cancer-associated stroma; TUM: colorectal adenocarcinoma epithelium.

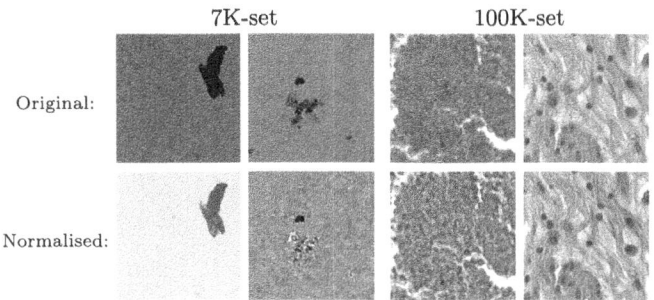

Fig. 4. Effects of normalisation. Left: two BACK patches from the 7K-set; one presents a large dark spot causing the rest of the normalised image to become extremely bright, while the other stays relatively uniform. Right: two very purple patches (from DEB and MUS classes), when normalised look visually more like the rest of the set. (Color figure online)

4 Methods

Two types of features were computed from the images from the train and test datasets. Topological features were obtained from the level-set filtration previously introduced. For comparison purposes, features using Gabor frequency filtering were also calculated. All the features were normalised to a range of 0-1. These methodologies are described below.

4.1 Topological Features

Topological features were calculated from images by the following process. First, the colour image was converted to greyscale. Then, a 5×5 median filter was applied to the greyscale image to reduce noise and make regions of similar intensities smoother. The size of the median filter was optimised heuristically and selected visually for the best results (results not shown). Next, the persistence diagram was calculated using level-set thresholds in the range $[0,255]$ at every integer. Figure 5 shows some example patches from the 100K-set together with the persistence diagram generated through this process. There is always exactly one component that makes it to the end of the filtration and, in strict mathematical notation, its death is given as ∞. This was also the value returned by the GUDHI [15] package used to compute the diagram. For simplicity, the point corresponding to this component was discarded from the persistence diagram before calculating the following features: number of components/holes, mean birth of components/holes, mean death of components/holes, standard deviation of the births of components/holes, standard deviation of the deaths of components/holes, mean persistence of components/holes, median persistence of components/holes, standard deviation of the persistences of components/holes, minimum birth of components/holes, maximum birth of components/holes, minimum death of components/holes, maximum death of components/holes, range of births of components/holes, range of deaths of components/holes, 1st, 5th, 25th, 50th (median), 75th, 95th, 99th percentiles of births of components/holes, 1st, 5th, 25th, 50th (median), 75th, 95th, 99th percentiles of deaths of components/holes. The ratio between the number of holes and the number of components was also calculated and added to the list of features, for a total of 57 topological features from each persistence diagram.

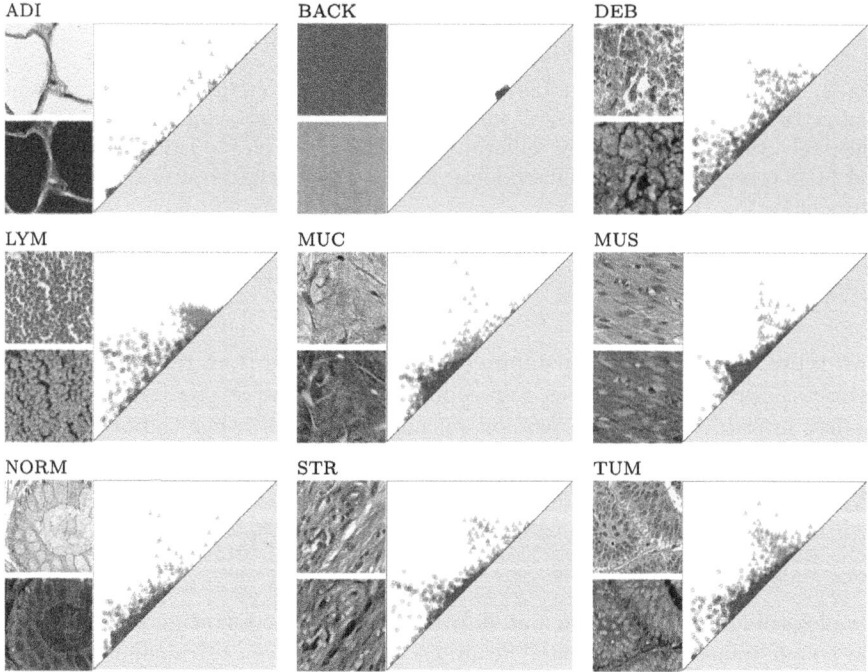

Fig. 5. Illustration of the persistence diagrams of the histological tissues from the 100K-set. One representative patch from each of the classes (ADI, BACK, DEB, LYM, MUC, MUS, NORM, STR, TUM) is converted to greyscale and inverted. Noise is removed on the greyscale image by applying a 5×5 median filter. A persistence diagram is calculated from the smoothed greyscale image where blue circles are components and red triangles are holes. The distribution of the scatterplots in the persistence diagram capture differences in the textures of different tissues. ADI: adipose tissue; BACK: background; CRC: colorectal cancer; DEB: debris; LYM: lymphocytes; MUC: mucus; MUS: smooth muscle; NORM: normal colon mucosa; STR: cancer-associated stroma; TUM: colorectal adenocarcinoma epithelium. (Color figure online)

4.2   Gabor Features

Gabor filters are filters which operate on an image through convolution. They can be described as made up of a spatial frequency and orientation within a two-dimensional Gaussian envelope. For an in-depth explanation of how Gabor filters are used, the reader is referred to [17]. Each Gabor filter is defined uniquely by a direction, a frequency, and the standard deviations in the horizontal and vertical coordinates. 36 different Gabor filters with four different angles $(0, \pi/4, \pi/2, 3\pi/4)$, three frequencies $(1/20, 1/10, 1/4)$, and three standard deviations $(1, 3, 5)$. [20]. To compute features using Gabor filters, each image was converted to greyscale and then convolved with the Gabor filters. This yields a filtered greyscale image, from which the mean pixel intensity and variance of pixel intensities were computed. The effects that different directions and frequencies for the Gabor filters have on the filtered image are shown in Fig. 6.

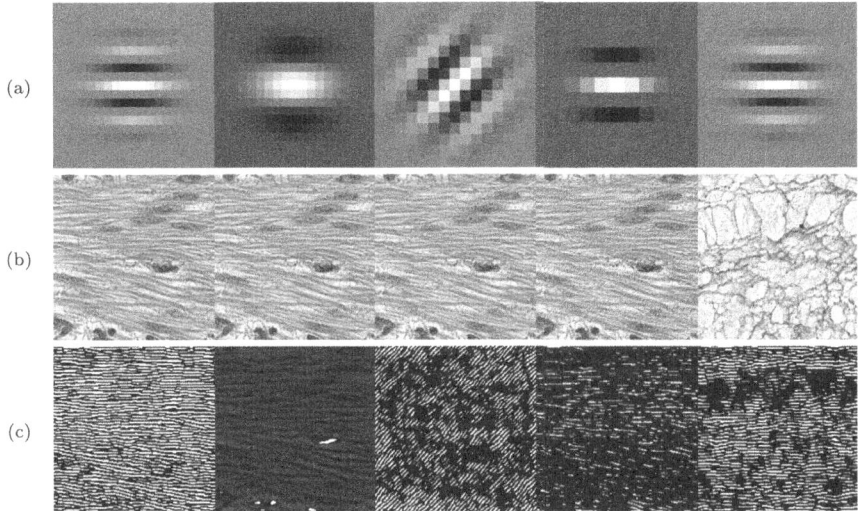

Fig. 6. Illustration of Gabor filters. (a) Gabor filters (b) Sample patches converted to greyscales (c) Filtered results.

4.3   Random Forest

Random forests are a supervised classification model introduced in 2001 by L. Breiman [4]. It is based on the much older decision tree classifiers [5]. In broad terms, a random forest classifier is created by building multiple decision trees and combining their outputs: the algorithm creates many subsets of the training data by randomly sampling with replacement (this is called "bootstrapping"), then each subset (bootstrapped set) is used to train a single decision tree. Additionally, not all features are considered for each tree - only a random subset of them. For classification, the label assigned to a new sample is given by majority voting from all the decision trees in the forest. A comprehensive overview on random forests can be found in [2].

A random forest model was trained on subsets of different sizes ($n = 100, 250, 500, 750, 1000, 2500, 5000, 7500, 10000, 20000$) of the 100K-set and tested on the complete 7K-set, using only topological features, only Gabor features, and the combination of both (combined features). The maximum depth and number of estimators for the Random Forest were also optimised. The criterion used to build the decision trees was the Gini index.

The accuracy on the 7K-set was calculated by taking the ratio of correctly classified samples to the total number of samples in the set. The *out-of-bag* (OOB) score of each model was also calculated [3]. As mentioned previously, the model works by bootstrapping the dataset many times; i.e. randomly sampling with replacement many times. Then, decision trees are built using the boot-strapped sets. The OOB score is calculated by classifying the samples which are not included in the bootstrapped sets for each tree. In other words, if a sample is not part of the bootstrapped set used to build a particular tree, the sample is labelled by that tree, and it is checked whether or not the assigned label is correct. The OOB score is a popular way to estimate how well a random for-est will generalise, as for large samples it approximates a k-fold cross-validation estimation [10]. For both the accuracy and OOB score, a correct classification was considered any sample that was assigned the correct tissue label. When a sample was assigned a different class, it was considered a misclassification.

5   Results

The t-SNE visualisations reveal clearly that the separability of the classes is greater in the 7K-set than in the 100K-set for the topological features (Fig. 7(a)), Gabor features (Fig. 7(b)) and Combined features (Fig. 7(c)). To emphasise the separability, 2D Gaussian distributions were fitted to the distributions of the points per class, and the equation of the ellipse containing the area 1.5 standard deviations away from the mean was calculated. Whilst the ellipses for 4 classes overlap substantially in the 100K, MUS and MUC (red and purple) are quite separate from NORM and TUM (green and yellow) in the 7K.

To confirm the separability of classes between sets, Random Forests were trained with an increasing number of topological, Gabor and Combined features and then tested on the 7K-set (Fig. 8). The results of the OOB score and accuracy follow similar patterns and stabilised between 5,000 and 10,000 samples, which suggested that around 7,000 samples were sufficient to obtain good results. With the samples restricted to 7,500, the random forest's parameters were tested and it was found that after 100 estimators and a maximum depth of 18 leaves, there was no major improvement in OOB-Score. Thus, these were the parameters chosen for the next experiment (results not shown).

Next, the number of samples of the 100K-set were restricted to 7,180 to perform a reverse experiment: train on the reduced 100K-set and classify the 7K-set and then train on the 7K-set and classify the reduced 100K-set. The results confirmed the higher separability of the 7K-set, reaching 0.96 OOB-Score but only a 0.55 when the 100K-set was classified with training on the 7K-set (Table 1). On the other hand, when training on the 100K-set, the OOB-Score was lower (0.88) and the classification of the 7K-set was 0.71.

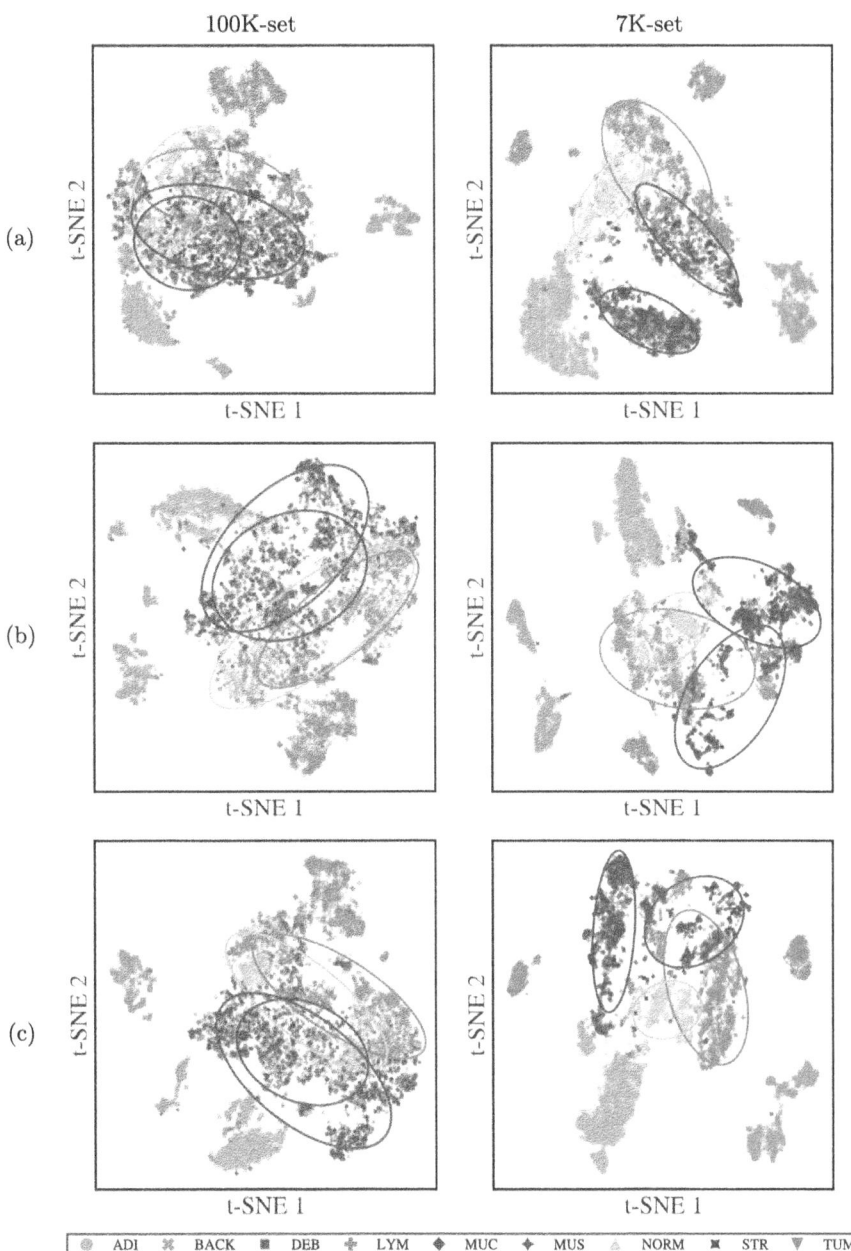

Fig. 7. t-SNE visualisation of the samples by feature type and set they belong to. (a) Visualisations created from topological features. (b) Visualisations created from Gabor features. (c) Visualisations created from Combined features. (Color figure online)

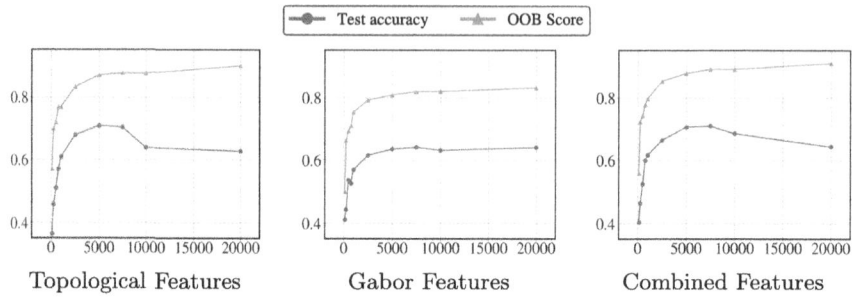

Fig. 8. Accuracy on the 7K-set and the OOB score when a Random Forest model is trained on random samples of differing sizes from the 100K-set and using topological, Gabor or combined features.

Table 1. Effects of training on the different sets. The model was trained on the combined features using 7180 samples from the 100K-set and tested on the 7K-set, then trained on the 7K-set and tested on the 7180 samples from the 100K-set. Note that training on 100K-set and testing on 7K-set yields a much higher Test Accuracy but lower OOB-Score than the reverse case.

Training set	Test Accuracy	OOB-Score
100K-set	0.7061	0.8801
7K-set	0.5557	0.9638

6   Discussion

Concerns about the bias in the colour profile of the classes and improper handling of the images 100K-set and the 7K-set had been highlighted [9]. However, up to the best knowledge of the authors, the differences in separability of classes of these important datasets had not been discussed. These were demonstrated with topological and Gabor features, which were used to extract textural and structural properties from the data, that is, properties unrelated to colour.

First, the problems related to **brightness** previously noted in [9] were confirmed. The intensity profiles of the BACK class in the 100K-set go to the extremes; very bright or very dark (Fig. 3). In contrast, the patches in the BACK class in the 7K-set have more uniform intensities. The few patches that are brighter almost always contain a very dark region, these are most likely due to issues of **normalisation**. Macenko's normalisation seems to have this effect when there is a dark region in the image.

Second, there were problems of **hue**, which are visible in the DEB and MUS classes of the 100K-set. In the DEB class, there are four patches that are visually more purple/violet (hue values around 270–280) than the majority, which are visually closer to pink/magenta (hue values around 300–320). In fact, it was found that the average hue of the four DEB patches was 277, while the average hue of the non-faulty patches was 312. These variations were also present in the

MUS class. These differences in colour seem to suggest that the 100K-set has not been properly normalised using Macenko's method.

Third, issues of **curation and labelling** were detected. The 100K-set shows signs of less consistent curation and labelling when compared to the 7K-set. For example, MUS patches of the 100K-set show white areas (possibly background). This will be further analysed below.

Fourth, there may be differences in **cell populations**, specifically there seem to exist two different types of LYM pathces in the 7K-set. An initial observation of these patches suggests that the difference arises from the brightness of the patches. However, a closer inspection suggests that there is also a difference in the sparseness and size of the lymphocytes (Fig. 3).

Fifth, the **differences in separability of classes** between the 100K-set and the 7K-set became evident with the extraction of topological and Gabor features and the visualisation with t-SNE (Fig. 7), and the previous visual observations were confirmed. Four classes (NORM - ▲, TUM - green ▼, MUC - purple ♦, MUS - magenta ⋆) were highlighted with ellipses as previously described. Whilst in the 100K-set, these four classes partially overlap in the topological, Gabor and combined features, in the 7K-set, these appear comparatively separated, especially MUC in the topological and TUM and NORM from MUS and MUC in Gabor and combined. Similarly, the ADI (grey ●) and the BACK (orange ×) are better separated in the 7K-set. For the topological features, the class BACK is strongly clustered in the 7K-set with just a few elements close to the ADI class, whilst in the 100K-set there are several clusters and the ADI class is surrounded by elements of BACK. For Gabor features, the BACK in 7K-set is totally separated from the ADI class but in the 100K-set again many elements overlap and presents more clusters.

As noted previously, the LYM class in the 100K-set always appears as a single cluster (pink crosses), whilst in the 7K-set always appears as two or even three large and distinctly located clusters (Fig. 7(a–c)). A smaller group is also visible and close to the other classes suggesting that there may be a third type of LYM patches not immediately distinguishable in Fig. 3.

To quantify the effects of the separability of classes, the following experiments were conducted: (1) Train on 7,180 samples from the 100K-set and classify the 7K-set, (2) train on the 7K-set and classify 7,180 samples from the 100K-set (Table 1). When trained on the 7K-set, a random forest model obtained a higher OOB-Score (0.9638) than when trained on 7180 samples of the 100K-set (0.8801). Yet, when the opposite set was classified, the results of the model trained on the 7K-set were far lower (0.5557) than those trained on the 100K-set (0.7061). Both of these results imply a higher separability of classes in the 7K-set.

Separability of classes can come from many factors: intrinsic differences in the classes (i.e. different textures, colours, or shape). However, it is to be expected that two sets of images treated in a similar manner should show the same degrees of separations between their classes. Some prominent factors can potentially influence the observed differences in separability between the sets, mainly differences in preprocessing and handling of the images. In the case of these two data sets, the most probable causes are problems of normalisation and problems of curation and labelling. In the case of normalisation, some patches show evidence of not having been properly normalised when compiling the dataset. This is especially noticeable in Fig. 3 when looking at the DEB and MUS classes and the effects shown in Fig. 4. An example of problems with curation and labelling is that MUS patches have a seemingly more even texture than the patches in the 100K-set: some of these patches seem to show more white areas (possibly background) than actual tissue (Fig. 3). However, other factors such as the probable existence of three different populations of lymphocytes could suggest that there may be intrinsic differences related to the nature of the tissue (healthy/diseased) in one particular patient.

To summarise, greyscale versions of images from two datasets (100K-set and 7K-set) were used to extract features from the corresponding persistence diagrams and the Gabor-filtered versions of the images. The features were used to train random forest models (Fig. 8) and compare the effects of training on one of the sets and testing on the other, then reversing the roles (Table 1). The difference in accuracies and OOB-Score of the experiment, together with a visual analysis of the images (Fig. 3) and a t-SNE visualisation of the classes reveal inconsistencies between the datasets. These inconsistencies go beyond what is expected between two different datasets of supposedly similar images, leading to very different generalisation scores of the random forest model.

The analysis performed to find compare the separability issues in these datasets can be applied to others. The use of topological and textural descriptors can be used as an initial feature extraction method that helps to evaluate separability of classes in other histopathological datasets. While not explored, it is thought that the feature extraction methods shown here can also be applied to datasets outside of the realm of histopathology, as long as patches differ between classes through texture. A limitation in the experiments carried out is that robustness to small changes in the hyperparameters was not tested.

To conclude, it is reasonable to expect that the datasets that one chooses to train and test on will impart some differences in the scores. However, in the case of these two datasets, it has been shown that the quality of the sets has a very large effect on the precision scores achieved by the machine learning model (Table 1) and researchers should be careful about the datasets used to train and test models. Even though NCT-CRC-HE-100K and CRC-VAL-HE-7K are popular datasets used to train and test machine learning and deep learning models, it seems the quality of the training set is lower than that of the test set, and researchers using these sets to train models should be wary of this fact.

References

1. Afshari Mirak, S., et al.: The growing nationwide radiologist shortage: current opportunities and ongoing challenges for international medical graduate radiologists. Radiology **314**(3), e232625 (2025)
2. Biau, G., Scornet, E.: A random forest guided tour. TEST **25**(2), 197–227 (2016). https://doi.org/10.1007/s11749-016-0481-7

3. Breiman, L.: Out-of-bag estimation. Technical report, University of California Berkeley (1996)
4. Breiman, L.: Random forests. Mach. Learn. **45**(1), 5–32 (2001). https://doi.org/10.1023/A:1010933404324
5. Breiman, L., et al.: Classification and Regression Trees. Chapman and Hall/CRC, New York (2017). https://doi.org/10.1201/9781315139470
6. Brito-Pacheco, D., et al.: Relationship between irregularities of the nuclear envelope and mitochondria in hela cells observed with electron microscopy. In: 2024 IEEE ISBI, pp. 1–5 (2024)
7. Brito-Pacheco, D., Giannopoulos, P., Reyes-Aldasoro, C.C.: Persistent homology in medical image processing: a literature review. medRxiv (2025). https://doi.org/10.1101/2025.02.21.25322669
8. Edelsbrunner, H., Harer, J.: Persistent homology—a survey, vol. 453, pp. 257–282. American Mathematical Society, Providence, Rhode Island (2008). https://doi.org/10.1090/conm/453/08802
9. Ignatov, A., Malivenko, G.: NCT-CRC-HE: not all histopathological datasets are equally useful (2024). https://doi.org/10.48550/arXiv.2409.11546
10. Janitza, S., Hornung, R.: On the overestimation of random forest's out-of-bag error. PLoS ONE **13**(8), e0201904 (2018). https://doi.org/10.1371/journal.pone.0201904
11. Kather, J.N., et al.: 100,000 histological images of human colorectal cancer and healthy tissue (2018). https://doi.org/10.5281/zenodo.1214456
12. Kather, J.N., et al.: Predicting survival from colorectal cancer histology slides using deep learning: a retrospective multicenter study. PLOS Med. **16**(1), e1002730 (2019). https://doi.org/10.1371/journal.pmed.1002730
13. Khvostikov, A., et al.: Tissue type recognition in whole slide histological images. In: Proceedings of the 31th International Conference on Computer Graphics and Vision, vol. 2, pp. 496–507. Keldysh Institute of Applied Mathematics (2021). https://doi.org/10.20948/graphicon-2021-3027-496-507
14. Maier-Hein, L., et al.: Why rankings of biomedical image analysis competitions should be interpreted with care. Nat. Commun. **9**(1), 5217 (2018)
15. GUDHI User and Reference Manual. GUDHI Editorial Board, 3.11.0 edn. (2025). https://gudhi.inria.fr/doc/3.11.0/
16. Ramos, J., Aung, P.P.: International medical graduates and the shortage of US pathologists: challenges and opportunities. Arch. Pathol. Lab. Med. **148**(6), 735–738 (2024)
17. Reyes-Aldasoro, C.C.: Multiresolution Volumetric Texture Segmentation. Doctoral, University of Warwick (2004). http://wrap.warwick.ac.uk/67756/
18. Russell, D.K., et al.: Analysis of 2023 cytologists employment survey. J. Am. Soc. Cytopathol. **14**(2), 78–85 (2025)
19. Sun, K., et al.: Automatic classification of histopathology images across multiple cancers based on heterogeneous transfer learning. Diagnostics **13**(77), 1277 (2023). https://doi.org/10.3390/diagnostics13071277
20. van der Walt, S., et al.: scikit-image: image processing in python. PeerJ **2**, e453 (2014). https://doi.org/10.7717/peerj.453
21. Wang, K.S., et al.: Accurate diagnosis of colorectal cancer based on histopathology images using artificial intelligence. BMC Med. **19**(1), 76 (2021). https://doi.org/10.1186/s12916-021-01942-5

SWIFT-Reg: Slide-Wide Intelligent Feature-Based Tissue Registration

Esha Sadia Nasir$^{(\boxtimes)}$ and Shan E. Ahmed Raza

Tissue Image Analytics (TIA) Centre, Department of Computer Science,
University of Warwick, Coventry, UK
{esha.nasir,shan.raza}@warwick.ac.uk

Abstract. Accurate alignment of histopathological whole slide images (WSIs) across different staining modalities is essential for comprehensive multimodal tissue analysis, yet remains challenging due to complex deformations, sectioning artefacts, and staining variations. This paper presents an efficient registration framework that effectively addresses these challenges through a progressive multi-stage approach. Our approach integrates efficient tissue segmentation using Florence2-SAM2 with a progressive three-stage registration strategy. Initial coarse alignment utilises tissue mask centroids and geometric transformations to establish preliminary correspondence. Subsequently, the accelerated feature extraction module (XFeat) identifies and matches distinctive tissue landmarks from the roughly aligned images, significantly reducing the computational burden of the final stage. The registration concludes with fine alignment using diffusive regulariser based iterative optimisation. Comprehensive evaluation on the ANHIR, ACROBAT and HyReCo datasets demonstrates that our method achieves superior registration accuracy (med-TRE 6.01 μm for restained and med-TRE 65.5 μm for consecutive sections) and computational efficiency (average runtime of 17 s) compared to state-of-the-art approaches. The proposed framework enables precise spatial correlation of histological features in differently stained modalities, facilitating advanced analysis for both diagnostic and research applications.

Keywords: whole slide image registration · image registration · H&E · IHC · tissue segmentation · cross-stain alignment

1 Introduction

Image registration refers to the process of determining a transformation that aligns two images, typically a source image and a target image, by mapping corresponding elements from one to the other. This transformation brings both images, which originate from different coordinate systems, into a common coordinate space, allowing for an accurate and meaningful comparison. One of the primary applications of image registration is in computational pathology, where the goal is to align multi-stained whole slide images (WSI) to facilitate a more precise and comprehensive analysis of tissue specimens.

© The Author(s), under exclusive license to Springer Nature Switzerland AG 2026
S. Ali et al. (Eds.): MIUA 2025, LNCS 15916, pp. 102–117, 2026.
https://doi.org/10.1007/978-3-031-98688-8_8

Tissue samples are often prepared using a variety of staining techniques to highlight distinct cellular structures and biomarkers. Common staining methods, such as Hematoxylin & Eosin (H&E), Immunohistochemistry (IHC), and multiplex immunofluorescence (miF), are employed to reveal specific tissue characteristics that are crucial for identifying abnormalities and disease-related changes. In this context, WSI registration plays a pivotal role in aligning these differently stained tissue sections. By doing so, it enables a more accurate comparison and integration of structural, molecular, and cellular data. This alignment is essential for tasks such as detecting affected tissues, identifying tumour markers, and conducting in-depth analyses that supports critical clinical decisions related to diagnosis, prognosis, and treatment planning.

However, WSI registration presents several challenges. The most significant of these is the large size of WSI files, which often exceeds several gigabytes when uncompressed, making the registration process computationally intensive and time consuming. Additionally, tissue deformations such as folds, stretching, missing tissue, tears, and variations in local structures between slices can severely impact the accuracy of image alignment. The absence of a common marker, particularly in immunohistochemical staining, further complicates the registration process. Finally, inter-user and inter-platform variations in staining intensity adds another layer of complexity.

Despite these challenges, WSI registration remains a critical first step in a broad range of downstream applications in automated computational pathology pipelines, such as to perform detailed WSI analyses, compensate for distortions, merge data from different modalities, and identify diseased tissues.

This leads to a need for a robust WSI registration tool that can work on differently stained WSI images, leading to accurate alignment for cases having tissue folds, missing tissues, stretches, tearing, and stain variation.

This paper introduces a unique registration framework (SWIFT-Reg) designed to achieve reliable WSI registration across diverse histopathological conditions in an efficient manner. The proposed method comprises four principal components:

1. **Tissue Mask Extraction:** An optimised Florence2 SAM2 instance segmentation technology to generate high-fidelity tissue masks, establishing a crucial foundation for subsequent registration processes.
2. **Affine Registration via TriMorph:** An integrated three-stage systematic estimation process, TriMorph, to align using both image data and tissue masks comprising of the following steps:
   - Initial spatial alignment via centre-of-mass (COM) based translation.
   - Precise scale factor determination derived from tissue boundary coordinates.
   - Comprehensive rotation optimisation through angular similarity evaluation across the complete $[-180°, 180°]$ range with $10°$ step intervals
3. **Accelerated Feature-Based Alignment:** An XFeat based feature alignment which couples accelerated dense feature extraction with efficient feature matching protocols to facilitate robust similarity metric computation between image pairs.

4. **Iterative Intensity based Registration:** A non-rigid registration via iterative multi-resolution intensity optimisation between fixed and transformed images, generating accurate deformation estimation and precise tissue registration.

Experimental validation demonstrates that the proposed integrated approach enables reliable WSI registration even in challenging scenarios characterised by significant tissue variations and imaging inconsistencies addressing a critical challenge in computational pathology workflows for multi-stained analysis.

2 Related Work

Various computational approaches have been developed for automatic WSI registration, differentiated primarily by stain compatibility and registration performance. These methods broadly fall into three categories: feature-based, frequency-based, and intensity-based approaches, each with distinct advantages for wholeslide image analysis. Numerous computational methods have been developed for automatic registration of whole-slide images (WSIs), each varying in terms of stain compatibility and registration accuracy. These methods are generally classified into three main categories: feature-based, frequency-based, and intensity-based approaches, each offering distinct advantages for WSI analysis. Lotz et al. [10] introduced a local-global registration method for multi-slide IHC fusion, combining low-resolution non-linear alignment with patch-level refinement to address both global and local tissue distortions. This was later extended into a more robust three-stage pipeline [11] incorporating rotation-based affine registration, Gauss-Newton optimization, and non-rigid B-spline regularization.

Wodzinski et al. [21] proposed a hybrid feature- and intensity-based registration framework with automatic failure detection, combining low-resolution affine alignment with demons-based non-rigid registration. To overcome computational limitations, they later introduced a pyramidal, patch-based refinement strategy supported by preprocessing steps such as Gaussian smoothing and background segmentation. Their most recent work [20] employs a two-step hybrid approach that integrates SuperPoint and SuperGlue for deep feature matching with intensity-based non-rigid registration using normalized cross-correlation and diffusive regularization. Paknezhad et al. [15] developed a multiscale attention-based registration method that narrows focus around (ROIs) as resolution increases. This strategy at all scales, improves robustness to large deformations outside the ROI. They further enhanced regional accuracy by selectively filtering SIFT keypoints to remove irrelevant matches.

Hoque et al. [6] presented a robust WSI registration framework based on classical methods. They used gradient SIFT for feature extraction from multi-stained images and introduced a novel keypoint matching algorithm that incorporates scale, orientation, and spatial information. Notably, their method performs large-scale registration without relying on patch-based strategies and demonstrated superior accuracy, recall, and processing speed compared to state-of-the-art methods like SIFT and SURF. Mahapatra et al. [13] proposed a self-supervised deep learning approach for non-linear histology registration, guided by segmentation maps generated via K-means clustering on multi-scale features extracted from a pre-trained U-Net.

Awan et al. [2] employed deep features from a pre-trained VGG model for rigid registration, and final high-resolution patch-based B-spline registration to capture local deformations.

Our approach differs fundamentally by addressing WSI registration as a generalised problem suitable for diverse histological preparations. We leverage accurate tissue masks as the registration foundation, accommodating tissue deformations, staining variations, and morphological differences by focusing specifically on relevant tissue regions while excluding background artefacts. This mask-based strategy achieves precise initial alignment even in challenging scenarios with significant tissue distortions or staining inconsistencies. The proposed approach enables adaptive parameter selection based on structural characteristics, optimising performance for each sample pair without requiring stain-specific or tissue-specific manual tuning, thereby offering a more generalised and robust solution for digital pathology workflows.

3   Datasets

In this study, we evaluated our proposed approach on three publicly available whole slide image registration datasets including ANHIR [5], ACROBAT [19] and HyReCo [7].

3.1   Automatic NonRigid Histological Image Registration - ANHIR

The ANHIR [5] dataset comprises a total of 481 image pairs, divided into 230 training pairs and 251 evaluation pairs. It features 8 distinct tissue types stained with 18 different stains, presenting significant challenges for analysis and registration tasks.

3.2   AutomatiC Registration Of Breast cAncer Tissue - ACROBAT

The ACROBAT [19] dataset comprises consecutive female breast cancer slides, including 750 training cases, 100 validation cases, and 303 test cases. These slides are stained using H&E, ER, KI67, PGR, and HER2, resulting in a total of 3,406 WSIs across the training, validation, and test sets.

3.3   Hybrid Re-stained and Consecutive Histological Serial Sections - HYRECO

Consecutive Slides. Subset A contains 9 sets of consecutive sections stained with H&E, CD8, CD45, and Ki67. PHH3-stained slides were created by bleaching and re-staining H&E slides using a t-CyCIF-like technique. Each section includes 11–19 manually verified landmarks (138 per stain, 690 total).

Restained Slides. Subset B comprises 54 H&E-PHH3 image pairs without cons sections, containing 2303 annotations (43 per pair).

4   Model Architecture

This section details SWIFT-Reg framework for multimodal whole slide image alignment, encompassing both rigid and non-rigid registration techniques. Figure 1 shows detailed framework of SWIFT-Reg model.

4.1   Preprocessing

Our preprocessing pipeline converts RGB images to greyscale, applies gamma correction to enhance poorly stained tissue features, resizes images for standardisation, and implements Macenko normalisation. For each image pair, we extract downsampled thumbnails at $1.25\times$ resolution and apply differential gamma correction—specifically, $\gamma = 1.0$ for H&E (which maintains the original image) and $\gamma = 0.4$ for IHC (enhancing tissue visibility). This stain-specific gamma adjustment significantly improves tissue mask extraction (as detailed in the following subsection), as prompt-based segmentation performs better on normalised images compared to raw IHC-stained slides. To maintain the integrity of the greyscale, we apply intensity rescaling based on the 0âĂŞ90th percentile interval, which enhances contrast while reducing the influence of extreme outlier pixels.

4.2   Tissue Segmentation

Tissue segmentation forms the critical foundation of our registration framework. We implement stain normalisation to standardise tissue appearance prior to mask extraction. Our approach incorporates a prompt-based approach using Florence2-SAM2 instance segmentation [22] with strategically selected prompts (**tissue, stain, histology, cell, tissue**) designed to detect tissue regions while excluding artefacts like pen marks. If the primary segmentation fails (as indicated by a None mask value), we activate a fallback mechanism based on UNet architecture. This secondary model was trained on 179 tissue samples from the ACROBAT dataset [19]. All outputs undergo post-processing to preserve only significant tissue regions based on connected component analysis. These refined masks enable our algorithm to focus exclusively on relevant tissue regions, facilitating precise alignment even in challenging scenarios with significant deformations or staining inconsistencies.

4.3   Rigid Registration

The SWIFT-Reg framework employs an efficient, intelligent approach to align WSIs across multiple staining modalities. Our method computes precise transformations by analysing tissue morphology and extracting dense features to calculate inter-image similarity.

For computational efficiency, the process begins with downsampled WSIs that undergo preprocessing and tissue mask extraction. These outputs are then

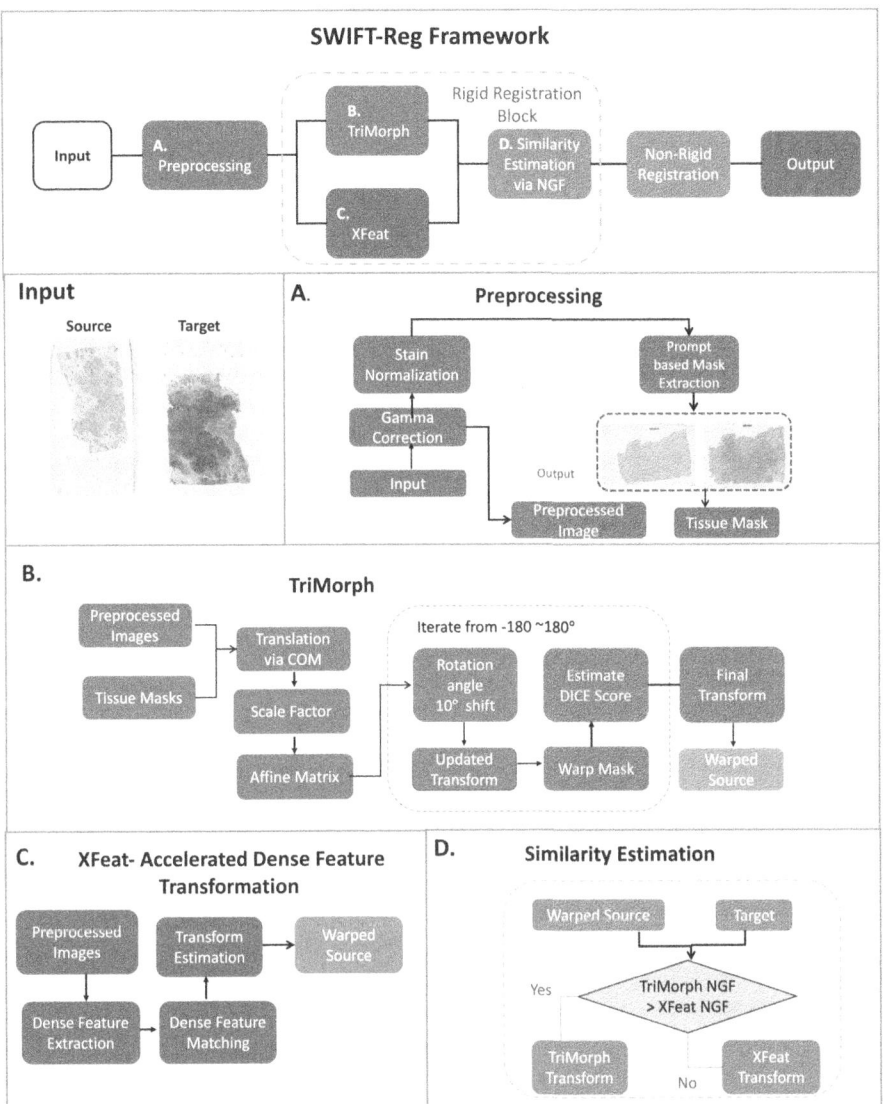

Fig. 1. Rigid Registration Architecture: (A) Preprocessing with gamma correction, Macenko stain normalisation, and Florence2-SAM2 mask extraction; (B) TriMorph module performing triple transformations for morphology-based registration; (C) XFeat module computing dense features. Both transformations are evaluated using Normalised Gradient Field (NGF) similarity metric, with the higher-scoring transformation selected for final warping.

processed by our TriMorph and XFeat modules for rigid transformation estimation, with the final transformation selected based on Normalised Gradient Fields (NGF) similarity metrics.

TriMorph. The TriMorph module establishes initial spatial correspondence between WSI pairs through a robust coarse registration approach based on tissue morphology. This specialised component estimates triple transformations, translation, rotation, and scaling to effectively align tissue specimens despite significant initial misalignments.

Transformation Estimation. Our registration pipeline begins with centre of mass alignment, where we compute a transformation matrix $\mathbf{T}_{\text{com}}$ that translates the moving image's centre (x_m, y_m) to align with the fixed image's centre (x_f, y_f).

To address scale discrepancies between slides, the algorithm analyses relative dimensions of tissue masks and computes appropriate scale factors. The system then explores rotational alignments at discrete angles (in increments of $\theta = 10°$), systematically evaluating each transformation using the Dice coefficient.

Optimal Alignment Selection. The transformation yielding the highest Dice coefficient above our empirically determined threshold ($\text{Dice}_{\text{threshold}} = 0.7$) is selected as the optimal coarse alignment.

Similarity Metric. For initial TriMorph transformation optimisation and similarity estimation on tissue masks we have used DICE score:

$$\text{Dice}(M_f, M_m) = \frac{2|M_f \cap M_m|}{|M_f| + |M_m|} \tag{1}$$

where in Eq. 1 M_f and M_m represent the tissue masks of fixed and moving images, respectively.

Accelerated Dense Extraction via XFeat. Our registration framework incorporates an accelerated feature-based alignment method utilising the XFeat algorithm [16], which leverages computationally efficient dense feature extractors. XFeat represents a lightweight architecture designed for resource-efficient visual correspondence, ideal for our histopathological registration pipeline.

Our implementation maintains higher resolution feature maps while limiting channel dimensionality to preserve fine tissue details. The method detects and matches up to 16,000 distinctive keypoints between histopathological image pairs, utilising XFeat's semi-dense matching to capture complex structural patterns in multi-stained specimens.

The extracted correspondences ($\mathbf{X} \in \mathbf{R}^{n \times 2}$ and $\mathbf{Y} \in \mathbf{R}^{n \times 2}$) undergo RANSAC-based outlier rejection, complementing XFeat's novel match refinement module. This approach enables precise estimation of a partial affine transformation matrix encompassing translation, rotation, and uniform scaling parameters.

XFeat delivers up to 5x faster processing compared to other deep learning-based feature extraction methods while maintaining comparable accuracy—a critical advantage when processing high-resolution whole slide images without specialized hardware acceleration.

Similarity Metric. The final assessment of warped source and target images for rigid transformation estimation utilises Normalised Gradient Fields (NGFs). This method evaluates alignment quality by calculating normalised image gradients and their dot products, effectively measuring the correlation between edge orientations.

$$\text{NGF} = \frac{1}{N} \sum_{i=1}^{N} \left(\frac{\nabla I_f}{\sqrt{|\nabla I_f|^2 + \epsilon}} \cdot \frac{\nabla I_m}{\sqrt{|\nabla I_m|^2 + \epsilon}} \right)^2 \tag{2}$$

Equation 2 defines NGF as ∇I_f and ∇I_m are the gradients of the fixed and moving images, and $\epsilon = 0.01$ prevents division by zero.

4.4 Deformable Registration of Wholeslide Images via Adaptive Regularisation

For non-rigid registration, we have applied an iterative, instance-specific optimization framework that builds upon the methodology introduced by Wodzinski et al. [20].

Our method employs a multi-resolution image pyramid, enabling a coarse-to-fine refinement of the displacement field. This hierarchical strategy commonly used in both traditional (e.g., ANTs [1]) and learning-based (e.g., Voxel-Morph [3]) registration approaches facilitates efficient convergence and mitigates the risk of local minima. It achieves this by capturing large-scale deformations at lower resolutions and progressively refining details at higher levels.

The registration process begins with a coarse alignment at the lowest resolution, ensuring computational efficiency and robust initialization. Subsequent higher-resolution stages incrementally fine-tune the displacement field. At each level of the pyramid, the displacement field is iteratively optimized using the Adam optimizer. The optimization objective combines normalized cross-correlation as the similarity metric with an adaptive regularization. Unlike the simple diffusive regularization used in the baseline model, the adaptive regularization is specifically designed to preserve local tissue rigidity and prevent unrealistic, large-scale deformations that could compromise structural integrity. The regulariser design is adapted from [18] that models transformation constraints through a combination of homogeneous and spatially varying penalties. The regularization term $R(T)$ comprises two components:

1. A **homogeneous smoothness penalty** that promotes spatial regularity in the deformation field, implemented via the squared Frobenius norm of the gradient, and
2. An **inhomogeneous penalty** weighted by a spatially varying stiffness factor $\gamma(x)$.

The stiffness factor $\gamma(x)$ is designed to be high in rigid structures and low in more elastic regions, thereby adaptively controlling the deformation smoothness.

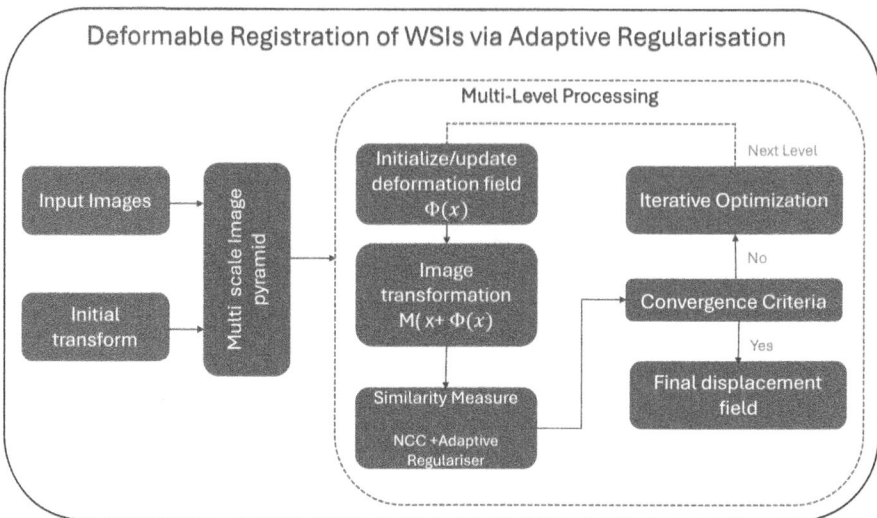

Fig. 2. Non-rigid registration framework. The process computes multi-level registration given input images and initial rigid transform displacement, compute loss using NCC and applies regularisation followed by optimisation using Adam optimiser and loss estimation until convergence (till number of iterations) end.

In this work, we consider only the homogeneous component (1). This decision follows a careful evaluation of existing first and second order regularisers, including total variation (TV), isotropic TV, and curvature-based regularisers. While isotropic TV often yields accurate deformation fields, it can introduce artifacts near tissue boundaries, potentially compromising cellular structure integrity. Based on these observations, we adopt an adaptive, spatially varying regularization strategy that maintains a balance between deformation accuracy and structural preservation.

$$R(\mathbf{D}) = \gamma_s \left\| \nabla \mathbf{D} \right\|^2_{Frob}$$

The implementation intelligently handles displacement field interpolation between different levels and supports incorporation of initial transformation estimates from initial rigid registration. The transformation applied through grid-based sampling using bilinear interpolation. The modular design allows for customisation of iteration counts and optimisation parameters per resolution level. Experimental results demonstrate robust performance across varied imaging scenarios, particularly in cases with significant variations and intensity inconsistencies between source and target images.

Experimental results demonstrate that the framework performs robustly across a wide range of imaging conditions, particularly in the presence of significant structural variation and intensity inconsistencies between the source and target slides. The overall system architecture is illustrated in Fig. 2.

To ensure practical feasibility for high-resolution WSIs, the framework implements grid-based spatial transformations with bilinear interpolation.

Similarity Metric. For our non-rigid iterative alignment, we employ Normalised Cross Correlation (NCC) as the primary similarity metric for cost estimation during each iteration:

$$\text{NCC} = \frac{\sum_{i=1}^{N}(I_f(i) - \bar{I}_f)(I_m(i) - \bar{I}_m)}{\sqrt{\sum_{i=1}^{N}(I_f(i) - \bar{I}_f)^2 \sum_{i=1}^{N}(I_m(i) - \bar{I}_m)^2}} \tag{3}$$

As given in Eq. 3 I_f and I_m represent the fixed and moving images, $\bar{I}_f$ and $\bar{I}_m$ denote their respective mean intensities, and N indicates the number of pixels in the overlap region.

5   Results

The qualitative evaluation reveals substantial improvement in whole slide image alignment post-registration. Fixed and moving WSI pairs demonstrate excellent structural correspondence after applying the rigid registration method, with precise matching of morphological features across different stain types. Notably, the muscle fiber orientations in the HyReCo dataset and the glandular structures in the ACROBAT dataset maintain their biological integrity while achieving spatial alignment. This registration approach effectively compensates for the inherent deformations between consecutive tissue sections, enabling accurate multi-stain analysis without compromising anatomical context.

Evaluation Metric. We conducted a comprehensive evaluation of our registration framework on ANHIR [5], ACROBAT [19] and HyReCo [7] datasets using Target Registration Error (TRE). The registration accuracy was assessed using two metrics:

$$\text{TRE} = \|P_f - T(P_m)\|_2 \qquad \text{rTRE} = \frac{\text{TRE}}{d_{\text{ref}}} \tag{4}$$

As shown in Eq. 4, TRE measures the Euclidean distance between a landmark point P_f in the fixed image and its corresponding transformed point $T(P_m)$ from the moving image after registration. TRE is an evaluation metric to assess registration error in ACROBAT [19] & HyReCo [12] and is used in state-of-the-art methods DFBR [2], DeeperHistReg [20] and HistokatFusion [12]. Since it provides an absolute measure of alignment precision and allows direct quantification of spatial errors.

Where rTRE (relative Target Registration Error) normalises the TRE by a reference distance d_{ref}, typically the image diagonal length. rTRE has been used as an evaluation metric for ANHIR [5] as it enables fair comparison across different image scales, and resolutions representing error as a dimensionless ratio

Table 1. Comparison of registration methods on multiple datasets. The upper section shows results on the ANHIR dataset using relative Target Registration Error (rTRE) **Average** and **Median** across all image pairs. The lower section presents performance on the ACROBAT dataset.

ANHIR Dataset							
Method	Average rTRE		Median rTRE		Max rTRE		Average time [min]
	Average (AArTRE)	Median	Average (AMrTRE)	Median	Average (AMxrTRE)	Median	
Proposed	**0.0040**	**0.0026**	**0.0026**	**0.0015**	**0.0240**	**0.0187**	**0.05**
UPENN	0.0042	0.0029	0.0029	0.0019	0.0239	0.0190	1.60
CKVST	0.0043	0.0032	0.0027	0.0023	0.0239	0.0189	7.80
HistokatFusion [12]	0.0044	0.0027	0.0029	0.0018	0.0251	0.0188	0.16
DeeperHistReg [20]	0.0044	0.0029	0.0029	0.0017	0.0280	0.0225	2.00
AGH [21]	0.0053	0.0032	0.0036	0.0019	0.0283	0.0225	6.55
DFBR [2]	0.0055	0.0029	0.0040	0.0018	0.0275	0.0203	4.00
ACROBAT Dataset							
Method	Average Median TRE (μm)						Avg Time (sec)
Proposed	**234.58**						**16**
DeeperHistReg [20]	396.38						120
DFBR [2]	1447.37						240

relative to image size. This normalisation is particularly important for multi-dataset i.e. ANHIR [5] evaluation where image dimensions vary significantly, ensuring that performance metrics remain comparable regardless of absolute image dimensions.

Table 1 presents quantitative results comparing our method against state-of-the-art techniques on the ANHIR dataset. Our approach outperforms existing methods including DFBR [2], DeeperHistReg [20], and HistokatFusion [12] across all four landmark selection strategies, achieving the lowest rTRE values, representing a 12% improvement. Table 1 demonstrates performance of the proposed method on the ACROBAT challenge dataset, achieving an Average Median TRE of 234.58 while requiring only 16 s of processing time—7.5× faster than competing approaches.

Figure 3 shows registration results at coarse and fine resolution. Table 2 shows Median TRE comparison of consecutive and restained section of HyReCo dataset with existing state of the art models. Our method achieved an average median TRE of 6.01 ± 2.14 μm on HyReCo restained sections and an average median TRE of 65.32 ± 2.14 μm on consecutive sections, outperforming state-of-the-art methods including DeeperHistReg [20] and DFBR [2]. While HistokatFusion [12] outperforms our method, it performs registration at 10×, thus producing a lower TRE compared to the other methods (registering at 1.25× resolution). In future, we plan to enhance our method to perform registration at higher power magnification which may produce lower TRE scores outperforming HistokatFusion.

Computational efficiency was evaluated on a CPU workstation, with our approach completing registration in an average of **16** seconds per WSI pair at $0.625\times$ and $1.25\times$, representing a $3.2\times$ speed-up over existing methods including DFBR [2], DeeperHistReg [20] and HistokatFusion [12]. Notably, the XFeat module reduced feature matching time by **67%** compared to traditional SIFT-based approaches while maintaining comparable accuracy.

Table 2. Performance Comparison on HyReCo Dataset: Consecutive and Re-stained Histological Sections. SWIFT-Reg (Proposed) demonstrates competitive performance across both tasks, especially in terms of runtime efficiency. HistokatFusion performs better in terms of accuracy at $10\times$ resolution, while SWIFT-Reg offers a faster alternative.

Technique	Consecutive Sections			Re-stained Sections	
	Median TRE	Avg. TRE	Avg-Time (sec)	Median TRE	Avg-Time (sec)
HistokatFusion [12]	45.9783	62.5768	—	**2.001**	50.1357
Proposed	**65.26**	**109.83**	**14.37**	**6.807**	**14.37**
Harris [17]	134.0032	142.9819	—	—	—
MSER [14]	143.12	1453.04	49.229	7.1641	49.229
BRISK [8]	149.89	150.53	40	—	—
SURF [4]	158.93	187.144	42.866	7.1134	42.866
DeeperHistReg [20]	174.9	234.5	120	12.24	70
AGH [21]	442.725	753.129	150	28.5786	120
DFBR [2]	542.42	1754.52	240	30.0339	50
SIFT [9]	—	—	—	13.2379	30.145
KAZE	—	—	—	27.2317	35.621

Limitations. One limitation of this approach is that the method focuses on lower resolution levels ($0.625\times$ and $1.25\times$) for deformation computation. While these levels offer a good balance between accuracy and computational efficiency, the method is yet to be fully evaluated at higher resolutions which are often required for detailed cellular-level analysis. The increased computational and memory demands at these resolutions pose a significant challenge, and addressing them will be a critical next step in extending the applicability of our method.

Table 3 presents a detailed breakdown of the execution time for each step in our proposed registration pipeline.

Table 3. Stepwise Execution Time of our Proposed Registration Method

Steps	Avg-Time CPU (sec)	Avg-Time GPU (sec)
Initial	0.29	0.5
Downsampling	0.80	0.67
Preprocessing	0.19	0
Tissue Mask Extraction	6.08	5.4
TriMorph	1.22	0.56
Evaluation	0.70	0.29
XFeat	2.91	0.8
Similarity Estimation	0.73	0.29
Warping	<0.01	0
Total	**13.23**	**8.68**

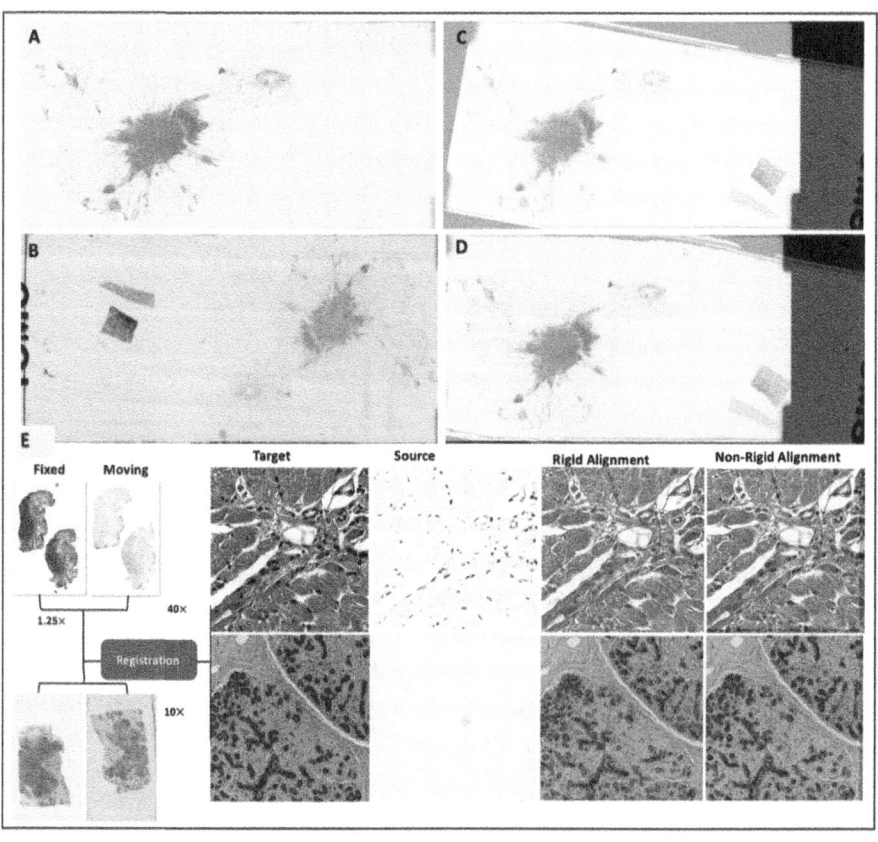

Fig. 3. Acrobat Registration Results at 0.625× and 10×. Block (A) shows fixed WSI, (B) shows Moving WSI, (C) Overlay of the rigid registration (D) Non-rigid registration overlay. (E) Top row shows fine registration results at full resolution for HyReCo (40×) and bottom row shows fine registration results at full resolution for ACROBAT (10×).

6   Conclusion

In this paper, we presented a robust and efficient registration framework for histopathological whole slide images with multiple staining modalities. Our hierarchical approach, combining tissue segmentation with coarse-to-fine registration, effectively addresses the challenges inherent in aligning histological specimens. The framework first employs Florence2-SAM2 for rapid tissue segmentation, followed by an initial alignment based on tissue mask centres and geometrical transformations. The subsequent fine registration refinement using iterative optimisation ensures precise spatial correspondence even in challenging cases. Experimental results on all datasets demonstrate that our method achieves good alignment accuracy while maintaining computational efficiency compared to most of the existing approaches. This registration framework provides a solid foundation for multimodal histopathological analysis, and enables to accurately correlate information across different staining modalities and potentially enhance computer-aided diagnosis systems. Future work will aim to extend this approach to handle more severe tissue deformations, develop a high-resolution registration framework for enhanced alignment precision, and incorporate deep learning-based similarity metrics to improve performance across a wide range of tissue types and pathologies.

Acknowledgments. SEAR reports financial support by the MRC (MR/X011585/1) and the BigPicture project, which has received funding from the Innovative Medicines Initiative 2 Joint Undertaking under grant agreement No 945358.

Disclosure of Interests. The authors have no competing interests.

References

1. Avants, B.B., et al.: A reproducible evaluation of ANTs similarity metric performance in brain image registration. NeuroImage **54**(3), 2033–2044 (2011). https://doi.org/10.1016/j.neuroimage.2010.09.025.   https://linkinghub.elsevier.com/retrieve/pii/S1053811910012061
2. Awan, R., et al.: Deep feature based cross-slide registration. Comput. Med. Imaging Graph. **104**, 102162 (2023). https://doi.org/10.1016/j.compmedimag.2022.102162
3. Balakrishnan, G., Zhao, A., Sabuncu, M.R., Guttag, J., Dalca, A.V.: VoxelMorph: A Learning Framework for Deformable Medical Image Registration (2018). https://doi.org/10.48550/ARXIV.1809.05231. https://arxiv.org/abs/1809.05231

4. Bay, H., Ess, A., Tuytelaars, T., Van Gool, L.: Speeded-up RobustFeatures (SURF). Comput. Vis. Image Underst. **110**(3), 346–359 (2008). https://doi.org/10.1016/j.cviu.2007.09.014. https://linkinghub.elsevier.com/retrieve/pii/S1077314207001555

5. Borovec, J., et al.: ANHIR: automatic non-rigid histological image registration challenge. IEEE Trans. Med. Imaging **39**(10), 3042–3052 (2020). https://doi.org/10.1109/TMI.2020.2986331

6. Hoque, M.Z., Keskinarkaus, A., Nyberg, P., Mattila, T., Seppänen, T.: Whole slide image registration via multi-stained feature matching. Comput. Biol. Med. **144**, 105301 (2022). https://doi.org/10.1016/j.compbiomed.2022.105301. https://linkinghub.elsevier.com/retrieve/pii/S0010482522000932

7. van der Laak, J., Lotz, J., Weiss, N., Heldmann, S.: HyReCo - Hybrid re-stained and consecutive histological serial sections (2021). https://doi.org/10.21227/PZJ5-BS61. https://ieee-dataport.org/open-access/hyreco-hybrid-re-stained-and-consecutive-histological-serial-sections

8. Leutenegger, S., Chli, M., Siegwart, R.Y.: BRISK: binary robust invariant scalable keypoints. In: 2011 International Conference on Computer Vision, Barcelona, Spain, pp. 2548–2555. IEEE (2011). https://doi.org/10.1109/ICCV.2011.6126542. http://ieeexplore.ieee.org/document/6126542/

9. Lindeberg, T.: Scale invariant feature transform. Scholarpedia**7**(5), 10491 (2012). https://doi.org/10.4249/scholarpedia.10491. http://www.scholarpedia.org/article/Scale_Invariant_Feature_Transform

10. Lotz, J., et al.: Patch-based nonlinear image registration for gigapixel whole slide images. IEEE Trans. Biomed. Eng. **63**(9), 1812–1819 (2016). https://doi.org/10.1109/TBME.2015.2503122. https://ieeexplore.ieee.org/document/7335576/

11. Lotz, J., Weiss, N., Heldmann, S.: Robust, fast and accurate: a 3-step method for automatic histological image registration (2019). https://doi.org/10.48550/ARXIV.1903.12063. https://arxiv.org/abs/1903.12063. version Number: 2

12. Lotz, J., Weiss, N., Laak, J.V.D., Heldmann, S.: Comparison of consecutive and re-stained sections for image registration in histopathology. J. Med. Imaging **10**(06) (2023). https://doi.org/10.1117/1.JMI.10.6.067501. http://arxiv.org/abs/2106.13150. arXiv:2106.13150

13. Mahapatra, D.: Registration of Histopathogy Images Using Structural Information From Fine Grained Feature Maps (2020). https://doi.org/10.48550/ARXIV.2007.02078. https://arxiv.org/abs/2007.02078. Version Number: 1

14. Matas, J., Chum, O., Urban, M., Pajdla, T.: Robust wide-baseline stereo from maximally stable extremal regions. Image Vis. Comput. **22**(10), 761–767 (2004). https://doi.org/10.1016/j.imavis.2004.02.006

15. Paknezhad, M., Loh, S.Y.: Regional registration of whole slide image stacks containing major histological artifacts. BMC Bioinform. **21**(1), 558 (2020). https://doi.org/10.1186/s12859-020-03907-6

16. Potje, G., Cadar, F., Araujo: XFeat: Accelerated Features for Lightweight Image Matching (2024). https://doi.org/10.48550/ARXIV.2404.19174. Version Number: 1

17. Rosten, E., Porter, R., Drummond, T.: Faster and better: a machine learning approach to corner detection. IEEE Trans. Pattern Anal. Mach. Intell. **32**(1), 105–119 (2010). https://doi.org/10.1109/TPAMI.2008.275. http://ieeexplore.ieee.org/document/4674368/

18. Ruan, D., Fessler, J.A., Roberson, M., Balter, J., Kessler, M.: Nonrigid registration using regularization that accomodates local tissue rigidity. In: Reinhardt, J.M., Pluim, J.P.W. (eds.) SPIE Proceedings, San Diego, CA, vol. 6144,

p. 614412. SPIE (2006). https://doi.org/10.1117/12.653870. http://proceedings. spiedigitallibrary.org/proceeding.aspx?doi=10.1117/12.653870. ISSN: 0277-786X

19. Weitz, P., Valkonen, M., Solorzano: The ACROBAT 2022 challenge: automatic registration of breast cancer tissue. Med. Image Anal. **97**, 103257 (2024). https:// doi.org/10.1016/j.media.2024.103257

20. Wodzinski, M., Marini, N., Atzori, M., Müller, H.: RegWSI. Comput. Methods Programs Biomed. **250**, 108187 (2024). https://doi.org/10.1016/j.cmpb.2024.108187

21. Wodzinski, M., Skalski, A.: Multistep, automatic and nonrigid image registrations. Phys. Med. Biol. (2020). https://doi.org/10.1088/1361-6560/abcad7

22. Xiao, B., et al.: Florence-2: Advancing a Unified Representation for a Variety of Vision Tasks (2023). https://doi.org/10.48550/ARXIV.2311.06242. https://arxiv. org/abs/2311.06242. Version Number: 1

Learnable Moran's Index for Modeling Spatial Autocorrelation in Whole Slide Images to Predict Breast Cancer Outcomes

Lucan DSilva[✉] and Fayyaz Minhas[iD]

The University of Warwick, Coventry CV4 7AL, UK
{Lucan.Dsilva,Fayyaz.Minhas}@warwick.ac.uk

Abstract. *Can spatial heterogeneity in whole slide images (WSIs) be automatically learned to predict patient survival outcomes?* Spatial heterogeneity within the tissue and tumour microenvironments is increasingly recognised as a critical indicator of cancer prognosis. However, most existing methods do not explicitly model spatial heterogeneity, and those that do typically require segmentation of cellular or tissue structures followed by the use of hand-crafted spatial metrics such as the Morisita-Horn index or colocalisation indices. These approaches are not learnable, and rely on manually defined features and relationships. In this work, we propose a novel neural network-based framework that learns a differentiable variant of Moran's Index, a classical measure of spatial autocorrelation, to automatically quantify spatial heterogeneity from point cloud representations of whole slide image patches. Guided by survival information in training, the proposed method adaptively learns which image-derived features correlate spatially, and how proximity influences their interaction, enabling the discovery of prognostic spatial patterns directly from patch-level features. Applied to the TCGA breast cancer dataset, the proposed method achieves a test concordance index of 0.662 ± 0.060, outperforming several competitive baselines while providing an interpretable quantification of spatial heterogeneity in WSIs. This approach opens new directions for interpretable, spatially informed prognostic modeling and biomarker discovery in computational pathology.

Keywords: Computational Pathology · Deep Learning · Moran's Index · Spatial Autocorrelation · Intratumour Heterogeneity · Disease-Specific Survival

1 Introduction

Intratumour Heterogeneity (ITH) refers to the diversity in cell types in a tumour microenvironment (TME) [4]. The existence of spatial ITH is known to influence crucial aspects of cancer prognosis, including cancer subtypes, survival and

S. Ali et al. (Eds.): MIUA 2025, LNCS 15916, pp. 118–130, 2026.
https://doi.org/10.1007/978-3-031-98688-8_9

other clinical outcomes [1,14]. For example, studies have shown that the spatial location of immune cells relative to invasive cancer cells can be a significant deterministic factor in breast cancer subtypes [15], breast-cancer specific survival [14], and disease-free survival in colorectal cancer [1]. Hence, methods that analyse and map the spatial patterns of cells within tumours can provide deeper insights into understanding the heterogeneous TME [2]. However, current methods do not explicitly learn spatial heterogeneity patterns from features of whole slide images (WSIs) based on survival time and event information. Here, we propose a novel method that can automatically learn to quantify spatial intra-tumour heterogeneity in terms of spatial autocorrelation patterns in cells and derive prognostic insights using this measure.

1.1 Related Work

Maley *et al.* [15] introduced a method using ecological metrics, including the Morisita-Horn index to measure colocalisation between cancer and immune cells, which can effectively predict breast cancer subtypes. This provides a valuable means of measuring spatial heterogeneity in terms of spatial colocalisation. However, the proposed workflow is not fully automated, in that, manual computation or intervention is required to compute indices and obtain results. Furthermore, the locations of cancer and immune cells need to be carefully extracted prior to computation, i.e. prior segmentation and annotation is required to compute colocalisation. In addition, the Morisita-Horn index is generally used to model predator-prey interactions, and would require explicit definitions of predator-prey communities before computing colocalisation indices. Work by Lu *et al.* [11] uses an artificial intelligence-based computational framework to determine spatial colocalisation patterns of Ki67 expression in tumours to predict survival. Furthermore, Lashen *et al.* [6] quantify and comprehensively evaluate ITH in breast cancer and its influence on tumour behaviour and patient outcomes, by learning ITH scores for each feature in consideration. However, these methods include cell segmentation and classification in the deep learning pipeline, and careful time-intensive feature annotation before use in the deep learning framework, respectively. A graph-based method using a graph neural network (GNN) for survival analysis by Mackenzie *et al.* [13] can implicitly capture prognosis-related spatial heterogeneity in the tumour by extracting node embeddings before the final pooling layer of the network. However, it does not provide any specific measure to quantify heterogeneity.

2 Proposed Method

Taking inspiration from the classical Moran's Index (Moran's I) [16], we propose a trainable neural network model, to automatically learn spatial autocorrelation patterns in whole slide images that can predict patient survival.

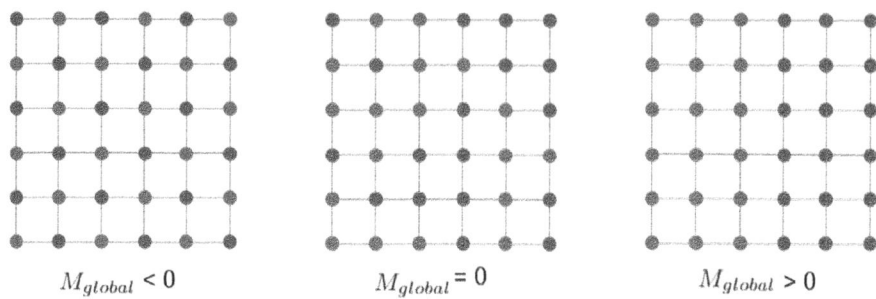

$M_{global} < 0$ $M_{global} = 0$ $M_{global} > 0$

Fig. 1. Example of spatial patterns corresponding to different values of global Moran's I, indicating spatial autocorrelation in the feature of interest. (Left) $M_{global} < 0$ depicts a checker-board pattern demonstrating negative spatial autocorrelation. (Center) $M_{global} = 0$ depicts a random spatial distribution of the feature indicating no spatial autocorrelation. (Right) $M_{global} > 0$ depicts clearly distinguishable spatial clusters, indicating positive spatial autocorrelation.

2.1   Classical Moran's I

Moran's I is a classical measure of spatial autocorrelation that indicates the degree to which a variable is correlated to itself through space, i.e., whether similar objects tend to be clustered together in space or dispersed [8,16]. Mathematically, given a set $X = \{x_i, i = 1...N\}$ of N spatial nodes each with a single feature x_i with non-negatively weighted edge connections w_{ij} between them, the global Moran's index is given by Eq. 1.

$$M_{global}(X) = \frac{N}{W} \frac{\sum_{i=1}^{N} \sum_{j=1}^{N} w_{ij}(x_i - \mu_x)(x_j - \mu_x)}{\sum_{i=1}^{N}(x_i - \mu_x)^2} \tag{1}$$

Here, μ_x is the feature mean of all nodes, i.e. $\mu_x = \frac{\sum_{i=1}^{N} x_i}{N}$. A core component in the computation of Moran's I is the definition of the edge weights, w_{ij}, which determines how feature similarity should influence the contribution of each neighbouring node. W is the sum aggregate of all edge weights, $W = \sum_{i=1}^{N} \sum_{j=1}^{N} w_{ij}$.

Figure 1 shows the relative distribution of global Moran's I values for different spatial feature distribution types. For example, a negative value indicates low spatial clustering, where similar objects are spaced as far apart as possible, reflecting a negative spatial autocorrelation. A value close to 0 would suggest a random dispersion, indicating no spatial autocorrelation between similar nodes. Likewise, a positive value of Moran's I signifies positive spatial autocorrelation, where similar features tend to be highly clustered together. In essence, higher values of Moran's I indicate a greater measure of spatial autocorrelation and hence a distinctively high amount of clustering in similar nodes.

While Moran's I can quantify spatial heterogeneity of a set of nodes with a single feature, its calculation using the formula from Eq. 1 for complex neighbourhoods of nodes with high dimensional features has significant limitations, including: (1) we must define a fixed weight matrix prior to computation, and (2) objects must have a single feature representation.

The proposed method uses Moran's I to quantify spatial intratumour heterogeneity while overcoming these limitations, by adaptively learning which features should be correlated, and how spatial proximity should modulate interobject interaction strength. In our context of whole slide images in computational pathology, Moran's I can capture how similar image patterns are across neighbouring spatial locations. We present Moran's I as a learnable and adaptive neural framework that can help identify spatially coherent patterns in images, enabling downstream tasks like survival analysis, tumour subtyping, niche discovery, or spatial phenotype classification.

2.2   Learnable Moran's Index on Whole Slide Images

The proposed method quantifies spatial autocorrelation in a whole slide image by modeling it as a point cloud $G = \{(\mathbf{p}_i, \mathbf{x}_i)\}_{i=1}^N$, where each of the N nodes is associated with a spatial location $\mathbf{p}_i \in \mathbb{R}^c$ and a corresponding feature vector $\mathbf{x}_i \in \mathbb{R}^d$. These node-level features may represent information derived from image patches or individual cells at the given locations.

Inspired by the classical formulation of the Moran's I statistic, we introduce a *learnable spatial autocorrelation index* composed of two key neural components:

- A **feature mapping network** $\phi(\mathbf{x}; \theta_\phi) : \mathbb{R}^d \to \mathbb{R}$, which transforms high-dimensional node features into scalar values. The parameters θ_ϕ are learned during training.
- A **distance-weighting network** $\psi(\mathbf{x}; \theta_\psi) : \mathbb{R}^d \to \mathbb{R}$, which modulates spatial influence between nodes. Specifically, the weight between nodes i and j is computed by Eq. 3 (Sect. 2.2), where ψ learns how node features control the spatial neighbourhood.

Given these components, the *learnable Moran's Index* for a single WSI is defined as:

$$I(G; \theta_\psi, \theta_\phi) = \frac{N}{W} \cdot \frac{\sum_{i=1}^N \sum_{j=1}^N \tilde{w}_{ij} \left(\phi(\mathbf{x}_i) - \mu_\phi\right) \left(\phi(\mathbf{x}_j) - \mu_\phi\right)}{\sum_{i=1}^N \left(\phi(\mathbf{x}_i) - \mu_\phi\right)^2}, \tag{2}$$

where $\mu_\phi = \frac{1}{N} \sum_{i=1}^N \phi(\mathbf{x}_i)$ is the mean of the mapped features, $\tilde{w}_{ij}$ is the learned adaptive spatial weight (Sect. 2.2) and $W = \sum_{i=1}^N \sum_{j=1}^N \tilde{w}_{ij}$ is the normalisation factor corresponding to the total pairwise weight.

Adaptive Spatial Weight Function. A spatial spread function with adaptive distance-weighting using node feature representations and a Gaussian decay of Euclidean distance aids the computation of Moran's I. This spatial exponential decay weight function is given by Eq. 3:

$$w_{ij} = e^{-\psi(\mathbf{x}_i; \theta_\psi)^2 D_{ij}} \tag{3}$$

D_{ij} is the pairwise Euclidean distance between nodes,

$$D_{ij} = ||p_i - p_j|| \tag{4}$$

The spread coefficient determined by the neural network described in Fig. 2, $\psi(\mathbf{x}_i; \theta_\psi)$, controls how sharply distance penalises the interaction between nodes i and j. Using exponential decay means closer points will have higher learned weights. The adaptive spread coefficient controls the scale of 'closeness' relative to the node. That is, a large value for $\psi(\mathbf{x}_i; \theta_\psi)$ implies a more rapid decay and consequently an increased emphasis on local (nearer) neighbourhoods, while a small value implies a slower decay or far-ranging influence. Additionally, each row of the learned weight matrix is made row-stochastic by normalising to sum to 1. This ensures that weights are comparable across rows (i.e., if relatively larger or smaller weights are computed for some nodes, they do not have a dominating effect on the Moran's I value):

$$\tilde{w}_{ij} = \frac{w_{ij}}{\sum_{j=1}^{N} w_{ij}} \tag{5}$$

This adaptive weight function allows the model to learn feature-dependent spatial decay independently for each node that adapts during training, as opposed to deciding on and assigning a constant spatial decay parameter. This also means that each node learns a different sensitivity to spatial distances between itself and other nodes.

Scalar Feature Mapping. For each node, we define a single scalar feature mapping from the d-dimensional node features,

$$z_i = f_{\text{map}}(\mathbf{x}_i) = \phi(\mathbf{x}; \theta_\phi) \tag{6}$$

where ϕ is a neural network with a *tanh* activation function, shown in Fig. 2. This encodes d node features into a single feature and overcomes the limitations of a classical Moran's I statistic mentioned in Sect. 2.1, without losing any information. This feature mapping can intuitively be thought of as a specification of the type of tissue at a given node.

Moran's Index Computation. The mapped features are centred using the feature mean:

$$\tilde{z}_i = z_i - \mu_z, \quad \text{where } \mu_z = \frac{1}{N} \sum_{i=1}^{N} z_i \tag{7}$$

We then compute the outer product of the centred feature matrix, $(\tilde{z}_i \cdot \tilde{z}_j) \forall i, j \in 1, \ldots, N$, and compute the weighted sum of centred feature products. This is then scaled by the sum aggregate of all weights, to give the numerator of Moran's I. The denominator consists of the variance of centred features,

$$\sigma_{\tilde{z}}^2 = \frac{1}{N} \sum_{i=1}^{N} (\tilde{z}_i)^2 + \varepsilon \tag{8}$$

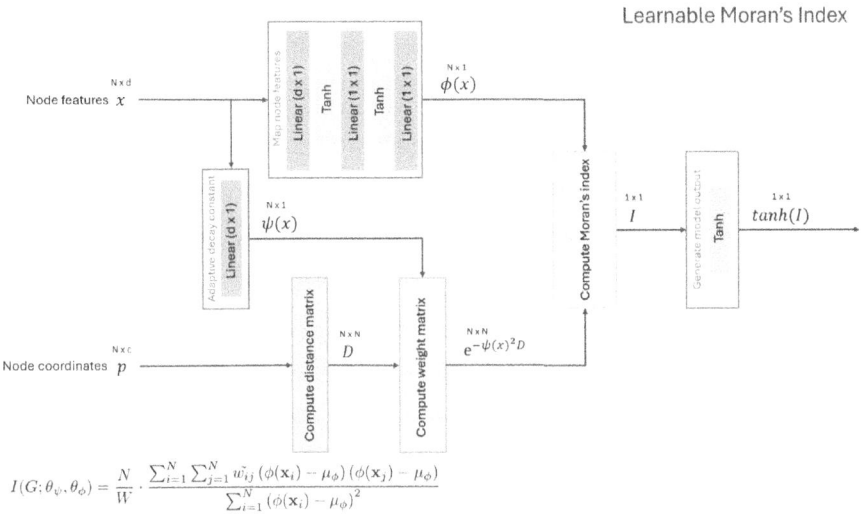

Fig. 2. Architecture of the proposed Learnable Moran's Index model for Disease-Specific Survival prediction.

A small constant ε is added to prevent division by zero. This gives the final computation of the learnable Moran's I given by Eq. 2, which at its core resembles Eq. 1. Figure 2 shows the architecture of the proposed model using learnable Moran's I and describes the details of the neural network architectures for ϕ and ψ. A final $tanh$ activation provides a non-linear mapping of the learned Moran's I value that is constrained to the range $(-1, 1)$, to generate survival scores for the disease-specific survival task described in Sect. 2.3.

2.3 Learnable Moran's Index for Disease-Specific Survival Prediction

Disease-Specific Survival (DSS) in breast cancer refers to the length of time from diagnosis (or the start of the study) until death attributable specifically to breast cancer, excluding deaths caused by any other, unrelated conditions. Unlike overall survival, DSS provides a more focused assessment of the lethality and progression of the disease itself.

Data. To train and evaluate the proposed model, we used data from 523 breast cancer patients in The Cancer Genome Atlas (TCGA) [3,5] dataset. DSS data used includes: (1) DSS event indicators, encoded as

- 0: the event of interest has not occurred until the end of the study is reached (after which outcomes are censored);
- 1: the event of interest has occurred within the study period;

where the *event of interest* is death due to breast cancer. (2) DSS time indicating the length of time in days until death or censoring [9].

As input to our model, point set representations of WSIs are used instead of the WSIs themselves [7]. The features for each node have been generated in line with the SlideGraph [12] approach in previous literature by Mackenzie *et al.* [13] using WSIs from the TCGA Breast Cancer dataset (TCGA-BRCA) [5]. To produce these representations, 512×512 pixel patches of the WSI are passed through a pre-trained ShuffleNet [18] model to encode each patch as a 1024-dimensional feature vector [13]. Samples for which no DSS data is available are omitted, giving a total of 523 graphs, whose nodes and coordinates (like point clouds) are used as inputs to the model.

Model Training and Performance Assessment. We train the model (with the architecture as shown in Fig. 2) to predict a survival score indicating how long a patient survives before experiencing death due to breast cancer (i.e. the event of interest). For training, we implement a ranking loss, defined by Eq. 9. This ranking loss function is used to tune model parameters such that the predicted scores from the model align with known survival times of these patients. We randomly pick two samples G_a and G_b based on their DSS times, t_a and t_b, and event indicators, δ_a and δ_b respectively, such that G_a has a survival time greater than that of G_b and G_b has experienced the event of interest. That is, $t_b < t_a \mid \delta_b = 1$, thus creating a pair-wise ranking set of patients $S = \{(G_a, G_b) \mid t_a > t_b, \delta_b = 1, a, b = 1 \ldots N\}$, and the predicted survival score $I(G_a)$ should be higher than $I(G_b)$. The ranking loss is optimised with a learning rate of 0.001 using Adaptive Moment Estimation with decoupled weight decay (AdamW) [10] as Eq. 9, where ϕ^* and ψ^* are the trainable weights of the constituent neural networks ϕ, and ψ.

$$\phi^*, \psi^* = \arg\min_{\phi,\psi} \sum_{(i,j)\in S} \max\left(0, \ 1 - (I(G_a; \phi, \psi) - I(G_b; \phi, \psi))\right) \qquad (9)$$

We perform stratified grouped 5-fold cross-validation, whereby the dataset is randomly split into 60% training, 20% validation and 20% test sets 5 times and performance is evaluated as the average across the 5 runs. Stratifying the splits using the DSS events ensures that each event indicator (0 or 1) occurs in equal proportions across each of the training, validation and test sets, while patient-wise grouping guarantees that all samples (if more than one) from a single patient occurs in exactly one fold (i.e. not split across training, validation or test sets) to prevent any data leakage.

3   Results

The model's predictive capability is evaluated using the concordance index (C-index) that measures the correctness of the relative ranking of high and low survival patients. The proposed model achieves an average test C-index of 0.662

Table 1. C-Index obtained on the test set using the proposed Learnable Moran's Index model compared to existing and baseline models.

Model	C-Index ± Std. Dev.
Mean pooling (Baseline 1.)	0.594 ± 0.030
Mean & std. dev. pooling (Baseline 2.)	0.604 ± 0.041
Deep learning MIL [17] (Existing)	0.616 ± 0.072
Learnable Moran's I (Proposed)	0.662 ± 0.060

across the 5 folds with a standard deviation of 0.060. This result is shown in Table 1, in comparison with existing (deep learning Multiple Instance Learning (MIL)) and performance baseline models in survival analysis [17]. The performance baseline models implemented include: (1) **Mean pooling**, that predicts survival scores using a mean-pooling of node features passed through a single linear neural layer, and (2) **Mean & std. dev.**, which uses mean-pooling as well as standard deviations of features across nodes, passed through a single linear neural layer to produce survival scores.

Figure 4 shows the Kaplan-Meier survival curves, with DSS times (in days) on the horizontal axis and the survival probabilities on the vertical axis. This plot shows the classification of samples produced by our model into low-risk and high-risk groups. The risk grouping is performed by thresholding the predicted survival scores using the median predicted survival score for the test set of each fold. These risk stratifications for each fold are then concatenated to give a stratification of all patients in the dataset into low and high-risk groups. The p-value obtained by a log-rank test for this stratification is $p = 0.0029$, indicating a meaningful distinction ($p << 0.05$) between the survival curves for the two groups, demonstrating the model's survival prediction capability based on learned slide-level spatial autocorrelation patterns.

3.1 Qualitative Results

Figure 3 shows the mapped scalar features ($\phi(x)$) for graphs in the test set from the best-performing fold that experienced the event (DSS event = 1), overlaid on the corresponding WSIs. Before visualisation, we scale the generated feature values to the range [0, 1] for mapping on a viridis colourmap. Samples with high predicted survival scores demonstrate higher learned Moran's I values, consequently showing higher visible spatial clustering of similar node features.

4   Discussion

As seen in Fig. 3, nodes with similar mapped feature values tend to be spatially clustered in low-risk (high survival) samples, while lower survival samples do not routinely display any distinguishable spatial clustering of nodes. For example, high survival sample in Fig. 3a with (Top-left) DSS time = 1699 and

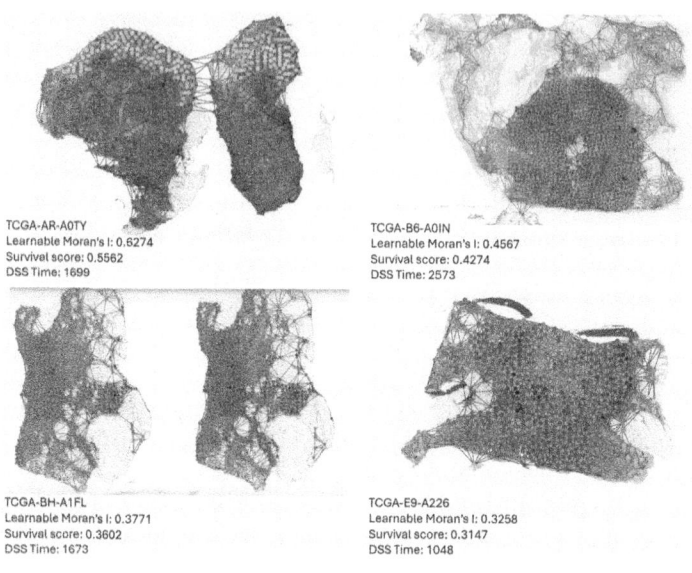

(a) Samples with higher predicted survival and computed Moran's I values.

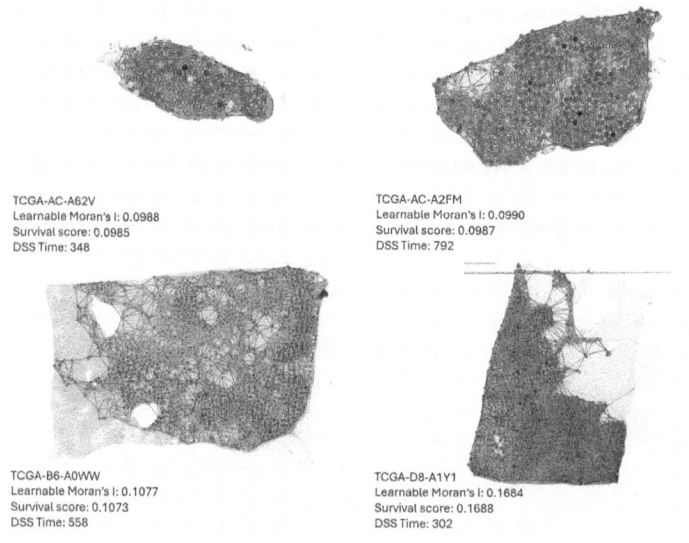

(b) Samples with lower predicted survival and computed Moran's I values.

Fig. 3. Mapped scalar features produced by the neural network ϕ in the proposed Learnable Moran's Index model for test set samples that experienced the DSS event, indicating learned node-level features for which Moran's I is computed. For each example, we show the computed Morans I value from the Learnable Moran's Index model (Learnable Moran's I), model output (Survival score) and ground truth DSS time. Notice the spatial clustering patterns in the graphs.

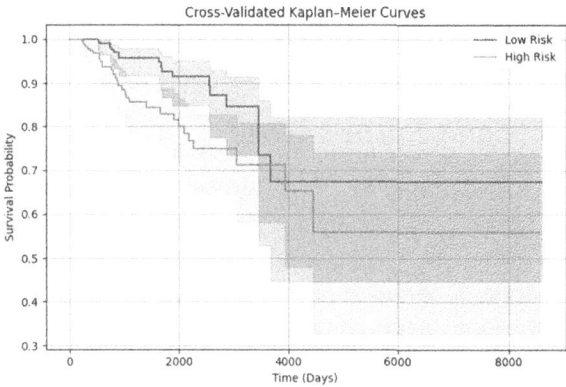

Fig. 4. Kaplan-Meier survival curves for low and high-risk patient groups across all 5 folds based on predicted survival scores using the Learnable Moran's Index model ($p = 0.0029$). A steeper slope of the high risk curve indicates a higher event rate (death rate) and therefore a worse survival prognosis, i.e. the survival probability for these samples decreases more rapidly as compared to the high survival or low-risk group.

predicted survival score = 0.5562 displays almost distinctly clustered regions with similar mapped-feature nodes (yellow-green indicating higher feature values, green-indigo indicating lower feature values). This clustering pattern can be compared to the demonstrative spatial distribution pattern for highly spatially-autocorrelated neighbourhoods in Fig. 1. Low survival samples displaying more dispersed or low spatial clustering patterns (Fig. 3b) suggests that more heterogeneous tumour microenvironments are prone to worse survival outcomes, as has been inferred in other related literature regarding ITH [6, 11].

Table 1 shows that the achieved average c-index value of 0.662 outperforms performance baselines and existing models [17] that emphasise interpretability of qualitative results and the effect of ITH on disease prognosis, indicating that the model can distinguish between high survival and low survival groups fairly well. The proposed model also presents significant advantages in being a computationally efficient end-to-end framework that explicitly quantifies and associates spatial ITH with survival outcomes. Furthermore, since only node features and their spatial coordinates are used for Moran's I computation, no explicit graph construction or edge definition of the input graphs is required. The proposed method presents avenues to systematically uncover object-level characteristics in selected tissue regions or patches to analyse and correlate mapped feature representations with histopathological features or tumour components in the WSI. This could potentially provide valuable insights into fundamental biological differences between the two patient survival groups (high and low survival). The learnable Moran's index measure could be employed to predict other target outcomes (e.g., receptor status, gene expression), demonstrating the impact of spatial autocorrelation on such clinical variables. This model can also be used as an intermediate layer in larger deep learning pipelines for further downstream classification or prediction tasks.

5   Conclusions and Future Work

Our work provides a learnable Moran's index of spatial autocorrelation using a neural network-based approach that can serve as an effective quantification of intratumour heterogeneity. The learned Moran's I values have shown to have effective use in survival analysis to predict patient survival outcomes. The proposed method allows us to automatically detect spatial clustering patterns in specific histological features, which reveal a significant distinction between high and low survival groups, directly from whole slide images without necessarily undergoing prior cell segmentation or annotation. Our work demonstrates that certain spatially localised tissue regions may encapsulate biologically or clinically relevant information reflecting the underlying mechanisms of disease progression or response. Further investigation into the mapped feature representations obtained from our model could point to potential biomarker discovery linked to disease prognosis. Furthermore, elucidating the nature and role of these spatial patterns offers new perspectives to inform prognostic assessments and guide the development of spatially-informed therapeutic strategies.

Although the proposed model demonstrates strong performance, further validation using larger datasets with more samples in each risk group could improve mapping patterns. Moreover, although the graph representations of WSIs used contained edge connections between nodes that were defined in line with the SlideGraph [12] pipeline, these have not been used in the proposed method for spatial autocorrelation computation. Future methods could incorporate this information to implement an edge-aware spatial association pattern of nodes that could further help derive more robust results and interpretation of the TME. Additionally, future developments could similarly implement other spatial statistical metrics in a trainable framework, to provide other forms of quantification of ITH.

6   Data and Code Availability

The graphs for the TCGA dataset are available on a public Google Drive[1] made available by Mackenzie et al. [13]. The DSS data for TCGA is publicly available on the TCGA Pan-Cancer Clinical Data Resource (TCGA-CDR) [9]. All code required to run the experiments and reproduce results is available in the associated Github repository[2].

---

[1] https://drive.google.com/drive/folders/1BBR0CRZKm5Oz3cmergZP_CemJFHk3 rxV?usp=sharingl.

[2] https://github.com/L-DSilva/LearnableMoransIndex.

Acknowledgments. FM is funded through EPSRC Grant EP/W02909X/1. We acknowledge initial model design and experimentation work undertaken by Farham Ahmad and Tomás Freitas Fernandes for non-prognostic histology models. We acknowledge Mark Eastwood for his contribution in initial pipeline design and data insights.

Disclosure of Interests. The authors declare no competing interests.

References

1. Galon, J., et al.: Type, density, and location of immune cells within human colorectal tumors predict clinical outcome. Science **313**(5795), 1960–1964 (2006). https://doi.org/10.1126/science.1129139
2. Heindl, A., Nawaz, S., Yuan, Y.: Mapping spatial heterogeneity in the tumor microenvironment: a new era for digital pathology. Lab. Invest. **95**(4), 377–384 (2015). https://doi.org/10.1038/labinvest.2014.155
3. Hoadley, K.A., et al.: Cell-of-origin patterns dominate the molecular classification of 10,000 tumors from 33 types of cancer. Cell **173**(2), 291-304.e6 (2018). https://doi.org/10.1016/j.cell.2018.03.022
4. Jamal-Hanjani, M., Quezada, S.A., Larkin, J., Swanton, C.: Translational implications of tumor heterogeneity. Clin. Cancer Res. **21**(6), 1258–1266 (2015). https://doi.org/10.1158/1078-0432.CCR-14-1429
5. Koboldt, D.C., et al.: Comprehensive molecular portraits of human breast tumours. Nature **490**(7418), 61–70 (2012). https://doi.org/10.1038/nature11412
6. Lashen, A.G., et al.: Characterization of breast cancer intra-tumor heterogeneity using artificial intelligence. Cancers **16**(22) (2024). https://doi.org/10.3390/cancers16223849
7. Lauro, G.R., et al.: Digital pathology consultations-a new era in digital imaging, challenges and practical applications. J. Digit. Imaging **26**(4), 668–677 (2013). https://doi.org/10.1007/s10278-013-9572-0
8. Li, H., Calder, C.A., Cressie, N.: Beyond Moran's I: testing for spatial dependence based on the spatial autoregressive model. Geogr. Anal. **39**(4), 357–375 (2007). https://doi.org/10.1111/j.1538-4632.2007.00708.x
9. Liu, J., et al.: An integrated tcga pan-cancer clinical data resource to drive high-quality survival outcome analytics. Cell **173**(2), 400–416.e11 (2018). https://doi.org/10.1016/j.cell.2018.02.052
10. Loshchilov, I., Hutter, F.: Decoupled weight decay regularization. arXiv: 1711.05101 [cs.LG] (2019)
11. Lu, W., et al.: AI-based intra-tumor heterogeneity score of Ki67 expression as a prognostic marker for early-stage ER+/HER2 breast cancer. J. Pathol.: Clin. Res. **10**(1), e346 (2024). https://doi.org/10.1002/cjp2.346
12. Lu, W., Toss, M., Rakha, E., Rajpoot, N., Minhas, F.: SlideGraph+: whole slide image level graphs to predict HER2Status in breast cancer. arXiv:2110.06042 [cs.CV] (2021)
13. Mackenzie, C.C., Dawood, M., Graham, S., Eastwood, M., ul Amir Afsar Minhas, F.: Neural graph modelling of whole slide images for survival ranking. In: Rieck, B., Pascanu, R.: Proceedings of the First Learning on Graphs Conference. Proceedings of Machine Learning Research, pp. 48:1–48:10. PMLR (2022)
14. Mahmoud, S.M., et al.: Tumor-infiltrating CD8$^+$ lymphocytes predict clinical outcome in breast cancer. J. Clin. Oncol. **29**(15), 1949–1955 (2011). https://doi.org/10.1200/JCO.2010.30.5037

15. Moran, P.: Notes on continuous stochastic phenomena. Biometrika **37**(1/2), 17 (1950). https://doi.org/10.2307/2332142
16. Maley, C.C., Koelble, K., Natrajan, R., Aktipis, A., Yuan, Y.: An ecological measure of immune-cancer colocalization as a prognostic factor for breast cancer. Breast Cancer Res. **17**(1) (2015). https://doi.org/10.1186/s13058-015-0638-4
17. Sandarenu, P., et al.: Survival prediction in triple negative breast cancer using multiple instance learning of histopathological images. Sci. Rep. **12**, (2022). https://doi.org/10.1038/s41598-022-18647-1
18. Zhang, X., Zhou, X., Lin, M., Sun, J.: ShuffleNet: an extremely efficient convolutional neural network for mobile devices. arXiv:1707.01083 [cs.CV] (2017)

Image Synthesis and Generative Artificial Intelligence

Augmenting Chest X-ray Datasets with Non-Expert Annotations

Veronika Cheplygina⬤, Cathrine Damgaard, Trine Naja Eriksen,
Dovile Juodelyte⬤, and Amelia Jiménez-Sánchez$^{(\boxtimes)}$⬤

IT University of Copenhagen, Copenhagen, Denmark
{vech,amji}@itu.dk

Abstract. The advancement of machine learning algorithms in medical image analysis requires the expansion of training datasets. A popular and cost-effective approach is automated annotation extraction from free-text medical reports, primarily due to the high costs associated with expert clinicians annotating medical images, such as chest X-rays. However, it has been shown that the resulting datasets are susceptible to biases and shortcuts. Another strategy to increase the size of a dataset is crowdsourcing, a widely adopted practice in general computer vision with some success in medical image analysis. In a similar vein to crowdsourcing, we enhance two publicly available chest X-ray datasets by incorporating non-expert annotations. However, instead of using diagnostic labels, we annotate shortcuts in the form of tubes. We collect 3.5k chest drain annotations for NIH-CXR14, and 1k annotations for four different tube types in PadChest, and create the Non-Expert Annotations of Tubes in X-rays (NEATX) dataset. We train a chest drain detector with the non-expert annotations that generalizes well to expert labels. Moreover, we compare our annotations to those provided by experts and show "moderate" to "almost perfect" agreement. Finally, we present a pathology agreement study to raise awareness about the quality of ground truth annotations. We make our dataset available on Zenodo at https://zenodo.org/records/14944064 and our code available at https://github.com/purrlab/chestxr-label-reliability.

1 Introduction

The use of machine learning (ML) algorithms is nowadays standard for medical image analysis, yet there are still issues with the size and representativeness of the datasets used to train the algorithms. While it is clear that we need large and high-quality datasets for the *validation* of the algorithms, there have been various efforts to reduce the number of expert labels needed during *training*. These efforts include methods development (*e.g.,* semi-supervised [8] or active learning [6]) or alternative labeling strategies, such as label extraction via natural language processing or crowdsourcing, we focus on the latter in this paper.

Supplementary Information The online version contains supplementary material available at https://doi.org/10.1007/978-3-031-98688-8_10.

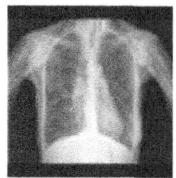 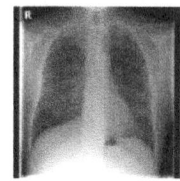 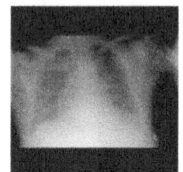 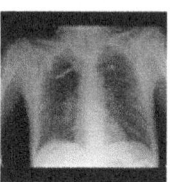

(a) Chest drain   (b) Tracheostomy   (c) NSG - Nasogastric   (d) Endotracheal

Fig. 1. Tube examples in PadChest dataset.

One popular strategy consists of creating larger datasets based on the automatic extraction of labels. For example, CheXpert [18] and NIH-CXR14 [43] extracted pathology labels from the free text clinical reports, and PadChest [7] combined expert diagnostic labels with ML-extracted annotations. However, CheXpert and NIH-CXR14 datasets have been shown to suffer from bias [15,26,39] or shortcuts [21,32].

In general computer vision tasks, crowdsourcing of non-expert labels has been a popular solution [25], with some successes reported in medical imaging as well [35]. For chest X-ray, Filice et al. [12] collected crowdsourced annotations from six board-certified radiologists for the "pneumothorax" class in NIH-CXR14. In chest CT scans, non-experts have assessed the similarity of lung tissue [34], and also annotated pathological patterns, [33], nodules [5] and airways [9].

While the previous work on chest X-rays focused on relabeling pathologies, we extend annotation types by labeling "shortcuts" in two datasets. We refer to shortcuts as spurious correlations between artifacts in images and diagnostic labels [4,20]. Our method is close in spirit to crowdsourcing, but rather than extending the dataset size in terms of diagnostic labels, we annotate possible shortcuts, increasing the richness of the annotations. Our contributions are:

- We introduce the Non-Expert Annotations of Tubes in X-rays (NEATX) dataset[1], which enriches two publicly available chest X-ray datasets with annotations from non-experts. We collect 3.5k drain annotations for NIH-CXR14, and 1k annotations for four different tube types in PadChest.
- We present a pathology agreement study on different labels created for NIH-CXR14 to raise awareness about potential limitations of the available ground truth annotations.
- We train a chest drain detector with our non-expert annotations and validate the performance showing that it generalizes well to expert drain annotations for NIH-CXR14.
- We train a tube classifier on PadChest and show that the non-expert annotations achieve similar, or better, performance than the extracted by ML.
- We make our code for the experiments available[2].

---

[1] https://zenodo.org/records/14944064.

[2] https://github.com/purrlab/chestxr-label-reliability.

2   Related Work

2.1   Experts-Provided Annotations

The cost of annotating medical image datasets influences algorithm development. In [24], this cost is defined as a function of three factors: *quantity*, *quality*, and *granularity* of the annotations. They found that cost-efficient annotations provide great value for training multi-label classification and segmentation in frontal chest X-ray, and that combining these annotations with a limited number of high-cost labels lead to competitive models at a much lower expense.

Building on a similar concept, [12,36] proposed techniques to automatically identify chest X-ray samples for expert validation. Mislabeled instances in a dataset might not only impact the performance of ML models negatively but also endanger the explainability and reliability of the predictions. Filice et al. [12] explored ML methods for generating annotations in chest X-rays for expert review, with multiple experts labeling pneumothorax in the NIH-CXR14 dataset. Rädsch et al. [36] proposed a ML approach for the automatic detection of mislabeled instances in CheXpert dataset. Their method identified 7.4% of mislabeled Cardiomegaly cases. Moreover, they validated mislabeled cases through a blind study with a professional radiologist, supporting ongoing data quality efforts. In contrast, our approach focuses on enhancing the dataset's richness with a different type of annotation (shortcuts), and does not rely on clinical expertise.

2.2   Annotations from Non-Experts

Crowdsourcing is popular in computer vision [25], but medical imaging presents several challenges that make the transferability of that success more difficult. Some approaches have successfully leveraged non-expert knowledge to gather annotations [3,22,40]. Ørting et al. [34] survey 57 papers applying crowdsourcing to medical imaging. They conclude that most published studies find that crowdsourcing is a viable solution, often for segmentation tasks which might be more intuitive to non-experts. Focusing on lung images, non-experts have annotated pathological patterns, [33], nodules [5] and airways [9], or assessed similarity of lung tissue [34], all in chest CT scans, reporting added value to ML algorithms.

One of the main limitations of crowdsourcing is that is non-trivial how to setup a crowdsourcing project for medical images, and the surveyed papers often do not provide enough details on how this is done. For example, papers often do not report how the annotators were recruited, incentivized, and trained to perform the annotation tasks.

Our work is similar in spirit to crowdsourcing, however, instead of enlarging the dataset with additional diagnostic labels, we annotate potential shortcuts, enhancing the depth of the annotation information. This alternative form of annotation allows us to assess whether shortcut issues may be present in medical image diagnosis tasks in chest X-rays.

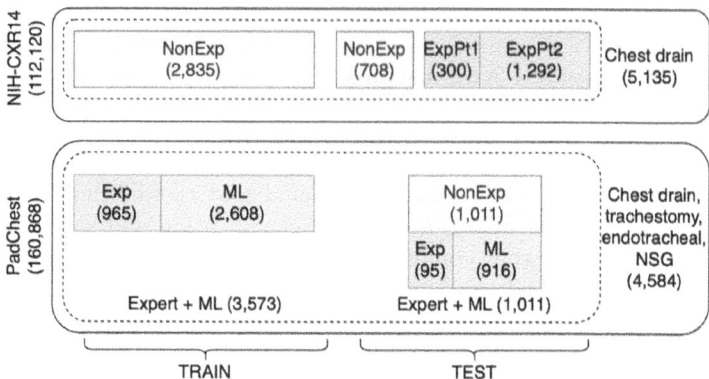

Fig. 2. Train and test subsets for NIH-CXR14 (top) and PadChest (bottom). ExptPt1, ExpPt2 refer to the annotations provided by an external expert at the beginning and end of our study, respectively. Exp are the original PadChest labels from clinicians looking at the reports.

3   Methods

3.1   Datasets

We create the **Non-Expert Annotations of Tubes in X-rays (NEATX)** dataset enriching the annotations of two publicly available chest X-ray datasets: NIH-CXR14 [43] and PadChest [7]. We release NEATX on Zenodo, a platform offering persistent storage and a Digital Object Identifier (DOI).

NIH-CXR14 originally has 112,120 images from 30,805 patients associated with 14 classes corresponding to different pathologies. We extracted 5,302 images labeled as pneumothorax cases. The annotations provided were text-mined from reports and may not always reflect the visual contents of the images [31].

For NIH-CXR14, multiple additional label sets are available. We investigate the following four: BBox dataset [43], released alongside NIH-CXR14; two GCS datasets—GCS16L [30] and GCS4L [29]—collected from two independent studies; and the RSNA set [41], designed to evaluate performance on pneumonia detection. Additional details about these datasets are provided in Table A1.

In addition, we received annotations about the presence/absence of chest drains in 1,592 images, created by a board-certified radiologist [32]. We filter the pneumothorax subset by excluding these expert-annotated images (to use them for evaluation of our annotations), as well as any images of the same patients, leaving a subset of 3,709 chest X-ray images. This selection process is illustrated in Fig. A1.

PadChest dataset consists of 160,868 chest X-ray images from 67,000 patients, labeled with pathologies but also other findings such as tubes, based on reports associated with the images. Of these reports, 27% were manually annotated by physicians, and the remaining set was labeled using a supervised Recurrent Neural Network (RNN). We extract a subset of 1,011 images labeled with one of the four tubes shown in Fig. 1: (a) chest drain, (b) tracheostomy, (c) nasogastric (NSG) and (d) endotracheal tubes.

3.2 Annotation

Two authors of this paper (CD and TNE) without a medical background provided annotations for 3,709 images from NIH-CXR14 and 1,011 images from PadChest, after studying annotator guidelines [19, 27, 28].

Both annotators first independently labeled the presence or absence of a tube (chest drain for NIH-CXR14, four types of tubes for PadChest). We used the following labels: {0, 0.25, 0.5, 0.75, 1, INVALID}, with 0 and 1 indicating absolute certainty about the absence (0) or presence (1). We also included the label 'INVALID' due to, for instance, the image not being a frontal chest X-ray. We then combined the raw annotations where both annotators were certain, which was the most prevalent case. This resulted in annotations for 3,543 images for NIH-CXR14 and 1,011 images for PadChest (see Fig. 2).

3.3 Experimental Setup

We investigate the added value of additional annotations in two main ways. Firstly, we use Cohen's kappa to evaluate the agreement between different annotators. Secondly, we train and evaluate ML models for tube classification tasks using subsets taking into account different annotators or labeling methods, detailed in Sect. 4. We evaluate the Area Under the Receiver Operating Characteristic Curve (AUC) across three model runs, each with a different initialization seed. We report the mean and standard deviation of the AUC over these runs. We always use disjoint subsets of patient-wise images for training and evaluation of the models.

For the models, we used four different architectures, all with pretrained ImageNet weights: ResNet50 [16], InceptionV3 [42], DenseNet121 [17], and Ours, which is a modified DenseNet121 with three additional layers (pooling, dense and dropout) between the backbone architecture and the flattened layer.

We performed a grid search to find the best hyperparameters for each setup. For the chest drain classification task with NIH-CXR14, we use a batch size of 32, a learning rate of 0.0001, and 200 epochs. For the tube classification with PadChest, we use a batch size of 32, a learning rate of 0.00001 fine-tuned for 250 epochs. All models use Adam as optimizer and binary cross-entropy as the loss function. Our implementations are based on the Keras library [10].

4 Results

4.1 Low to Moderate Agreement on Pathology in NIH-CXR14

We compare different label sets for pathologies available for NIH-CXR14 using the Cohen's kappa scores in Fig. 3. Note that not all combinations of label sets

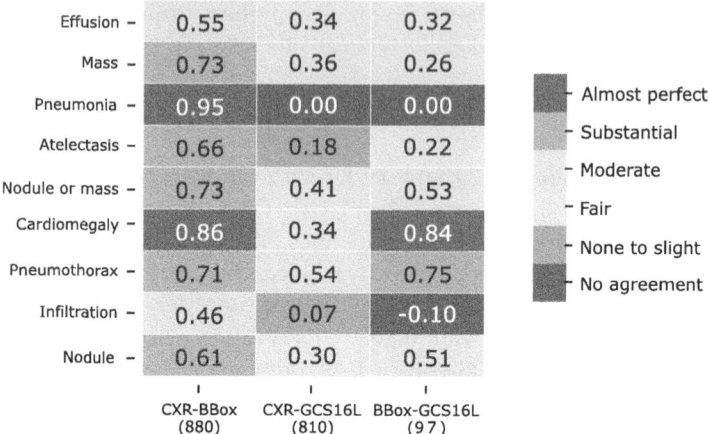

Fig. 3. Cohen's Kappa scores of labels from different datasets, all on NIH-CXR14 images. Labels from NIH-CXR14 ('CXR') are from report parsing, the other label sets are from expert image reviews. We include the number of shared images in the parenthesis below the dataset names.

Table 1. Chest drain detection (AUC average ± standard deviation). All models are fine-tuned on NIH-CXR14 training data, and evaluated on disjoint NIH-CXR14 test subsets: our annotations (NonExp), expert annotations part 1 (ExpPt1) and part 2 (ExpPt2). Bold = highest average AUC per column.

Model	NonExp	ExpPt1	ExpPt2
ResNet	59.7 ± 11.8	62.4 ± 11.5	62.2 ± 14.1
Inception	86.1 ± 0.3	85.2± 0.4	86.2± 0.1
DenseNet	90.9 ± 0.3	90.8 ± 0.1	89.3 ± 0.1
Ours	**92.1 ± 1.3**	**92.6 ± 0.2**	**89.6 ± 0.6**

are shown since some did share a few categories while others did not share any images, we report the sample sizes in the same figure.

Overall, we observe almost perfect or substantial agreement for NIH-CXR14 and BBox set, which were released together. Agreements between NIH-CXR14 and three other pathology label sets are at best moderate. Agreement between the other sets varies across pathologies, however, the sample sizes are lower in these cases. The pneumonia class has none to slight agreement, which could be due to the fact that it is a differential diagnosis and requires clinical information beyond X-ray images [7]. We also find none to slight agreement for emphysema, edema, pleural thickening, consolidation, and fibrosis categories.

4.2 Detector Trained with Non-expert Chest Drain Annotations Generalizes Well to Expert Labels

We train models for the chest drain detection task using our NonExpert labels, and evaluate on three scenarios:

- NonExp: test set of images annotated by two authors of this paper (CD and TNE).
- ExpPt1 (part 1): 20% of the expert annotations, provided to the annotators for training purposes at the beginning of this study.
- ExpPt2 (part 2): hold-out test set of the expert annotations, provided for evaluation towards the end of this study.

Table 1 shows the mean AUC and standard deviation over three model runs for the backbone models and our proposed detection model (Ours). We observe very similar results across the evaluation scenarios for all the models when considering each model's performance individually. The general good performance on ExpPt2 scenario indicates that the models generalize well overall to the hold-out test set with expert annotations.

4.3 Higher Agreement and Good Generalization with Tube Annotations in PadChest

We consider the annotations of four tube types in PadChest dataset: chest drain, tracheostomy, NSG, and endotracheal tube. Figure 4 shows that our annotations, compared to PadChest, present almost perfect agreement ($\kappa = 0.91$) on the tracheostomy tube annotations, substantial agreement ($\kappa = 0.72$) on the chest drains, and moderate agreement on the remaining two tube types.

We now use our modified DenseNet121 architecture for the tube classification task. We train the model on the PadChest dataset and evaluate it using four different sets of annotations:

- NonExp: test set annotated by the authors of this paper (CD and TNE).
- Exp+ML: test set in PadChest with a tube label.
- ML: test subset of images automatically extracted with a RNN (90.4% of the annotated tube set).
- Exp: test subset of images where physicians annotated from the reports (9.6% of the annotated tube set).

Table 2 shows the mean AUC and standard deviation over three model runs for the tube classification task in PadChest dataset. Our model evaluated on the NonExpert set shows higher AUC for chest drains and tracheostomy tubes. These two tubes showed a Cohen's kappa that corresponded with almost perfect agreement with PadChest original annotations. Moreover, our results suggest that a small number of expert annotations may be more effective than mixing them with automatically extracted annotations.

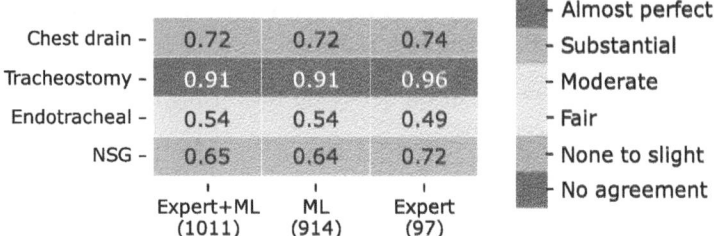

Fig. 4. Cohen's Kappa scores between the `NonExpert` and PadChest annotations (`Expert+ML`, `ML`, `Expert`). We include the number of shared images in the parenthesis below.

Table 2. Tube classification AUC ± standard deviation). We fine-tune on PadChest training data and evaluate on PadChest test set with our annotations (`NonExp`), Pad-Chest original annotations (`Exp+ML`) and the two subsets thereof (`Exp` and `ML`). Bold = highest average AUC per tube.

Tube	NonExp	Exp+ML	ML	Exp
Drain	**83.7** ± 4.5	77.8 ± 3.5	77.9 ± 3.5	79.0 ± 4.5
Trach	**87.6** ± 2.0	86.4 ± 2.5	83.3 ± 3.3	86.6 ± 2.5
Endo.	74.9 ± 0.4	75.7 ± 0.1	75.7 ± 0.1	**77.1** ± 2.2
NSG	68.4 ± 1.1	74.8 ± 1.3	73.5 ± 1.7	**81.1** ± 1.8

5   Discussion and Conclusions

Ground Truth and Task Difficulty. Our results show that available pathology labels in a public dataset should not be taken for granted, and not merely seen as benchmarks for ML models. The labels we might consider as "ground truth", might not actually reflect the ground truth status of the patient, for example if the labels are automatically (but with errors) extracted from reports, and/or because some diseases require a differential diagnosis. This is in particular reflected in the low agreement for pneumonia, which would typically require additional information next to the chest X-ray [7].

Given the sometimes low agreement from experts on established pathologies, our results suggest that annotating tubes is an "easier" task, since our non-expert annotations show high agreement with those of a certified radiologist, despite the fact that our annotators did not have access to the radiologist's annotations, nor any contact with the radiologist. While this is a small-scale study, we believe non-expert annotations for such "easier" tasks could still provide additional value in exploring different strategies for training pathology detection models.

Training Strategies for Non-expert Annotations. There are several strategies how non-expert annotations could be used to improve ML training, here we describe three possibilities. The first strategy is to incorporate the annotations into a multi-task learning setup. The additional annotations act as a regularizer, since the model is trained to both predict both the diagnosis and the presence of a visual element, like chest tubes. Such regularization helps the model learn better pathology representations. A study on the classification of skin lesions, which included non-expert annotations of features such as "asymmetry" (a more intuitive feature than a diagnosis), showed that using these non-expert annotations with multi-task learning improved the model performance [37]. We have conducted similar, preliminary, experiments with chest X-ray classification with our additional annotations. Our early results indeed tend to show increased performance, but would still require further validation, so we have chosen not to focus on this aspect in this paper.

A second strategy for using additional annotations is to avoid shortcut learning in an adversarial [45] setup, where the model optimizes the learning towards features that are discriminative for the pathology while minimizing the effect of the shortcut. This strategy is similar to work on bias and fairness, where the model learns to minimize the effect of a protected attribute, like sex or age, on the model, for example [1,2].

A third strategy could be based on contrastive learning [23], where pairs of positive (similar) and negative (dissimilar) samples can guide the model towards capturing the discriminative predictive features. Additional annotations could be used here to define or refine the (dis)similarity functions.

Limitations. A limitation of our study is that the authors who labeled the images (with a data science but no medical background) dedicated significant effort to understanding the annotation task. This included reading medical literature and tutorials [19,27,28]. As a result, our findings might not be applicable to other non-expert annotators, such as those on crowdsourcing platforms, where due to the financial incentives annotators would likely take on a variety of annotation tasks (not just medical images), and spend less time on each specific task.

Concluding Remarks. Our work is in spirit close to other studies that add additional information to existing datasets, for example in the form of additional documentation (e.g., Datasheets [14] or the later introduced Healthsheet [38]), additional annotations, segmentation masks [13], or experimental results that show evidence of shortcuts [11,15,21,32,44]. These extensions of existing datasets have been referred to as "research artifacts" [20]. As a community aiming to build upon previous work, we recommend that we not simply treat datasets "as-is", but thoughtfully consider such existing research artifacts when interpreting and drawing conclusions from our results.

To conclude, while our work shows that non-expert annotations could be advantageous in the training stage, we want to emphasize that there is *no free lunch* for evaluation, and one should never use such annotations to claim superiority of one algorithm over another. For reliable evaluation of models, we always need reliable ground truth, more diverse datasets, and expert involvement.

References

1. Abbasi-Sureshjani, S., Raumanns, R., Michels, B.E., Schouten, G., Cheplygina, V.: Risk of training diagnostic algorithms on data with demographic bias. In: MICCAI LABELS workshop. Lecture Notes in Computer Science, vol. 12446, pp. 183–192. Springer (2020)
2. Adeli, E., et al.: Representation learning with statistical independence to mitigate bias. In: Proceedings of the IEEE/CVF Winter Conference on Applications of Computer Vision, pp. 2513–2523 (2021)
3. Albarqouni, S., Baur, C., Achilles, F., Belagiannis, V., Demirci, S., Navab, N.: AggNet: deep learning from crowds for mitosis detection in breast cancer histology images. IEEE Trans. Med. Imaging **35**(5), 1313–1321 (2016)
4. Banerjee, I., et al.: "Shortcuts" causing bias in radiology artificial intelligence: causes, evaluation and mitigation. J. Am. Coll. Radiol. (2023)
5. Boorboor, S., Nadeem, S., Park, J.H., Baker, K., Kaufman, A.: Crowdsourcing lung nodules detection and annotation. In: Medical Imaging 2018: Imaging Informatics for Healthcare, Research, and Applications, vol. 10579, p. 105791D. International Society for Optics and Photonics (2018)
6. Budd, S., Robinson, E.C., Kainz, B.: A survey on active learning and human-in-the loop deep learning for medical image analysis. Med. Image Anal. **71**, 102062 (2021). https://doi.org/10.1016/j.media.2021.102062, https://www.sciencedirect.com/science/article/pii/S1361841521001080
7. Bustos, A., Pertusa, A., Salinas, J.M., de la Iglesia-Vayá, M.: PadChest: a large chest X-ray image dataset with multi-label annotated reports. Med. Image Anal. **66**, 101797 (2020). https://doi.org/10.1016/j.media.2020.101797, https://www.sciencedirect.com/science/article/pii/S1361841520301614
8. Cheplygina, V., de Bruijne, M., Pluim, J.P.: Not-so-supervised: a survey of semi-supervised, multi-instance, and transfer learning in medical image analysis. Med. Image Anal. **54**, 280–296 (2019)
9. Cheplygina, V., Perez-Rovira, A., Kuo, W., Tiddens, H.A., de Bruijne, M.: Crowdsourcing airway annotations in chest computed tomography images. PLoS ONE **16**(4), e0249580 (2021)
10. Chollet, F., et al.: Keras: deep learning for humans (2015). https://github.com/fchollet/keras
11. DeGrave, A.J., Janizek, J.D., Lee, S.I.: Ai for radiographic COVID-19 detection selects shortcuts over signal. Nat. Mach. Intell. 1–10 (2021)
12. Filice, R.W., et al.: Crowdsourcing pneumothorax annotations using machine learning annotations on the NIH chest X-ray dataset. J. Digit. Imaging **33**, 490–496 (2020)
13. Gaggion, N., et al.: ChexMask: a large-scale dataset of anatomical segmentation masks for multi-center chest X-ray images. Sci. Data **11**(1), 511 (2024)
14. Gebru, T., et al.: Datasheets for datasets. Commun. ACM **64**(12), 86–92 (2021)
15. Gichoya, J.W., et al.: AI recognition of patient race in medical imaging: a modelling study. Lancet Digit. Health **4**(6), e406–e414 (2022)
16. He, K., Zhang, X., Ren, S., Sun, J.: Deep residual learning for image recognition. In: Proceedings of the IEEE Conference on Computer Vision and Pattern Recognition, pp. 770–778 (2016)
17. Huang, G., Liu, Z., Van Der Maaten, L., Weinberger, K.Q.: Densely connected convolutional networks. In: Proceedings of the IEEE Conference on Computer Vision and Pattern Recognition, pp. 4700–4708 (2017)

18. Irvin, J., et al.: CheXpert: a large chest radiograph dataset with uncertainty labels and expert comparison. In: Proceedings of the AAAI Conference on Artificial Intelligence, vol. 33, pp. 590–597 (2019)

19. Jain, S.N.: A pictorial essay: radiology of lines and tubes in the intensive care unit. Indian J. Radiol. Imaging **21**(03), 182–190 (2011)

20. Jiménez-Sánchez, A., et al.: In the picture: Medical imaging datasets, artifacts, and their living review. In: Proceedings of the 2025 ACM Conference on Fairness, Accountability, and Transparency, pp. 511–531 (2025)

21. Jiménez-Sánchez, A., Juodelyte, D., Chamberlain, B., Cheplygina, V.: Detecting shortcuts in medical images - a case study in chest X-rays. In: 2023 IEEE 20th International Symposium on Biomedical Imaging (ISBI), pp. 1–5 (2023). https://doi.org/10.1109/ISBI53787.2023.10230572

22. Keshavan, A., Yeatman, J., Rokem, A.: Combining citizen science and deep learning to amplify expertise in neuroimaging. bioRxiv, p. 363382 (2018)

23. Khosla, P., et al.: Supervised contrastive learning. Adv. Neural. Inf. Process. Syst. **33**, 18661–18673 (2020)

24. Kim, T.S., Jang, G., Lee, S., Kooi, T.: Did you get what you paid for? Rethinking annotation cost of deep learning based computer aided detection in chest radiographs. In: Medical Image Computing and Computer Assisted Intervention– MICCAI 2022: 25th International Conference, Singapore, 18–22 September 2022, Proceedings, Part III, pp. 261–270. Springer (2022)

25. Kovashka, A., Russakovsky, O., Fei-Fei, L., Grauman, K.: Crowdsourcing in computer vision. Found. Trends Comput. Graph. Vision **10**(3), 177–243 (2016)

26. Larrazabal, A.J., Nieto, N., Peterson, V., Milone, D.H., Ferrante, E.: Gender imbalance in medical imaging datasets produces biased classifiers for computer-aided diagnosis. Proc. Natl. Acad. Sci. **117**(23), 12592–12594 (2020)

27. Lloyd-Jones, D.G.: Chest X-ray - tubes (2019). https://www.radiologymasterclass.co.uk/tutorials/chest/chest_tubes/chest_xray_tubes_start. Accessed 03 Mar 2023

28. MacDuff, A., Arnold, A., Harvey, J.: Management of spontaneous pneumothorax: British thoracic society pleural disease guideline 2010. Thorax **65**(Suppl 2), ii18–ii31 (2010)

29. Majkowska, A., et al.: Chest radiograph interpretation with deep learning models: assessment with radiologist-adjudicated reference standards and population-adjusted evaluation. Radiology **294**(2), 421–431 (2020). https://doi.org/10.1148/radiol.2019191293. pMID: 31793848

30. Nabulsi, Z., et al.: Deep learning for distinguishing normal versus abnormal chest radiographs and generalization to two unseen diseases tuberculosis and COVID-19. Sci. Rep. **11**(1) (2021). https://doi.org/10.1038/s41598-021-93967-2

31. Oakden-Rayner, L.: Exploring large-scale public medical image datasets. Acad. Radiol. **27**(1), 106–112 (2020)

32. Oakden-Rayner, L., Dunnmon, J., Carneiro, G., Ré, C.: Hidden stratification causes clinically meaningful failures in machine learning for medical imaging. In: ACM Conference on Health, Inference, and Learning, pp. 151–159 (2020)

33. O'Neil, A.Q., Murchison, J.T., van Beek, E.J., Goatman, K.A.: Crowdsourcing labels for pathological patterns in CT lung scans: Can non-experts contribute expert-quality ground truth? In: Intravascular Imaging and Computer Assisted Stenting, and Large-Scale Annotation of Biomedical Data and Expert Label Synthesis (MICCAI LABELS), pp. 96–105. Springer (2017)

34. Ørting, S.N., Cheplygina, V., Petersen, J., Thomsen, L.H., Wille, M.M.W., de Bruijne, M.: Crowdsourced emphysema assessment. In: Intravascular Imaging and Computer Assisted Stenting, and Large-Scale Annotation of Biomedical Data and Expert Label Synthesis (MICCAI LABELS), pp. 126–135. Springer (2017)

35. Ørting, S.N., et al.: A survey of crowdsourcing in medical image analysis. Hum. Comput. **7**, 1–26 (2020)

36. Rädsch, T., Eckhardt, S., Leiser, F., Pandl, K.D., Thiebes, S., Sunyaev, A.: What your radiologist might be missing: using machine learning to identify mislabeled instances of X-ray images (2021)

37. Raumanns, R., Schouten, G., Joosten, M., Pluim, J.P., Cheplygina, V., et al.: Enhance (enriching health data by annotations of crowd and experts): a case study for skin lesion classification. Mach. Learn. Biomed. Imaging **1**(December 2021 issue), 1–26 (2021)

38. Rostamzadeh, N., et al.: HealthSheet: development of a transparency artifact for health datasets. In: Proceedings of the 2022 ACM Conference on Fairness, Accountability, and Transparency, pp. 1943–1961 (2022)

39. Seyyed-Kalantari, L., Liu, G., McDermott, M., Chen, I.Y., Ghassemi, M.: CheXclusion: fairness gaps in deep chest X-ray classifiers. In: Pacific Symposium on Biocomputing, pp. 232–243. World Scientific (2020)

40. Sharma, M., Saha, O., Sriraman, A., Hebbalaguppe, R., Vig, L., Karande, S.: Crowdsourcing for chromosome segmentation and deep classification. In: Computer Vision and Pattern Recognition Workshops (CVPRW), pp. 786–793. IEEE (2017)

41. Shih, G., et al.: Augmenting the national institutes of health chest radiograph dataset with expert annotations of possible pneumonia. Radiol.: Arti. Intell. **1**, e180041 (2019). https://doi.org/10.1148/ryai.2019180041

42. Szegedy, C., Vanhoucke, V., Ioffe, S., Shlens, J., Wojna, Z.: Rethinking the inception architecture for computer vision. In: Proceedings of the IEEE Conference on Computer Vision and Pattern Recognition, pp. 2818–2826 (2016)

43. Wang, X., Peng, Y., Lu, L., Lu, Z., Bagheri, M., Summers, R.M.: ChestX-ray8: hospital-scale chest X-ray database and benchmarks on weakly-supervised classification and localization of common thorax diseases. In: Proceedings of the IEEE Conference on Computer Vision and Pattern Recognition (CVPR). IEEE (2017). https://doi.org/10.1109/cvpr.2017.369

44. Winkler, J.K., et al.: Association between surgical skin markings in dermoscopic images and diagnostic performance of a deep learning convolutional neural network for melanoma recognition. JAMA Dermatol. **155**(10), 1135–1141 (2019)

45. Zhang, B.H., Lemoine, B., Mitchell, M.: Mitigating unwanted biases with adversarial learning. In: Proceedings of the 2018 AAAI/ACM Conference on AI, Ethics, and Society, pp. 335–340 (2018)

Leveraging Synthetic Data for Whole-Body Segmentation in X-Ray Images

Ahmed Alshenoudy$^{(\boxtimes)}$ [iD], Bertram Sabrowsky-Hirsch [iD], Stefan Thumfart [iD], and Michael Giretzlehner [iD]

Research Unit Medical Informatics, RISC Software, Hagenberg, Austria
`ahmed.alshenoudy@risc-software.at`

Abstract. Automatic segmentation of anatomical structures in X-ray images is essential for clinical and research applications, particularly as the increasing volume of medical examinations necessitates workflow automation and efficient data screening. While numerous public X-ray imaging datasets exist, they are predominantly limited to chest X-rays, hindering AI-driven solutions for whole-body segmentation. In this paper, we propose a method for whole-body anatomical segmentation in X-ray images using synthetic data. We generate synthetic X-ray projections from an existing CT dataset using the DiffDRR framework and train five multi-class 2D UNet models, each targeting distinct anatomical groups. To assess generalization, we validate a subset of our models on two real X-ray imaging databases. Our models achieve a per-class median Dice Similarity Coefficient (DSC) above 0.88 for nearly 79 anatomical structures on the synthetic test set and perform on par with models trained on real data for rib segmentation with a similar architecture. We further highlight key challenges in transferring models from simulation to real-world datasets. Our models are made publicly available on GitHub (github.com/risc-mi/totalsegmentator2D) to facilitate further development.

Keywords: X-ray · Segmentation · Synthetic Data

1 Introduction

X-ray imaging is a cornerstone modality in both diagnostic and interventional medicine, playing a critical role in clinical workflows. In England alone, 22.9 million X-ray scans were performed between 2023 and 2024 [23], highlighting the vast scale and clinical dependence on this modality. This underscores a significant opportunity to develop robust and comprehensive AI-based segmentation models that can improve diagnostic accuracy and reduce clinicians' workload [3,15,22]. These models can also streamline various tasks, such as large-scale database screening, precise content-based image retrieval, and dataset curation. However,

S. Ali et al. (Eds.): MIUA 2025, LNCS 15916, pp. 145–158, 2026.
https://doi.org/10.1007/978-3-031-98688-8_11

their development is hindered by the limited availability of high-quality, annotated, and publicly accessible large-scale X-ray imaging databases beyond chest X-rays [4,9,26]. While prior research has explored X-ray image analysis, most efforts have focused on specific anatomical structures (e.g., heart, lungs, ribs, and clavicles) [11,17,18,24] rather than developing a comprehensive whole-body segmentation solution.

A promising approach to overcoming this data limitation is the *in silico* generation of synthetic data. This can be achieved through two main strategies within the X-ray imaging context: generative modeling and digitally reconstructed radiographs (DRRs). Generative modeling leverages methods such as Denoising Diffusion Probabilistic Models (DDPMs) to synthesize new samples by learning the underlying data distribution [7]. In contrast, DRRs reconstruct 2D X-ray images from existing 3D computed tomography (CT) scans using various ray-tracing techniques [6,25]. A major advantage of DRRs over generative models is their ability to produce anatomically accurate and geometrically consistent synthetic X-ray projections. This enables the generation of novel views (e.g., lateral images) without requiring additional training data, unlike generative models. Moreover, generative models such as DDPMs may suffer from hallucinations in the generated samples [1], resulting in anatomically implausible structures or subtle inconsistencies that could undermine their reliability in clinical applications. Although DRRs rely on the availability of CT imaging studies, a wealth of publicly accessible, annotated CT datasets [14,16,20] provides a valuable resource for generating large-scale, annotated synthetic X-ray datasets. Additionally, recent advancements in simulation-to-reality (Sim2Real) transfer [10,29], particularly in the X-ray domain [5,25], further enhance the potential of DRRs in addressing data limitations and enabling robust AI-based models for improved X-ray imaging analysis in diverse clinical settings.

In this paper, we present a method for whole-body segmentation of anatomical structures from X-ray images, addressing the scarcity of annotated X-ray datasets beyond chest X-rays. By leveraging existing annotated CT databases in combination with the realistic simulation framework DiffDRR, we construct a synthetic dataset of X-ray images with corresponding annotations. We then train five different multi-class 2D UNet models to segment various anatomical structures, following the grouping defined by the TotalSegmentator Toolkit [27]. Additionally, we evaluate a subset of our models on two real X-ray datasets. The **contributions** of our work can be summarized as follows:

- We present five multi-class 2D UNet models for whole-body segmentation of anatomical structures in X-ray images, trained on synthetic data.
- We highlight key challenges in transferring models trained on synthetic data to real X-ray databases.

2   Related Work

Recent studies have increasingly explored the *in silico* generation of X-ray images using both generative models and DRR frameworks for various downstream tasks, including classification and segmentation.

Due to the abundance of large-scale chest X-ray imaging databases [4,9,26], many prior works employing generative models have primarily focused on synthesizing thoracic-region images. Synthetic data has been leveraged to address class imbalance, augment existing datasets [8,12], and improve anomaly detection [19] and disease classification [2]. Additionally, some studies have integrated both generative models and DRRs to facilitate automatic segmentation of anatomical structures in X-ray images, utilizing unsupervised domain adaptation [31].

On the other hand, recent works utilizing DRR methods have benefited from advanced frameworks such as DeepDRR and DiffDRR [6,25], which enable the realistic synthesis of X-ray images from CT data. Killeen et al. [13] employed DeepDRR to generate large-scale synthetic data for training a language-aligned foundation model capable of segmenting 128 anatomical structures and 464 non-anatomical objects. Additionally, DRRs have been applied in vascular segmentation of X-ray angiography, as demonstrated by Zhang et al. [29], where they employed self-supervised and contrastive learning techniques on unlabeled X-ray angiography images, achieving performance comparable to supervised methods requiring manual annotations. Furthermore, Gao et al. [5] introduced SynthX and demonstrated that models trained on synthetic X-ray images, combined with domain randomization techniques, can match or even surpass the performance of models trained on native X-ray images, particularly in novel scenarios where real data is scarce. DRRs have also been employed in various segmentation tasks, including disease segmentation [30], surgical tool segmentation [28], and rib segmentation [32].

3   Materials and Methods

3.1   Method

Our proposed method consists of two main steps: synthetic data generation followed by supervised multi-class training, as illustrated in Fig. 1. In the first step, we generate synthetic X-ray projection images using the DiffDRR framework [6] from 3D CT data. Alongside the simulated X-ray images, corresponding ground-truth annotations are also projected, which we categorize into five anatomical groups based on the TotalSegmentator toolkit's grouping: Cardiac, Ribs, Organs, Muscles, and Vertebrae. For each subject, a single synthetic X-ray image is projected along the anterior-posterior (AP) axis, along the center of the volume. To minimize magnification and skew distortions in both the projected images and their corresponding annotations, we increase the source-to-detector distance while reducing the object-to-detector distance. Our aim is to project images that are similar to orthogonal projections. In the second step, we train a set of multi-class 2D U-Net models using an in-house adapted version of the nnUNet v2 framework. Each model is trained separately for one of the five anatomical groups.

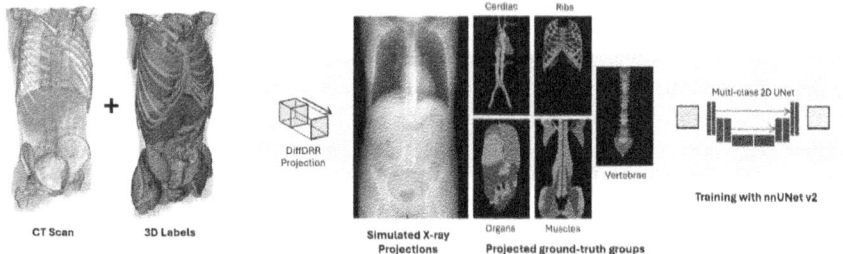

Fig. 1. Overview of our proposed method, 3D CT data and corresponding ground-truth annotations are projected to synthetic X-ray images using DiffDRR, where ground-truth annotations are grouped following the same structure in TotalSegmentator. The generated data is then used to train different models for each ground-truth group in a multi-class setting using nnUNet v2 framework.

3.2 Data

We utilize the publicly available TotalSegmentator dataset (version 2) as the primary source for simulating X-ray training data. This dataset comprises 1,228 3D CT scans covering various body regions, along with ground-truth annotations for 117 anatomical structures. To maintain consistency and reproducibility, we adhere to the original training, validation, and testing splits provided with the dataset. The data is split into 1,081 images for training, 58 for validation, and 89 images for the hold-out test set. All simulated images are projected with their original physical spacing of 1.5×1.5 mm.

Furthermore, we evaluate a subset of our trained models on publicly available native X-ray imaging datasets, specifically: (1) VinDR-RibsCXR [18] and (2) the Japanese Society of Radiological Technology (JSRT) Database [21]. We preprocess the data to match the same physical spacing our models were trained on, and evaluate on the entire databases. The first dataset comprises of 245 images of both AP and PA scans, with ground-truth annotations for individual 20 ribs. The second database contains 246 images with ground-truth annotations for lungs, heart and clavicles.

3.3 Implementation Details

We train all of our models using an in-house adapted version of the nnUNet framework (version 2.5.1) that enables multi-class segmentation using PyTorch (version 2.5.1) and CUDA (version 12.4). All models were trained with mirroring disabled to correctly differentiate between left and right anatomies, in terms of

Table 1. Ablation results on different anatomical groups, attenuation levels, and training with or without augmentation. Values represent both DSC and NSD scores with 95% confidence intervals.

		DSC				
Training	Atten.	Ribs	Vertebrae	Muscles	Organs	Cardiac
500 Epochs	$\mu = 1$	$0.775_{[0.755,0.795]}$	$0.819_{[0.790,0.845]}$	$0.917_{[0.898,0.935]}$	$0.695_{[0.590,0.781]}$	$0.682_{[0.627,0.733]}$
	$\mu = 3$	$0.823_{[0.806,0.840]}$	$0.857_{[0.833,0.879]}$	$0.924_{[0.907,0.940]}$	$0.680_{[0.576,0.766]}$	$0.672_{[0.617,0.724]}$
	$\mu = 6$	$\mathbf{0.832}_{[0.811,0.852]}$	$\mathbf{0.860}_{[0.834,0.883]}$	$\mathbf{0.927}_{[0.911,0.943]}$	$0.675_{[0.570,0.759]}$	$0.666_{[0.612,0.717]}$
500 Epochs + DA5	$\mu = 1$	$0.773_{[0.750,0.795]}$	$0.806_{[0.774,0.836]}$	$0.899_{[0.877,0.920]}$	$\mathbf{0.697}_{[0.590,0.783]}$	$\mathbf{0.690}_{[0.638,0.738]}$
	$\mu = 3$	$0.814_{[0.794,0.834]}$	$0.858_{[0.834,0.879]}$	$0.905_{[0.885,0.922]}$	$0.688_{[0.581,0.772]}$	$0.672_{[0.616,0.723]}$
	$\mu = 6$	$0.821_{[0.800,0.841]}$	$0.856_{[0.828,0.881]}$	$0.910_{[0.890,0.929]}$	$0.680_{[0.580,0.763]}$	$0.671_{[0.617,0.722]}$
		NSD				
Training	Atten.	Ribs	Vertebrae	Muscles	Organs	Cardiac
500 Epochs	$\mu = 1$	$0.806_{[0.772,0.833]}$	$0.810_{[0.788,0.830]}$	$0.841_{[0.796,0.884]}$	$\mathbf{0.552}_{[0.495,0.605]}$	$\mathbf{0.681}_{[0.629,0.727]}$
	$\mu = 3$	$0.855_{[0.817,0.884]}$	$0.871_{[0.856,0.885]}$	$0.858_{[0.812,0.899]}$	$0.521_{[0.467,0.571]}$	$0.667_{[0.617,0.713]}$
	$\mu = 6$	$\mathbf{0.862}_{[0.821,0.894]}$	$\mathbf{0.876}_{[0.862,0.889]}$	$\mathbf{0.866}_{[0.822,0.906]}$	$0.502_{[0.450,0.551]}$	$0.655_{[0.609,0.697]}$
500 Epochs + DA5	$\mu = 1$	$0.807_{[0.769,0.838]}$	$0.786_{[0.762,0.809]}$	$0.796_{[0.743,0.845]}$	$0.545_{[0.489,0.599]}$	$0.673_{[0.620,0.720]}$
	$\mu = 3$	$0.846_{[0.807,0.877]}$	$0.870_{[0.854,0.884]}$	$0.811_{[0.755,0.860]}$	$0.524_{[0.470,0.574]}$	$0.662_{[0.611,0.710]}$
	$\mu = 6$	$0.850_{[0.807,0.884]}$	$0.866_{[0.850,0.882]}$	$0.819_{[0.763,0.867]}$	$0.487_{[0.422,0.545]}$	$0.652_{[0.602,0.699]}$

data augmentation we utilize the DA5 trainer. For simulating X-ray images, we use DiffDRR (version 0.4.4) to create datasets at three attenuation levels and to project labels from 3D to 2D. All of our experiments were conducted on a workstation with an Intel Core i7-13700F CPU and an Nvidia GeForce RTX 4090 GPU. In our experiments, we report both the Dice Similarity Coefficient (DSC) and the Normalized Surface Distance (NSD) at a 3 mm threshold.

4   Experiments and Results

4.1   Ablation Results

We conduct an ablation study to assess the impact of simulating X-ray images at different attenuation levels ($\mu = 1, 3, 6$) on segmentation performance across various anatomical structure groups. Additionally, we examine the effect of data augmentation when using the DA5 trainer. All experiments were conducted over 500 epochs with a batch size of 8. The results are presented in Table 1.

As expected, models generally perform better on high-density anatomical structures, such as skeletal structures. These structures are more prominent in X-ray images and become even more visible at higher attenuation levels, where soft-tissue structures are increasingly suppressed. Most of these structures belong to the Ribs, Vertebrae, and Muscles anatomical groups. Despite its name, the Muscles group also includes several skeletal structures, such as the femur, hip bones, scapula, and humerus, which explains its significantly higher scores compared to other groups. Figure 2 shows the distribution of scores for all anatomical structures across different groups when evaluated using the 500-epoch model on the synthetic dataset with $\mu = 3$.

The Cardiac and Organs groups, which primarily consist of soft-tissue structures, exhibited significantly lower segmentation performance in terms of both DSC and NSD. Performance further declined as soft-tissue suppression increased at higher attenuation levels. While overall segmentation performance for these groups was relatively poor, some major anatomical structures such as: the heart, lungs, kidneys, liver, stomach, and spleen, still achieved good segmentation performance, as illustrated in Fig. 2. We attribute the lower performance in soft-tissue segmentation to the challenge of transferring labels from 3D CT scans to 2D X-ray images. Not all structures that are clearly visible in 3D scans transfer well to X-ray images or are even relevant in this context. For example, several labels within the Cardiac group might be best visualized with contrast material, which is not typically available in standard X-ray imaging. Furthermore, the overlap of multiple soft-tissue structures creates ambiguous boundaries and similar appearances, making segmentation particularly challenging for soft-tissue structures. Finally, training using the DA5 data augmentation trainer, resulted in little-to-no effect on segmentation performance. Possibly model training would have benefited from more samples projected for each scan in combination with domain randomization, on this specific dataset.

4.2 Evaluation on Native X-Ray Data

We evaluate and present the results of a subset of our trained models on publicly available native X-ray imaging datasets, specifically: (1) VinDR-RibsCXR [18] and (2) the Japanese Society of Radiological Technology (JSRT) Database [21]. We preprocess the data to match the same physical spacing our models were trained on, and evaluate on the entire databases. The first dataset comprises of 245 images of both AP and PA scans, with ground-truth annotations for individual 20 ribs. The second database contains 246 images with ground-truth annotations for lungs, heart and clavicles. This evaluation helps us better understand the Sim2Real transfer and highlights key challenges.

For VinDR-RibsCXR, we found negligible performance differences with models trained with the data augmentation trainer. Despite being trained on different attenuation levels, their segmentation performance remained largely the same, with a mean class DSC of 0.744 (95% CI: 0.725, 0.766) and NSD of 0.778 (95% CI: 0.761, 0.793) for the model trained with data at $\mu = 3$. To further improve generalization, we trained a combined model using data across all attenuation levels, effectively tripling the dataset size and increasing variability in attenuation. This allowed the model to learn more robustly. The combined model, trained for 500 epochs, achieved a higher mean class DSC of 0.767 (95% CI: 0.752, 0.784) and an NSD of 0.800 (95% CI: 0.786, 0.812), demonstrating improved robustness across variations in attenuation. The distribution of individual class scores is presented in Fig. 3, and sample model predictions are shown in Fig. 4. In comparison with a similar 2D UNet architecture, the authors of VinDR-RibsCXR reported a DSC performance 0.765 (95% CI: 0.737, 0.788) on the validation set, when training on

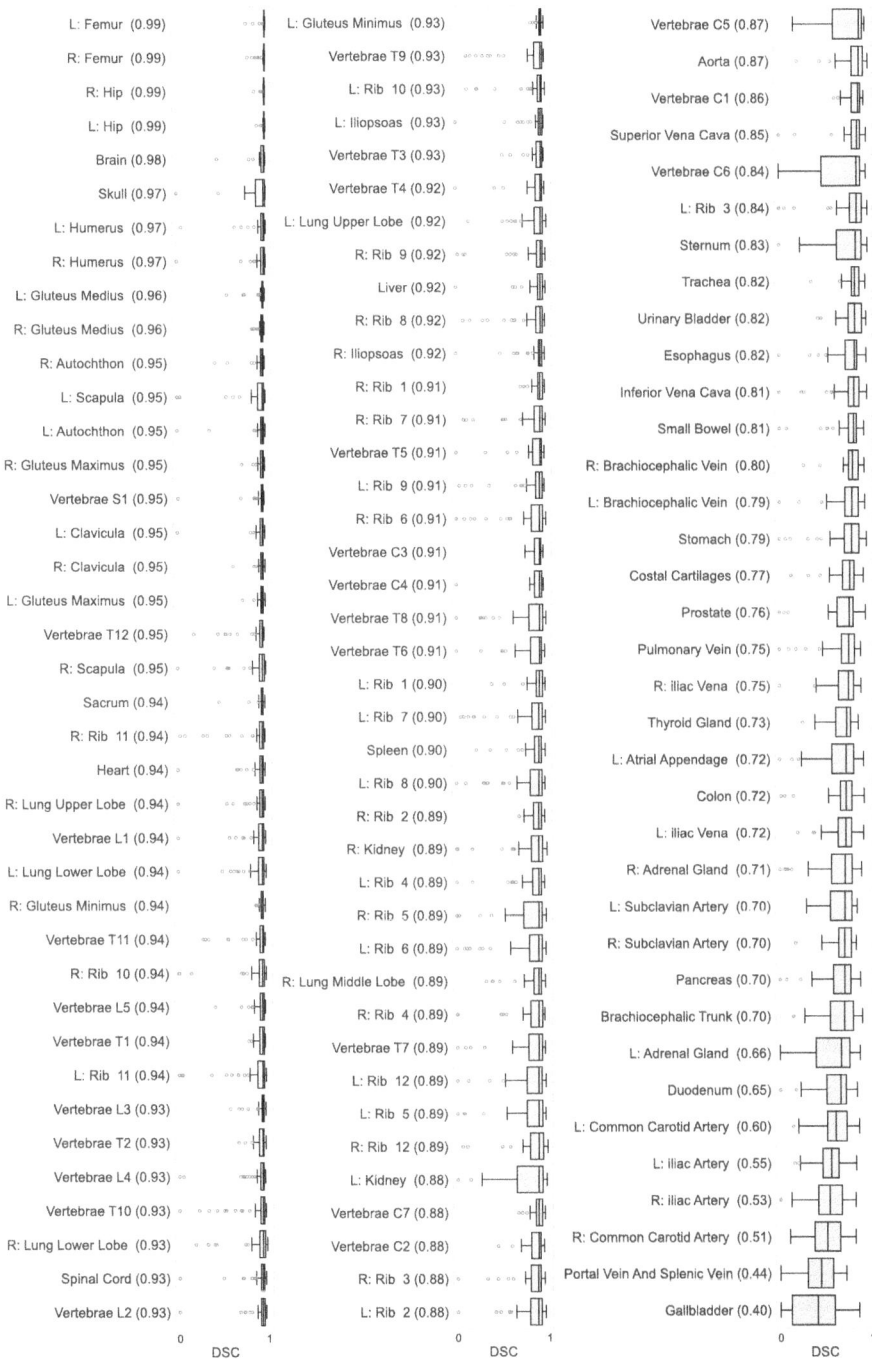

Fig. 2. DSC distribution results for all anatomical structures across all anatomical groups. Scores are sorted in descending order based on the median value of each label, which is noted between brackets for reference. Results are for the synthetic hold-out test data at attenuation level $\mu = 3$.

native X-ray images from the same distribution. We report a DSC performance of 0.754 (95% CI: 0.734, 0.776) when evaluating our combined model on the same validation set, using only synthetic data.

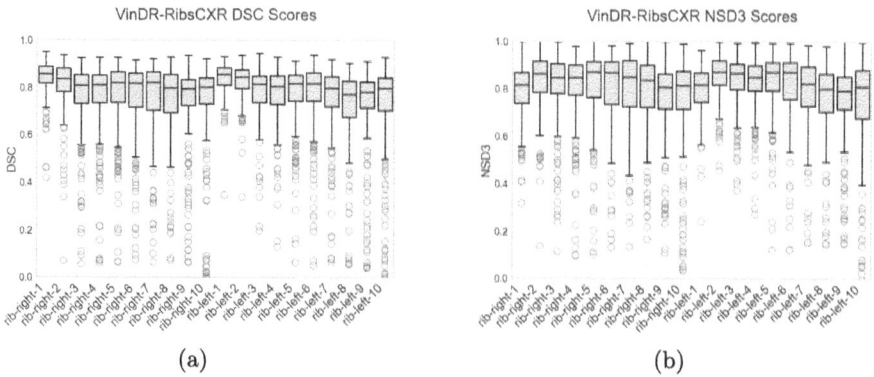

Fig. 3. Segmentation performance for each individual class in VinDR-RibsCXR Database using our combined model, (a) DSC results and (b) NSD results.

To better understand cases with poor segmentation performance, we analyze common errors made by our models. One frequent issue is misidentifying the anatomical extent of a rib, where the model correctly segments parts of the rib but inaccurately follows its curvature. Another challenge is the discontinuity in predictions, where the model fails to segment the rib as a continuous structure. A third common error is incorrect class assignment, such as predicting the 10th rib as the 9th. Notably, when a portion of a rib is misclassified, it often leads to further errors in adjacent ribs, compounding the overall reduction in prediction scores.

For the JSRT database, we report results for individual structures in Fig. 5, we use this dataset to highlight potential pitfalls when evaluating synthetically trained models on real X-ray images. Our reported results are for the models trained on the synthetic data at attenuation of $\mu = 3$. We highlight two main factors that can contribute to discrepancies in performance: (1) differences between annotations delineated on a 3D CT scan and ones directly performed on X-ray images, and (2) variations in the extent of delineated anatomy.

The first factor can be explained within the context of lung segmentation. Our models were trained on annotations delineated on 3D CT scans and then projected to 2D X-ray images. In 3D CT scans, the lungs are typically fully delineated, whereas in X-ray images, portions of the lungs are obscured by structures such as the mediastinum, and only the air-filled regions are usually annotated. As a result, directly comparing annotations delineated from different modalities can lead to misleading conclusions, since the lungs are represented differently. To address this discrepancy, we apply a simple post-processing step to our model

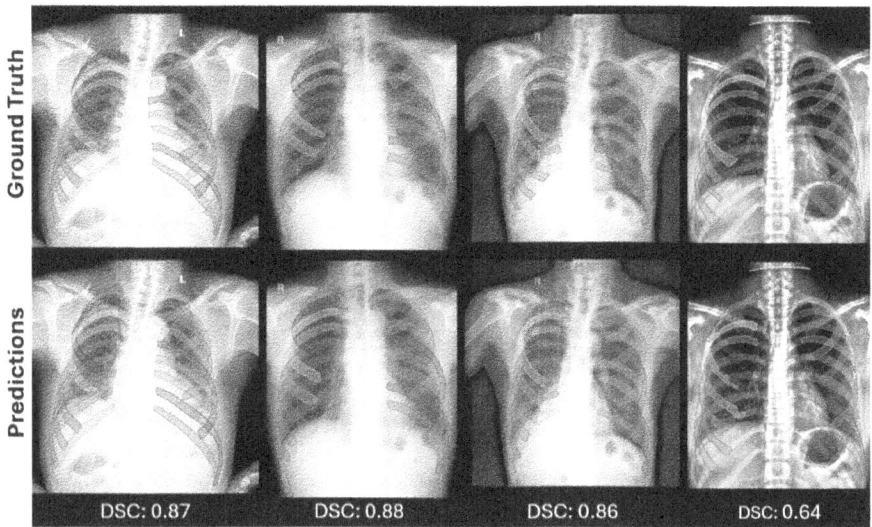

Fig. 4. Sample predictions from the combined model on VinDR-RibCXR validation patients 05, 08, 47, and 41 (from left to right). The top row displays ground-truth annotations overlaid on the original images, while the bottom row shows the model's predictions.

outputs. Because our models also predict additional organs occluding or overlapping the lungs, such as the liver, stomach, and spleen, we remove these labels from the lung predictions. This adjustment accounts for anatomical overlap and occlusion in X-rays, aligning the model's output more closely with how lungs are typically annotated in native X-ray images. This improves the DSC from 0.842 (95% CI: 0.829, 0.845) and 0.745 (95% CI: 0.740, 0.749) to 0.934 (95% CI: 0.932, 0.936) and 0.922 (95% CI: 0.919, 0.925) for the right and left lungs, respectively, while also improving the NSD from 0.396 (95% CI: 0.390, 0.401) and 0.468 (95% CI: 0.464, 0.473) to 0.619 (95% CI: 0.611, 0.627) and 0.640 (95% CI: 0.634, 0.648), respectively.

Moreover, the second factor can be explained from the performance results of the heart as well both right and left clavicles. Our model achieved a DSC score of 0.831 (95% CI: 0.827, 0.835) and a NSD score of 0.375 (95% CI: 0.362, 0.388). This discrepancy between a both metrics is due to differences of what is defined as heart between the 3D CT data and also what is annotated in the JSRT database. Furthermore, for clavicle segmentation, in the JSRT database, clavicles are segmented to around their visual intersection with the ribcage, while our models predict the entire bone. These differences explain the low segmentation performance as well as discrepancy between DSC and NSD scores. We illustrate a sample prediction and the corresponding ground-truth in Fig. 6, to better understand these annotation differences.

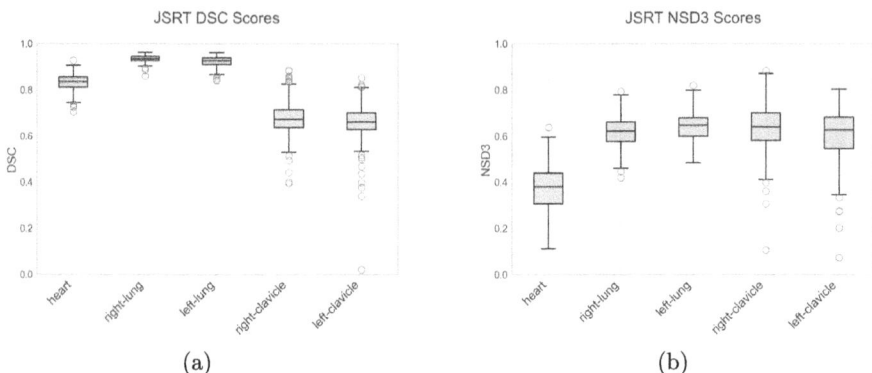

Fig. 5. DSC (a) and NSD (b) scores for the entire JSRT dataset. Results shown for the model trained for 500 epochs on synthetic data at attenuation level $\mu = 3$, including post-processing of lung labels to match what is usually visible on an X-ray image.

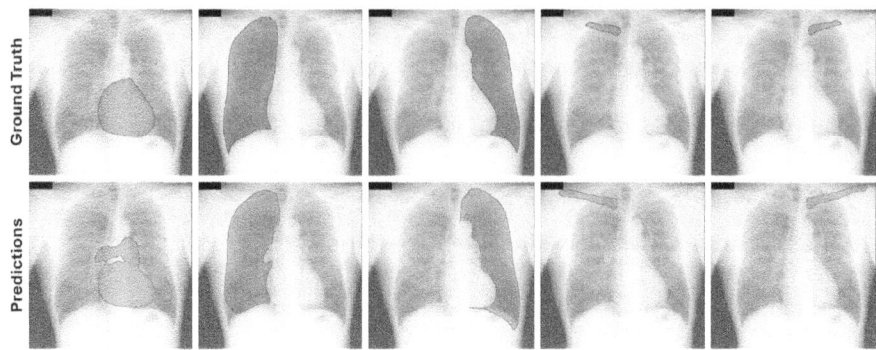

Fig. 6. Sample predictions of different structures on JSRT database, highlighting potential pitfalls when evaluating models trained on synthetic data and evaluated on native X-ray images. From left to right: heart, right-lung, left-lung, right-clavicle and left-clavicle, respectively. Ground-truth and predictions are visualized in green and red. Both lung labels are post-processed by subtracting the organs obstructing the lungs, to better match the ground-truth and what is visible on an X-ray image. (Color figure online)

5   Discussion and Conclusion

In this paper, we present a method for whole-body segmentation of anatomical structures in X-ray images, leveraging synthetic data simulated from 3D CT scans for model training. Our approach closely follows the structure of the TotalSegmentator toolkit, ensuring reproducibility and consistency. We utilize CT data from the TotalSegmentator dataset in combination with DiffDRR to generate synthetic X-ray images for training, adhering to the same training, validation, and testing splits. Additionally, we train five 2D UNet models to segment different anatomical groups, namely: Ribs, Vertebrae, Muscles, Cardiac, and Organs, following the original dataset's label structure. Our models are trained in a multi-class setting using an in-house adapted version of the nnUNet v2 framework. To assess generalization performance, we evaluate a subset of our models on two native X-ray imaging databases, identifying key challenges in transferring models trained on synthetic data to real X-ray images.

Our results demonstrate that models trained on synthetic data can achieve strong segmentation performance, particularly for skeletal structures and major organs such as the heart, liver, and kidneys. Our trained models achieved a median DSC above 0.88 for approximately 79 different classes on the synthetic test set. While the scores for anatomical groups such as cardiac structures and organs were lower, this was largely due to the high number of classes within these groups (24 and 18, respectively), most of which correspond to soft tissues. Some of these structures may be partially obscured by other anatomical features in the simulated X-ray images, exhibit indistinct boundaries, or simply that X-ray might not be the modality of choice.

Furthermore, in our evaluation on the VinDR-RibsCXR dataset, we achieved a DSC of 0.754 (95% CI: 0.734, 0.776) on the validation subset, closely matching the performance of a similar UNet architecture trained on real data from the same distribution [18]. We also found that incorporating different attenuation levels during model training improves generalization, as demonstrated by our combined model. Moreover, we highlight two key challenges when transferring models trained on synthetic data to native X-ray images. First, there are differences between annotations acquired from 3D CT scans and those directly delineated from 2D X-ray images. Second, variations exist in the extent of the delineated anatomy. We illustrate these challenges in our evaluation on the JSRT database and show that simple post-processing techniques can address some of these discrepancies. This is possible because our models were trained to segment a comprehensive set of anatomical structures, allowing us to refine predictions to more closely match X-ray-derived annotations.

Finally, our models can be incorporated into an active learning pipeline to construct large-scale X-ray imaging datasets. Because most publicly available, annotated X-ray datasets focus on chest X-rays, we primarily evaluated our models on such datasets. However, we encourage further evaluation on native imaging datasets to validate our models across different demographics and pathologies. While we used the nnUNet framework for reproducibility, exploring alternative architectures or projecting additional samples per volume could be valuable directions for future work.

Acknowledgments. This work was funded by research subsidies granted by the government of Upper Austria. RISC Software GmbH is a member of UAR (Upper Austrian Research) Innovation Network.

References

1. Aithal, S.K., Maini, P., Lipton, Z.C., Kolter, J.Z.: Understanding hallucinations in diffusion models through mode interpolation. In: Advances in Neural Information Processing Systems, vol. 37, pp. 134614–134644 (2024). https://proceedings.neurips.cc/paper_files/paper/2024/hash/f29369d192b13184b65c6d2515474d78-Abstract-Conference.html
2. Albahli, S.: Efficient GAN-based chest radiographs (CXR) augmentation to diagnose coronavirus disease pneumonia. Int. J. Med. Sci. **17**(10), 1439–1448 (2020). https://doi.org/10.7150/ijms.46684, https://www.ncbi.nlm.nih.gov/pmc/articles/PMC7330663/
3. Annarumma, M., Withey, S.J., Bakewell, R.J., Pesce, E., Goh, V., Montana, G.: Automated triaging of adult chest radiographs with deep artificial neural networks. Radiology **291**(1), 196–202 (2019). https://doi.org/10.1148/radiol.2018180921, https://pubs.rsna.org/doi/10.1148/radiol.2018180921
4. Gaggion, N., et al.: CheXmask: a large-scale dataset of anatomical segmentation masks for multi-center chest X-ray images. Scientific Data **11**(1), 511 (2024). https://doi.org/10.1038/s41597-024-03358-1, https://www.nature.com/articles/s41597-024-03358-1
5. Gao, C., et al.: Synthetic data accelerates the development of generalizable learning based algorithms for X-ray image analysis. Nat. Mach. Intell. **5**(3), 294–308 (2023). https://doi.org/10.1038/s42256-023-00629-1, https://www.nature.com/articles/s42256-023-00629-1
6. Gopalakrishnan, V., Golland, P.: Fast auto-differentiable digitally reconstructed radiographs for solving inverse problems in intraoperative imaging. In: Workshop on Clinical Image-Based Procedures, pp. 1–11. Springer (2022). https://link.springer.com/chapter/10.1007/978-3-031-23179-7_1
7. Ho, J., Jain, A., Abbeel, P.: Denoising diffusion probabilistic models. In: Advances in Neural Information Processing Systems, vol. 33, pp. 6840–6851. Curran Associates, Inc. (2020). https://proceedings.neurips.cc/paper/2020/hash/4c5bcfec8584af0d967f1ab10179ca4b-Abstract.html
8. Huijben, E.M.C., Pluim, J.P.W., van Eijnatten, M.A.J.M.: Denoising diffusion probabilistic models for addressing data limitations in chest X-ray classification. Inform. Med. Unlock. **50**, 101575 (2024). https://doi.org/10.1016/j.imu.2024.101575, https://www.sciencedirect.com/science/article/pii/S235291482400131X
9. Johnson, A.E.W., et al.: MIMIC-CXR, a de-identified publicly available database of chest radiographs with free-text reports. Sci. Data **6**(1), 317 (2019). https://doi.org/10.1038/s41597-019-0322-0, https://www.nature.com/articles/s41597-019-0322-0
10. Kausch, L., et al.: Toward automatic C-arm positioning for standard projections in orthopedic surgery. Int. J. Comput. Assist. Radiol. Surg. **15**(7), 1095–1105 (2020). https://doi.org/10.1007/s11548-020-02204-0
11. Kholiavchenko, M., et al.: Contour-aware multi-label chest X-ray organ segmentation. Int. J. Comput. Assist. Radiol. Surg. **15**(3), 425–436 (2020). https://doi.org/10.1007/s11548-019-02115-9
12. Khosravi, B., et al.: Synthetically enhanced: unveiling synthetic data's potential in medical imaging research. eBioMedicine **104** (2024). https://doi.org/10.1016/j.ebiom.2024.105174, https://www.thelancet.com/journals/ebiom/article/PIIS2352-3964(24)00209-3/fulltext

13. Killeen, B.D., et al.: FluoroSAM: a language-aligned foundation model for X-ray Image segmentation (2024). https://doi.org/10.48550/arXiv.2403.08059, arXiv:2403.08059 [cs]

14. Koitka, S., et al.: SAROS: a dataset for whole body region and organ segmentation in CT imaging. Sci. Data **11**(1), 483 (2024). https://doi.org/10.1038/s41597-024-03337-6, https://www.nature.com/articles/s41597-024-03337-6

15. Lauritzen, A.D., Lillholm, M., Lynge, E., Nielsen, M., Karssemeijer, N., Vejborg, I.: Early indicators of the impact of using AI in mammography screening for breast cancer. Radiology **311**(3), e232479 (2024). https://doi.org/10.1148/radiol.232479, https://pubs.rsna.org/doi/10.1148/radiol.232479

16. Li, W., et al..: AbdomenAtlas: a large-scale, detailed annotated, & multi-center dataset for efficient transfer learning and open algorithmic benchmarking. Med. Image Anal. **97**, 103285 (2024). https://doi.org/10.1016/j.media.2024.103285, https://www.sciencedirect.com/science/article/pii/S136184152400210X

17. Liu, W., Luo, J., Yang, Y., Wang, W., Deng, J., Yu, L.: Automatic lung segmentation in chest X-ray images using improved U-Net. Sci. Rep. **12**(1), 8649 (2022). https://doi.org/10.1038/s41598-022-12743-y, https://www.nature.com/articles/s41598-022-12743-y

18. Nguyen, H.C., Le, T.T., Pham, H., Nguyen, H.Q.: VinDr-RibCXR: a benchmark dataset for automatic segmentation and labeling of individual ribs on chest X-rays (2021). https://openreview.net/forum?id=oJi6xpSLdsj

19. Packhäuser, K., Folle, L., Thamm, F., Maier, A.: Generation of anonymous chest radiographs using latent diffusion models for training thoracic abnormality classification systems. In: 2023 IEEE 20th International Symposium on Biomedical Imaging (ISBI), pp. 1–5 (2023). https://doi.org/10.1109/ISBI53787.2023.10230346, https://ieeexplore.ieee.org/abstract/document/10230346. iSSN 1945-8452

20. Rister, B., Yi, D., Shivakumar, K., Nobashi, T., Rubin, D.L.: CT-ORG, a new dataset for multiple organ segmentation in computed tomography. Sci. Data **7**(1), 381 (2020). https://doi.org/10.1038/s41597-020-00715-8, https://www.nature.com/articles/s41597-020-00715-8

21. Shiraishi, J., et al.: Development of a digital image database for chest radiographs with and without a lung nodule: receiver operating characteristic analysis of radiologists' detection of pulmonary nodules. AJR Am. J. Roentgenol. **174**(1), 71–74 (2000). https://doi.org/10.2214/ajr.174.1.1740071

22. Sridharan, S., et al.: Real-World evaluation of an AI triaging system for chest X-rays: a prospective clinical study. Eur. J. Radiol. **181** (2024). https://doi.org/10.1016/j.ejrad.2024.111783, https://www.ejradiology.com/article/S0720-048X(24)00499-6/fulltext, publisher: Elsevier

23. Statistics: Statistics » Diagnostic Imaging Dataset 2024-25 Data. https://www.england.nhs.uk/statistics/statistical-work-areas/diagnostic-imaging-dataset/diagnostic-imaging-dataset-2024-25-data/

24. Ullah, I., Ali, F., Shah, B., El-Sappagh, S., Abuhmed, T., Park, S.H.: A deep learning based dual encoder–decoder framework for anatomical structure segmentation in chest X-ray images. Sci. Rep. **13**(1), 791 (2023). https://doi.org/10.1038/s41598-023-27815-w, https://www.nature.com/articles/s41598-023-27815-w

25. Unberath, M., et al.: DeepDRR – a catalyst for machine learning in fluoroscopy-guided procedures (2018). https://doi.org/10.48550/arXiv.1803.08606, arXiv:1803.08606 [physics]

26. Wang, X., Peng, Y., Lu, L., Lu, Z., Bagheri, M., Summers, R.M.: ChestX-Ray8: hospital-scale chest X-ray database and benchmarks on weakly-supervised

classification and localization of common thorax diseases. In: 2017 IEEE Conference on Computer Vision and Pattern Recognition (CVPR), pp. 3462–3471 (2017). https://doi.org/10.1109/CVPR.2017.369, https://ieeexplore.ieee.org/document/8099852. iSSN 1063-6919

27. Wasserthal, J., et al.: TotalSegmentator: robust segmentation of 104 anatomic structures in CT images. Radiol.: Artif. Intell. **5**(5), e230024 (2023). https://doi.org/10.1148/ryai.230024, https://pubs.rsna.org/doi/10.1148/ryai.230024

28. Yang, L., Gu, Y., Bian, G., Liu, Y.: DRR-net: a dense-connected residual recurrent convolutional network for surgical instrument segmentation from endoscopic images. IEEE Trans. Med. Robot. Bionics **4**(3), 696–707 (2022). https://doi.org/10.1109/TMRB.2022.3193420

29. Zhang, B., Zhang, Z., Liu, S., Faghihroohi, S., Schunkert, H., Navab, N.: XA-Sim2Real: adaptive representation learning for vessel segmentation in X-ray angiography. In: Linguraru, M.G., et al. (eds.) MICCAI 2024. LNCS, vol. 15006, pp. 747–756. Springer, Cham (2024). https://doi.org/10.1007/978-3-031-72089-5_70

30. Zhang, P., Zhong, Y., Deng, Y., Tang, X., Li, X.: DRR4Covid: learning automated COVID-19 infection segmentation from digitally reconstructed radiographs. IEEE Access **8**, 207736–207757 (2020). https://doi.org/10.1109/ACCESS.2020.3038279

31. Zhang, Y., Miao, S., Mansi, T., Liao, R.: Task driven generative modeling for unsupervised domain adaptation: application to X-ray image segmentation. In: Frangi, A.F., Schnabel, J.A., Davatzikos, C., Alberola-López, C., Fichtinger, G. (eds.) MICCAI 2018. LNCS, vol. 11071, pp. 599–607. Springer, Cham (2018). https://doi.org/10.1007/978-3-030-00934-2_67

32. Zhao, J., Nie, Z., Shen, J., He, J., Yang, X.: Rib segmentation in chest X-ray images based on unsupervised domain adaptation. Biomed. Phys. Eng. Express **10**(1), 015021 (2023). https://doi.org/10.1088/2057-1976/ad1663

Transform(AI)ng Radiology with CheXSBT: Integrating Dual-Attention Swin Transformer with BERT for Seamless Chest X-Ray Report Generation

Aradhya Khandeparker$^{(\boxtimes)}$ (ID) and Ping Lu$^{(\boxtimes)}$ (ID)

School of Computer Science, University of Leeds, Leeds LS2 9JT, UK
{lmfx5605,P.Lu}@leeds.ac.uk

Abstract. Radiology reports are crucial for diagnosing diseases, yet generation them is time-consuming, places a significant workload on medical professionals, and is subject to inter-expert variability, as different radiologists may interpret the same X-ray differently. This paper presents a novel hybrid AI model called CheXSBT, which combines our custom-designed Dual-Attention Swin Transformer (DAST) for vision processing with BERT for natural language understanding to automate the generation of chest X-ray (CXR) reports. Leveraging the MIMIC-CXR dataset, which includes over 370,000 X-ray images and their corresponding reports, CheXSBT learns to interpret chest X-ray images and convert them into structured, meaningful text. Our study focuses on two main objectives: (1) automating report generation to accelerate the diagnostic process and (2) improving model interpretability to foster trust among radiologists. The approach involves preprocessing chest X-ray images and their corresponding text reports using the pre-trained BLIP processor, training the novel hybrid vision-language model on paired data, and fine-tuning it for clinical relevance and coherence. The performance of CheXSBT is rigorously evaluated using established metrics such as BLEU, ROUGE, and METEOR, achieving scores of 0.232 for BLEU-4 and 0.392 for ROUGE-L, outperforming other state-of-the-art models and ensuring high-quality report generation. By reducing radiologists' workload and providing quick, accurate information, CheXSBT aims to transform the intersection between AI and clinical practice, making radiology reporting more efficient, consistent, and accessible.

Keywords: Vision-language models · Chest X-ray · Radiology report generation · Transformer · Swin transformer · BERT

1 Introduction

Radiology is a cornerstone of modern healthcare, providing essential diagnostic insights through medical imaging. However, increasing demand for imaging

© The Author(s), under exclusive license to Springer Nature Switzerland AG 2026
S. Ali et al. (Eds.): MIUA 2025, LNCS 15916, pp. 159–173, 2026.
https://doi.org/10.1007/978-3-031-98688-8_12

services, particularly in chest X-ray (CXR), has led to a growing workload for radiologists, contributing to delays in diagnosis and variability in the quality of the report. Artificial intelligence (AI) offers a promising solution to these challenges by automating radiology report generation using vision-language models (VLMs).

A standard chest X-ray (CXR) report typically consists of three key sections: (i) the *indications* section, which outlines the referring clinician's reasons for requesting the CXR and relevant aspects of the patient's medical history; (ii) the *findings* section, which details observations derived from the radiology image; and (iii) the *impression* section, which provides the clinical diagnostic information [18]. An example of such a report is shown in Fig. 1. Among these, the indications section is particularly important as it guides the interpretation of the X-ray by highlighting the relevant clinical context. We propose an approach to automatically generate the findings section by utilising both the indications and the CXR.

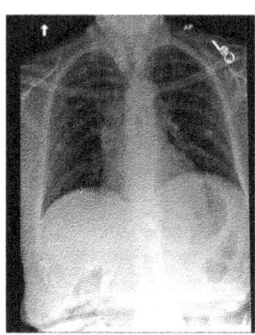

FINAL REPORT

INDICATION: History: __F with malignancy, recent cycle chemo last week, DVT last month, now w/ SIRS+ presentation, malaise, JVD, epig abd pain since last night

FINDING: Herat size is normal. The mediastinal and hilar contours are unchanged, with tortuosity of the thoracic aorta again noted. Atherosclerotic calcifications are seen throughout the aorta. Pulmonary vasculature is normal. No focal consolidation, pleural effusion or pneumothorax is present. Multilevel degenerative changes are seen in the thoracic spine. Clips in the right upper quadrant of the abdomen are re- demonstrated.

IMPRESSION: No acute cardiopulmonary abnormality.

Fig. 1. An example of a Chest X-Ray and corresponding report from the MIMIC-CXR dataset.

In this work, we present a novel hybrid vision-language model called as **CheXSBT**, which is designed to automate the generation of chest X-ray (CXR) reports. The model is built by combining our custom-designed **Dual-Attention Swin Transformer (DAST)** for vision processing and **BERT** (Bidirectional Encoder Representations from Transformers) [2] for natural language understanding, creating a hybrid vision-language framework that generates structured, context-aware, and clinically relevant reports. This approach not only improves accuracy but also enhances the interpretability of the generated findings.

Our model is designed to process multimodal data by integrating visual features from chest X-ray images with textual embeddings from corresponding reports. This fusion of modalities enhances the generation of more informative and coherent reports, closely aligning with expert-written radiology interpretations.

The model is trained on the MIMIC-CXR [4–6] dataset, which comprises over 370,000 chest X-ray images paired with corresponding radiology reports. We evaluate the performance of CheXSBT using well-established natural language generation (NLG) metrics such as BLEU [15], ROUGE [8], and METEOR [1] to ensure both linguistic quality and diagnostic accuracy. Our results demonstrate that the integration of visual and textual representations significantly enhances the coherence and reliability of generated reports compared to unimodal approaches.

The main contributions of our work are:

- We present CheXSBT, a novel hybrid vision-language model that integrates our custom-designed Dual-Attention Swin Transformer (DAST) for visual feature extraction with a BERT-based encoder for language processing, specifically tailored for radiology report generation. To the best of our knowledge, this is the first work to combine DAST with BERT for automated chest X-ray report generation.
- Our custom-designed Dual-Attention Swin Transformer (DAST) employs a two-stage structure in each block, incorporating Window Multi-head Self-Attention (W-MSA) followed by Shifted Window Multi-head Self-Attention (SW-MSA), which enables the model to capture both local and global dependencies. Additionally, Layer Normalisation (LN) is applied before each attention operation to stabilise training and improve convergence. A residual connection is also included to preserve gradient flow and prevent vanishing gradients during deep network training. These modifications improve the effectiveness of the Swin Transformer in visual tasks, contributing to better performance in feature extraction.
- Our model learns to interpret medical images effectively and generate structured, clinically meaningful textual descriptions, improving diagnostic consistency. We conduct rigorous evaluations using well-established NLG metrics, demonstrating the effectiveness of CheXSBT in generating high-quality, diagnostically valuable reports.

2   Related Work

Recent advancements in AI, particularly in vision-language modeling, have greatly enhanced automated medical report generation. Earlier approaches relied on CNN-RNN architectures, but modern research has increasingly adopted transformer based models due to their superior performance in capturing complex relationships between images and text [18]. In this section, we discuss the works related to CheXSBT.

You et al. [21] addressed the challenge of limited image-text pairs in chest X-ray (CXR) datasets by generating synthetic pairs using radiologist-designed prompts. Their method employs two contrastive losses—Image Contrastive Loss and Text Contrastive Loss—to enhance image-text retrieval and classification. Sanjeev et al. [16] introduced TiBiX, a transformer-based model with causal attention, which integrates temporal data from prior scans to enhance report generation.

Windsor et al. [19] explored improving vision-language models (VLMs) under low-data conditions, utilising unimodal self-supervision and contrastive loss functions to enhance model generalisation in report generation. Nooralahzadeh et al. [14] proposed a multi-stage generation approach (M^2TR P), where global image concepts were first extracted and then refined into detailed, coherent radiology reports using a transformer-based sequence-to-sequence model.

Liu et al. [9] introduced a contrastive attention (CA) model that enhances the representation of abnormal regions by leveraging contrastive mechanisms. Zeiser et al. [22] proposed CheXReport, a fully transformer-based encoder-decoder framework employing Swin Transformer blocks to improve the integration of visual and textual features. Nicolson et al. [13] investigated transfer learning by initialising the encoder with a Convolutional Vision Transformer (CvT) pre-trained on ImageNet-21K and the decoder with DistilGPT2, demonstrating effective performance gains. Sîrbu et al. [17] introduced GIT-CXR, an end-to-end transformer-based model for generating factually complete X-ray reports, incorporating curriculum learning to enhance model performance. Wang et al. [18] proposed a multimodal approach combining R2Gen and CvT2DistilGPT2 for automated chest X-ray report generation.

Building on these advancements, we propose a novel hybrid vision-language architecture for CXR report generation. Hybrid transformer architectures remain underexplored in this domain but have demonstrated effectiveness in various natural language processing tasks, including language modeling and machine translation. By leveraging a hybrid transformer for CXR report generation, we aim to capture complex relationships between CXR images and corresponding reports while mitigating issues such as hallucination.

3   Methodology

Our novel hybrid model, CheXSBT, employs a vision-language approach for automated radiology report generation. As shown in Fig. 2(a), the architecture comprises three key components: a Vision Encoder, a Language Encoder, and a Multimodal Fusion module. By utilising a hybrid transformer architecture—with our custom-designed Dual-Attention Swin Transformer (DAST) as the Vision Encoder and BERT as the Language Encoder—CheXSBT effectively extracts richer visual features and relationships from X-ray images, while enhancing the integration of these visual insights with textual elements.

3.1   Vision Encoder

The Vision Encoder in CheXSBT is based on the Swin Transformer [10], a state-of-the-art vision transformer architecture known for its efficiency in handling large-scale visual data. The Swin Transformer utilises a hierarchical structure with shifted windows to capture both local and global features in images [10]. Unlike traditional convolution-based models, it processes images using a patch-based approach with self-attention mechanisms, enabling better scalability and efficiency [3]. In our model, the Vision Encoder extracts high-level visual features from input chest X-ray images.

As illustrated in Fig. 2(b), we have custom-designed Dual-Attention Swin Transformer (DAST) to enhance feature extraction. Each block consists of two consecutive stages, where each stage includes a Window Multi-head Self-Attention (W-MSA) layer followed by a Shifted Window Multi-head Self-Attention (SW-MSA) layer. These attention mechanisms enable the model to capture both local and global dependencies by processing patches within fixed windows and then shifting those windows in subsequent layers.

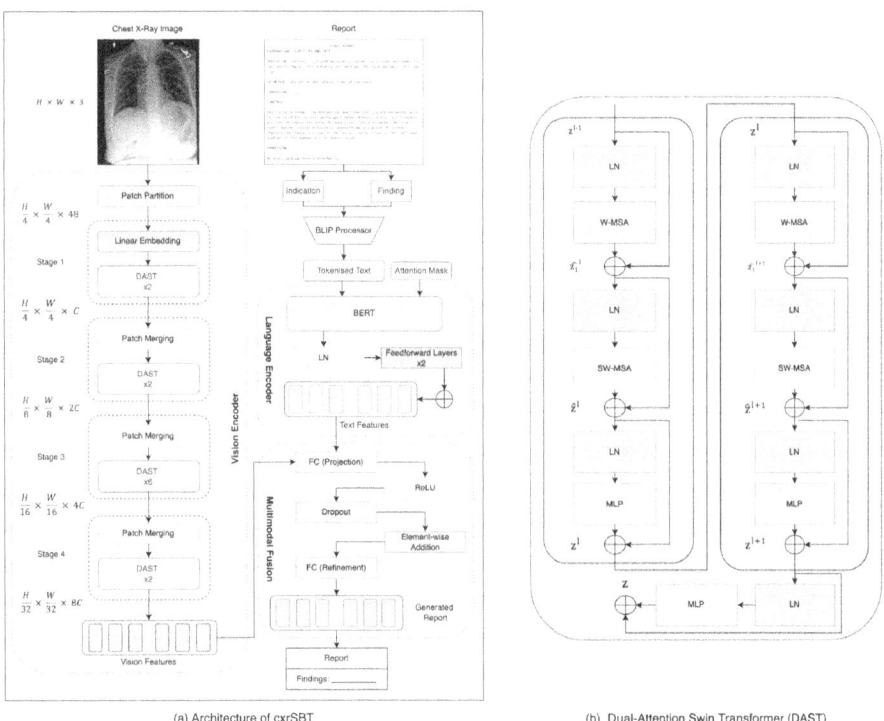

(a) Architecture of cxrSBT   (b) Dual-Attention Swin Transformer (DAST)

Fig. 2. (a) The detailed architecture of CheXSBT. (b) The custom-designed Dual-Attention Swin Transformer (DAST). Each block is formed by two sets of Window Multi-head Self-Attention (W–MSA) and Shifted Window Multi-head Self-Attention (SW–MSA) layers, three sets of Multi-Layer Perceptrons (MLP), and a set of Linear Normalisations (LN) before each attention and MLP operation.

The feature extraction process begins with Layer Normalisation (LN) applied before each attention operation. The output of W-MSA is computed as:

$$\hat{Z}_1^l = \text{W-MSA}(\text{LN}(Z^{l-1})) + Z^{l-1} \tag{1}$$

This is followed by the SW-MSA operation:

$$\hat{Z}^l = \text{SW-MSA}(\text{LN}(\hat{Z}_1^l)) + \hat{Z}_1^l \tag{2}$$

After the attention mechanisms, another Layer Normalisation (LN) layer is applied, followed by a Multi-Layer Perceptron (MLP) block, which refines the extracted features:

$$Z^l = \text{MLP}(\text{LN}(\hat{Z}^l)) + \hat{Z}^l \tag{3}$$

Each operation is also accompanied by a residual connection to maintain information flow. This entire process is repeated twice within a DAST Block to allow for deeper feature representation and we obtain the final equations:

$$\hat{Z}_1^{l+1} = \text{W-MSA}(\text{LN}(Z^l)) + Z^l \tag{4}$$

$$\hat{Z}^{l+1} = \text{SW-MSA}(\text{LN}(\hat{Z}_1^{l+1})) + \hat{Z}_1^{l+1} \tag{5}$$

$$Z^{l+1} = \text{MLP}(\text{LN}(\hat{Z}^{l+1})) + \hat{Z}^{l+1} \tag{6}$$

$$Z = \text{MLP}(\text{LN}(Z^{l+1})) + Z^{l+1} \tag{7}$$

The final output of the Vision Encoder is a set of embeddings representing crucial visual features of the input image:

$$V_f \in \mathbb{R}^{\frac{H}{32} \times \frac{W}{32} \times 8C} \tag{8}$$

These embeddings are subsequently utilised by the Multimodal Fusion component to generate radiology reports.

Comparison with Original Swin Transformer Blocks. The original Swin Transformer Blocks employ a standard W-MSA and SW-MSA sequence with Layer Normalisation and MLP layers. While effective, they maintain a relatively simple design in terms of feature extraction depth and computational complexity. In contrast, our custom DAST introduce an additional MLP block at the end and an enhanced attention mechanism configuration, which allows for deeper feature abstraction and improved learning capacity.

Another key difference is in the hierarchical depth and the number of attention heads used in our design. By adjusting these factors, our modified architecture is better tailored for the fine-grained and complex features present in medical imaging, particularly chest X-rays. Additionally, our implementation optimises gradient flow and convergence stability by refining the residual connections and Layer Normalisation placements, making it more robust for training on large-scale medical datasets.

3.2   Language Encoder

The Language Encoder in CheXSBT is based on BERT-based architecture, a well-established framework for natural language understanding and generation. BERT (Bidirectional Encoder Representations from Transformers) [2] utilises a transformer-based encoder to learn rich contextual representations by considering both left and right contexts of a given token. In our model, the Language Encoder is responsible for generating textual descriptions in conjunction with the visual features extracted by the Vision Encoder.

The language encoder processes two primary inputs: text features (i.e., textual embeddings from medical reports) and attention masks, which guide the model to focus on relevant portions of the text while ignoring padding tokens. The architecture consists of multiple layers of self-attention, feedforward neural networks, and residual connections, which collectively enable the model to learn robust textual representations. During training, the language encoder is optimised to predict the next token in the sequence using both textual and visual context, ensuring that the generated text remains clinically relevant and coherent.

Given a sequence of tokenised input text X_t, the encoder outputs contextualised embeddings:

$$T_f = \text{Encoder}(X_t) \in \mathbb{R}^{n \times d} \qquad (9)$$

where n is the number of tokens and d is the hidden dimension. These embeddings capture the semantic structure of the input text and are used for downstream fusion with visual features.

To improve generalisation and reduce overfitting, the language encoder incorporates layer normalisation, dropout, and feedforward layers. By fine-tuning the model on domain-specific radiology texts, the Language Encoder effectively aligns textual features with visual cues, supporting the generation of accurate and contextually meaningful radiology reports.

3.3   Multimodal Fusion

The Multimodal Fusion Network is central to integrating the visual and textual modalities in our framework. After extracting high-level visual features via the Vision Encoder and contextualised textual features via the Language Encoder, the fusion network combines these representations into a unified format suitable for report generation.

In our model, the Multimodal Fusion Network first projects both, the visual and textual embeddings into a shared representation space using a fully connected layer, followed by a ReLU activation and dropout for regularisation.

An element-wise addition is then applied to align the visual and textual information effectively. Although simple, this fusion method enables the model to leverage complementary cues from both modalities. The fused representation is then refined through another fully connected layer, consisting of linear projections followed by non-linear activation, to enhance the integration of multimodal information and produces the final output—the generated report.

Let $V_f \in \mathbb{R}^{\frac{H}{32} \times \frac{W}{32} \times 8C}$ be the vision features and $T_f \in \mathbb{R}^{n \times d}$ the text features, the fused representation is computed as:

$$M_f = V_f + T_f \tag{10}$$

where M_f represents the combined multimodal features, used to generate the final radiology report.

The Multimodal Fusion Network is designed to balance contributions from both modalities, ensuring that neither dominates the final prediction. By learning a joint representation space, the model effectively captures complex relationships between images and text, improving its ability to generate accurate and informative outputs in multimodal tasks.

4   Experiments

4.1   Dataset

Our study leverages the MIMIC-CXR [4–6] dataset for training, evaluating, and testing. The dataset is publicly available and contains 377,110 chest X-ray images corresponding to 227,835 radiographic studies performed at the Beth Israel Deaconess Medical Center in Boston, MA, USA. We have structured the dataset as a CSV file, which links image file paths to their corresponding reports. To facilitate training, we implement a custom dataset class that reads the CSV file, loads images from the specified directory, and applies necessary preprocessing steps. We used the MIMIC-CXR dataset's predefined split for training, validation and testing.

4.2   Data Preprocessing

To ensure compatibility with deep learning models, the preprocessing pipeline involves handling image preprocessing, text preprocessing, and data alignment.

Image Preprocessing. Chest X-ray images are resized to 224×224 pixels to maintain uniform input dimensions. Pixel intensity values are normalised using standard mean and deviation values to ensure stability in training. To improve model generalisation and robustness, data augmentation techniques such as random rotations, scaling, and contrast adjustments are applied.

Text Preprocessing. The Radiology reports undergo standardisation to reduce variability in medical terminology. Tokenisation is performed using the pre-trained BLIP [7] processor from Hugging Face, which converts text into structured sequences suitable for transformer-based models. Additionally, noise removal is applied to eliminate redundant or irrelevant information, ensuring high-quality textual inputs.

Data Alignment. The dataset undergoes verification to maintain correct image-text pairings, ensuring consistency between the chest X-ray images and their corresponding reports. Any missing or corrupted data entries are filtered out to maintain data integrity and improve training performance.

4.3   Implementation

Our model, CheXSBT, is trained on the MIMIC-CXR dataset to generate radiology reports from chest X-ray images. For the vision encoder, we use our custom-designed Dual-Attention Swin Transformer (DAST), while for the language encoder, we employ a BERT-based architecture.

For model optimisation, we employed the AdamW [11] optimiser with an initial learning rate of $1e^{-3}$ and a weight decay of $1e^{-3}$. A StepLR scheduler is applied to decrease the learning rate by 15% after each epoch, ensuring stable convergence. The model is trained with a batch size of 8, balancing computational feasibility and performance. We perform five runs of the model with same training, validation, and test splits to ensure consistency in results.

During training, we leverage a multi-GPU setup when available, which allows for more efficient processing of larger batches. The training loop involves feeding the model pre-processed chest X-ray images along with tokenised indication texts. Predictions are generated, and the loss is computed using the cross-entropy function. Validation is performed at the end of each epoch to track performance trends and adjust hyper parameters accordingly.

We trained CheXSBT on Aire HPC at the University of Leeds, which consists of 28 GPU nodes, each containing 3 NVIDIA L40S GPUs, offering a total of 84 GPUs. For our experiments, we used a single GPU node with 8 CPUs per task and 24 GB memory per CPU. Training each epoch required approximately 8 h. Our implementation was built using PyTorch, ensuring a robust and scalable framework for generating chest X-ray reports.

4.4   Evaluation Metrics

To quantitatively evaluate the performance of our model, we used several established Natural Language Generation (NLG) metrics such as BLEU (Bilingual Evaluation Understudy) [15], METEOR (Metric for Evaluating Translation with Explicit Ordering) [1], and ROUGE-L (Recall-Oriented Understudy for Gisting Evaluation - Longest Common Subsequence) [8].

5   Results and Discussion

In this section, we provide a comprehensive analysis of CheXSBT's performance. We begin with an ablation study to evaluate the impact of different architectural components on the model's performance. This is followed by a comparison with state-of-the-art models. Finally, we present a qualitative analysis, including both visual and textual comparisons, to showcase the model's capabilities in generating chest X-ray reports. This in-depth evaluation aims to validate the effectiveness of CheXSBT in producing accurate and informative chest X-ray reports.

5.1   Ablation Study

We conducted an ablation study to evaluate the performance of the model by utilising different architectural components. The study began with training a pre-trained BLIP model [7] from Hugging Face on the MIMIC-CXR dataset. We then evaluated the original Swin Transformer with BERT, followed by our custom-designed Dual-Attention Swin Transformer (DAST) integrated with BERT. All models are trained with a batch size of 8, balancing computational feasibility and performance. We perform five runs of the model with same training, validation, and test splits to ensure consistency in results, and the reported scores represent the mean ± standard deviation of all runs. Table 1 presents a summary of the scores achieved by the models across the evaluation metrics.

Table 1. Ablation study using different architectural components for CheXSBT on MIMIC-CXR dataset. To ensure consistency, the models were trained and tested five times using the same training, validation, and test splits, and the reported scores represent the mean ± standard deviation of all runs. Higher values in bold denote the best results in all columns.

Model	Pre-trained BLIP	Swin Transformer + BERT	CheXSBT DAST + BERT
BLEU 1	0.323 ± 0.12	0.408 ± 0.06	**0.502 ± 0.06**
BLEU 2	0.265 ± 0.10	0.319 ± 0.08	**0.397 ± 0.06**
BLEU 3	0.198 ± 0.13	0.256 ± 0.05	**0.306 ± 0.04**
BLEU 4	0.154 ± 0.08	0.198 ± 0.05	**0.232 ± 0.03**
ROUGE-L	0.257 ± 0.09	0.301 ± 0.07	**0.392 ± 0.06**
METEOR	0.166 ± 0.11	0.199 ± 0.09	**0.229 ± 0.03**

The results from the ablation study indicate that our model, CheXSBT with the custom-designed Dual-Attention Swin Transformer (DAST) integrated with BERT, outperforms the other models across all evaluation metrics. This suggests that our model is particularly effective at generating longer, more detailed captions that accurately capture the essence of the input image. The improved performance, as reflected in the higher scores across BLEU [15], ROUGE-L [8], and METEOR [1] metrics, demonstrates that the incorporation of DAST with BERT significantly enhances the quality of medical image captions.

5.2   Comparison with State-of-the-Art Models

We compare our CheXSBT with several other state-of-the-art models for generating chest X-ray reports on the MIMIC-CXR dataset, including Contrastive Attention (CA) [9], CheXReport [22], Convolutional Vision Transformer with the Distilled Generative Pre-trained Transformer 2 (CvT2DistilGPT2) [13], Meshed-Memory Transformer (M^2 TR P) [14], GIT-CXR (MV+C+CL) [17], Auxiliary Signal Guidance and Memory-Driven(ASGMD) [20] and Automated Generation of Accurate & Fluent Medical X-ray Reports with Multi-view (MV), w/ clinical text (T), and interpreter (I) (AGAFMXR (MV+T+I)) [12].

Table 2. Comparison with state-of-the-art models on MIMIC-CXR dataset. All metrics for the state-of-the-art models are directed cited from the original paper. Higher values in bold denote the best results in all columns. The Δ indicates that the model was trained and tested five times using the same training, validation, and test splits, and the reported scores represent the mean $\pm$ standard deviation of all runs.

Model	BLEU 1	BLEU 2	BLEU 3	BLEU 4	ROUGE-L	METEOR
CA [9]	0.350	0.219	0.152	0.109	0.283	0.151
CheXReport [22]	0.354	0.225	0.145	0.127	0.286	0.147
CvT2DistilGPT2 [13]	0.392	0.247	0.171	0.126	0.286	0.154
M^2 TR P [14]	0.378	0.232	0.154	0.107	0.272	0.145
GIT-CXR (MV+C+CL) [17]	0.403	0.286	0.215	0.168	–	**0.369**
ASGMD [20]	0.372	0.233	0.154	0.112	0.286	0.152
AGAFMXR (MV+T+I) [12]	0.495	0.360	0.278	0.224	0.390	0.222
CheXSBT DAST + BERT Δ	**0.502 ± 0.06**	**0.397 ± 0.06**	**0.306 ± 0.04**	**0.232 ± 0.03**	**0.392 ± 0.06**	0.229 ± 0.03

Table 2 presents the performance metrics reported by previous studies on the MIMIC-CXR dataset. The results demonstrate that CheXSBT achieves state-of-the-art performance across multiple metrics. Notably, CheXSBT outperforms existing models in BLEU-1 (0.502), BLEU-2 (0.397), BLEU-3 (0.306), BLEU-4 (0.232), and ROUGE (0.392), while also achieving competitive results in METEOR (0.229).

Despite its strong overall performance, CheXSBT exhibits slightly lower scores in METEOR compared to GIT-CXR (MV+C+CL) [17] (0.229 vs. 0.369). However, its superior performance in BLEU-4 and ROUGE suggests that

Table 3. Comparison of ground truth with the results generated by the original Swin Transformer with BERT and CheXSBT DAST with BERT models on randomly selected chest X-ray images from the MIMIC-CXR dataset. The first case demonstrates a strong alignment with the ground truth, while the second case fails to accurately replicate the reference report, highlighting the possible variability in model performance.

Chest X-ray Image	Ground Truth	Swin Transformer + BERT	CheXSBT DAST + BERT
INDICATION: ___ year old woman with lymphoma, no blood return from her port // port misplacement	The lungs are clear. The cardiomediastinal silhouette, hilar contours, pleural surfaces are normal. The tip of the right Port-A-Cath is in the upper SVC. No pneumothorax, pulmonary edema, pneumonia, or pleural effusions. Right tracheal deviation is due to enlargement of the left thyroid gland.	Lungs are clear with no signs of pneumothorax, pleural effusion, or pulmonary edema. The cardiomediastinal silhouette and hilar contours appear normal. The right Port-A-Cath tip is positioned in the upper SVC. Rightward tracheal deviation noted.	The lungs are clear with no evidence of pneumothorax, pleural effusion, pulmonary edema, or pneumonia. The cardiomediastinal silhouette, hilar contours, and pleural surfaces appear normal. The right Port-A-Cath tip is correctly positioned in the upper SVC. Mild rightward tracheal deviation is observed, likely due to an enlarged left thyroid gland.
INDICATION: ___ year old man with 2.5 week history of cough.	Lungs are well expanded and clear. No pleural effusion or pneumothorax. The cardiac and mediastinal silhouettes are unremarkable. Hilar contours are normal. No acute cardiopulmonary process.	The lung fields are underinflated with basal opacities. Moderate left-sided pneumothorax is suspected. Cardiomediastinal silhouette is distorted. Findings are concerning for possible pulmonary edema.	There is evidence of mild pulmonary infiltrates. A small right pleural effusion is present. The heart appears mildly enlarged. Prominent hilar markings are noted. These findings may indicate an early cardiopulmonary abnormality.

CheXSBT excels in generating longer, more coherent, and contextually rich reports. This capability is crucial in medical report generation, where detailed and accurate descriptions are paramount.

The ability of CheXSBT to generate longer, more informative reports makes it particularly well-suited for clinical applications, where clarity and comprehensiveness are critical. While some state-of-the-art models prioritise shorter, more structured outputs, CheXSBT's proficiency in capturing long-term dependencies through Transformer-based architectures aligns well with the requirements of medical documentation. Its effectiveness in aligning generated reports with ground truth radiological descriptions highlights its potential for real-world deployment in automated radiology report generation.

5.3   Qualitative Analysis

In Table 3, we present a qualitative comparison of results generated by the original Swin Transformer with BERT and our CheXSBT DAST with BERT models, using randomly selected chest X-ray images from the MIMIC-CXR dataset. For each image, we include the clinical indication provided to the model and compare the generated reports with the ground truth, which contain detailed findings from radiologists.

In the first case, the ground truth describes a patient with lymphoma and a port misplacement, with no signs of pneumothorax or other respiratory issues. Both models generate similar reports, differing slightly in phrasing but consistently identifying key features such as clear lungs, a normal cardiomediastinal silhouette, and proper Port-A-Cath placement. Our CheXSBT DAST with BERT model provides a more comprehensive description, particularly noting the mild rightward tracheal deviation likely caused by thyroid enlargement.

The second case represents a normal chest X-ray, with no pleural effusion, pneumothorax, or cardiopulmonary abnormalities. However, both models fail to replicate the ground truth accurately. Notably, the CheXSBT DAST with BERT model introduces hallucinated findings such as mild infiltrates and an enlarged cardiac silhouette—none of which are supported by the ground truth. Furthermore, the generated report lacks fluency and coherence, deviating significantly from the concise and factual style expected in clinical documentation.

Overall, our CheXSBT DAST with BERT model demonstrates the ability to produce accurate and fluent radiology reports in many cases, there are instances where the models either omit critical information or hallucinate pathological findings. These failure cases highlight the need for improved model grounding and finer control over clinical accuracy. In future work, we aim to address these limitations by incorporating pathology-aware training objectives and fine-grained error analysis frameworks.

6   Conclusion, Limitations and Future Work

In this paper, we introduced CheXSBT, a novel hybrid vision-language model that advances the automated generation of chest X-ray reports. By combining our custom-designed Dual-Attention Swin Transformer (DAST) for visual feature extraction with a BERT-based language encoder, CheXSBT provides a state-of-the-art solution that improves both the accuracy and clinical relevance of radiology reports. This integrated architecture enables the generation of coherent, contextually rich, and diagnostically meaningful text, facilitating effective communication in medical settings. Evaluated on the MIMIC-CXR dataset, CheXSBT demonstrates superior performance over existing models in key metrics such as BLEU and ROUGE, underscoring its capability to produce comprehensive and detailed reports.

Despite these promising results, our work has several limitations. First, we acknowledge the use of element-wise addition for multimodal fusion, which may oversimplify interactions between modalities. Future work will explore more sophisticated fusion strategies, such as cross-attention mechanisms. Second, while token-level metrics like BLEU and METEOR provide useful baselines, they do not fully capture the clinical correctness or contextual relevance of generated reports. We plan to adopt more advanced, semantics-aware metrics like BERTScore in future evaluations.

We also recognise the absence of pathology-specific evaluation in this study, which could provide deeper insights into clinical performance. Future iterations of CheXSBT will incorporate fine-grained, disease-specific assessments. Furthermore, although the MIMIC-CXR dataset is one of the largest and most widely used benchmark in this field—offering broad and diverse imaging data—we acknowledge the need for generalisation across datasets. We aim to extend our evaluation to other datasets such as CheXpert Plus to assess robustness and domain transferability.

Additionally, while CheXSBT shows potential for clinical integration, embedding the model within radiology workflows—such as integration with PACS systems via DICOM-SR interfaces—to support real-world deployment can be explored in the future.

In conclusion, CheXSBT represents a significant step forward in automated radiology report generation. With further methodological refinements, broader evaluation, and clinical integration, this approach holds strong potential to improve efficiency, consistency, and scalability in radiological practice.

Acknowledgments. This work was undertaken on the Aire HPC system at the University of Leeds, UK.

References

1. Banerjee, S., Lavie, A.: METEOR: an automatic metric for MT evaluation with improved correlation with human judgments. In: ACL Workshop on Intrinsic and Extrinsic Evaluation Measures for MT and/or Summarization, pp. 65–72 (2005)
2. Devlin, J., Chang, M.W., Lee, K., Toutanova, K.: BERT: pre-training of deep bidirectional transformers for language understanding. In: Proceedings of NAACL-HLT, pp. 4171–4186 (2019)
3. Dosovitskiy, A., Beyer, L., Kolesnikov, A., et al.: An image is worth 16×16 words: transformers for image recognition at scale. arXiv preprint arXiv:2010.11929 (2020)
4. Goldberger, A.L., et al.: PhysioBank, PhysioToolkit, and PhysioNet: components of a new research resource for complex physiologic signals. Circulation **101**(23), e215–e220 (2000)
5. Johnson, A., Pollard, T., Mark, R., Berkowitz, S., Horng, S.: MIMIC-CXR database (version 2.1.0). PhysioNet (2024). https://doi.org/10.13026/4jqj-jw95

6. Johnson, A.E., Pollard, T.J., Berkowitz, S.J., et al.: MIMIC-CXR, a de-identified publicly available database of chest radiographs with free-text reports. Sci. Data **6**, 317 (2019). https://doi.org/10.1038/s41597-019-0322-0

7. Li, J., Li, D., Xiong, C., Hoi, S.C.: BLIP: bootstrapping language-image pre-training for unified vision-language understanding and generation. In: International Conference on Machine Learning, pp. 12888–12900. PMLR (2022)

8. Lin, C.Y.: ROUGE: a package for automatic evaluation of summaries. In: Text Summarization Branches Out, pp. 74–81 (2004)

9. Liu, F., Yin, C., Wu, X., et al.: Contrastive attention for automatic chest X-ray report generation. arXiv preprint arXiv:2106.06965 (2021)

10. Liu, Z., et al.: Swin transformer: hierarchical vision transformer using shifted windows. In: Proceedings of the IEEE/CVF International Conference on Computer Vision, pp. 10012–10022 (2021)

11. Loshchilov, I., Hutter, F.: Decoupled weight decay regularization. arXiv preprint arXiv:1711.05101 (2017)

12. Nguyen, H.T., Nie, D., Badamdorj, T., et al.: Automated generation of accurate & fluent medical X-ray reports. arXiv preprint arXiv:2108.12126 (2021)

13. Nicolson, A., Dowling, J., Koopman, B.: Improving chest X-ray report generation by leveraging warm starting. Artif. Intell. Med. **144**, 102633 (2023)

14. Nooralahzadeh, F., Gonzalez, N.P., Frauenfelder, T., Fujimoto, K., Krauthammer, M.: Progressive transformer-based generation of radiology reports. arXiv preprint arXiv:2102.09777 (2021)

15. Papineni, K., Roukos, S., Ward, T., Zhu, W.J.: BLEU: a method for automatic evaluation of machine translation. In: Proceedings of the 40th Annual Meeting of the Association for Computational Linguistics, pp. 311–318 (2002)

16. Sanjeev, S., et al.: TiBiX: leveraging temporal information for bidirectional X-ray and report generation. In: MICCAI Workshop on Deep Generative Models, pp. 169–179. Springer (2024)

17. Sîrbu, I., Sîrbu, I.R., Bogojeska, J., Rebedea, T.: GIT-CXR: end-to-end transformer for chest X-ray report generation. arXiv preprint arXiv:2501.02598 (2025)

18. Wang, C., Janjic, V., McKenna, S.: Generating chest radiology report findings using a multimodal method. In: Yap, M.H., Kendrick, C., Behera, A., Cootes, T., Zwiggelaar, R. (eds.) Medical Image Understanding and Analysis. LNCS, vol. 14859, pp. 177–188. Springer, Cham (2024). https://doi.org/10.1007/978-3-031-66955-2_13

19. Windsor, R., Jamaludin, A., Kadir, T., Zisserman, A.: Vision-language modelling for radiological imaging and reports in the low data regime. arXiv preprint arXiv:2303.17644 (2023)

20. Xue, Y., Tan, Y., Tan, L., Qin, J., Xiang, X.: Generating radiology reports via auxiliary signal guidance and a memory-driven network. Expert Syst. Appl. **237**, 121260 (2024)

21. You, K., et al.: CXR-CLIP: toward large scale chest x-ray language-image pre-training. In: International Conference on Medical Image Computing and Computer-Assisted Intervention, pp. 101–111. Springer (2023)

22. Zeiser, F.A., da Costa, C.A., de Oliveira Ramos, G., Maier, A., da Rosa Righi, R.: CheXreport: a transformer-based architecture to generate chest x-ray reports suggestions. Expert Syst. Appl. **255**, 124644 (2024). https://doi.org/10.1016/j.eswa.2024.124644

Cardiac Ultrasound Video Generation Using a Diffusion Model with Temporal Transformer

Wenbin Wang$^{(\boxtimes)}$ and Ping Lu

School of Computing, University of Leeds, Leeds, UK
{cnml0744,p.lu}@leeds.ac.uk

Abstract. Cardiac ultrasound is widely used for the diagnosis and monitoring of cardiovascular diseases due to its noninvasive nature, real-time imaging capability, and low cost. However, its clinical utility is often limited by noise sensitivity and acquisition variability, which adversely affect automated interpretation and sequence consistency. To overcome these limitations, this paper presents a multimodal deep learning framework that combines a denoising diffusion model with a Temporal Transformer to generate high-quality cardiac ultrasound videos. A unified preprocessing pipeline with intensity normalisation and standardisation is employed to reduce intersample variation and enhance anatomical structures. Spatial features are first extracted from individual frames, followed by temporal modelling across sequences using the Temporal Transformer. These features guide the latent-space denoising process, optionally augmented by ControlNet for structure-aware generation. The experimental results demonstrate that the proposed method achieves robust performance, with an FID of 43.50, an FVD of 274.52, and an inception score of 8.62. Ablation studies further verify the critical contributions of ControlNet and composite loss design, highlighting the effectiveness of the framework in ensuring both spatial fidelity and temporal coherence.

Keywords: Cardiac Ultrasound · Diffusion Model · Temporal Transformer · ControlNet · Multimodal Generation

1 Introduction

Cardiac ultrasound plays a critical role in the clinical diagnosis and research of cardiovascular diseases due to its noninvasiveness, high resolution, and excellent contrast. However, current cardiac ultrasound acquisition often faces significant noise interference, unstable image quality, and data format variability caused by diverse medical equipment and imaging protocols, greatly restricting the efficiency and precision of subsequent clinical analyses [1]. Furthermore, traditional imaging techniques often lack effective control over frame-to-frame continuity when handling temporal sequence data, leading to temporal inconsistency that compromises the reliability of diagnostic results [2].

© The Author(s), under exclusive license to Springer Nature Switzerland AG 2026
S. Ali et al. (Eds.): MIUA 2025, LNCS 15916, pp. 174–186, 2026.
https://doi.org/10.1007/978-3-031-98688-8_13

In recent years, diffusion models, known for their powerful generative capabilities, have gradually been applied in medical imaging reconstruction and synthesis, outperforming traditional generative models such as Generative Adversarial Networks (GANs) in certain tasks [3]. Simultaneously, Transformers have become prominent in vision tasks due to their exceptional global information-capturing abilities, progressively replacing conventional Convolutional Neural Networks (CNNs) [4]. However, existing studies mostly concentrate on spatial feature extraction, rarely addressing precise temporal feature modelling, especially lacking joint spatial-temporal modelling tailored to the specific characteristics of medical imaging data.

To address the above issues, we first propose a deep learning framework combining diffusion models and temporal transformers. Through unified data preprocessing strategies with intensity normalisation and standardisation, noise suppression and key structural information extraction are effectively enhanced. Furthermore, a comprehensive loss function integrating the Structural Similarity Index Measure (SSIM), Temporal Mean Squared Error (Temporal MSE), which computes the mean squared difference between adjacent frames to reflect temporal consistency, is adopted as one of the loss components [34], and pixel-level error (L1) is designed to significantly enhance the temporal stability and image quality of cardiac ultrasound videos generated.

The primary innovative contributions of this paper are summarised as follows:

1. A flexible architecture is proposed, utilising a Temporal Transformer module to model temporal relationships in cardiac ultrasound sequences.
2. ControlNet is optionally integrated into the diffusion model, using original cardiac ultrasound images as structural guidance conditions to significantly enhance the structural fidelity of the generated images.
3. A comprehensive loss function based on SSIM, Temporal MSE, and L1 loss is designed to balance image quality and temporal continuity effectively.

2   Related Works

2.1   Overview of Medical Image Generation Techniques

In recent years, deep learning-based generative models have been widely applied to medical image reconstruction, enhancement, and synthesis. Among them, **Generative Adversarial Networks (GANs)** and **Variational Autoencoders (VAEs)** have emerged as two of the most prevalent frameworks. GANs are known for generating visually realistic images, whilst VAEs offer a principled latent space for data representation. However, both methods face limitations that hinder their broad adoption in clinical scenarios. GANs suffer from training instability and mode collapse, which often leads to the generation of limited or repetitive patterns [17]. VAEs, on the other hand, tend to produce blurry outputs due to the nature of their probabilistic reconstruction.

To address these issues, **Flow-based** and **Score-based** models have been proposed as alternatives. These methods offer advantages in terms of generation stability and likelihood estimation, enabling better modelling of complex medical data distributions [18]. Nevertheless, their adoption remains limited due to high computational demands and difficulty in scaling to high-resolution 3D medical data.

Recent work in multi-modal medical generation has also seen progress in report generation tasks. For example, a multinodal method for chest radiology report synthesis [28] leverages visual-textual alignment to generate semantically rich findings. While our framework focuses purely on visual generation, the concept of incorporating semantic priors into medical generative models remains a promising direction.

2.2 Diffusion Models and Their Applications in Medical Imaging

In recent years, **Transformer architectures** have garnered significant attention in the field of medical imaging, particularly in tasks that require modelling **long-range dependencies** and **temporal dynamics**. Unlike convolutional neural networks (CNNs), which are primarily effective at extracting local features, Transformers leverage self-attention mechanisms to capture **global contextual relationships**, making them especially suitable for modelling complex **temporal interactions**.

An increasing number of studies have explored the use of Transformers for **dynamic medical imaging**, such as cardiac ultrasound, cine MRI, and functional brain imaging, where data is represented as temporal sequences. For instance, some works introduce **temporal attention mechanisms** or stack frame-wise features across the time axis to learn organ motion patterns more effectively, leading to improved recognition of cardiac cycles and physiological rhythms [4,6,21].

However, most existing Transformer-based models are still designed with a **spatial modelling focus**, and **temporal continuity**—which is critical in medical image sequences—has not been adequately addressed. In particular, for generative tasks involving dynamic image synthesis, current approaches often fail to maintain **inter-frame structural consistency** and **motion coherence**, resulting in artefacts such as flickering, anatomical distortion, or loss of periodic motion. Therefore, designing Transformer modules that can **jointly capture spatial structures and temporal evolution** has become a critical challenge in the domain of dynamic medical image generation [22,23].

Recent studies have also explored counterfactual video generation as a means to model alternative outcomes or plausible trajectories. For instance, D'ARTAGNAN [31] proposes a generative architecture that conditions video synthesis on hypothetical interventions, demonstrating promising results in generating temporally coherent counterfactual sequences. While our method does not explicitly model causality, future extensions could integrate such mechanisms for interpretability in clinical contexts.

3   Method

3.1   Model Architecture and Feature Extraction

We propose *HeartDiffusionModel*, a modular deep generative framework tailored for cardiac ultrasound sequence generation. The model integrates transformer-based temporal encoding [6], diffusion-based generation in latent space [8], and a structure-aware ControlNet module [24]. The overall design aims to ensure both **spatial fidelity** and **temporal coherence**, two essential factors for clinical-quality video synthesis (Fig. 1).

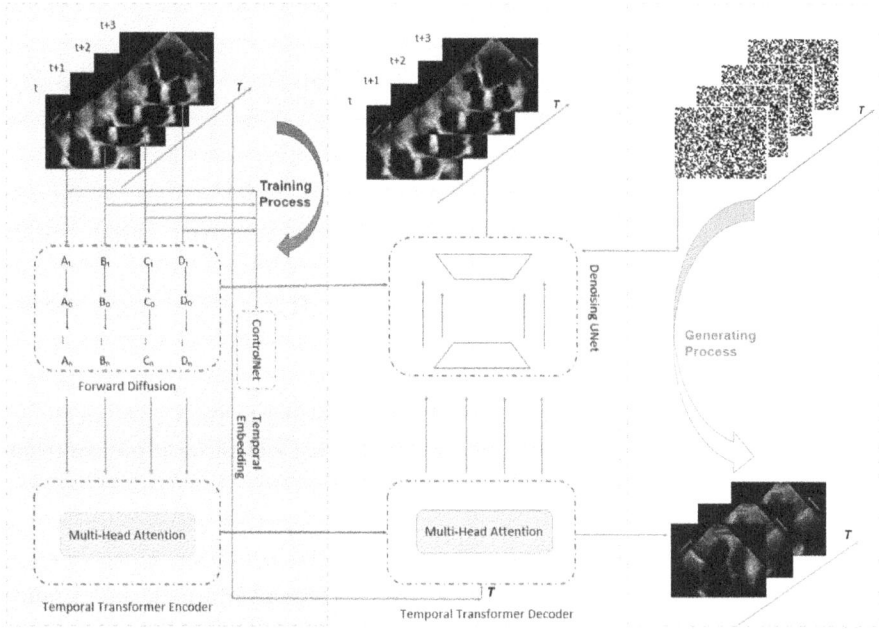

Fig. 1. Our model is structured as a modular architecture consisting of ControlNet, a Temporal Transformer, and a Diffusion model.

Temporal Feature Encoding. Given an input sequence of frames $x_i \in \mathbb{R}^{1 \times H \times W}$, a U-Net encoder is employed to extract spatial features f_i^{unet} for each frame. These features are then stacked along the temporal dimension to form a temporal feature sequence:

$$\mathbf{F}^{\text{unet}} = [\mathbf{f}_1^{\text{unet}}, \mathbf{f}_2^{\text{unet}}, \ldots, \mathbf{f}_T^{\text{unet}}] \in \mathbb{R}^{T \times C \times H' \times W'} \tag{1}$$

To capture long-range temporal dependencies, we adopt a **Temporal Transformer** [21], which operates along the time axis. With positional encoding and multi-head self-attention, the temporally enriched features are defined as:

$$\mathbf{F}^{\text{temp}} = \text{TemporalTransformer}(\mathbf{F}^{\text{cnn}} + \mathbf{E}_{\text{pos}}) \tag{2}$$

where $\mathbf{E}_{\text{pos}}$ denotes the learnable positional encoding. This module models long-range motion patterns in the cardiac cycle and improves rhythm consistency in the generated sequences.

Latent Diffusion and Feature Projection. The output features are projected to match the latent space of the diffusion backbone:

$$\mathbf{F}^{\text{proj}} = \mathbf{W}_{\text{proj}} \cdot \mathbf{F}^{\text{temp}} + \mathbf{b}_{\text{proj}} \tag{3}$$

A denoising diffusion probabilistic model (DDPM) [8] operates in latent space. Given the initial latent code $\mathbf{z}_0$, Gaussian noise is gradually added to generate corrupted latents $\mathbf{z}_t$:

$$\mathbf{z}_t = \sqrt{\alpha_t} \cdot \mathbf{z}_0 + \sqrt{1 - \alpha_t} \cdot \boldsymbol{\epsilon}, \quad \boldsymbol{\epsilon} \sim \mathcal{N}(0, \mathbf{I}) \tag{4}$$

The denoising network predicts the noise component:

$$\hat{\boldsymbol{\epsilon}} = \text{UNet}(\mathbf{z}_t, t, \mathbf{F}^{\text{proj}}, \mathbf{R}_{\text{down}}, \mathbf{R}_{\text{mid}}) \tag{5}$$

Structure Guidance via ControlNet. To enhance anatomical consistency, we integrate a ControlNet module [7] that runs parallel to the UNet backbone. Given the conditional input $\mathbf{x}$ and projected features, ControlNet produces residual conditions:

$$\{\mathbf{R}_{\text{down}}, \mathbf{R}_{\text{mid}}\} = \text{ControlNet}(\mathbf{z}_t, t, \mathbf{F}^{\text{proj}}, \mathbf{x}) \tag{6}$$

These residuals are injected into the UNet's corresponding blocks to guide structural generation, particularly effective for preserving cardiac anatomical features. The module is switchable for ablation studies.

3.2 Loss Function Design

To jointly optimise for spatial detail and temporal smoothness, we define a composite loss function [9,11,25]:

$$\mathcal{L}_{\text{total}} = \alpha \cdot \mathcal{L}_{\text{SSIM}} + \beta \cdot \mathcal{L}_{\text{Temporal}} + \gamma \cdot \mathcal{L}_{\text{L1}} \tag{7}$$

Structural Similarity Loss (SSIM): This loss promotes high-level structural similarity between the predicted and ground truth frames:

$$\mathcal{L}_{\text{SSIM}} = \frac{1}{B \cdot T} \sum_{b=1}^{B} \sum_{t=1}^{T} \left[\frac{1 - \text{SSIM}(\mathbf{X}_{b,t}, \hat{\mathbf{X}}_{b,t})}{2} \right] \tag{8}$$

Temporal Consistency Loss: To enforce smooth motion between frames:

$$\mathcal{L}_{\text{Temporal}} = \frac{1}{B \cdot (T-1)} \sum_{b=1}^{B} \sum_{t=1}^{T-1} \text{MSE}(\hat{\mathbf{X}}_{b,t}, \hat{\mathbf{X}}_{b,t+1}) \tag{9}$$

Pixel-wise L1 Loss: To maintain pixel-level fidelity:

$$\mathcal{L}_{\text{L1}} = \frac{1}{B \cdot T \cdot C \cdot H \cdot W} \sum_{b,t,c,h,w} \left| \mathbf{X}_{b,t,c,h,w} - \hat{\mathbf{X}}_{b,t,c,h,w} \right| \tag{10}$$

However, most existing studies primarily focus on **spatial aspects** of medical images, with limited attention to **temporal modelling**—a crucial factor in dynamic imaging modalities such as cardiac ultrasound or cine MRI. Moreover, whilst diffusion models offer strong performance in static image generation, their adaptation to **temporal consistency** and **sequence-level coherence** remains an open research challenge.

4   Experiments

4.1   Data Acquisition

We conducted our experiments on the publicly available EchoNet-Dynamic dataset provided by Stanford University [5]. The EchoNet-Dynamic dataset consists of 10,030 echocardiographic videos collected from patients undergoing echocardiography examinations. Each video captures cardiac cycles and includes important cardiac function metrics such as ejection fraction (EF), which are crucial to assessing cardiac functionality. To evaluate the performance of the proposed model, we randomly selected 1,500 frames from the EchoNet-Dynamic dataset. These frames were split into training, validation, and testing sets(8:1:1). This dataset has also been extended in EchoNet-Synthetic [27], which demonstrates the value of privacy-preserving video generation for secure and ethical sharing of medical imaging data.

4.2   Setup

Training: The experiments were conducted using four H20-NVLink GPUs, each equipped with 20 cores and 96 GB memory. During training, distributed data parallelism was employed to efficiently utilise computational resources and reduce training time. To investigate the contribution of each key component in our proposed architecture, we conducted comprehensive ablation studies by selectively removing individual modules, including the Temporal Transformer, ControlNet, MISS loss, and Temporal loss.

Table 1. Configurations of model variants for ablation studies

Model Configuration	Temporal Transformer	ControlNet	MISS Loss	Temporal Loss
Ours (full components)	✓	✓	✓	✓
w/o Temporal Transformer	×	✓	✓	✓
w/o ControlNet	✓	×	✓	✓
w/o MISS Loss	✓	✓	×	✓
w/o Temporal Loss	✓	✓	✓	×

Note: Each ablation variant (denoted as "w/o", short for "without") removes one core component from the baseline model to evaluate its unique contribution to spatial fidelity and temporal coherence in the generated ultrasound sequences.

4.3   Comparative Study Design

Ablation Study Design. Five model variants were created by removing key modules from the full architecture to isolate the effects of each component. Table 1 details these variants:

All configurations were trained under the same conditions and assessed using the same metrics to ensure reproducible comparisons. Each variant was trained for 200 epochs with early stopping based on validation performance, keeping learning rate (1e−5), batch size, and optimiser settings consistent across experiments.

Comparison with Representative Models. We further validated our approach by comparing it against another widely known video generation models:

– **TATS (Temporally-Aware Token Synthesis)** [29]: A Transformer-driven video generation technique that synthesises frame tokens in an autoregressive manner whilst modelling temporal features explicitly. Its progressive generation process is comparable to ours in its ability to recover structured video content from noise.

We implemented these baselines following their official specifications, adapting only the minimum domain-specific elements for cardiac ultrasound data. All models were trained under identical computational constraints for impartial evaluation.

4.4   Evaluation Metrics

To quantitatively assess the quality and fidelity of our generated videos, we employ three well-established metrics that evaluate both perceptual quality and statistical similarity:

– **FID (Fréchet Inception Distance)** [12]:

$$\text{FID} = \|\mu_r - \mu_g\|^2 + \text{Tr}\left(\Sigma_r + \Sigma_g - 2\left(\Sigma_r \Sigma_g\right)^{1/2}\right), \tag{11}$$

where μ_r, μ_g and Σ_r, Σ_g represent the mean and covariance matrices of real and generated image feature distributions, respectively. FID measures the distributional similarity between real and generated images through feature representations extracted from InceptionV3 network.

- **FVD (Fréchet Video Distance)** [13]: An extension of FID to the video domain that captures temporal dynamics by utilising features from a pre-trained 3D convolutional network. FVD is defined analogously to FID but operates on spatio-temporal features:

$$\text{FVD} = \|\mu_r^v - \mu_g^v\|^2 + \text{Tr}\left(\Sigma_r^v + \Sigma_g^v - 2\left(\Sigma_r^v \Sigma_g^v\right)^{1/2}\right), \tag{12}$$

where the superscript v indicates features extracted from video sequences.

- **IS (Inception Score)** [16]:

$$\text{IS} = \exp\left(\mathbb{E}_x\left[D_{KL}(p(y|x)\|p(y))\right]\right), \tag{13}$$

where $p(y|x)$ represents the conditional class distribution for a generated sample x as predicted by the Inception model, and $p(y)$ is the marginal class distribution. IS jointly quantises quality and diversity by measuring how distinctive and recognisable the generated samples are.

For all metrics, we calculate the scores across multiple samples to ensure robust evaluation. Lower FID and FVD values indicate better quality and temporal consistency, with values closer to zero representing perfect alignment with the real data distribution. Conversely, higher IS values signify improved quality and diversity. Through this complementary set of metrics, we comprehensively evaluate both the spatial fidelity and temporal coherence of our generated cardiac ultrasound sequences.

5   Results

5.1   Quantitative Results

Table 2. Quantitative comparison of the proposed method, its ablation variants, and TATS on ultrasound video generation.

Model Configuration	FID↓	FVD ↓	IS↑
TATS	41.40	**174.30**	7.06
w/o Temporal Transformer	**41.30**	–	5.32
w/o ControlNet	72.26	310.72	5.29
w/o MISS Loss	53.32	297.20	6.62
w/o Temporal Loss	48.10	291.74	7.78
Ours (Full Model)	43.50	274.52	**8.62**

As shown in Table 2, we conduct a comprehensive comparison between the proposed full model, its ablation variants, and the TATS baseline. While TATS achieves the best FID (41.40) and FVD (174.30), indicating strong image-level fidelity and temporal coherence, it lags behind in perceptual quality, with an IS score of 7.06. In contrast, our full model achieves the highest IS (8.62), suggesting superior perceptual sharpness and diversity, while maintaining competitive FID (43.50) and FVD (274.52), which reflects a good balance between spatial quality and temporal consistency.

Among the ablation variants, removing the ControlNet module leads to the most significant performance degradation, with FID and FVD increasing to 72.26 and 310.72 respectively, and IS dropping to 5.29. This underscores the importance of ControlNet in preserving spatial structures during generation. The MISS loss also plays a key role, as its removal causes FID to rise to 53.32 and FVD to 297.20, indicating a loss of fine-grained anatomical consistency.

Interestingly, removing the Temporal Loss results in the highest IS score (7.78), yet degrades FVD to 291.74, suggesting a trade-off where improved perceptual clarity comes at the cost of motion coherence. The variant without the Temporal Transformer yields the lowest FID (41.30), outperforming TATS in this metric. However, it lacks FVD evaluation due to unstable video generation, indicating compromised temporal modeling despite strong spatial accuracy.

Overall, our full model delivers a robust and well-rounded performance, effectively integrating spatial fidelity, perceptual realism, and temporal coherence, validating the superiority of our proposed architecture for high-quality cardiac ultrasound video synthesis.

5.2   Representative Examples

(See Fig. 2).

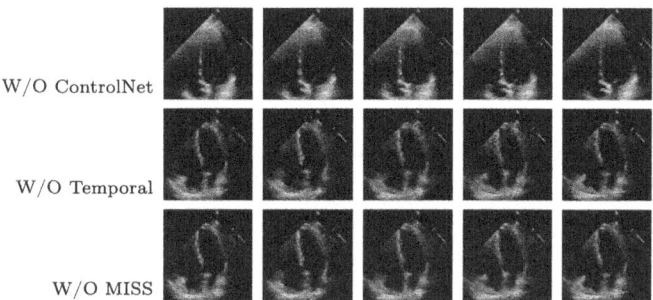

Fig. 2. Qualitative comparison of five internal frames for ablation model variants. Frames are sampled at every 12-frame interval from the generated videos.

5.3 Discussion

The experimental findings underscore the effectiveness of our proposed model in generating high-quality cardiac ultrasound sequences that preserve both spatial fidelity and temporal consistency. Compared to the TATS baseline [29], our model achieves a higher Inception Score, indicating enhanced perceptual realism and diversity, while maintaining competitive FID and FVD metrics. This performance highlights the advantage of combining diffusion-based generation [3,8] with dedicated temporal modeling (Fig. 3).

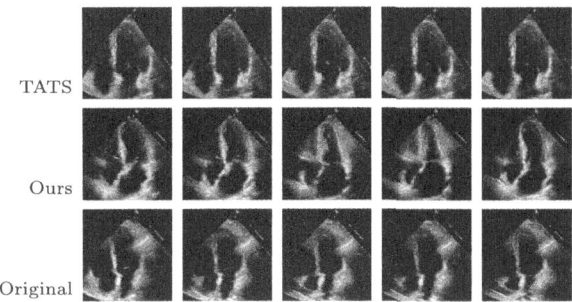

Fig. 3. Qualitative comparison of five consecutive frames generated by TATS and our proposed model, alongside the corresponding ground truth (Original). The frames are uniformly sampled every 12 frames from each video sequence.

Ablation experiments further validate the significance of individual modules. The removal of ControlNet leads to severe degradation across all metrics, confirming its role in preserving anatomical structure. Likewise, the MISS Loss contributes to multi-scale structural consistency, and its absence results in decreased spatial fidelity. Interestingly, eliminating the Temporal Loss yields sharper individual frames (higher IS), but leads to unstable motion patterns, emphasizing the trade-off between perceptual quality and temporal coherence.

Despite its demonstrated robustness, the proposed model exhibits limitations in accurately capturing fine-grained cardiac motion and managing noisy real-world ultrasound inputs. In future work, we will explore more advanced spatio-temporal architectures, including the incorporation of recurrent units such as LSTM [30] or GRU, to better model long-term temporal dependencies. Moreover, adaptive attention mechanisms and context-aware diffusion control strategies may further enhance generation fidelity in clinically complex scenarios. In addition, we plan to extend our evaluation across multiple datasets such as the CAMUS [32] and EchoNet-LVH datasets [33]—to improve the generalizability and reliability of the results under diverse imaging protocols and patient populations. As a potential clinical application, we also intend to incorporate ejection fraction (EF) estimation as a downstream task, enabling quantitative assessment of cardiac function from the generated ultrasound sequences.

6   Conclusion

In this work, we present a novel multimodal framework for cardiac ultrasound video generation by integrating diffusion models [3,8] with temporal transformers. The architecture leverages ControlNet for spatial conditioning, MISS Loss for structural consistency, and a Temporal Loss for maintaining motion coherence. A unified preprocessing pipeline also ensures normalization across highly variable ultrasound inputs.

Quantitative experiments on the EchoNet-Dynamic dataset [5] and qualitative comparisons with the TATS model [29] demonstrate that our approach generates perceptually realistic and temporally smooth sequences. Ablation results confirm that each component contributes meaningfully to the overall performance, particularly in balancing visual quality and anatomical correctness.

In the future, we aim to explore LSTM-based temporal modeling [30] and spatio-temporal attention mechanisms to further improve long-range motion continuity and fine detail reconstruction. These improvements could enhance the utility of generative models in clinical simulation, diagnostic support, and privacy-preserving data augmentation.

References

1. Bernard, O., et al.: Deep learning techniques for automatic MRI cardiac multi-structures segmentation and diagnosis: is the problem solved? IEEE Trans. Med. Imaging **37**(11), 2514–2525 (2018)
2. Qin, C., et al.: Convolutional recurrent neural networks for dynamic MR image reconstruction. IEEE Trans. Med. Imaging **38**(1), 280–290 (2018)
3. Wolleb, J., et al.: Diffusion models for medical anomaly detection. In: International Conference on Medical Image Computing and Computer-Assisted Intervention, pp. 35–45 (2022)
4. Chen, J., et al.: TransUNet: transformers make strong encoders for medical image segmentation. arXiv preprint arXiv:2102.04306 (2021)
5. Ouyang, D., et al.: Video-based AI for beat-to-beat assessment of cardiac function. Nature **580**(7802), 252–256 (2020)
6. Vaswani, A., et al.: Attention is all you need. In: Advances in Neural Information Processing Systems, pp. 5998–6008 (2017)
7. Zhang, L., et al.: Adding conditional control to text-to-image diffusion models. In: Proceedings of the of ICCV, pp. 18436–18446 (2023)
8. Ho, J., Jain, A., Abbeel, P.: Denoising diffusion probabilistic models. In: Advances in Neural Information Processing Systems, vol. 33, pp. 6840–6851 (2020)
9. Wang, Z., Bovik, A.C., Sheikh, H.R., Simoncelli, E.P.: Image quality assessment: from error visibility to structural similarity. IEEE Trans. Image Process. **13**(4), 600–612 (2004)
10. Huang, M., et al.: Learning temporal coherence via self-supervision for GAN-based video generation. ACM Trans. Graph. (TOG) **39**(4), 1–12 (2020)
11. Zhao, H., Gallo, O., Frosio, I., Kautz, J.: Loss functions for image restoration with neural networks. IEEE Trans. Comput. Imaging **3**(1), 47–57 (2016)

12. Heusel, M., Ramsauer, H., Unterthiner, T., Nessler, B., Hochreiter, S.: GANs trained by a two time-scale update rule converge to a local Nash equilibrium. In: Advances in Neural Information Processing Systems, pp. 6626–6637 (2017)
13. Unterthiner, T., et al.: FVD: A new metric for video generation. In: ICLR Workshop on Deep Generative Models for Highly Structured Data (2019)
14. Voleti, V., et al.: MCVD: masked conditional video diffusion for prediction, generation, and interpolation. arXiv preprint arXiv:2205.09853 (2022)
15. Ge, S., et al.: Long video generation with time-agnostic VQGAN and time-sensitive Transformer. In: European Conference on Computer Vision, pp. 370–386. Springer (2022)
16. Salimans, T., Goodfellow, I., Zaremba, W., Cheung, V., Radford, A., Chen, X.: Improved techniques for training GANs. In: Advances in Neural Information Processing Systems, pp. 2234–2242 (2016)
17. Yi, X., Walia, E., Babyn, P.: Generative adversarial network in medical imaging: a review. Med. Image Anal. **58**, 101552 (2019)
18. Song, Y., Ermon, S.: Generative modelling by estimating gradients of the data distribution. In: Advances in Neural Information Processing Systems (NeurIPS) (2019)
19. Wolleb, J., Van Gool, L., & Lüthi, M.: Diffusion models for medical image analysis: a comprehensive survey. arXiv preprint arXiv:2211.07804 (2022)
20. Vaswani, A., et al.: Attention is all you need. In: Advances in Neural Information Processing Systems, vol. 30 (2017)
21. Arnab, A., Dehghani, M., Heigold, G., Sun, C., Lučić, M., Schmid, C.: ViViT: a video vision transformer. In: Proceedings of the IEEE/CVF International Conference on Computer Vision (ICCV), pp. 6836–6846 (2021)
22. Yan, K., Wang, C., Yu, H., Liang, D.: Neural motion fields for dynamic MRI reconstruction. IEEE Trans. Med. Imaging **42**(2), 427–438 (2023)
23. Shi, X., et al.: Video diffusion models. arXiv preprint arXiv:2204.03458 (2022)
24. Zhang, L., Chen, H., Zhang, J., et al.: Adding conditional control to text-to-image diffusion models. In: CVPR 2023, pp. 14065–14075 (2023)
25. Huang, Y., Wu, W., et al.: Learning of temporal consistency for video super-resolution. IEEE Trans. Image Process. **29**, 9140–9153 (2020)
26. Author(s). D'ARTAGNAN: counterfactual video generation. Proceedings of [Conference Name] (2023)
27. Author(s). EchoNet-synthetic: privacy-preserving video generation for safe medical data sharing. In: Proceedings of [Conference Name] (2023)
28. Author(s). Generating chest radiology report findings using a multinodal method. Journal or Conference (2023)
29. Ge, Y., Dai, B., Wu, J., Torralba, A., Freeman, W. T., Liu, C.: Long-term video synthesis with time-agnostic VQGAN and time-aware transformer. In: Advances in Neural Information Processing Systems (NeurIPS) (2022)
30. Hochreiter, S., Schmidhuber, J.: Long short-term memory. Neural Comput. **9**(8), 1735–1780 (1997)
31. Yuan L., et al.: D'ARTAGNAN: counterfactual video generation with latent diffusion. In: Proceedings of the IEEE/CVF International Conference on Computer Vision (ICCV), pp. 20187–20197 (2023)
32. Leclerc, S., Smistad, E., Pedrosa, J., Ostvik, A., et al.: Deep learning for segmentation using an open large-scale dataset in 2D echocardiography. IEEE Trans. Med. Imaging **38**(9), 2198–2210 (2019). https://doi.org/10.1109/TMI.2019.2900516

33. Hannun, A.Y., Rajpurkar, P., Saeed, M.S.M., et al.: A large-scale benchmark for automated cardiac view classification and disease detection. In: NeurIPS 2019 Machine Learning for Health Workshop (2019). https://echonet.github.io/dataset/download.html
34. Villegas, R., Yang, J., Hong, S., Lin, X., Lee, H.: Decomposing motion and content for natural video sequence prediction. In: International Conference on Learning Representations (ICLR) (2017)

KCLVA: Knowledge-Enhanced Contrastive Learning and View-Specific Attention for Chest X-Ray Report Generation

Jinlong Zhu[✉] and Ping Lu

University of Leeds, Leeds LS2 9JT, UK
{bfbs2497,p.lu}@leeds.ac.uk

Abstract. In clinical scenarios, radiologists analyse multiple chest X-ray (CXR) images from various view positions to identify diseases and abnormalities. To replicate the diagnostic approach of experienced radiologists, we propose an encoder-decoder-based CXR report generation architecture, KCLVA, which leverages the Unified Medical Language System (UMLS) to extract view-specific information from diagnostic reports, focusing on posteroanterior, anteroposterior, and lateral views. This extracted information facilitates view-specific attention (VA) mechanisms and is subsequently used to construct a similarity matrix that enables many-to-many contrastive learning. In the encoder, we employ a knowledge distillation architecture to guide the learning of the student model by freezing the teacher model. Within the student text encoder, the VA mechanism is utilised to automatically assign higher weights to tokens corresponding to a specific view in diagnostic reports based on the view position of the CXR, while assigning lower weights to other tokens. The image and text features are then integrated using contrastive learning. In the decoder, a transformer-based backbone architecture is employed to decode the encoder output and generate a medical diagnosis report. This strategy leverages UMLS to extract view-specific information, employs VA to adjust token weights, and utilises many-to-many contrastive learning through a weighted contrastive loss. Together, these components enable our model to closely simulate the diagnostic process of professional radiologists. Consequently, our method achieves significant improvements of 0.185 on METEOR and 0.078 on ROUGE compared to previous approaches.

Keywords: Chest X-ray Report Generation · Contrastive Learning · Knowledge Distillation · Unified Medical Language System · View-specific Attention

1 Introduction

Chest X-ray (CXR) images are extensively utilised in medical practice, with approximately 500,000 images requested by physicians annually in the Netherlands alone [29]. While CXR images effectively reflect chest conditions, physicians require substantial expertise to accurately identify abnormalities and produce diagnostic reports. To alleviate this burden on physicians, automated radiology report generation systems aim to generate reports directly from radiographs. Current research primarily focuses on multimodal learning approaches, including contrastive learning [13,16,26,36,40], multi-view CXR images fusion [10,12,22,37,42], and knowledge enhancement strategies [5,17,24,41].

In clinical practice, as abnormalities often occupy only a small portion of each radiograph, physicians must systematically analyse multi-view CXR images—including posteroanterior (PA), anteroposterior (AP), and lateral (LTA) views—to develop effective treatment plans. Our proposed KCLVA model emulates this approach through an encoder-decoder architecture designed to learn from paired view-specific reports and radiographs.

Each sample in standard CXR datasets, such as IU-Xray [8] and MIMIC-CXR [11], typically contains one report associated with multiple CXR images from different view, each conveying distinct information. However, the report for each sample provides a comprehensive summary of multiple images, without assigning individual diagnoses to each image. To address this limitation, we extract view-specific medical terms from reports prior to training and align them with corresponding radiographs using view-specific attention (VA). These terms are then utilised to construct a similarity matrix via text similarity calculations.

Given the specialised nature of medical terminology, we incorporate the Unified Medical Language System (UMLS) [4] to enhance both the quantity and accuracy of extracted medical terms. Our model employs knowledge distillation to learn from pre-trained clinical encoders, with the VA automatically assigning higher weights to view-specific terms in reports. To address the many-to-many relationship between images and reports in CXR datasets [33], we utilise many-to-many contrastive learning for modality fusion. Our contributions include:

- We are the first to propose a novel architecture that utilises the Unified Medical Language System to extract medical terms from original reports as view-specific guided terms, leveraging these terms to construct a similarity matrix. This architecture can be applied to other datasets with multi-view X-ray images, provided that each patient is associated with a single report.
- We are the first to introduce the view-specific attention mechanism, which directs the model to assign weights to words based on extracted medical terms in diagnostic reports. This novel approach enables models to learn more effectively by emphasising view-specific terms in diagnostic reports.
- We propose a many-to-many contrastive learning objective function, weighted contrastive loss, which consists of structured matched loss and soft contrastive loss. As demonstrated by our experiments, the many-to-many contrastive learning approach enhances model performance effectively.

2   Related Work

Multi-view Chest X-Ray Report Generation. Multi-view CXR report generation has emerged as a significant research area with promising results.

Zhu & Feng [42] introduced MVC-Net, which employs separate networks for different radiograph views and an additional network for feature fusion. However, their model could not adaptively adjust to the varying importance of pathologies across views. Rubin et al. [27] trained separate CNN models for different view positions but achieved limited success. Yang et al. [37] proposed a multi-view encoder for AP and LTA X-rays that leveraged complementary information but focused solely on image-level fusion.

While these approaches have advanced multi-view CXR analysis, they primarily emphasise image-level fusion without addressing text-level alignment between images and reports. The critical connection between specific views and their corresponding textual descriptions remains largely unexplored.

Chest X-Ray Report Generation with Contrastive Learning. Since CLIP [26] demonstrated the effectiveness of contrastive learning for multi-modal tasks, this approach has become central to CXR report generation. Yan et al. [36] developed a weakly supervised contrastive loss that identified and weighted hard negative samples. Yang et al. [38] proposed triplet sample construction with double contrast learning across modalities. Liu et al. [16] introduced aggregate and differential attention mechanisms to extract distinguishing information by contrasting input images with normal ones.

While these approaches show promise, they primarily address one-to-one or one-to-many relationships between images and text. However, they fail to capture the many-to-many relationships inherent in CXR images and reports.

Chest X-Ray Report Generation with Knowledge Enhancement. The specialised nature of medical diagnosis has made knowledge enhancement highly effective for CXR report generation. Liu et al. [17] integrated multiple knowledge sources and developed Case-Based and Disease-Based Retrieval mechanisms. Prabhakar et al. [24] were the first to employ UMLS for zero-shot CXR classification. Zhang et al. [41] extracted medical entities using heuristic rules, RadGraph, and ChatGPT to guide visual representation learning.

Despite these advancements, existing approaches have not fully utilised established medical knowledge bases, either relying on limited knowledge sources or applying comprehensive bases to more narrowly defined tasks than report generation.

3   Method

We present the technical details of KCLVA, following the workflow illustrated in Fig. 1. KCLVA consists of the following components: (1) a medical view-specific term extractor that identifies view-specific medical terms and constructs a similarity matrix, (2) view-specific attention, which assigns weights to words based on the extracted view-specific terms of each radiograph, (3) vision and text encoders, comprising both student and teacher encoders, (4) a decoder that integrates image and text features to generate captions for each radiograph, and (5) objective functions employed to optimise the model. The architectural details are illustrated in Fig. 1b.

3.1 Medical View-Specific Terms Extractor

Medical View-Specific Terms Extraction. The proposed medical view-specific terms extractor module employs a multi-layered approach to extract view-specific medical terms from radiology reports, enabling precise alignment between CXR images and their corresponding textual descriptions. This component is essential to the KCLVA architecture, as it establishes the foundation for view-specific attention (VA) and many-to-many contrastive learning.

Our extraction methodology integrates natural language processing (NLP) with specialised medical knowledge to identify terms relevant to different radiographic views. The extraction process follows a comprehensive pipeline:

(1) Text Preprocessing: The module begins with text preprocessing to normalise the input, including case conversion, removal of redundant spaces, and correction of common abbreviations and spelling variations. This step enhances the accuracy of subsequent NLP tasks.
(2) Term Identification: A medical-domain-specific spaCy model (`en_core_sci_scibert` [19]), enhanced with custom term rules, is used to identify basic medical terms. Dependency syntax analysis is then applied to extract complete medical phrases, capturing relationships between anatomical structures and their associated findings.
(3) Pattern Matching: Regular expression pattern matching is employed to identify standardised medical expressions and complex medical phrases specific to chest radiology, such as cardiomediastinal descriptions.
(4) Negation Context Analysis: Specialised processors handle the nuanced nature of medical language by accurately identifying and representing negated findings (e.g., "no pleural effusion"). Status descriptions of anatomical structures and complex negation structures (e.g., "no X, Y, or Z") are also processed to ensure comprehensive term capture.
(5) Integration with Unified Medical Language System: A critical feature of the extractor is its integration with the UMLS knowledge base, which provides external medical knowledge for term validation and classification. UMLS enables the verification of extracted terms' medical relevance, expansion of terminology through related concepts, classification of terms based on semantic types, and view-specific filtering to identify terms particularly relevant to AP, PA, or LTA views.

Similarity Matrix Construction. After extraction, post-processing steps such as term normalisation, deduplication, conflict resolution, and filtering are performed to ensure that the extracted terms accurately represent radiographic findings. The extracted view-specific medical terms are subsequently utilised to

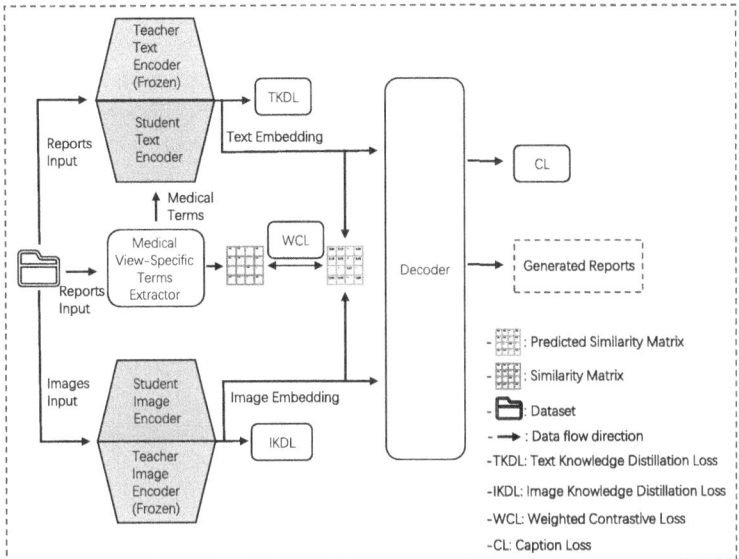

(a) An overview of the proposed KCLVA workflow.

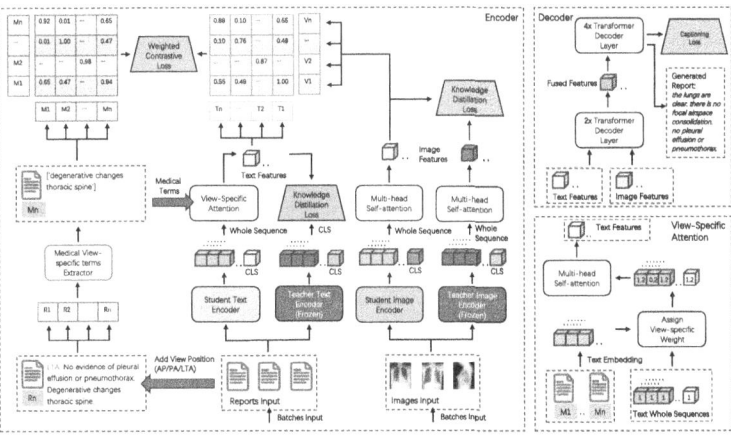

(b) An overview of KCLVA detailed architecture.

Fig. 1. The proposed KCLVA architecture consists of: (a) an overview of the KCLVA workflow and (b) the detailed KCLVA architecture. This multi-modal architecture employs a dual-encoder structure comprising frozen teacher encoders and trainable student encoders for both textual and visual pathways. The medical view-specific terms extractor identifies medical terms from input reports and constructs a similarity matrix. The architecture leverages multiple loss functions: text knowledge distillation loss (TKDL) and image knowledge distillation loss (IKDL) to transfer knowledge from teacher to student models, weighted contrastive loss (WCL) to establish many-to-many relationships between radiographs and reports, and caption loss (CL) to optimise report generation. The decoder employs a fusion layer (2x cross-modal transformer layers) to amalgamate these multi-modal representations, which are subsequently processed by 4x transformer decoder layers [30] to generate comprehensive medical reports that maintain clinical accuracy while capturing relevant visual findings.

construct a similarity matrix that quantifies the relationships between different radiographs and their textual descriptions.

The extracted medical terms are mapped to their corresponding UMLS Concept Unique Identifiers (CUIs) by considering semantic types, source vocabularies, and context-aware similarity calculations to ensure precise term matching. Using the mapped CUIs, semantic similarity between terms is computed by accounting for direct relationships such as synonyms, parent-child, and sibling relationships within the UMLS semantic type hierarchy. Furthermore, adjustments are applied to account for negation contexts and term types. The similarity scores are then used to construct a matrix where rows and columns represent terms from different CXR views. The matrix values reflect the degree of semantic similarity between each pair of terms, as represented by the following equation:

$$\text{Similarity Matrix} = \begin{bmatrix} sim(e_{11}, e_{12}) & \cdots & sim(e_{11}, e_{1n}) \\ \vdots & \ddots & \vdots \\ sim(e_{m1}, e_{12}) & \cdots & sim(e_{1m}, e_{1n}) \end{bmatrix} \quad (1)$$

where, e_{ij} represents the j-th term from the i-th CXR view, and $sim(e_{ij}, e_{kl})$ denotes the semantic similarity between term e_{ij} and term e_{kl}.

The similarity matrix is further refined by applying view-specific filtering, ensuring that only terms relevant to the specific CXR view are considered in the similarity calculations. This refinement enhances the alignment between CXR images and their associated textual descriptions.

This approach addresses a fundamental challenge in CXR datasets, where multiple images from different views are frequently associated with a single report. By extracting view-specific medical terms, fine-grained connections are established between individual radiographs and their corresponding textual descriptions, enabling more precise image-text alignment. The similarity matrix derived from these extracted terms serves as the foundation of our many-to-many contrastive learning approach, facilitating the identification of potential positive samples and the definition of appropriate margins for negative samples.

3.2 View-Specific Attention

The View-specific Attention (VA) within the KCLVA architecture is designed to dynamically allocate attention weights to medical terms in radiology reports based on their relevance to specific CXR views. This mechanism is essential for improving the alignment between images and textual descriptions by focusing on view-specific information while simultaneously considering the global context of the report.

The first step involves tokenisation and position tracking. The module tokenises the reports and medical terms, tracking token positions to ensure accurate attention distribution. Let T represent the set of all tokens in the report, and S denote the set of view-specific medical terms: $T = \{t_1, t_2, \ldots, t_n\}$, $S = \{s_1, s_2, \ldots, s_m\}$, where n is the total number of tokens, and m is the number of medical terms.

The next step is the computation of attention weights. A relevance mask is calculated for each token t_i in the report, assigning higher weights to tokens within medical terms that correlate with the current CXR view. Tokens outside these terms receive lower but non-zero weights, enabling the model to capture the global context:

$$\text{Relevance Mask}(t_i) = \begin{cases} 1.0, & \text{if } t_i \in S_{\text{view-specific}} \\ \lambda, & \text{otherwise} \end{cases} \tag{2}$$

where λ is a learnable parameter representing the base weight for tokens outside the view-specific sentences.

Terms identified as medically significant (e.g., derived from UMLS) are assigned an additional weight boost to emphasise their importance:

$$\text{Medical Term Weight}(t_i) = \mu \times \text{Relevance Mask}(t_i) \tag{3}$$

where μ is a learnable parameter that enhances the weight of medical terms.

The module computes self-attention scores among tokens, adjusting these scores based on the relevance masks and medical term weights:

$$A = \text{softmax}\left(\frac{QK^T}{\sqrt{d_k}} \odot M\right) \tag{4}$$

where, Q, K, and V are the query, key, and value matrices derived from the input tokens, d_k is the dimension of the key vectors, and M is the matrix of attention weights derived from the relevance mask:

$$M = \text{diag}(\text{Relevance Mask}(t_1), \ldots, \text{Relevance Mask}(t_n)) \tag{5}$$

The attention weights are then applied to the value matrix:

$$\text{Attention}(Q, K, V) = AV \tag{6}$$

3.3   Vision and Text Encoder

The proposed KCLVA architecture comprises a student image encoder, a student text encoder, a teacher image encoder, and a teacher text encoder.

Vision Encoder. The vision encoder in KCLVA employs a dual-architecture architecture comprising teacher and student image encoders to facilitate efficient knowledge transfer in radiographic image processing. The encoder first transforms input images $I \in \mathbb{R}^{B \times C \times W \times H}$ through the teacher or student encoder preprocessor E_{pre} to obtain V_0. Subsequently, the images are encoded using the teacher or student vision encoder E_{img} to produce CLS_V and P_V. To leverage both global and local information, we implement an attention refinement mechanism E_{Att}, which combines the CLS token (global representation) and patch tokens (local features) to generate V_1. Finally, a projection head maps the refined embeddings into a normalised embedding space to produce V:

$$V_0 = E_{pre}(I) \tag{7}$$
$$CLS_V, P_V = E_{img}(V_0) \tag{8}$$
$$V_1 = E_{Att}(CLS_V, P_V) \tag{9}$$
$$V = f_{pv}(V_1) \tag{10}$$

where, $CLS_V \in \mathbb{R}^{B \times 1 \times d_{hidden}}$ and $P_V \in \mathbb{R}^{B \times (N-1) \times d_{hidden}}$, while f_{pv} denotes the projection head.

Text Encoder. The Text Encoder in KCLVA employs a dual-architecture architecture comprising teacher and student text encoders. It is further enhanced by a VA mechanism to optimise the representation of radiological reports. The encoder processes input text tokens $T_0 \in \mathbb{R}^{B \times L}$ with an attention mask $M \in \mathbb{R}^{B \times L}$ through the following sequential pipeline:

$$T_1 = E_{text}(T_0, M) \tag{11}$$
$$CLS_T, P_T = E_{VA}(T_1) \tag{12}$$
$$T = f_{pt}(P_T) \tag{13}$$

where, E_{text} represents either the teacher or student text encoder, producing hidden representations $T_1 \in \mathbb{R}^{B \times L \times d_{hidden}}$. E_{VA} denotes the VA module, $P_T \in \mathbb{R}^{B \times d_{hidden}}$ represents the weighted average representation, and $CLS_T \in \mathbb{R}^{B \times d_{hidden}}$ corresponds to the CLS token representation. f_{pt} denotes the projection head.

3.4   Decoder

The Decoder in KCLVA employs a transformer-based architecture to generate radiological reports and align visual and textual representations. The decoder module processes the encoded features and generates text in an autoregressive manner:

$$L = D(V, T, T_{in}, M, \alpha_1) \tag{14}$$

where, D denotes the decoder function, T is normalised text embeddings, T_{in} represents the input token IDs, M is the attention mask, α_1 is the training phase parameter, and L corresponds to the output logits.

3.5   Objective Functions

Weighted Contrastive Loss. The weighted contrastive loss (WCL) in KCLVA is designed to address the many-to-many relationships inherent in medical image-text pairs. Unlike conventional contrastive learning, which treats each image-text pair as strictly positive or negative, our approach integrates a structured matching loss and a soft contrastive loss to more effectively capture the nuanced relationships between radiological images and reports.

The structured matching loss measures the alignment between normalised prediction logits and the ground truth similarity matrix:

$$L_{str} = \frac{1}{B^2} \sum_{i=1}^{B} \sum_{j=1}^{B} w_{ij} \cdot \left(\sigma(4 \cdot V_i \cdot T_j^T - S_{ij} \cdot \gamma_1 - \delta_{ij} \cdot (1 - \gamma_1)) \right)^2 \qquad (15)$$

where, B is the batch size, V_i and T_j are normalised image and text embeddings, σ is the sigmoid function, S_{ij} is the similarity matrix value, γ_1 is a reliability factor, δ_{ij} is the Kronecker delta function (1 for $i = j$, 0 otherwise), and w_{ij} are dynamic weights with enhanced diagonal values based on similarity:

$$w_{ij} = \begin{cases} 1 + \lambda_{diag} \cdot S_{ii}, & \text{if } i = j \\ 1, & \text{otherwise} \end{cases} \qquad (16)$$

The soft contrastive loss extends traditional contrastive learning to handle many-to-many relationships:

$$L_{soft} = \frac{1}{2B}(L_{i2t} + L_{t2i}) \qquad (17)$$

where, L_{i2t} and L_{t2i} represent the image-to-text and text-to-image directional losses:

$$L_{i2t} = \alpha_1 \cdot L_{i2t}^{pos} + \beta_1 \cdot L_{i2t}^{neg} \qquad (18)$$
$$L_{t2i} = \alpha_1 \cdot L_{t2i}^{pos} + \beta_1 \cdot L_{t2i}^{neg} \qquad (19)$$

The positive and negative components are defined as:

$$L_{i2t}^{pos} = \sum_{i=1}^{B} \frac{1}{n_i^{pos}} \sum_{j=1}^{B} -\frac{(V_i \cdot T_j^T)}{\text{Temp}_i} \cdot \mathbb{K}[S_{ij} > \theta] \qquad (20)$$

$$L_{i2t}^{neg} = \sum_{i=1}^{B} \frac{1}{n_i^{neg}} \sum_{j=1}^{B} \max\left(0, \frac{(V_i \cdot T_j^T)}{\text{Temp}_i} + m_{ij} \right) \cdot \mathbb{K}[S_{ij} < \theta] \qquad (21)$$

where, θ is the similarity threshold, n_i^{pos} and n_i^{neg} are the number of positive and negative samples for the i-th image, Temp_i is an adaptive temperature parameter, and m_{ij} is a dynamic margin:

$$m_{ij} = m_{base} + \gamma_1 \cdot (1 - S_{ij}) \cdot \mathbb{K}[S_{ij} < \theta] \qquad (22)$$

The adaptive temperature Temp_i is computed based on the contrast between positive and negative similarities:

$$\text{Temp}_i = \text{Temp}_{base} \cdot (1 - 0.3 \cdot \max(0, S_i^{pos} - S_i^{neg})) \qquad (23)$$

where, S_i^{pos} and S_i^{neg} are the mean similarities of positive and negative samples for the i-th image, Temp_{base} is the initial temperature parameter.

The overall weighted contrastive loss is formulated as:

$$L_{total}^{WCL} = \alpha_2 \cdot L_{str} + \beta_2 \cdot L_{soft} \tag{24}$$

where, α_2 and β_2 are dynamic weights that adjust based on training progress, with α_2 decreasing from 0.6 to 0.2 and β_2 increasing from 0.4 to 0.8 as training progresses.

Knowledge Distillation Loss. Our knowledge distillation architecture employs a comprehensive loss function to facilitate effective knowledge transfer while preserving the semantic relationships essential for medical image-text alignment. The architecture combines cosine similarity loss, Kullback-Leibler (KL) divergence loss, and mean squared error (MSE) loss.

The cosine similarity loss preserves the directional alignment between student and teacher embeddings:

$$L_{mod}^{cos} = \frac{1}{B} \sum_{i=1}^{B} \left(1 - \cos\left(\hat{z}_i^{(mod,S)}, \hat{z}_i^{(mod,T)}\right)\right) \tag{25}$$

where, $\hat{z}_i$ represents the normalised feature vectors. S and T separately represents student vectors and teacher vertors.

The KL divergence loss ensures that the student model learns the distributional characteristics of the teacher embeddings:

$$L_{mod}^{KL} = \tau^2 \cdot D_{KL}\left(p_\tau\left(z^{(mod,S)}\right) \| p_\tau\left(z^{(mod,T)}\right)\right) \tag{26}$$

where, τ is the temperature parameter (default: 2.0), and p_τ represents the softmax-normalised feature distributions.

Additionally, the MSE loss is computed between raw feature vectors to capture absolute differences:

$$L_{mod}^{MSE} = \frac{1}{BD} \sum_{i=1}^{B} \left\| \hat{z}_i^{(mod,S)} - \hat{z}_i^{(mod,T)} \right\|_2^2 \tag{27}$$

The overall knowledge distillation loss is formulated as:

$$L_{total}^{KD} = \alpha_3 \cdot L_{mod}^{MSE} + \beta_3 \cdot L_{mod}^{KL} + \gamma_3 \cdot L_{mod}^{cos} \tag{28}$$

where, α_3, β_3 and γ_3 are weighted parameters (0.33, 0.33, 0.34).

Caption Loss. The caption loss in the proposed KCLVA is designed to optimise the generation of radiological reports by training the decoder to predict the next token in the sequence, given the preceding tokens and the aligned image-text features. This loss is computed using teacher forcing and a cross-entropy objective. The caption loss is defined as:

$$L_{caption} = -\frac{1}{N} \sum_{i=1}^{N} \sum_{t=1}^{T} m_{i,t} \cdot \log p \left(y_{i,t} \mid y_{i,<t}, z_i^{img}, z_i^{txt} \right) \qquad (29)$$

where, N is the batch size, T is the sequence length, $y_{i,t}$ is the ground truth token at position t for sample i, $\log p \left(y_{i,t} \mid y_{i,<t}, z_i^{img}, z_i^{txt} \right)$ is the predicted probability of the token $y_{i,t}$ conditioned on all previous tokens $y_{i,<t}$, the image features z_i^{img}, and the text features z_i^{txt}. Additionally, $m_{i,t}$ is the attention mask value, which is 1 if the token is valid and 0 if it is padding.

To implement teacher forcing, the predicted logits are shifted by one position relative to the ground truth labels. Specifically:

$$\text{logits}_{i,t} = \text{decoder} \left(y_{i,<t}, z_i^{img}, z_i^{txt} \right) \qquad (30)$$

Here, the predicted logits are shifted to exclude the last token:

$$y_{i,t} = \text{labels}_{i,t+1} \qquad (31)$$

Similarly, the ground truth labels are shifted to exclude the first token.

Total Loss. Total loss is the combination of caption loss, knowledge distillation loss and caption loss:

$$L_{total} = \alpha_4 \cdot L_{total}^{KD} + \beta_4 \cdot L_{total}^{WCL} + \gamma_4 \cdot L_{caption} \qquad (32)$$

where, α_4, β_4 and γ_4 are weighted parameters (0.5, 0.5, 1.0).

4   Experiment

4.1   Dataset

In our experiments, we utilised the widely used benchmark dataset, Indiana University Chest X-ray Collection (IU-Xray), for evaluation. The IU-Xray dataset comprises 7,470 chest X-ray images and 3,955 radiology reports. Each report is divided into three sections: 'Indication', 'Findings', and 'Impression'.

The 'Indication' section details symptoms (e.g., hypoxia) or reasons for the examination (e.g., age); the 'Findings' section lists radiological observations; and the 'Impression' section outlines the final diagnosis. Ideally, a system should generate the 'Findings' and 'Impression' sections, potentially linking them to provide a cohesive diagnostic report. Following previous work [1,6,7,9,15,25,32,35,39], we split the dataset into training, validation, and test sets in a 7:1:2 ratio to ensure a fair comparison.

4.2   Experimental Settings

Data Preprocessing. Our data preprocessing primarily focuses on text preprocessing, while image preprocessing is managed by the processors of pre-trained image encoders. Specifically, images are resized to 224×224 pixels to standardise input dimensions.

The text preprocessing pipeline for medical reports consists of several sequential steps designed to standardise and normalise the textual data while preserving critical medical information. First, the system employs a comprehensive medical abbreviation dictionary to expand common medical acronyms and abbreviations (e.g., "ct", "copd", "ecg") into their complete forms. Simultaneously, it ensures that the capitalisation of specific medical terms (e.g., "COVID", "COPD") is retained.

Next, the preprocessing workflow applies a series of text cleaning operations. These include the removal of non-medical punctuation using regex patterns, elimination of redundant characters, and normalisation of whitespace and punctuation marks. Privacy-related placeholders (e.g., "XXXX") are systematically removed to ensure compliance with data privacy regulations. Additionally, the text undergoes case normalisation while preserving the integrity of domain-specific terminology. Finally, the process concludes with sentence-level formatting to ensure proper punctuation and maintain semantic coherence.

Implementation Details. For the student encoder, we use "vit-base-patch16-224-in21k" [34] as the image encoder and "distilbert-base-uncased" [28] as the text encoder. For the teacher encoder, we select "rad-dino" [23] as the image encoder and "Bio_ClinicalBERT" [2] as the text encoder. The teacher encoder remains frozen during training.

The view-specific attention mechanism is based on multi-head attention, consisting of a single layer with four heads. The output of the student image encoder is processed using one multi-head attention layer, also configured with four heads. For the decoder, we employ two cross-modal transformer layers to fuse the image and text features, followed by four transformer decoder layers for decoding.

The training setup includes a learning rate of 1e-4 with cosine decay, a batch size of 80, a contrastive learning temperature of 0.07, and a knowledge distillation temperature of 2.0. The model is trained for 40 epochs, on the University of Leeds HPC system Aire, using 1 NVIDIA L40S GPU for approximately 5 h. Additionally, we extract medical terms and construct the similarity matrix, on the University of Leeds HPC system Aire, using 1 NVIDIA L40S GPU and 16×3G CPU cores, which takes approximately 5 h.

Evaluation Metrics. Following the standard evaluation paradigm, we employ the widely-used metrics BLEU [21], METEOR [3], ROUGE-L [14], and CIDEr [31] to assess the quality of generated diagnostic reports.

BLEU evaluates n-gram overlap between the generated and reference texts, capturing precision at different granularities, which is critical for ensuring accurate medical terminology. METEOR complements BLEU by accounting for synonyms, stemming, and word order, providing a more nuanced evaluation of linguistic variations common in medical reports. ROUGE-L emphasises recall by focusing on the longest common subsequence, ensuring that the generated text retains the essential content of the reference. CIDEr, designed for consensus-based evaluation, measures the similarity of the generated text to multiple references using TF-IDF weighting. This makes CIDEr particularly effective for assessing the relevance and informativeness of medical reports.

4.3   Results and Discussion

Result. The comparison results are presented in Table 1. Several baseline methods are complex and, in some cases, not open source. Due to limitations in time and computational resources, we were unable to perform multiple runs for these baselines. Therefore, our comparisons are based on single-run results. Our proposed KCLVA architecture demonstrates superior performance across several evaluation metrics. Specifically, KCLVA achieves the highest BLEU-1 (0.511), BLEU-2 (0.345), BLEU-3 (0.246), METEOR (0.432), and ROUGE-L (0.462) scores, surpassing all other methods in these categories. These results underscore the model's ability to generate captions with improved semantic alignment and greater phrase overlap with the ground truth, producing clinically meaningful and coherent reports. Although KCLVA achieves competitive performance on BLEU-4 (0.173), it is marginally lower than MRCL (0.180), indicating scope for improvement in capturing finer-grained n-gram overlaps. Furthermore, the CIDEr score of KCLVA (0.303) exceeds that of most methods but is lower than METransformer (0.435) and AMLMA (0.381). This suggests that while KCLVA excels in semantic and structural alignment, there is potential to further enhance its ability to capture consensus information across multiple reference reports.

Table 1. Result of comparison on IU-Xray. Comparison results are from test set and the best performance is indicated in bold. * indicates the results are quoted from their published literatures.

Model	BLEU-1	BLEU-2	BLEU-3	BLEU-4	METEOR	ROUGE	CIDEr
$R2Gen^*$ [7]	0.470	0.304	0.219	0.165	0.187	0.371	-
$R2GenCMN^*$ [6]	0.475	0.309	0.222	0.170	0.191	0.375	-
$CMCL^*$ [15]	0.473	0.305	0.217	0.162	0.186	0.378	-
$CDGPT2^*$ [1]	0.387	0.245	0.166	0.111	0.164	0.289	0.257
$AlignTransformer^*$ [39]	0.484	0.313	0.225	0.173	0.204	0.379	-
$QinandSong^*$ [25]	0.494	0.321	0.235	0.109	0.201	0.384	-
$AMLMA^*$ [9]	0.471	0.315	0.231	0.172	0.247	0.376	0.381
$MRCL^*$ [35]	0.458	0.324	0.238	**0.180**	0.206	0.369	0.287
$METransformer^*$ [32]	0.483	0.322	0.228	0.172	0.192	0.380	**0.435**
Ours(KCLVA)	**0.511**	**0.345**	**0.246**	0.173	**0.432**	**0.462**	0.303

Figure 2 presents a comparison between the generated reports and the reference reports. Two examples, including one AP view and one LTA view, are showcased. Similar words between generated reports and reference reports are highlighted in green text, demonstrating the system's ability to generate clinically relevant observations that align closely with the reference reports

Discussion. Although our KCLVA model demonstrates promising performance on standard metrics, several limitations remain. The reliability and scalability of the knowledge base are critical—if the knowledge base is insufficient, accurate extraction of medical terms becomes challenging and may introduce noise into the training process. The model's performance is closely tied to the quality of UMLS term extraction, a process that is not only time-consuming—requiring up to 5 h for preprocessing on the IU-Xray dataset—but also prone to instability and inaccuracy, particularly in the absence of sufficient clinical guidance. Additionally, the model may focus excessively on view-specific diagnoses while neglecting the global context. Furthermore, the model is constrained by long-tail data distributions in the dataset, resulting in reduced accuracy when generating reports for rare or uncommon pathologies. In such cases, it often defaults to descriptions associated with more prevalent conditions, reflecting a tendency toward majority class bias when confronted with unusual presentations.

To address these challenges, future work could focus on enhancing the reliability and scalability of the knowledge base, as well as improving medical term extraction through closer collaboration with medical experts and optimizing both UMLS search and similarity computation. Specifically, to mitigate the impact of long-tail data distributions—such as the overrepresentation of normal conditions like "no pleural effusions" and "lungs are clear" in the dataset compared to rarer conditions—incorporating explicit medical knowledge graphs may enhance the model's reasoning about rare conditions. Such approaches could help balance

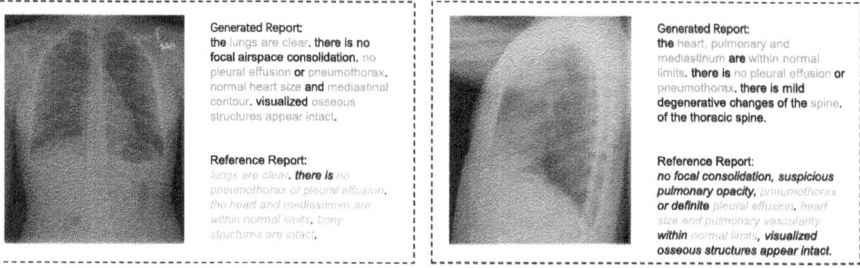

Fig. 2. Two examples of the generated reports and their comparison with reference reports for chest X-ray images. The figure shows one anteroposterior case (the left image) and one lateral case (the right image), each containing a chest X-ray image with its corresponding AI-generated report (top) and the radiologist's reference report (bottom). The color coding (dark green for generated reports and light green for reference reports) highlights the similar words between the AI-generated report and the radiologists' report.

the training environment and improve the model's ability to generate accurate reports for both common and uncommon pathologies.

4.4 Ablation Study

We conducted an ablation study to evaluate the effectiveness of VA and the WCL by replacing the WCL with one-to-one Noise Contrastive Estimation (InfoNCE) [20] loss and adding or removing the VA. Notably, the VA is always utilised in conjunction with the UMLS-based term extractor. The extractor is not employed when VA is omitted. In this study, each architecture is trained five times [18] to validate the effect of the proposed WCL and VA, using the same split of training, validation, and test datasets. The results are presented in Table 2.

The results demonstrate that the combination of WCL and VA achieves the best performance across all metrics, with significant improvements in BLEU-4, METEOR, ROUGE, and CIDEr scores, underscoring their complementary benefits. When comparing WCL with InfoNCE, WCL+VA consistently outperforms InfoNCE+VA across all evaluation criteria, reaffirming the advantages of WCL in multimodal learning tasks. However, without VA integration, the performance gap between WCL and InfoNCE narrows, with WCL-VA showing only modest improvements over InfoNCE-VA in most metrics. This suggests that the benefits of WCL are amplified when paired with attention mechanisms.

Interestingly, InfoNCE-VA slightly outperforms InfoNCE+VA on several metrics (BLEU-1, BLEU-2, and METEOR), indicating potential challenges in integrating InfoNCE with VA effectively. This highlights the importance of designing loss functions tailored to structured attention mechanisms. In contrast, WCL demonstrates consistent improvements when combined with VA, validating that many-to-many relationship learning provides significant advantages over traditional one-to-one contrastive approaches in multimodal contexts.

Table 2. Ablation Study Results. "-VA" indicates that VA is not used, "+VA" indicates that VA is utilised, "InfoNCE" refers to replacing the WCL with InfoNCE, and "WCL" denotes the use of the proposed WCL. The best performance is indicated in bold. Each evaluation metrics is composed of "five-time result average ± five-time result standard deviation", representing the range of evaluation metrics.

Model	BLEU-1	BLEU-2	BLEU-3	BLEU-4	METEOR	ROUGE	CIDEr
InfoNCE-VA	0.455	0.285	0.195	0.137	0.387	0.405	0.258
	±0.024	±0.017	±0.013	±0.011	±0.019	±0.003	±0.021
InfoNCE+VA	0.460	0.286	0.196	0.138	0.392	0.406	0.244
	±0.008	±0.012	±0.012	±0.010	±0.012	±0.012	±0.024
WCL-VA	0.462	0.288	0.196	0.139	0.398	0.401	0.268
	±0.009	±0.004	±0.002	±0.002	±0.015	±0.011	±0.050
WCL+VA	**0.487**	**0.315**	**0.219**	**0.153**	**0.418**	**0.429**	**0.278**
	±0.022	**±0.022**	**±0.018**	**±0.013**	**±0.012**	**±0.020**	**±0.042**

The results further emphasize the robustness of WCL+VA in achieving best performance.

5   Conclusions

In this paper, we propose a novel encoder-decoder-based architecture, KCLVA, for chest X-ray (CXR) report generation. By leveraging UMLS, view-specific attention, and a weighted contrastive loss, our model effectively aligns multiview CXR images with their corresponding diagnostic reports. The proposed architecture emulates the diagnostic process of radiologists by focusing on view-specific features while preserving the global context. Experimental results on the IU-Xray dataset demonstrate the effectiveness of the KCLVA architecture. Nonetheless, KCLVA is constrained by the long-tail distribution and its reliance on the medical knowledge base, as it is highly dependent on the time-consuming process of term extraction and the construction of the similarity matrix. To address these issues, we plan to construct a more scalable knowledge resource and collaborate with radiologists to supervise preprocessing. Additionally, we aim to optimize preprocessing to enhance scalability. For future work, we plan to further assess the generalizability of our model by evaluating it on larger and more diverse datasets, such as MIMIC-CXR.

References

1. Alfarghaly, O., Khaled, R., Elkorany, A., Helal, M., Fahmy, A.: Automated radiology report generation using conditioned transformers. Inform. Med. Unlocked **24**, 100557 (2021)
2. Alsentzer, E., et al.: Publicly available clinical BERT embeddings. arXiv preprint arXiv:1904.03323 (2019)
3. Banerjee, S., Lavie, A.: Meteor: an automatic metric for MT evaluation with improved correlation with human judgments. In: Proceedings of the ACL Workshop on Intrinsic and Extrinsic Evaluation Measures for Machine Translation and/or Summarization, pp. 65–72 (2005)
4. Bodenreider, O.: The unified medical language system (UMLS): integrating biomedical terminology. Nucleic Acids Res. **32**(suppl_1), D267–D270 (2004)
5. Cao, W., et al.: Bootstrapping chest CT image understanding by distilling knowledge from X-ray expert models. In: Proceedings of the IEEE/CVF Conference on Computer Vision and Pattern Recognition, pp. 11238–11247 (2024)
6. Chen, Z., Shen, Y., Song, Y., Wan, X.: Cross-modal memory networks for radiology report generation. arXiv preprint arXiv:2204.13258 (2022)
7. Chen, Z., Song, Y., Chang, T.H., Wan, X.: Generating radiology reports via memory-driven transformer. arXiv preprint arXiv:2010.16056 (2020)
8. Demner-Fushman, D., et al.: Preparing a collection of radiology examinations for distribution and retrieval. J. Am. Med. Inform. Assoc. **23**(2), 304–310 (2016)
9. Gajbhiye, G.O., Nandedkar, A.V., Faye, I.: Translating medical image to radiological report: adaptive multilevel multi-attention approach. Comput. Methods Programs Biomed. **221**, 106853 (2022)

10. Hosseinzadeh, H.: Deep multi-view feature learning for detecting Covid-19 based on chest X-ray images. Biomed. Signal Process. Control **75**, 103595 (2022)
11. Johnson, A.E., et al.: MIMIC-CXR, a de-identified publicly available database of chest radiographs with free-text reports. Sci. Data **6**(1), 317 (2019)
12. Kim, D.: Chexfusion: effective fusion of multi-view features using transformers for long-tailed chest X-ray classification. In: Proceedings of the IEEE/CVF International Conference on Computer Vision, pp. 2702–2710 (2023)
13. Li, M., Lin, B., Chen, Z., Lin, H., Liang, X., Chang, X.: Dynamic graph enhanced contrastive learning for chest X-ray report generation. In: Proceedings of the IEEE/CVF Conference on Computer Vision and Pattern Recognition, pp. 3334–3343 (2023)
14. Lin, C.Y.: Rouge: a package for automatic evaluation of summaries. In: Text Summarization Branches Out, pp. 74–81 (2004)
15. Liu, F., Ge, S., Zou, Y., Wu, X.: Competence-based multimodal curriculum learning for medical report generation. arXiv preprint arXiv:2206.14579 (2022)
16. Liu, F., et al.: Contrastive attention for automatic chest X-ray report generation. arXiv preprint arXiv:2106.06965 (2021)
17. Liu, Z., Zhu, Z., Zheng, S., Zhao, Y., He, K., Zhao, Y.: From observation to concept: a flexible multi-view paradigm for medical report generation. IEEE Trans. Multimed. **26**, 5987–5995 (2023)
18. Lu, P., et al.: Improving classification of tetanus severity for patients in low-middle income countries wearing ECG sensors by using a CNN-transformer network. IEEE Trans. Biomed. Eng. **70**(4), 1340–1350 (2022)
19. Neumann, M., King, D., Beltagy, I., Ammar, W.: Scispacy: fast and robust models for biomedical natural language processing. arXiv preprint arXiv:1902.07669 (2019)
20. van den Oord, A., Li, Y., Vinyals, O.: Representation learning with contrastive predictive coding. arXiv preprint arXiv:1807.03748 (2018)
21. Papineni, K., Roukos, S., Ward, T., Zhu, W.J.: Bleu: a method for automatic evaluation of machine translation. In: Proceedings of the 40th Annual Meeting of the Association for Computational Linguistics, pp. 311–318 (2002)
22. Paul, A., et al.: Generalized zero-shot chest X-ray diagnosis through trait-guided multi-view semantic embedding with self-training. IEEE Trans. Med. Imaging **40**(10), 2642–2655 (2021)
23. Pérez-García, F., et al.: Rad-dino: exploring scalable medical image encoders beyond text supervision. arXiv preprint arXiv:2401.10815 (2024)
24. Prabhakar, C., et al.: Improving generalized zero-shot learning for multi-labelchest X-ray classification using knowledge graphs (2021)
25. Qin, H., Song, Y.: Reinforced cross-modal alignment for radiology report generation. In: Findings of the Association for Computational Linguistics: ACL 2022, pp. 448–458 (2022)
26. Radford, A., et al.: Learning transferable visual models from natural language supervision. In: International Conference on Machine Learning, pp. 8748–8763. PMLR (2021)
27. Rubin, J., Sanghavi, D., Zhao, C., Lee, K., Qadir, A., Xu-Wilson, M.: Large scale automated reading of frontal and lateral chest X-rays using dual convolutional neural networks. arXiv preprint arXiv:1804.07839 (2018)
28. Sanh, V., Debut, L., Chaumond, J., Wolf, T.: Distilbert, a distilled version of BERT: smaller, faster, cheaper and lighter. arXiv preprint arXiv:1910.01108 (2019)
29. Speets, A.M., et al.: Chest radiography in general practice: indications, diagnostic yield and consequences for patient management. Br. J. Gen. Pract. **56**(529), 574–578 (2006)

30. Vaswani, A., et al.: Attention is all you need. In: Advances in Neural Information Processing Systems, vol. 30 (2017)
31. Vedantam, R., Lawrence Zitnick, C., Parikh, D.: Cider: consensus-based image description evaluation. In: Proceedings of the IEEE Conference on Computer Vision and Pattern Recognition, pp. 4566–4575 (2015)
32. Wang, Z., Liu, L., Wang, L., Zhou, L.: Metransformer: radiology report generation by transformer with multiple learnable expert tokens. In: Proceedings of the IEEE/CVF Conference on Computer Vision and Pattern Recognition, pp. 11558–11567 (2023)
33. Wang, Z., Wu, Z., Agarwal, D., Sun, J.: Medclip: contrastive learning from unpaired medical images and text. In: Proceedings of the Conference on Empirical Methods in Natural Language Processing. Conference on Empirical Methods in Natural Language Processing, vol. 2022, p. 3876 (2022)
34. Wu, B., et al.: Visual transformers: token-based image representation and processing for computer vision. arXiv preprint arXiv:2006.03677 (2020)
35. Wu, X., Li, J., Wang, J., Qian, Q.: Multimodal contrastive learning for radiology report generation. J. Ambient. Intell. Humaniz. Comput. **14**(8), 11185–11194 (2023)
36. Yan, A., et al.: Weakly supervised contrastive learning for chest X-ray report generation. arXiv preprint arXiv:2109.12242 (2021)
37. Yang, S., Niu, J., Wu, J., Liu, X.: Automatic medical image report generation with multi-view and multi-modal attention mechanism. In: International Conference on Algorithms and Architectures for Parallel Processing, pp. 687–699. Springer, Cham (2020)
38. Yang, Y., Yu, J., Jiang, H., Han, W., Zhang, J., Jiang, W.: A contrastive triplet network for automatic chest X-ray reporting. Neurocomputing **502**, 71–83 (2022)
39. You, D., Liu, F., Ge, S., Xie, X., Zhang, J., Wu, X.: AlignTransformer: hierarchical alignment of visual regions and disease tags for medical report generation. In: de Bruijne, M., et al. (eds.) MICCAI 2021. LNCS, vol. 12903, pp. 72–82. Springer, Cham (2021). https://doi.org/10.1007/978-3-030-87199-4_7
40. You, K., et al.: CXR-clip: toward large scale chest X-ray language-image pre-training. In: International Conference on Medical Image Computing and Computer-Assisted Intervention, pp. 101–111. Springer, Cham (2023)
41. Zhang, X., Wu, C., Zhang, Y., Xie, W., Wang, Y.: Knowledge-enhanced visual-language pre-training on chest radiology images. Nat. Commun. **14**(1), 4542 (2023)
42. Zhu, X., Feng, Q.: MVC-net: multi-view chest radiograph classification network with deep fusion. In: 2021 IEEE 18th International Symposium on Biomedical Imaging (ISBI), pp. 554–558. IEEE (2021)

BlastDiffusion: A Latent Diffusion Model for Generating Synthetic Embryo Images to Address Data Scarcity in In Vitro Fertilization

Alejandro Golfe$^{(\boxtimes)}$ ⓘ, Natalia P. García-de-la-Puente ⓘ, Adrián Colomer ⓘ, and Valery Naranjo ⓘ

Instituto de Investigación sobre Tecnología Centrada en el Ser Humano (Human-Tech), Universidad Politécnica de Valencia, Valencia, Spain
algolsan@upv.es

Abstract. Accurately identifying oocytes that progress to the blastocyst stage is crucial in reproductive medicine, but the limited availability of annotated high-quality embryo images presents challenges for developing automated diagnostic tools. To address this, we propose BlastDiffusion, a generative model based on Latent Diffusion Models (LDMs) that synthesizes realistic oocyte images conditioned on developmental outcomes. Our approach utilizes a pretrained Variational Autoencoder (VAE) for latent space representation, combined with a diffusion process to generate images that distinguish between oocytes that reach the blastocyst stage and those that do not. When compared to Blastocyst-GAN, a GAN-based model we trained for this task, BlastDiffusion achieves superior performance, with a global Frechet Inception Distance (FID) of 94.32, significantly better than Blastocyst-GAN's FID of 232.73. Additionally, our model shows improvements in perceptual (LPIPS) and structural (SSIM) similarity to real oocyte images. Qualitative analysis further demonstrates that BlastDiffusion captures key morphological differences linked to developmental outcomes. These results highlight the potential of diffusion models in reproductive medicine, offering an effective tool for data augmentation and automated embryo assessment.

Keywords: latent diffusion models · synthetic data generation · blastocyst · embryo · oocyte selection

1 Introduction

Reliable identification of oocytes that progress to the blastocyst stage is vital in reproductive biology and clinical medicine. Blastocysts represent a key phase in embryonic development, as this is when embryos are most likely to implant successfully in the recipient's uterus, increasing the chances of a viable pregnancy [1]. Furthermore, analyzing embryos at this stage provides valuable insights into

S. Ali et al. (Eds.): MIUA 2025, LNCS 15916, pp. 205–217, 2026.
https://doi.org/10.1007/978-3-031-98688-8_15

developmental quality and helps select the best embryos for transfer in vitro fertilization (IVF) treatments [2].

However, there is a significant scarcity of annotated datasets containing high-quality images of embryos at the blastocyst stage, which limits both research progress and clinical applications of computer vision algorithms. The absence of consistent and standardized labelling of the ground truth in training data hinders artificial intelligence (AI) models' reliability and predictive capability in embryo selection [3]. In this context, generating synthetic images could provide a solution to expand the available data, allowing the training of more robust models for oocyte identification and classification at this crucial stage.

Generative models have evolved significantly in recent years, from Variational Autoencoders (VAEs) [4], which capture latent data distributions, to Generative Adversarial Networks (GANs) [5], which enable the creation of realistic images. More recently, diffusion models, which rely on transforming data through a series of noise and restoration steps, have demonstrated exceptional performance in generating high-quality images [6]. Due to their ability to generate complex and realistic images, these models present a promising tool for creating images of embryos at the blastocyst stage, contributing to the expansion of annotated datasets and improving the accuracy of automated diagnostic systems. The contributions of this work can be summarized as follows:

- We introduce the first Latent Diffusion Model (LDM) that generates synthetic oocyte images conditioned on their capacity to reach the blastocyst stage, directly addressing the scarcity of annotated data for research and clinical applications.
- By leveraging diffusion models to produce high-quality synthetic images, this work expands the data available for embryo-selection research and clinical practice in IVF, illustrating the promise of advanced generative models in biomedical applications.
- We perform benchmarking against Blastocyst-GAN, a GAN-based architecture we trained for oocyte image generation, highlighting the superior performance of our diffusion-based approach in key metrics like FID, LPIPS, and SSIM.

2   Related Work

Accurately identifying and selecting blastocysts in reproductive medicine have been extensively studied, with various approaches proposed to improve embryo assessment. Traditional embryo evaluation methods rely on morphological grading systems [1], which, while effective, are subjective and prone to interobserver variability [7]. To address these limitations, automated systems using machine learning and deep learning have been explored to enhance embryo selection in IVF treatments [8].

The availability of well-labelled embryo images is critical for training robust classification and predictive models, yet existing datasets are limited in size and diversity [8]. To overcome this challenge, data augmentation techniques, including synthetic image generation, have been proposed to expand training datasets and improve model performance [9]. However, traditional data augmentation techniques, such as colour jittering, flips, rotations, and random cropping, are limited in capturing complex morphological variations. These methods alter pixel-level features without introducing new structural patterns, which may be crucial for modelling fine-grained biological differences.

Generative models have played a key role in synthetic data generation. LDMs have emerged as a powerful alternative for image synthesis, offering a more computationally efficient approach that operates in a lower-dimensional latent space [10]. These models iteratively transform noise into detailed images through a learned denoising process, enabling the generation of highly realistic and diverse datasets [6]. LDMs have been successfully applied in various biomedical imaging tasks, including histopathology [11] and embryo generation [12].

Recent developments in diffusion models have emphasized the integration of cross-attention layers, which allow the generative process to condition on additional input information such as class labels, textual descriptions, or clinical metadata. Cross-attention improves the model's ability to focus on relevant spatial and semantic features, making it particularly effective for conditional image generation tasks. In biomedical imaging, this facilitates the synthesis of images that reflect subtle biological variations linked to specific phenotypes or clinical outcomes [13,14].

In the context of reproductive medicine, applying diffusion models with cross-attention layers enables conditioning synthetic oocyte images on developmental outcomes–specifically, whether an oocyte develops into a blastocyst or not. This conditional generation is crucial because oocytes that do or do not reach the blastocyst stage exhibit distinct morphological features that should be accurately represented in the synthetic data to better reflect biological variability.

Given their superior image generation capabilities, diffusion models represent a promising approach to address dataset limitations in embryo classification. Previous studies have demonstrated that augmenting training data with synthetic images generated by diffusion or other generative models can significantly enhance classification performance and model robustness in biomedical imaging tasks [15,16]. Unlike previous work focusing on direct embryo generation [12], our approach leverages latent diffusion models (LDMs) to generate synthetic oocyte images conditioned on developmental outcome information, specifically whether they reach the blastocyst stage or not. To the best of the authors' knowledge, this is the first work to apply LDMs for conditional oocyte image generation based on developmental viability.

3 Materials

3.1 Database

The protocol and procedures for oocyte analysis were approved by the Institutional Review Board (IRB reference 2303-VLC-035-MM), which oversees database analyses and clinical IVF research procedures at IVI (Instituto Valenciano de Infertilidad) and RMA (Reproductive Medicine Associates), now known as IVIRMA Global. This retrospective study examined 2,217 oocyte images captured before intracytoplasmic sperm injection (ICSI) using a Basler acA3088-57uc camera connected to a microinjection microscope. Patient data, stimulation protocols, clinical outcomes, and work environment variables were collected from the center's internal registry.

All data used in this study was pseudonymized, as the investigator receives the data without any identification. The individual responsible for data extraction retained re-identification information, ensuring a clear functional and technical separation between the researcher and data collector. The compiled data were divided into training, validation, and testing sets while ensuring that samples from the same patient did not appear in both training and testing sets simultaneously. The training and validation set comprised 90% of the total data, with 10% of this portion further allocated for validation. The remaining 10% of the data was reserved for testing. In the dataset, 44.8% of the oocytes correspond to those that reach the blastocyst stage, while 55.2% correspond to those that do not. The partitioning was performed at the patient level to prevent data leakage and ensure a robust model evaluation.

A key preprocessing step involves isolating the region in each image containing the oocyte. To achieve this, we use a pretrained YOLO model [17], which is well-known for its effectiveness in object detection and real-time detection capabilities and facilitates its integration into oocyte analysis software. This architecture has been widely adopted in various medical imaging applications, including tumor localization, fracture detection, and histopathological analysis, demonstrating its versatility and robustness across domains [18]. This process reduces the image dimensions from approximately 3000×2000 to 1500×1500 pixels. For retraining the YOLOv8n model, bounding boxes were manually labelled on 61 images, with a train/validation/test split of 26/24/11 [19].

4 Methodology

Our approach leverages a LDM for conditional oocyte image generation. First, the VAE encoder compresses the input image into a lower-dimensional latent space, facilitating efficient processing. Then, the LDM is applied within this latent space, iteratively refining noisy representations into realistic embeddings. A class embedding mechanism conditions the generation process on whether the oocyte reaches the blastocyst stage, guiding the diffusion model toward biologically relevant image synthesis. Finally, the VAE decoder reconstructs the high-resolution image from the generated latent representation (see Fig. 1).

4.1 BlastDiffusion Framework

Variational Autoencoder (VAE) Encoder. To obtain a compact and structured latent representation, we employ a pretrained Variational Autoencoder

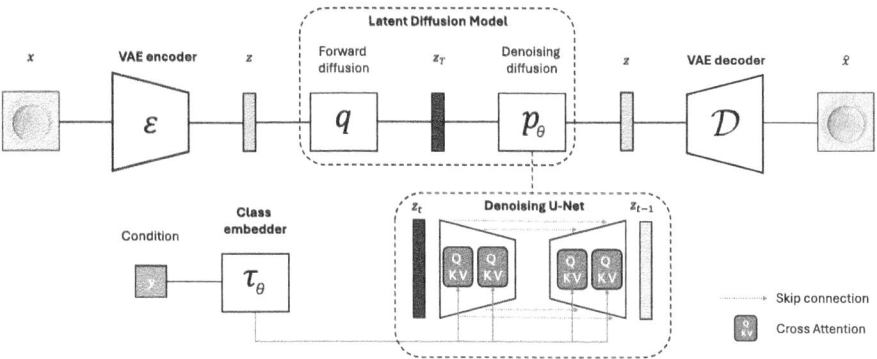

Fig. 1. Overview of BlastDiffusion framework. A Variational Autoencoder (VAE) encodes the input image into a latent space, where a LDM refines noisy representations into realistic embeddings. The process is conditioned on developmental outcome, allowing the generation of biologically relevant synthetic images.

(VAE) from the Stable Diffusion framework. This VAE, originally trained on the LAION-5B dataset [20], filtered to exclude sensitive content, serves as a feature extractor. Given an input image $x \in \mathbb{R}^{H \times W \times C}$, the VAE encoder $\mathcal{E}$ compresses it into a lower-dimensional latent representation $z \in \mathbb{R}^{h \times w \times c}$, where typically $h < H$, $w < W$, and $c < C$. This transformation preserves the most relevant features of the data while significantly reducing computational overhead compared to operating directly in pixel space. The latent representation z is then used as input for the diffusion process.

Mathematically, the encoder $\mathcal{E}$ can be expressed as:

$$z = \mathcal{E}(x) \quad \text{where} \quad z \sim q_\phi(z|x)$$

where $\mathcal{E}(x)$ represents the encoder function mapping the input image x to the latent variable z, and $q_\phi(z|x)$ is the approximate posterior distribution of z given x, parameterized by ϕ.

The VAE decoder $\mathcal{D}$ reconstructs the input image from the latent representation. Given the latent variable z, the VAE decoder $\mathcal{D}$ generates the reconstructed image $\hat{x} \in \mathbb{R}^{H \times W \times C}$, which can be expressed as:

$$\hat{x} = \mathcal{D}(z) \quad \text{where} \quad p_\theta(x|z) = \mathcal{N}(\hat{x}, \sigma^2)$$

where $\mathcal{D}(z)$ is the decoder function that maps the latent representation z back to the image space to produce the reconstruction $\hat{x}$, and $p_\theta(x|z)$ is the likelihood of observing the image x given the latent variable z, modeled as a Gaussian distribution with mean $\hat{x}$ and variance σ^2.

Diffusion Process. The diffusion model learns to generate samples by gradually corrupting a data distribution with noise and then training a neural network
to reverse this process. Given a latent representation z_0 obtained from the VAE
encoder, a *forward diffusion process* progressively adds Gaussian noise through a
predefined schedule, producing a sequence of latent variables $z_1, z_2, \ldots, z_T$. This
process follows the formulation:

$$q(z_t \mid z_{t-1}) = \mathcal{N}(z_t; \sqrt{\alpha_t} z_{t-1}, (1 - \alpha_t)I) \tag{1}$$

where $q(z_t \mid z_{t-1})$ represents the transition probability at time step t. The term
α_t is a noise scheduling coefficient that controls the amount of noise added at
each step, ensuring a smooth transition from structured data to pure noise. Here,
I is the identity matrix of appropriate size, which is used to model the covariance
structure of the added noise, ensuring that the noise is independent across the
dimensions of z_t.

During training, the model learns to approximate the reverse process, denoted
as:

$$p_\theta(z_{t-1} \mid z_t) = \mathcal{N}(z_{t-1}; \mu_\theta(z_t, t), \Sigma_\theta(z_t, t)) \tag{2}$$

where $p_\theta(z_{t-1} \mid z_t)$ models the probability distribution of recovering z_{t-1} given
z_t. The function $\mu_\theta(z_t, t)$ represents the predicted mean of the denoised latent
variable, while $\Sigma_\theta(z_t, t)$ is the learned variance. The parameters θ are optimized
to minimize the divergence between the true reverse process and its approxima-
tion.

Conditioning Mechanism. To guide image synthesis toward meaningful biological relevance, we incorporate a conditioning mechanism that introduces information about whether an oocyte develops into a blastocyst. The diffusion model
is conditioned on an embedding vector y that encodes this classification (blastocyst or non-blastocyst). This embedding is processed through a learnable transformation τ_θ, yielding a conditioning vector:

$$c = \tau_\theta(y)$$

which is then injected into the diffusion process via *cross-attention layers*, as
illustrated in Fig. 1. The conditional reverse process is formulated as:

$$p_\theta(z_{t-1} \mid z_t, c) = \mathcal{N}(z_{t-1}; \mu_\theta(z_t, c, t), \Sigma_\theta(z_t, c, t)) \tag{3}$$

where $\mu_\theta(z_t, c, t)$ and $\Sigma_\theta(z_t, c, t)$ now depend on both the noisy latent variable z_t
and the conditioning vector c. This conditioning enables the model to generate
synthetic oocyte images that are representative of the specified developmental
outcome, thereby augmenting datasets in a targeted manner.

4.2   Blastocyst-GAN Framework

The Blastocyst-GAN is a conditional generator based on the ProGleason-GAN architecture [15]. Although the original ProGleason-GAN was trained on prostate histology patches, the Blastocyst-GAN model has been trained from scratch using our oocyte dataset. This adaptation enables the generation of synthetic samples conditioned on whether the oocytes develop into viable blastocysts or not. This tailored training ensures that the model captures oocytes' unique characteristics and developmental outcomes.

We used this newly trained Blastocyst-GAN model as a comparison baseline to evaluate our proposed method more robustly. By comparing the results of our method with the outcomes generated by this model, we can assess the strengths and weaknesses of our approach, offering a comprehensive evaluation.

In the original ProGleason-GAN model, the generator was conditioned on the Gleason grade in prostate tissue patches. However, for our study, this mechanism was modified so that the synthesis process is conditioned on the developmental status of oocytes (viable or non-viable blastocyst).

The ProGAN [21] architecture enables the model to learn high-level image features and refine them as training progresses. The generator and the discriminator are provided with information about the specific condition of the oocyte (whether it results in a viable or non-viable blastocyst), allowing for conditional image synthesis without needing to incorporate a specific term in the loss function.

The training process is conducted in multiple stages, beginning with low-resolution patches of 4×4 pixels and progressively increasing to a final resolution of 512×512 pixels. Additionally, the model employs a technique called fade-in, which smoothly transitions between different resolutions, helping to stabilize the training process. Techniques such as minibatch standard deviation and pixel normalization are also used to improve the quality of the generated images.

The model is trained using the Wasserstein GAN with Gradient Penalty (WGAN-GP) loss function [22], which minimizes the discrepancy between real and synthetic data distributions, thereby improving the quality of the generated synthetic oocyte images.

5   Experiments and Results

5.1   Experimental Setup

Training Configuration. The BlastDiffusion model was trained using the Adam optimizer with a learning rate of 0.00005. A batch size of 24 was used, and the training was carried out for 4,000 epochs. The latent space parameters for the denoising U-net included downsampling channels of [64, 128, 256, 512] and the middle layers of [512, 256]. The time embedding dimension was set to 512. The upsampling process was carried out in two stages, using layers that mirror the downsampling process for efficient reconstruction. A conditional dropout probability of 0.2 was applied to introduce diversity in the generated images, and the training data was augmented using random horizontal flips (p=0.5) and random vertical flips (p = 0.3). Finally, a perceptual loss weight of 1 was used to ensure high-quality image generation.

Implementation. The experiments were conducted on an NVIDIA DGX A100 system with six NVIDIA A100 GPUs, each having 40 GB of HBM2 memory. Multi-GPU training was utilized to accelerate model training. The environment used was PyTorch 2.1.2 and Python 3.10.

Evaluation Metrics. We used multiple metrics to evaluate the synthetic images to assess their quality and similarity to real images. The primary metric employed was the Frechet Inception Distance (FID) [23], which measures the distance between two distributions of images: real and generated images. It uses features extracted from a pre-trained Inception v3 model [24], providing a high-dimensional image embedding.

Formally, FID is defined as the Frechet distance between the Gaussian distributions fitted to these embeddings:

$$FID = \|\mu_r - \mu_g\|_2^2 + \mathrm{Tr}(\Sigma_r + \Sigma_g - 2(\Sigma_r \Sigma_g)^{1/2})$$

where μ_r and Σ_r represent the mean and covariance of the real images' embeddings, while μ_g and Σ_g represent the mean and covariance of the generated images' embeddings. The term $\|\cdot\|_2$ denotes the L2 norm, which measures the Euclidean distance between the means of the two distributions. The trace operator denoted as Tr, is applied to the sum of the covariance matrices of both real and generated images. Lower FID values indicate that the generated images are closer to the real images in terms of both distribution and visual quality.

In addition to FID, we also computed the Learned Perceptual Image Patch Similarity (LPIPS) metric [25], which evaluates the perceptual similarity between real and synthetic images based on deep neural network activations. Lower LPIPS values indicate higher perceptual similarity between the images.

Furthermore, the Structural Similarity Index (SSIM) was used to evaluate the structural similarity between real and generated images. This metric compares the luminance, contrast, and structural information between images.

5.2   Quantitative Evaluation

The results presented in Table 1 show that our proposed method, BlastDiffusion, outperforms Blastocyst-GAN across all evaluated metrics. Specifically, BlastDiffusion achieves a significant reduction in FID across all categories, indicating a higher similarity to real data. For the LPIPS metric, it also obtains lower values, with a particularly notable improvement in the blastocyst class, suggesting that the generated images are perceptually closer to real ones. Additionally, the SSIM values demonstrate better structural preservation in BlastDiffusion-generated images, with consistent improvements across all categories, especially in the blastocyst class. These results confirm that BlastDiffusion generates images of higher quality, more realistic and structurally coherent than Blastocyst-GAN, establishing itself as a superior alternative for oocyte generation.

Table 1. Comparison of different methods for FID, LPIPS, and SSIM metrics across different classes.

Method	Class	FID ↓	LPIPS ↓	SSIM ↑
Blastocyst-GAN	Non-Blastocyst	223.588	0.392 ± 0.054	0.312 ± 0.056
	Blastocyst	278.581	0.397 ± 0.064	0.308 ± 0.052
	Total	232.733	0.394 ± 0.059	0.310 ± 0.054
BlastDiffusion	Non-Blastocyst	**101.166**	**0.2745 ± 0.0540**	**0.3913 ± 0.0506**
	Blastocyst	**105.503**	**0.2659 ± 0.0511**	**0.3863 ± 0.0572**
	Total	**94.318**	**0.2877 ± 0.0461**	**0.4462 ± 0.0534**

The limited dataset size is a key factor in interpreting these results, which challenges capturing fine details and full variability within each class. Despite this, the results highlight the model's ability to conditionally generate images, effectively distinguishing embryos that reach the blastocyst stage from those that do not.

5.3 Qualitative Evaluation

To assess the quality of the images generated by Blastocyst-GAN and Blast-Diffusion, we compare them visually against real oocytes. Figure 2 shows real oocytes, Fig. 4 shows oocytes generated by Blastocyst-GAN and Fig. 3 oocytes generated by BlastDiffusion. In each set, the first row corresponds to oocytes that do not reach the blastocyst stage, while the second row represents those that do.

From a biological perspective, the model must differentiate between oocytes that reach the blastocyst state and oocytes that do not. In the images generated by BlastDiffusion (Fig. 3), a clearer separation between these two categories is observed. Row (a) oocytes display characteristics often associated with lower developmental potential, including an irregular and granular cytoplasm (as highlighted in the second image of row a), and a zona pellucida that appears less smooth and may exhibit adherent debris within the perivitelline space (noticeable in the fourth image of row a). Furthermore, the perivitelline space in row (a) sometimes appears wider and less uniform (observe the third image of row a).

In contrast, row (b) oocytes, which reached the blastocyst stage, show a smooth and homogeneous cytoplasm (evident in the third image of row b), a clean perivitelline space often devoid of visible debris (clearly seen in all images of row b, especially the fourth), and a seemingly more uniformly structured zona pellucida (as indicated in the fourth image of row b). In particular, the oocytes in the second row exhibit a more homogeneous internal structure and a more distinct and regular zona pellucida, characteristics also present in the real images (Fig. 2). In contrast, Blastocyst-GAN (Fig. 4) tends to generate less differentiated patterns, suggesting a lower capacity to capture key biological differences.

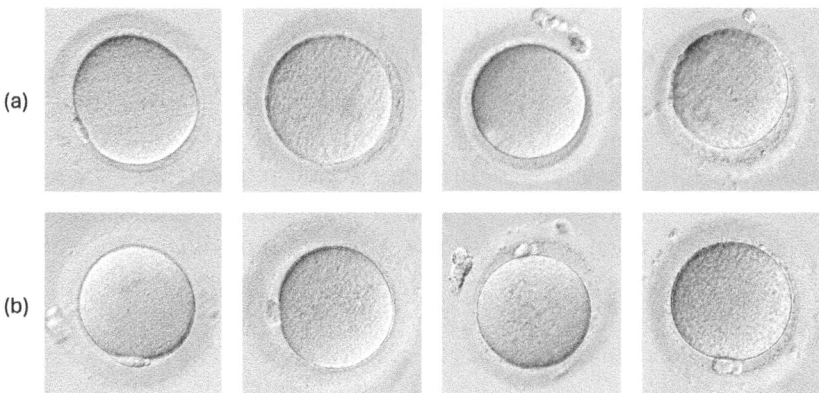

Fig. 2. Real oocyte images. The first row (a) corresponds to oocytes that did not reach the blastocyst stage, while the second row (b) shows oocytes that successfully developed into blastocysts.

BlastDiffusion demonstrates a notable improvement in visual fidelity compared to Blastocyst-GAN. While the images generated by Blastocyst-GAN exhibit noticeable artefacts and unnatural textures, BlastDiffusion produces oocytes with more defined structures and a smoother texture that closely resembles real samples. In particular, peripheral cellular structures and the zona pellucida appear to be more naturally defined in the images generated by BlastDiffusion.

In conclusion, the conditional synthesis of BlastDiffusion shows significant improvements in oocyte generation, both in terms of visual realism and the accurate representation of relevant biological features. These results indicate that BlastDiffusion produces more realistic images and is a more reliable tool for computational embryology studies. Although the limited size of the data set may restrict the model's ability to learn fine-grained morphological features associated with blastocyst formation, BlastDiffusion still demonstrates a remarkable capacity to capture intrinsic class characteristics despite data limitations, highlighting its potential for applications in oocyte analysis. One possible explanation for its superior performance compared to Blastocyst-GAN is the architectural difference between the models: while BlastDiffusion leverages diffusion-based generation with cross-attention mechanisms that enable finer control over conditional synthesis, Blastocyst-GAN is based on a progressive growing GAN framework, which may be less effective in capturing complex, high-resolution

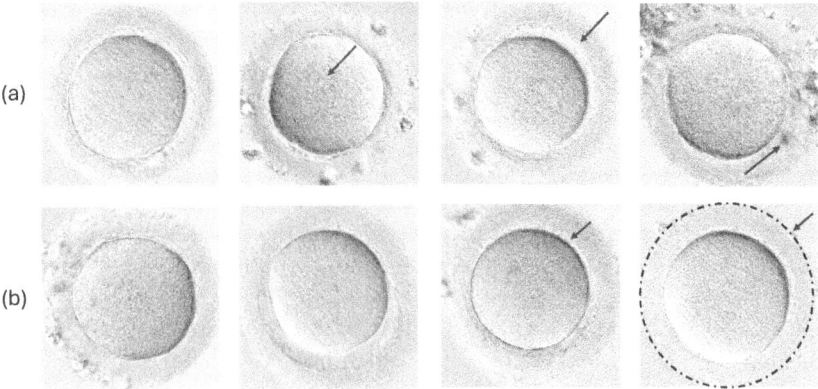

Fig. 3. Generated oocytes using BlastDiffusion. The first row (a) consists of generated oocytes that did not reach the blastocyst stage, while the second row (b) represents those predicted to develop into blastocysts. Specific features are highlighted with arrows.

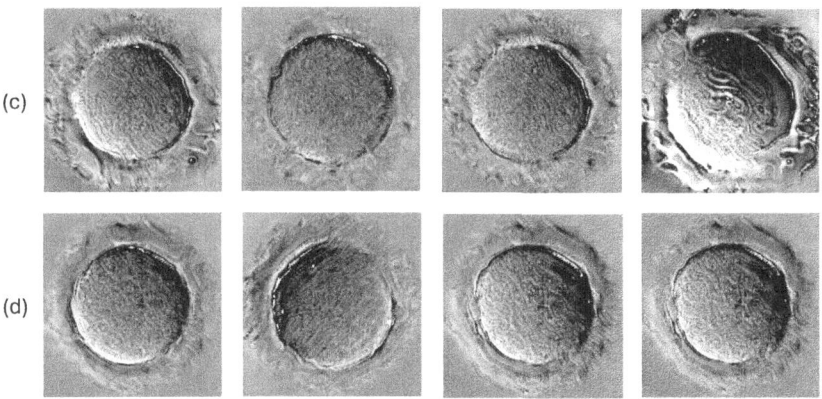

Fig. 4. Generated oocytes using Blastocyst-GAN. The first row (a) represents generated oocytes that did not reach the blastocyst stage, while the second row (b) corresponds to those predicted to develop into blastocysts.

biological details under limited data conditions. These observations highlight the potential of conditional generative models in reproductive biology and the importance of further improving dataset diversity.

6 Conclusion

BlastDiffusion, a conditional latent-diffusion model trained with a pretrained VAE backbone, synthesizes oocyte images conditioned on later blastocyst formation. Despite using only binary class labels, it achieves markedly superior realism and biological relevance over our GAN baseline, improving FID from 232.7 to 94.3 and surpassing it in LPIPS and SSIM while faithfully reproducing morphological cues that distinguish oocytes that reach the blastocyst stage from those that do not.

While our model relies on a compact dataset and uses only binary class-label conditioning, these choices mark clear opportunities for growth rather than shortcomings. Scaling the dataset and complementing the class labels with richer signals–such as text annotations or molecular markers–should further sharpen image specificity and widen the spectrum of oocyte phenotypes the model can represent.

Future work should enlarge and diversify the training corpus and enrich conditioning with multimodal biological metadata. Crucially, synthetic images ought to be validated by an independent embryo-quality classifier and, eventually, through prospective clinical evaluation to confirm their utility in IVF practice.

Acknowledgment. This work has received funding from the Spanish Ministry of Economy and Competitiveness through the project PID2022-140189OB-C21 (ASSIST). The work of Natalia P. García de la Puente was supported by the grant PID2022-140189OB-C21 funded by MICIU/AEI/10.13039/ 501100011033 ERDF/UE and FSE+.

References

1. Gardner, D.K., Lane, M.: Culture and selection of viable blastocysts: a feasible proposition for human IVF? Hum. Reprod. Update **3**(4), 367–382 (1997)
2. Gardner, D.K., Schoolcraft, W.B., Wagley, L., Schlenker, T., Stevens, J., Hesla, J.: A prospective randomized trial of blastocyst culture and transfer in in-vitro fertilization. Hum. Reprod. (Oxford, England) **13**(12), 3434–3440 (1998)
3. Salih, M., et al.: Embryo selection through artificial intelligence versus embryologists: a systematic review. Hum. Reprod. Open **2023**(3), hoad031 (2023)
4. Kingma, D.P.: Auto-encoding variational bayes. arXiv preprint arXiv:1312.6114 (2013)
5. Goodfellow, I., et al.: Generative adversarial nets. In: Advances in Neural Information Processing Systems, vol. 27 (2014)
6. Croitoru, F.-A., Hondru, V., Ionescu, R.T., Shah, M.: Diffusion models in vision: a survey. IEEE Trans. Pattern Anal. Mach. Intell. **45**(9), 10 850–10 869 (2023)
7. Martínez-Granados, L., et al.: Inter-laboratory agreement on embryo classification and clinical decision: conventional morphological assessment vs. time lapse. PLoS ONE **12**(8), e0183328 (2017)
8. Hew, Y., Kutuk, D., Duzcu, T., Ergun, Y., Basar, M.: Artificial intelligence in IVF laboratories: elevating outcomes through precision and efficiency. Biology **13**(12), 988 (2024)
9. Wang, Z., et al.: Enhance image classification via inter-class image mixup with diffusion model. In: Proceedings of the IEEE/CVF Conference on Computer Vision and Pattern Recognition, pp. 17 223–17 233 (2024)

10. Herron, E., et al.: Latent diffusion models for structural component design. Comput. Aided Des. **171**, 103707 (2024)
11. Yellapragada, S., Graikos, A., Prasanna, P., Kurc, T., Saltz, J., Samaras, D.: PathLDM: text conditioned latent diffusion model for histopathology. In: Proceedings of the IEEE/CVF Winter Conference on Applications of Computer Vision, pp. 5182–5191 (2024)
12. Presacan, O., et al.: Embryo 2.0: merging synthetic and real data for advanced AI predictions. arXiv preprint arXiv:2412.01255 (2024)
13. Rombach, R., Blattmann, A., Lorenz, D., Esser, P., Ommer, B.: High-resolution image synthesis with latent diffusion models. In: Proceedings of the IEEE/CVF Conference on Computer Vision and Pattern Recognition, pp. 10 684–10 695 (2022)
14. Dhariwal, P., Nichol, A.: Diffusion models beat GANs on image synthesis. Adv. Neural. Inf. Process. Syst. **34**, 8780–8794 (2021)
15. Golfe, A., Del Amor, R., Colomer, A., Sales, M.A., Terradez, L., Naranjo, V.: Progleason-GAN: conditional progressive growing GAN for prostatic cancer Gleason grade patch synthesis. Comput. Methods Programs Biomed. **240**, 107695 (2023)
16. Oh, H.-J., Jeong, W.-K.: Diffmix: diffusion model-based data synthesis for nuclei segmentation and classification in imbalanced pathology image datasets. In: International Conference on Medical Image Computing and Computer-Assisted Intervention, pp. 337–345. Springer, Cham (2023)
17. Varghese, R., Sambath, M.: YOLOv8: a novel object detection algorithm with enhanced performance and robustness. In: 2024 International Conference on Advances in Data Engineering and Intelligent Computing Systems (ADICS), pp. 1–6. IEEE (2024)
18. Soni, A., Rai, A.: YOLO for medical object detection (2018–2024). In: 2024 IEEE 3rd International Conference on Electrical Power and Energy Systems (ICEPES), pp. 1–7. IEEE (2024)
19. García-de-la Puente, N.P., Paya, E., Murria, L., López-Pérez, M., Meseguer, M., Naranjo, V.: Unsupervised prediction of blastocyst development from oocyte images. In: Decision Science Alliance International Summer Conference, pp. 199–209. Springer, Cham (2024)
20. Schuhmann, C., et al.: Laion-5b: an open large-scale dataset for training next generation image-text models. In: Advances in Neural Information Processing Systems, vol. 35, pp. 25 278–25 294 (2022)
21. Karras, T., Aila, T., Laine, S., Lehtinen, J.: Progressive growing of GANs for improved quality, stability, and variation. arXiv preprint arXiv:1710.10196 (2017)
22. Gulrajani, I., Ahmed, F., Arjovsky, M., Dumoulin, V., Courville, A.C.: Improved training of Wasserstein GANs. In: Advances in Neural Information Processing Systems, vol. 30 (2017)
23. Heusel, M., Ramsauer, H., Unterthiner, T., Nessler, B., Hochreiter, S.: GANs trained by a two time-scale update rule converge to a local Nash equilibrium. In: Advances in Neural Information Processing Systems, vol. 30 (2017)
24. Szegedy, C., Vanhoucke, V., Ioffe, S., Shlens, J., Wojna, Z.: Rethinking the inception architecture for computer vision. In: Proceedings of the IEEE Conference on Computer Vision and Pattern Recognition, pp. 2818–2826 (2016)
25. Johnson, J., Alahi, A., Fei-Fei, L.: Perceptual losses for real-time style transfer and super-resolution. In: Leibe, B., Matas, J., Sebe, N., Welling, M. (eds.) ECCV 2016. LNCS, vol. 9906, pp. 694–711. Springer, Cham (2016). https://doi.org/10.1007/978-3-319-46475-6_43

MediAug: Exploring Visual Augmentation in Medical Imaging

Xuyin Qi[1,2], Zeyu Zhang[1,3], Canxuan Gang[4], Hao Zhang[5], Lei Zhang[5],
Zhiwei Zhang[6], and Yang Zhao[1(✉)]

[1] La Trobe, Melbourne, Australia
y.zhao2@latrobe.edu.au
[2] AIML, Adelaide, Australia
[3] ANU, Canberra, Australia
[4] UNSW, Sydney, Australia
[5] UCAS, Cheltenham, UK
[6] PSU, Canberra, Australia

Abstract. Data augmentation enhances medical imaging tasks but faces domain gaps and fragmented studies. We propose a unified framework applying six mix-based methods on brain tumor MRI and eye disease datasets with convolutional and transformer backbones. Our contributions are threefold. (1) We present **MediAug**, a benchmark for advanced data augmentation in medical imaging. (2) Six methods (MixUp, YOCO, CropMix, CutMix, AugMix, SnapMix) are evaluated with ResNet-50 and ViT-B backbones. (3) Experiments show MixUp achieves **79.19%** accuracy on brain tumor classification with ResNet-50, SnapMix **99.44%** with ViT-B, YOCO **91.60%** on eye disease classification with ResNet-50, and CutMix **97.94%** with ViT-B. Code will be available at https://github.com/AIGeeksGroup/MediAug.

Keywords: Data Augmentation · Low-Level Vision · Medical Imaging

1 Introduction

Data augmentation generates label-preserving synthetic samples via flips, rotations and elastic deformations, expanding limited datasets and underpinning deep learning [22]. In medical imaging, where annotations are scarce, classes imbalanced and diagnostic cues subtle, it enhances screening, triage and treatment planning. Two challenges remain. First, ImageNet-based policies often distort or remove critical disease features under low contrast, high noise and dense semantics [18]. Second, DA studies in medical imaging are fragmented and task or model specific, leaving unclear which image mixing strategies improve performance and why [14].

MediAug is a pipeline evaluating six mix-based DA methods–MixUp [29], YOCO [9], CropMix [10], CutMix [28], AugMix [12], SnapMix [13]–on the brain

---

X. Qi, Z. Zhang and C. Gang—Equal contribution.
Z. Zhang—Project lead.

S. Ali et al. (Eds.): MIUA 2025, LNCS 15916, pp. 218–232, 2026.
https://doi.org/10.1007/978-3-031-98688-8_16

tumour MRI dataset [1] and the eye disease fundus dataset [5] using ResNet-50 [11] and ViT-B [6] backbones.

- We introduce **MediAug**, a comprehensive and reproducible study of advanced DA strategies for medical imaging that offers a unified reference and practical guidance for the research community.
- Our study provides a systematic evaluation of MixUp, CutMix, SnapMix, AugMix, CropMix and YOCO across convolutional and transformer backbones, highlighting their respective strengths and limitations.
- We conducted comprehensive experiments on the brain tumour and eye disease datasets, achieving **79.19%** with MixUp on ResNet-50 and **99.44%** with SnapMix on ViT-B for brain tumour classification and **91.60%** with YOCO on ResNet-50 and **97.94%** with CutMix on ViT-B for eye disease classification, indicating that MixUp on ResNet-50 and SnapMix on ViT-B are optimal for brain tumours and YOCO on ResNet-50 and CutMix on ViT-B are optimal for eye diseases.

2 Related Work

Visual data augmentation is foundational in computer vision. In natural images, techniques like random crops [15], flips [19], rotations, and color jitter [22] enhance generalization, robustness, and diversity, while noise injection and elastic deformations [19] improve resilience to artifacts. In medical imaging, where annotated scans are scarce and costly, DA improves classification [17,21,27,32], detection [2,3,34,36,37], and segmentation [8,24–26,30,33,35,38] by reducing reliance on large annotated datasets [16], improving automated systems [23], supporting semi-supervised and transfer learning [4], lowering diagnostic costs [7,31], and enabling consistent lesion and organ segmentation in MRI and CT [16,20]. Beyond traditional methods, advanced mix-based approaches generate richer samples. MixUp blends images and labels for smoother decision boundaries [29], YOCO applies independent augmentations to subregions [9], CropMix merges multi-scale crops [10], CutMix swaps patches between images [28], AugMix ensembles augmentation chains for better calibration [12], and SnapMix uses activation maps for fine-grained classification [13]. These methods show promise for robust medical image analysis.

3 Method

3.1 Overview

Our method, shown in Fig. 1, enhances medical representation learning with six augmentations: MixUp [29], YOCO [9], CropMix [10], CutMix [28], AugMix [12], and SnapMix [13], plus the original image. Two backbones, Vit-B [6] (JointViT [32]) and ResNet-50 [11] (MedConv [21]), process these for disease classification, learning robust representations.

3.2   MixUp

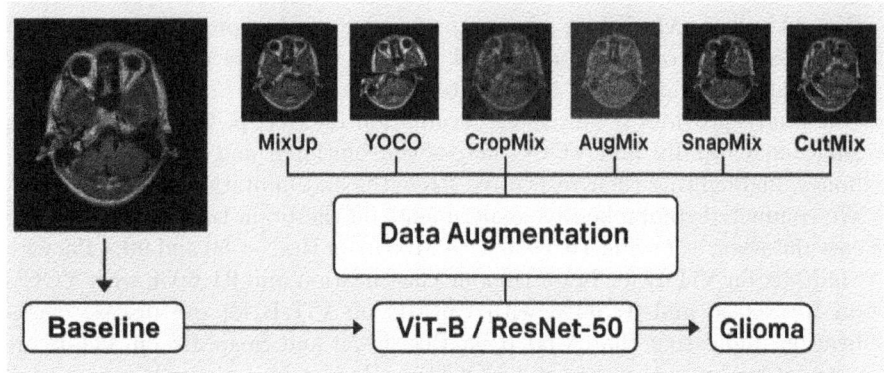

Fig. 1. *Architecture of MediAug*: We enhance medical representation learning via advanced visual augmentation.

Mixup [29] is a data augmentation technique that improves the generalization ability of neural networks by interpolating images and labels. Let I_a and I_b represent two randomly selected input images from the training dataset, and y_a and y_b be their corresponding one-hot encoded labels. A mixing coefficient λ is sampled from a Beta distribution, denoted as $\lambda \sim \text{Beta}(\alpha, \alpha)$, where $\alpha > 0$ controls the strength of interpolation. The mixed image $\tilde{I}$ and label $\tilde{y}$ are computed as:

$$\tilde{I} = \lambda I_a + (1 - \lambda)I_b, \quad \tilde{y} = \lambda y_a + (1 - \lambda)y_b. \tag{1}$$

I_a and I_b are two randomly selected input images, while y_a and y_b are their corresponding one-hot encoded labels. The parameter λ represents the mixing coefficient, sampled from a Beta distribution with parameter $\alpha > 0$, which determines the interpolation ratio between I_a and I_b. The interpolated image $\tilde{I}$ and label $\tilde{y}$ are obtained by combining I_a and I_b, as well as y_a and y_b, respectively, using λ and $1 - \lambda$ as weights.

During training, the loss function is defined as:

$$\mathcal{L} = \frac{1}{n} \sum_{i=1}^{n} \ell(f(\tilde{I}_i), \tilde{y}_i), \tag{2}$$

where f denotes the neural network model, ℓ represents the loss function (e.g., cross-entropy), n is the batch size, and $(\tilde{I}_i, \tilde{y}_i)$ are the mixed image and label for the i-th training example.

In medical imaging, Mixup, shown in panels (b) of Figs. 2 and 3, addresses limited data and class imbalance by interpolating images and labels. It enhances datasets, reduces overfitting, and improves robustness, benefiting medical image analysis.

3.3   YOCO

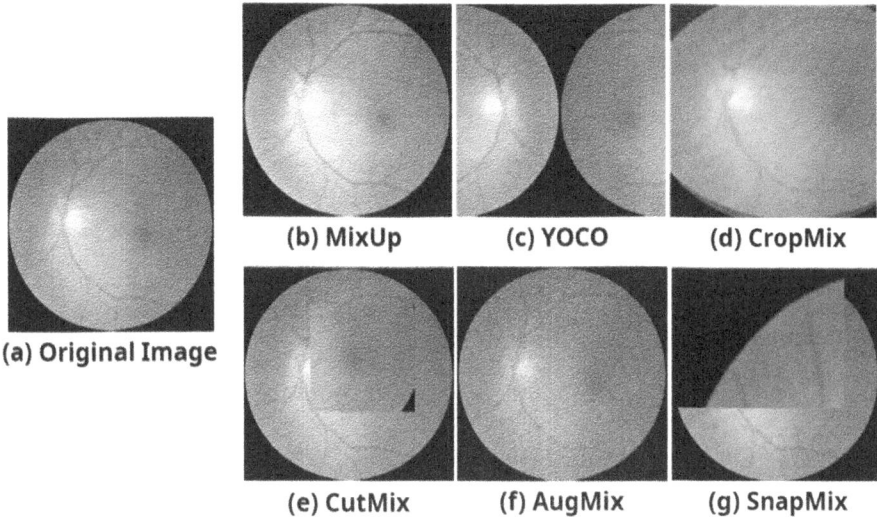

(a) Original Image

(b) MixUp   **(c) YOCO**   **(d) CropMix**

(e) CutMix   **(f) AugMix**   **(g) SnapMix**

Fig. 2. *Augmentation in Eye diseases classification dataset* [5]: (a) An image of a cataract. (b) *MixUp* [29]: Original image and contrast-enhanced image is mixed with a mixing parameter $\lambda = 0.42$. (c) *YOCO* [9]: splits, flips, and recombines the image for augmentation. (d) *CropMix* [10]: combines three 25% cropped views using MixUp [29] for augmentation. (e) *CutMix* [28]: augments by relocating a 1/4 cropped region within the image. (f) *AugMix* [12]: AugMix blends blurring, sharpening, and color adjustments with the original. (g) *SnapMix* [13]: SnapMix blends interpolated regions, weighted by saliency maps, with the original.

The YOCO method [9], as illustrated in panels (c) of Figs. 2 and 3, is designed for processing medical images $X \in \mathbb{R}^{C \times H \times W}$, where C represents the number of image channels (e.g., grayscale or RGB), H is the height, and W is the width of the image. The goal of YOCO is to apply data augmentation in a way that enhances both local and global diversity while maintaining the structural integrity of the image. A data augmentation function $a(\cdot) : \mathbb{R}^{C \times H \times W} \rightarrow \mathbb{R}^{C \times H \times W}$ transforms the input image X into an augmented image $X' = a(X)$.

Unlike traditional augmentation methods, YOCO first splits the input image into sub-regions. To achieve this, the image is randomly split into two parts along either the height or width dimension. Specifically, if the random variable $p \sim U(0, 1)$ (a uniformly distributed random number between 0 and 1) satisfies $0 < p \leq 0.5$, the image is split along the height, resulting in two sub-images $[X_1, X_2] = \text{cutH}(X)$. Alternatively, if $0.5 < p \leq 1$, the image is split along the width, resulting in $[X_1, X_2] = \text{cutW}(X)$. The dimensions of these sub-images depend on the splitting direction: - For height splitting, $X_1, X_2 \in \mathbb{R}^{C \times \frac{H}{2} \times W}$, - For width splitting, $X_1, X_2 \in \mathbb{R}^{C \times H \times \frac{W}{2}}$.

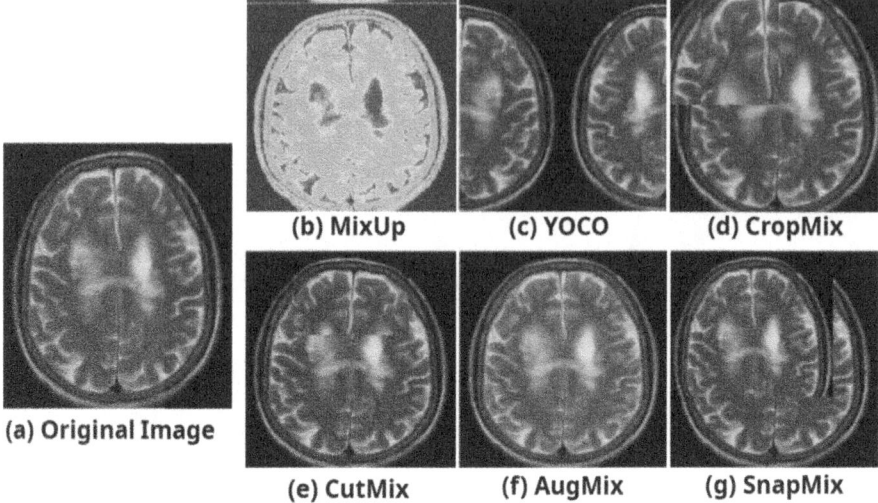

Fig. 3. *Augmentation in Brain Tumor Classification (MRI) dataset* [1]: (a) An image of a no_tumor in Testing. (b) ***MixUp*** [29]: Contrast-adjusted and mixed ($\lambda = 0.30$), in grayscale and pseudo-color. (c) ***YOCO*** [9]: The image was resized, contrast-enhanced, flipped, and concatenated. (d) ***CropMix*** [10]: It from a contrast-enhanced, randomly cropped image using CutMix. (e) ***CutMix*** [28]: Original image flipped and mixed using random CutMix enhancement ($\lambda = 0.70$). (f) ***AugMix*** [12]: It enhances the image with flipping and brightness adjustment. (g) ***SnapMix*** [13]: It enhances by blending resized cropped regions with the original image.

After splitting, independent augmentation functions $a_1(\cdot)$ and $a_2(\cdot)$ are applied to the two sub-images X_1 and X_2, respectively. These augmentations may involve operations such as rotation, flipping, or intensity adjustment. The final augmented image X' is then reconstructed by concatenating the two augmented sub-images along the original splitting axis:

$$X' = \text{concat}[a_1(X_1), a_2(X_2)]. \tag{3}$$

To generalize this approach for more complex scenarios, YOCO can split the image into $M + 1$ parts along the height and $N + 1$ parts along the width, producing $(M + 1) \times (N + 1)$ sub-images. This is represented as:

$$[X_{i,j}] = \text{cut}^{M,N}(X), \quad i = 1, \ldots, M + 1, \ j = 1, \ldots, N + 1, \tag{4}$$

where $X_{i,j}$ denotes the sub-image located in the i-th row and j-th column of the grid. Each sub-image $X_{i,j}$ is independently augmented using a corresponding augmentation function $a_{i,j}(\cdot)$. The final augmented image is then reconstructed by concatenating all augmented sub-images:

$$X' = \text{concat}_{i=1,j=1}^{M+1,N+1}[a_{i,j}(X_{i,j})]. \tag{5}$$

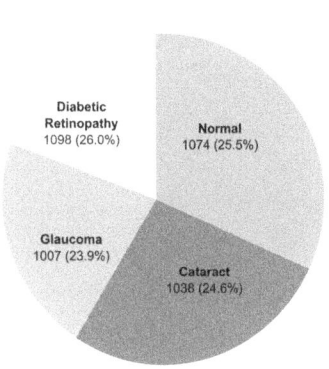

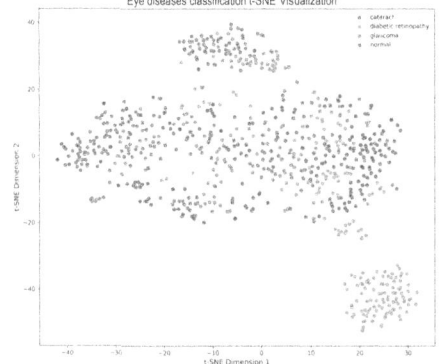

Fig. 4. Eye disease classification dataset [5] with four categories (23.9%-26.0%).

Fig. 5. t-SNE visualization of eye diseases [5], showing clustering patterns across cataract, diabetic retinopathy, glaucoma, and normal cases.

By augmenting sub-regions while preserving global structure, YOCO boosts data diversity, aiding detection of localized features in medical imaging and improving model robustness.

3.4 CropMix

CropMix [10] enhances generalization by using multi-scale random crops to increase diversity and reduce labeling errors, benefiting medical imaging with limited data and complex lesions.

Let I represent the original input medical image, and I_i denote a cropped view of I, obtained through random resized cropping (RRC) with crop scale s_i, where $s_i \in [s_{\min}, s_{\max}]$. The cropped views I_i are generated to capture both fine-grained and coarse-grained information from the image. To combine these views, a mixing coefficient λ is sampled from a Beta distribution, denoted as $\lambda \sim \text{Beta}(\alpha, \alpha)$, where $\alpha > 0$ controls the interpolation strength. The mixed image $\tilde{I}$ is computed using the following formula:

$$\tilde{I} = \lambda I_1 + (1 - \lambda)I_2, \tag{6}$$

where I_1 and I_2 are two randomly selected cropped views of I, and λ determines the mixing ratio. Since all cropped views are derived from the same image, the label y of the original image I remains unchanged, ensuring semantic consistency:

$$\tilde{y} = y. \tag{7}$$

In medical imaging applications, CropMix, as illustrated in panels (d) of Figs. 2 and 3, leverages the multi-scale information captured from the cropped

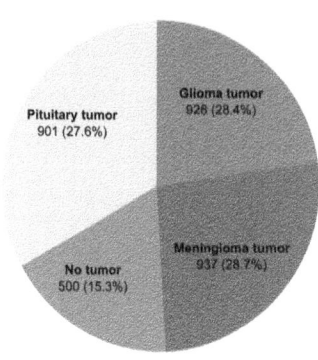
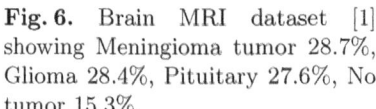

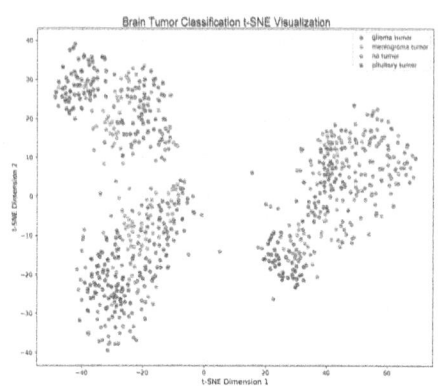

Fig. 6. Brain MRI dataset [1] showing Meningioma tumor 28.7%, Glioma 28.4%, Pituitary 27.6%, No tumor 15.3%.

Fig. 7. t-SNE visualization of brain tumor categories [1] showing clustering of glioma, meningioma, pituitary, and non-tumor cases.

views to enhance the model's ability to learn localized lesion features while retaining global anatomical structures. For example, in lesion classification tasks, the combination of fine-grained and coarse-grained information helps the model focus on both detailed lesion characteristics and broader contextual cues. By interpolating cropped views and preserving labels, CropMix effectively reduces sensitivity to label noise, alleviates overfitting, and improves robustness, making it highly valuable for medical image analysis.

3.5   CutMix

CutMix [28] is a data augmentation technique that improves the generalization ability of neural networks by combining regions from different images and interpolating their labels. Let I_A and I_B represent two randomly selected input images from the training dataset, and y_A and y_B be their corresponding one-hot encoded labels. A binary mask M is used to define the region in I_A that is replaced with a patch from I_B. The mixing ratio λ is sampled from a Beta distribution, denoted as $\lambda \sim \text{Beta}(\alpha, \alpha)$, where $\alpha > 0$ controls the interpolation strength. The mixed image $\tilde{I}$ and label $\tilde{y}$ are computed as:

$$\tilde{I} = M \odot I_A + (1 - M) \odot I_B, \quad \tilde{y} = \lambda y_A + (1 - \lambda)y_B. \tag{8}$$

I_A and I_B are two randomly selected input images, while y_A and y_B are their corresponding one-hot encoded labels. The binary mask M defines the region in I_A that is replaced with pixels from I_B, and λ represents the mixing ratio, which is proportional to the area of M. The mixed image $\tilde{I}$ is obtained by combining I_A and I_B based on M, while the mixed label $\tilde{y}$ interpolates y_A and y_B using λ and $1 - \lambda$ as weights.

Table 1. Comparative performance on **brain tumor classification dataset** [1]

Method	Backbone	Accuracy	Precision	Recall	Sensitivity	Specificity	F1 Score	ROC AUC
Baseline	ResNet-50	76.4	83.18	76.14	75.26	91.69	72.22	92.34
	ViT-B	85.20	84.78	82.58	81.55	93.94	82.55	96.61
AugMix	ResNet-50	$76.65_{+0.25}$	$82.35_{-0.83}$	$76.65_{+0.51}$	$75.94_{+0.68}$	$91.92_{+0.23}$	$73.72_{+1.5}$	$94.11_{+1.77}$
	ViT-B	$97.51_{+12.31}$	$84.63_{-0.15}$	$84.32_{+1.74}$	$83.39_{+1.84}$	$94.53_{+0.59}$	$84.32_{+1.77}$	$95.39_{-1.22}$
CropMix	ResNet-50	$73.35_{-3.05}$	$78.58_{-4.60}$	$73.35_{-2.79}$	$71.20_{-4.06}$	$90.78_{-0.91}$	$70.85_{-1.37}$	$91.47_{-0.87}$
	ViT-B	$99.05_{+13.85}$	$86.10_{+1.32}$	$86.06_{+3.48}$	$85.40_{+3.85}$	$95.16_{+1.22}$	$86.00_{+3.45}$	$96.80_{+0.19}$
CutMix	ResNet-50	$74.37_{-2.03}$	$81.82_{-1.36}$	$74.37_{-1.77}$	$72.63_{-2.63}$	$91.04_{-0.65}$	$72.73_{+0.51}$	$91.87_{-0.47}$
	ViT-B	$97.61_{+12.41}$	$87.57_{+2.79}$	$87.28_{+4.70}$	$86.63_{+5.08}$	$95.59_{+1.65}$	$87.29_{+4.74}$	$96.41_{-0.20}$
MixUp	ResNet-50	$79.19_{+2.79}$	$84.50_{+1.32}$	$74.36_{-1.78}$	$79.19_{+3.93}$	$78.53_{-13.16}$	$92.77_{+20.55}$	$76.55_{-15.79}$
	ViT-B	$98.52_{+13.42}$	$89.05_{+4.27}$	$89.02_{+6.44}$	$89.14_{+7.59}$	$96.27_{+2.33}$	$88.98_{+6.43}$	$97.42_{+0.81}$
SnapMix	ResNet-50	$78.68_{+2.28}$	$84.21_{+1.03}$	$78.68_{+2.54}$	$77.25_{+1.99}$	$92.58_{+0.89}$	$76.72_{+4.50}$	$93.70_{+1.36}$
	ViT-B	$99.44_{+14.24}$	$90.68_{+5.90}$	$90.59_{+8.01}$	$90.83_{+9.28}$	$96.72_{+2.78}$	$90.62_{+8.07}$	$97.82_{+1.21}$
YOCO	ResNet-50	$74.37_{-2.03}$	$79.73_{-3.45}$	$74.37_{-1.77}$	$72.78_{-2.48}$	$91.11_{-0.58}$	$71.92_{-0.30}$	$91.79_{-0.55}$
	ViT-B	$95.02_{+9.82}$	$87.64_{+2.86}$	$87.63_{+5.05}$	$87.92_{+6.37}$	$95.75_{+1.81}$	$87.54_{+4.99}$	$97.21_{+0.60}$

The binary mask M is determined by sampling the bounding box coordinates r_x and r_y, and dimensions r_w and r_h. The coordinates r_x and r_y are sampled uniformly:

$$r_x \sim \text{Unif}(0, W), \quad r_y \sim \text{Unif}(0, H), \tag{9}$$

where W and H are the width and height of the image. The dimensions r_w and r_h are computed as:

$$r_w = W\sqrt{1 - \lambda}, \quad r_h = H\sqrt{1 - \lambda}. \tag{10}$$

During training, the loss function is defined as:

$$\mathcal{L} = \frac{1}{n} \sum_{i=1}^{n} \ell(f(\tilde{I}_i), \tilde{y}_i), \tag{11}$$

where f denotes the neural network model, ℓ represents the loss function (e.g., cross-entropy), n is the batch size, and $(\tilde{I}_i, \tilde{y}_i)$ are the mixed image and label for the i-th training example.

In medical imaging, CutMix, shown in panels (e) of Figs. 2 and 3, tackles limited data and class imbalance by replacing regions and interpolating labels. It enhances datasets, reduces overfitting, and improves robustness, benefiting medical image analysis.

3.6 AugMix

AugMix [12] improves robustness and uncertainty estimation, addressing data corruption and unseen perturbations in medical imaging for reliable predictions.

Table 2. Comparative performance on **eye diseases classification dataset** [5]

Method	Backbone	Accuracy	Precision	Recall	Sensitivity	Specificity	F1 Score	ROC AUC
Baseline	ResNet-50	90.77	87.95	85.78	85.79	85.98	85.98	96.12
	ViT-B	80.36	80.61	78.81	78.90	92.99	79.17	95.45
AugMix	ResNet-50	$83.31_{-7.46}$	$84.55_{-3.40}$	$83.31_{-2.47}$	$83.33_{-2.46}$	$94.46_{+8.48}$	$83.53_{-2.45}$	$95.85_{-0.27}$
	ViT-B	$93.71_{+13.35}$	$82.13_{+1.52}$	$81.63_{+2.82}$	$81.51_{+2.61}$	$93.91_{+0.92}$	$81.51_{+2.34}$	$94.70_{-0.75}$
CropMix	ResNet-50	$73.25_{-17.52}$	$77.15_{-10.80}$	$73.25_{-12.53}$	$73.57_{-12.22}$	$91.13_{+5.15}$	$72.90_{-13.08}$	$92.24_{-3.88}$
	ViT-B	$97.32_{+16.96}$	$83.91_{+3.30}$	$83.56_{+4.75}$	$83.55_{+4.65}$	$94.54_{+1.55}$	$83.66_{+4.49}$	$95.13_{-0.32}$
CutMix	ResNet-50	$73.25_{-17.52}$	$77.15_{-10.80}$	$73.25_{-12.53}$	$73.57_{-12.22}$	$91.13_{+5.15}$	$72.90_{-13.08}$	$92.24_{-3.88}$
	ViT-B	$97.94_{+17.58}$	$81.08_{+0.47}$	$81.04_{+2.23}$	$80.87_{+1.97}$	$93.69_{+0.70}$	$80.96_{+1.79}$	$94.74_{-0.71}$
MixUp	ResNet-50	$88.99_{-1.78}$	$89.50_{+1.55}$	$88.99_{+3.21}$	$88.68_{+2.89}$	$96.33_{+10.35}$	$88.75_{+2.77}$	$97.69_{+1.57}$
	ViT-B	$90.55_{-0.22}$	$83.88_{+3.27}$	$83.26_{+4.45}$	$83.14_{+4.24}$	$94.44_{+1.45}$	$83.47_{+4.30}$	$95.96_{+0.51}$
SnapMix	ResNet-50	$87.69_{-3.08}$	$88.81_{+0.86}$	$87.69_{+1.91}$	$87.32_{+1.53}$	$95.89_{+9.91}$	$87.59_{+1.61}$	$96.51_{+0.39}$
	ViT-B	$93.93_{+3.16}$	$81.14_{+0.53}$	$81.04_{+2.23}$	$80.76_{+1.86}$	$93.69_{+0.70}$	$80.99_{+1.82}$	$94.20_{-1.25}$
YOCO	ResNet-50	$91.60_{+0.83}$	$91.78_{+3.83}$	$91.60_{+5.82}$	$91.37_{+5.58}$	$97.20_{+11.22}$	$91.51_{+5.53}$	$97.89_{+1.77}$
	ViT-B	$97.72_{+17.36}$	$87.65_{+7.04}$	$87.56_{+8.75}$	$87.36_{+8.46}$	$95.86_{+2.87}$	$87.52_{+8.35}$	$97.27_{+1.82}$

Let x_{orig} represent the original input medical image, and O denote the set of augmentation operations (e.g., rotation, translation, posterization). AugMix generates augmented images by combining multiple augmentation chains, where k is the number of chains, and w_i is the mixing weight for the i-th chain, sampled from a Dirichlet distribution: $w \sim \mathrm{Dirichlet}(\alpha, \ldots, \alpha)$. The augmented image x_{aug} is computed as:

$$x_{\mathrm{aug}} = \sum_{i=1}^{k} w_i \cdot \mathrm{chain}_i(x_{\mathrm{orig}}), \qquad (12)$$

where $\mathrm{chain}_i(\cdot)$ represents an augmentation chain composed of multiple operations. The final AugMix image x_{augmix} is interpolated between x_{orig} and x_{aug}, with interpolation weight m sampled from a Beta distribution: $m \sim \mathrm{Beta}(\alpha, \alpha)$. The interpolation is defined as:

$$x_{\mathrm{augmix}} = m \cdot x_{\mathrm{orig}} + (1 - m) \cdot x_{\mathrm{aug}}. \qquad (13)$$

To enforce consistency across embeddings, AugMix introduces the Jensen-Shannon divergence consistency loss $\mathcal{L}_{\mathrm{JS}}$. This loss measures the divergence between the model's predicted distributions for the original image x_{orig} and two independently generated AugMix images x_{augmix1} and x_{augmix2}. The loss is defined as:

$$\mathcal{L}_{\mathrm{JS}} = \mathrm{JS}(p(y|x_{\mathrm{orig}}), p(y|x_{\mathrm{augmix1}}), p(y|x_{\mathrm{augmix2}})), \qquad (14)$$

where $p(y|x)$ is the model's predicted distribution for image x, and $\mathrm{JS}(\cdot)$ represents the Jensen-Shannon divergence.

In medical imaging, AugMix, shown in panels (f) of Figs. 2 and 3, enhances robustness to perturbations and uncertainty estimation. The augmented image

x_{aug} ensures variability with semantic consistency, while x_{augmix} interpolates with the original image. The Jensen-Shannon loss $\mathcal{L}_{\text{JS}}$ improves calibration and reduces sensitivity, benefiting tasks like disease classification and lesion segmentation.

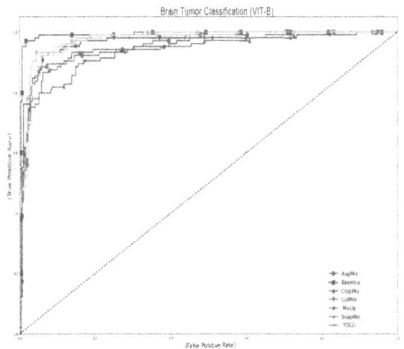
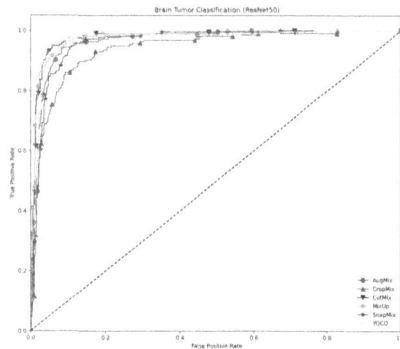

Fig. 8. ROC curves with ViT-B on brain tumor dataset [1].

Fig. 9. ROC curves with ResNet-50 on brain tumor dataset [1].

3.7 SnapMix

SnapMix [13] uses class activation maps (CAM) to maintain semantic consistency in image-label mixing, enhancing performance in medical imaging by focusing on lesions, reducing overfitting, and improving robustness in tasks like disease classification.

Let I_i denote an input medical image with label y_i (e.g., disease class or lesion type). The class activation map CAM_i for I_i is normalized to sum to 1, producing a semantic percent map SPM_i that represents pixel-level semantic relevance. A region R_i is cropped from I_i, and its semantic ratio SR_i is computed as:

$$\text{SR}_i = \sum_{p \in R_i} \text{SPM}_i(p), \tag{15}$$

where p represents a pixel in the cropped region R_i. The semantic ratio SR_i quantifies the semantic importance of the region R_i based on the values in SPM_i.

To create a mixed image $\tilde{I}$, SnapMix combines cropped regions R_a and R_b from two input images I_a and I_b:

$$\tilde{I} = R_a + R_b. \tag{16}$$

The mixed label $\tilde{y}$ for $\tilde{I}$ is computed by weighting the original labels y_a and y_b of I_a and I_b according to their semantic ratios SR_a and SR_b:

$$\tilde{y} = \frac{\text{SR}_a}{\text{SR}_a + \text{SR}_b} \cdot y_a + \frac{\text{SR}_b}{\text{SR}_a + \text{SR}_b} \cdot y_b. \tag{17}$$

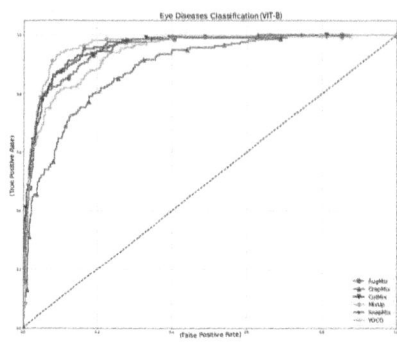 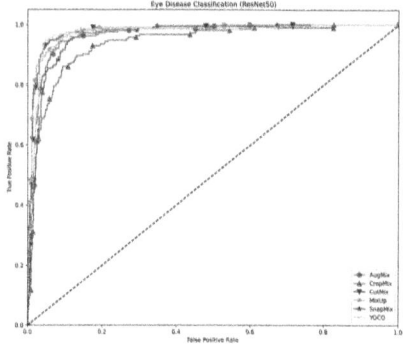

Fig. 10. ROC curves with ViT-B on eye diseases dataset [5].

Fig. 11. ROC curves with ResNet-50 on eye diseases dataset [5].

Table 3. Ablation study on the CutMix interpolation parameter α using the ViT-B backbone on the eye diseases dataset, demonstrating CutMix performance across different α values

α value	Accuracy	Precision	Recall	Sensitivity	Specificity	F1 Score	ROC AUC
$\alpha = 1.0$	**97.94**	**81.08**	**81.04**	**80.87**	**93.69**	**80.96**	**94.74**
$\alpha = 0.8$	96.78	80.42	80.33	80.15	93.21	80.37	94.32
$\alpha = 0.6$	95.35	79.76	79.82	79.64	92.87	79.79	93.86
$\alpha = 0.4$	93.21	78.45	78.61	78.40	92.35	78.53	93.12
$\alpha = 0.2$	90.64	76.92	77.18	76.95	91.83	77.05	92.47

This ensures that the mixed label $\tilde{y}$ accurately reflects the semantic contributions of R_a and R_b to the mixed image $\tilde{I}$.

In medical imaging, SnapMix, shown in panels (g) of Figs. 2 and 3, uses CAMs to preserve semantic information, with the semantic ratio SR_i focusing on diagnostically relevant regions. This reduces overfitting, enhances robustness, and improves generalization, proving valuable in medical image analysis.

4 Experiments

4.1 Datasets and Evaluation Matrices

Brain Tumor Classification Dataset. [1] includes four categories: glioma tumor, meningioma tumor, no tumor, and pituitary tumor. A pie chart Fig. 6 reveals an imbalanced class distribution. t-SNE visualization Fig. 7 shows pituitary tumor forms distinct clusters, while glioma tumor and meningioma tumor partially overlap. No tumor is dispersed and overlaps significantly with other categories, increasing classification difficulty.

Table 4. Ablation study on the CutMix interpolation parameter α using ResNet-50 backbone on the eye diseases dataset, demonstrating CutMix performance across different α values

α value	Accuracy	Precision	Recall	Sensitivity	Specificity	F1 Score	ROC AUC
$\alpha = 1.0$	**91.83**	**91.97**	**91.83**	**91.67**	**97.29**	**91.86**	**98.22**
$\alpha = 0.8$	91.25	91.39	91.25	91.08	97.05	91.32	97.86
$\alpha = 0.6$	90.86	90.98	90.86	90.72	96.84	90.92	97.43
$\alpha = 0.4$	90.42	90.58	90.42	90.25	96.65	90.50	97.12
$\alpha = 0.2$	90.15	90.28	90.15	90.04	96.42	90.21	96.85

Eye Diseases Classification Dataset [5] includes cataract, diabetic retinopathy, glaucoma, and normal. Balanced classes Fig. 4 support classification, while t-SNE Fig. 5 shows clustering with some overlap, adding difficulty.

Evaluation Matrices: Accuracy measures correctness, *Precision* evaluates positive prediction accuracy, *Recall/Sensitivity* assesses positive detection, *Specificity* measures negative identification, *F1-Score* balances Precision and Recall, and *ROC AUC* indicates class distinction.

4.2   Implementation Details

Datasets were split 8:2 for Training and Testing with a fixed seed. Six augmentations were applied only to training sets. Models trained for 50 epochs at a 0.001 learning rate using Adam on an NVIDIA A100 GPU, CUDA 12.4, Intel Xeon CPU @ 2.20 GHz, and 80G memory.

4.3   Comparative Study

Tables 1 and 2 present our comparative experiments on augmentation techniques for medical image classification. For brain tumour classification (Table 1), **MixUp** with ResNet-50 achieves the highest performance gains, increasing accuracy to **79.19%**, while **SnapMix** with ViT-B achieves the highest gains, increasing accuracy to **99.44%**, as evidenced by the ROC curves in Figs. 8 and 9.

For eye diseases classification (Table 2), **YOCO** with ResNet-50 achieves the highest performance gains, increasing accuracy by 0.83% to **91.60%** and ROC AUC by 1.77% to **97.89%**. Meanwhile, **CutMix** with ViT-B achieves the highest gains, increasing accuracy by 17.58% to **97.94%**, as shown in Figs. 10 and 11.

Our study indicates that specific combinations excel in particular applications, with MixUp on ResNet-50 and SnapMix on ViT-B optimal for brain tumour classification and YOCO on ResNet-50 and CutMix on ViT-B optimal for eye disease classification.

4.4   Ablation Study

Tables 3 and 4 show that increasing the CutMix interpolation parameter α improves performance, with $\alpha = 1.0$ yielding the best results where ViT-B achieves **97.94%** accuracy and ResNet-50 reaches **91.83%**. This highlights the importance of hyperparameter tuning for mix-based augmentations. However, the optimal strategies remain unchanged where MixUp with ResNet-50 and SnapMix with ViT-B perform best for brain tumors and YOCO with ResNet-50 and CutMix with ViT-B perform best for eye diseases. This tuning approach applies to MixUp, SnapMix, and YOCO, demonstrating its broad utility.

5   Conclusion

MediAug benchmarks six mix-based augmentations on brain tumor MRI and eye disease classification. Optimal combinations are MixUp with ResNet-50 and SnapMix with ViT-B for brain tumors, and YOCO with ResNet-50 and CutMix with ViT-B for eye diseases. Hyperparameter tuning is emphasized as crucial, providing guidance for robust and generalizable AI in medical imaging.

References

1. Bhuvaji, S., Kadam, A., Bhumkar, P., Dedge, S., Kanchan, S.: Brain tumor classification (MRI) (2020). https://doi.org/10.34740/KAGGLE/DSV/1183165. https://www.kaggle.com/dsv/1183165
2. Cai, G., et al.: Medical AI for early detection of lung cancer: a survey. arXiv preprint arXiv:2410.14769 (2024)
3. Cai, G., et al.: MSDet: receptive field enhanced multiscale detection for tiny pulmonary nodule. arXiv preprint arXiv:2409.14028 (2024)
4. Cheplygina, V., de Bruijne, M., Pluim, J.P.: Not-so-supervised: a survey of semi-supervised, multi-instance, and transfer learning in medical image analysis. Med. Image Anal. **54**, 280–296 (2019). https://doi.org/10.1016/j.media.2019.02.010
5. Doddi, G.: Eye diseases classification dataset (2023). https://www.kaggle.com/datasets/gunavenkatdoddi/eye-diseases-classification/data. Accessed 28 Mar 2025
6. Dosovitskiy, A., et al.: An image is worth 16 × 16 words: transformers for image recognition at scale. In: International Conference on Learning Representations (2021)
7. Esteva, A., et al.: Dermatologist-level classification of skin cancer with deep neural networks. Nature **542**(7639), 115–118 (2017)
8. Ge, J., Zhang, Z., Phan, M.H., Zhang, B., Liu, A., Zhao, Y.: ESA: annotation-efficient active learning for semantic segmentation. arXiv preprint arXiv:2408.13491 (2024)
9. Han, J., et al.: You only cut once: boosting data augmentation with a single cut. In: International Conference on Machine Learning, pp. 8196–8212. PMLR (2022)
10. Han, J., Petersson, L., Li, H., Reid, I.: Cropmix: sampling a rich input distribution via multi-scale cropping. arXiv preprint arXiv:2205.15955 (2022)
11. He, K., Zhang, X., Ren, S., Sun, J.: Deep residual learning for image recognition. In: Proceedings of the IEEE Conference on Computer Vision and Pattern Recognition, pp. 770–778 (2016)

12. Hendrycks, D., Mu, N., Cubuk, E.D., Zoph, B., Gilmer, J., Lakshminarayanan, B.: Augmix: a simple data processing method to improve robustness and uncertainty. arXiv preprint arXiv:1912.02781 (2019)
13. Huang, S., Wang, X., Tao, D.: Snapmix: semantically proportional mixing for augmenting fine-grained data. In: Proceedings of the AAAI Conference on Artificial Intelligence, vol. 35, pp. 1628–1636 (2021)
14. Islam, T., Hafiz, M.S., Jim, J.R., Kabir, M.M., Mridha, M.: A systematic review of deep learning data augmentation in medical imaging: recent advances and future research directions. Healthcare Anal. **5**(1), 100340 (2024). https://doi.org/10.1016/j.health.2024.100340
15. Krizhevsky, A., Sutskever, I., Hinton, G.E.: Imagenet classification with deep convolutional neural networks. In: Advances in Neural Information Processing Systems, vol. 25, pp. 1097–1105 (2012)
16. Litjens, G., et al.: A survey on deep learning in medical image analysis. Med. Image Anal. **42**, 60–88 (2017)
17. Luo, Y., et al.: Pathohr: breast cancer survival prediction on high-resolution pathological images. arXiv preprint arXiv:2503.17970 (2025)
18. Ma, Y., Zhang, H., Si, Z., Li, A.: On the transferability of data augmentation approaches from natural images to medical imaging. Med. Image Anal. **81**, 102533 (2022). https://doi.org/10.1016/j.media.2022.102533
19. Perez, L., Wang, J.: The effectiveness of data augmentation in image classification using deep learning. arXiv preprint arXiv:1712.04621 (2017)
20. Qi, X., et al.: Projectedex: enhancing generation in explainable AI for prostate cancer. arXiv preprint arXiv:2501.01392 (2025)
21. Qi, X., et al.: Medconv: convolutions beat transformers on long-tailed bone density prediction. arXiv preprint arXiv:2502.00631 (2025)
22. Shorten, C., Khoshgoftaar, T.M.: A survey on image data augmentation for deep learning. J. Big Data **6**(1), 1–48 (2019)
23. Tajbakhsh, N., et al.: Convolutional neural networks for medical image analysis: full training or fine tuning? IEEE Trans. Med. Imaging **35**, 1299–1312 (2016). https://doi.org/10.1109/TMI.2016.2535302
24. Tan, S., et al.: Segkan: high-resolution medical image segmentation with long-distance dependencies. arXiv preprint arXiv:2412.19990 (2024)
25. Tan, S., et al.: Segstitch: multidimensional transformer for robust and efficient medical imaging segmentation. arXiv preprint arXiv:2408.00496 (2024)
26. Wu, B., et al.: BHSD: a 3D multi-class brain hemorrhage segmentation dataset. In: International Workshop on Machine Learning in Medical Imaging, pp. 147–156. Springer, Cham (2023)
27. Wu, B., et al.: Xlip: cross-modal attention masked modelling for medical language-image pre-training. arXiv preprint arXiv:2407.19546 (2024)
28. Yun, S., Han, D., Oh, S.J., Chun, S., Choe, J., Yoo, Y.: Cutmix: regularization strategy to train strong classifiers with localizable features. In: Proceedings of the IEEE/CVF International Conference on Computer Vision, pp. 6023–6032 (2019)
29. Zhang, H., Cisse, M., Dauphin, Y.N., Lopez-Paz, D.: mixup: beyond empirical risk minimization. arXiv preprint arXiv:1710.09412 (2017)
30. Zhang, R., Guo, H., Zhang, Z., Yan, P., Zhao, S.: Gamed-snake: gradient-aware adaptive momentum evolution deep snake model for multi-organ segmentation. arXiv preprint arXiv:2501.12844 (2025)
31. Zhang, Z., Ahmed, K.A., Hasan, M.R., Gedeon, T., Hossain, M.Z.: A deep learning approach to diabetes diagnosis. In: Asian Conference on Intelligent Information and Database Systems, pp. 87–99. Springer, Cham (2024)

32. Zhang, Z., et al.: Jointvit: modeling oxygen saturation levels with joint supervision on long-tailed octa. In: Annual Conference on Medical Image Understanding and Analysis, pp. 158–172. Springer, Cham (2024)
33. Zhang, Z., et al.: Segreg: segmenting oars by registering MR images and CT annotations. In: 2024 IEEE International Symposium on Biomedical Imaging (ISBI), pp. 1–5. IEEE (2024)
34. Zhang, Z., et al.: Meddet: generative adversarial distillation for efficient cervical disc herniation detection. In: 2024 IEEE International Conference on Bioinformatics and Biomedicine (BIBM), pp. 4024–4027. IEEE (2024)
35. Zhang, Z., et al.: Thin-thick adapter: segmenting thin scans using thick annotations. OpenReview (2023)
36. Zhao, R., et al.: Peddet: adaptive spectral optimization for multimodal pedestrian detection. arXiv preprint arXiv:2502.14063 (2025)
37. Zhao, Y., et al.: A landmark-based approach for instability prediction in distal radius fractures. In: 2024 IEEE International Symposium on Biomedical Imaging (ISBI), pp. 1–5. IEEE (2024)
38. Zhu, H., et al.: Doei: dual optimization of embedding information for attention-enhanced class activation maps. arXiv preprint arXiv:2502.15885 (2025)

On the Robustness of Medical Vision-Language Models: Are They Truly Generalizable?

Raza Imam$^{(\boxtimes)}$ [ID], Rufael Marew [ID], and Mohammad Yaqub [ID]

Mohamed bin Zayed University of Artificial Intelligence, Abu Dhabi, UAE
{raza.imam,rufael.marew,mohammad.yaqub}@mbzuai.ac.ae

Abstract. Medical Vision-Language Models (MVLMs) have achieved *par excellence* generalization in medical image analysis, yet their performance under noisy, corrupted conditions remains largely untested. Clinical imaging is inherently susceptible to acquisition artifacts and noise; however, existing evaluations predominantly assess generally clean datasets, overlooking robustness—*i.e.*, the model's ability to perform under real-world distortions. To address this gap, we first introduce MediMeta-C, a corruption benchmark that systematically applies several perturbations across multiple medical imaging datasets. Combined with MedMNIST-C, this establishes a comprehensive robustness evaluation framework for MVLMs. We further propose RobustMedCLIP, a visual encoder adaptation of a pretrained MVLM that incorporates few-shot tuning to enhance resilience against corruptions. Through extensive experiments, we benchmark 5 major MVLMs across 5 medical imaging modalities, revealing that existing models exhibit severe degradation under corruption and struggle with domain-modality tradeoffs. Our findings highlight the necessity of diverse training and robust adaptation strategies, demonstrating that efficient low-rank adaptation when paired with few-shot tuning, improves robustness while preserving generalization across modalities.

Keywords: Medical VLM · Generalization · Robustness · Healthcare

1 Introduction

In recent years, Medical Vision-Language Models (MVLMs) have emerged as powerful tools for analyzing medical imaging data by leveraging large-scale multimodal learning [18,26,29]. These models have demonstrated impressive accuracy in zero-shot and few-shot medical image classification, making them promising candidates for real-world deployment. However, despite improvements in generalization accuracy, the *robustness* of MVLMs under real-world distribution shifts, from the point of corruptions, remains largely unexplored. Clinical imaging in practice is often affected by artifacts and noise introduced during acquisition and

---

Dataset and Code is available at: Github.
Accepted at: Medical Image Understanding and Analysis (MIUA) 2025.

© The Author(s), under exclusive license to Springer Nature Switzerland AG 2026
S. Ali et al. (Eds.): MIUA 2025, LNCS 15916, pp. 233–256, 2026.
https://doi.org/10.1007/978-3-031-98688-8_17

Table 1. Overview of dataset statistics for MediMeta [27] and MedMNIST [3], covering the common imaging modalities analyzed in this study. #Val/Test represents the number of validation and test samples. Extended statistics are provided in **Appendix**.

Modality ↓	MediMeta			MedMNIST		
	Data Name	#Val/Test	Description	Data Name	#Val/Test	Description
Cell Microscopy	PBC	1,709/3,149	Blood cells	BloodMNIST	1,712/3,421	Blood cells
Breast Imaging	Mammo	214/326	Calcifications	BreastMNIST	78/156	Breast tumors
Chest X-ray	Pneumonia	817/624	Lung infection	PneumoniaMNIST	524/624	Lung infection
Fundoscopy	Fundus	640/640	Eye diseases	RetinaMNIST	120/400	Eye diseases
Retinal OCT	OCT	16,694/1,000	Retinal layers	OCTMNIST	10,832/1,000	Retinal layers

preprocessing, which can significantly degrade model performance. Existing evaluations [2,4,30] predominantly focus on clean datasets, overlooking the impact of such corruptions. Without systematic robustness assessment, the reliability of MVLMs in practical medical scenarios remains uncertain, raising concerns about their safety and effectiveness in clinical decision-making.

Although datasets such as CheXpert [14] and MedMNIST [3] are carefully curated to ensure high-quality images through fixed resolutions and rigorous normalization, they fail to capture the range of corruptions and distribution shifts encountered in real-world clinical settings. Inspired by ImageNet-C [10], MedMNIST-C [5] was proposed to introduce controlled distortions. However, its reliance on low-resolution MedMNIST data, use of modality-specific corruptions, and disregard for the inherently lower high-frequency content of medical images limit its ability to fully represent authentic imaging challenges [28]. This highlights the need for a more comprehensive corruption benchmark that effectively evaluates the robustness of MVLMs and other medical AI models.

A critical aspect of robustness evaluation is understanding how different types and severities of corruptions impact MVLM performance across various medical imaging modalities (Table 1). Traditional learning models typically rely on extensive dataset curation and domain-specific adaptations to improve resilience [17]. In contrast, MVLMs introduced a paradigm where contrastive learning could play a pivotal role in addressing robustness challenges. Given their strong generalization capabilities, it is necessary to investigate whether contrastively learned pretrained MVLMs, when effectively combined with robust adaptation techniques, can mitigate the impact of corruptions and enhance MVLMs reliability. These challenges motivate us to answer the following:

Research Questions

Q1. Do MVLMs maintain performance when facing visual corruptions?

Q2. How do corruption types and their severities affect MVLM generalization across clinical modalities?

Q3. Do accurate MVLMs directly correlate with robustness against corruptions and distribution shifts?

Q4. How can few-shot sampling be *efficiently* infused with the presence of strong MVLMs to address generalization despite corruptions?

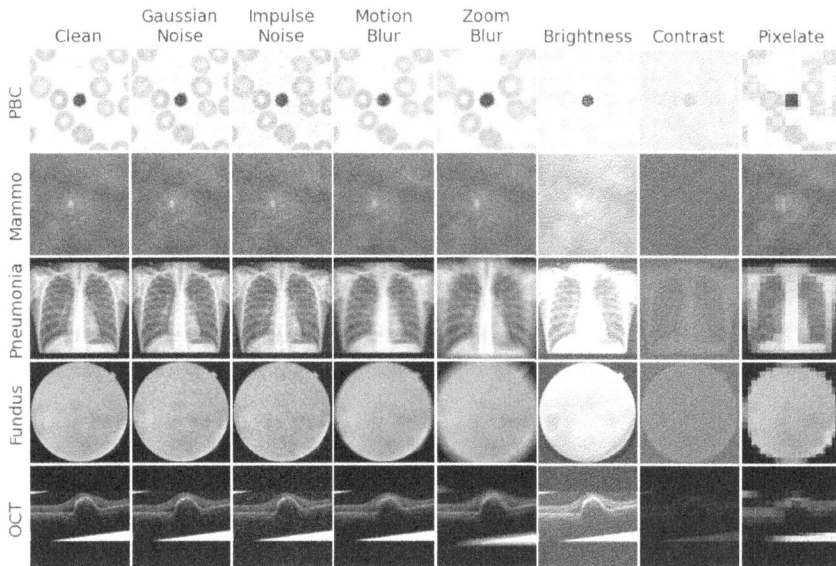

Fig. 1. Corrupted samples from our MediMeta-C dataset. The y-axis shows dataset names by modality and the x-axis displays corruption types at a fixed severity level.

To answer these research questions, we introduce **MediMeta-C**, a corruption benchmark specifically designed for medical imaging. By combining MediMeta-C with MedMNIST-C [5], we establish a comprehensive evaluation framework to assess model robustness across multiple imaging modalities. Furthermore, we propose **RobustMedCLIP**, a novel adaptation of a pretrained MVLM (such as BioMedCLIP [29] and MedCLIP [26]) that incorporates few-shot fine-tuning to enhance performance under corrupted conditions. Through extensive experiments, we benchmark MVLMs against a range of seven corruptions, providing valuable insights into their resilience and adaptability in real-world medical settings. Overall, our key contributions are summarized as follows:

1. **MediMeta-C Dataset**: A corruption classification benchmark for evaluation that applies 7 systematic perturbations to 5 medical imaging datasets to simulate real-world OOD shifts.
2. **Corruption MVLM Benchmarking**: A unified evaluation framework combining MediMeta-C and MedMNIST-C to analyze the robustness of 5 major MVLMs across 5 medical imaging modalities across classification tasks.
3. **RobustMedCLIP**: A robust adaptation of pretrained MVLM that integrates efficient few-shot-tuning to enhance visual representations to achieve better generalization and robustness against corruptions.
4. **Extensive Evaluations**: A systematic study assessing the impact of various corruption types and severities across multiple MVLMs robustness, while evaluating the true generality of existing MVLMs.
5. **Datasets and Code**: We release our benchmark dataset and APIs, promoting standardized robustness evaluation practices in medical AI research.

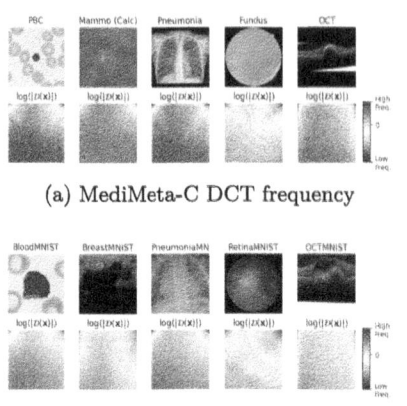

(a) MediMeta-C DCT frequency

(b) MedMNIST-C DCT frequency

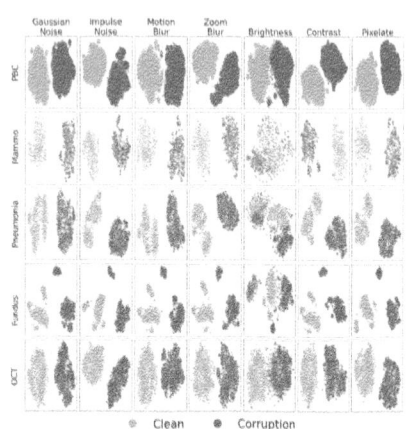

● Clean ● Corruption

Fig. 2. Comparison of average **DCT frequency distributions** across datasets. Medical images generally exhibit *higher density* of low-frequency content compared to natural images and vice-versa [28]. Among the two, MediMeta-C (a) more clearly demonstrates this assumption than MedMNIST-C (b).

Fig. 3. t-SNE visualization of the **clean and corrupted feature distributions**, showing how the *distributions shift* occur at the latent-level due to introduced corruption. MediMeta-C's Corrupted features differ notably than MediMeta's Clean features. Here RN50 backbone is used to extract features.

2   Background

A. Vision-Language Models in Medical Imaging: The adaptation of vision-language models to the medical domain has advanced by modifying dual-encoder architectures. For example, CLIP [23] has been fine-tuned on medical image-text pairs, resulting in variants such as MedCLIP [26] and BioMed-CLIP [29] that employ domain-specific tokenization and contrastive loss adjustments. However, training on clean, curated datasets leaves these models vulnerable to the distribution shifts and noise present in real-world clinical imaging. This vulnerability underscores the need for corruption-specific adaptations—such as fine-tuning on distorted samples and robust weak or unsupervised strategies [13]—to improve resilience against imaging artifacts and ensure reliable performance.

B. Robustness in Healthcare: Among the reliable strategies in trustworthy solutions, approaches such as adversarial training [6,7,22] and domain adaptation have been shown to achieve consistent and generalizable model robustness across various recognition tasks [19]. To enhance robustness in healthcare AI, multimodal fusion architectures with knowledge distillation have improved patient outcome predictions by integrating chest X-rays, clinical texts, and tabular data [9]. Additionally, combining clinical time-series data with chest X-rays

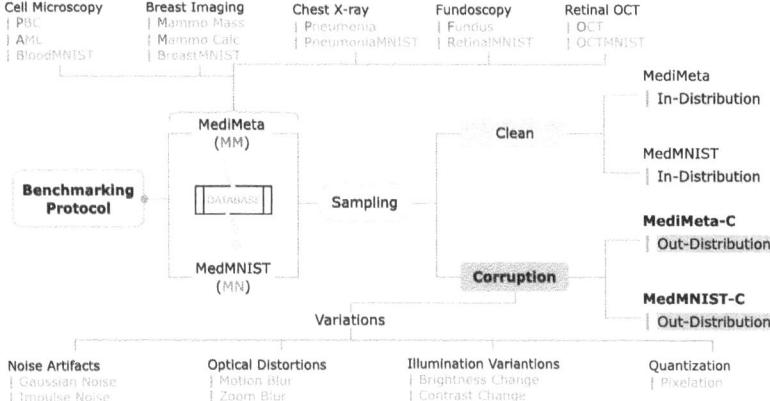

Fig. 4. Benchmarking protocol used in our evaluation, where clean samples represent *In-Distribution* data seen by RMC, while corrupted samples correspond to *Out-Distribution* shifts. *Sampling* refers to selecting the *testset* from each dataset.

using transformer-based models has boosted diagnostic performance, highlighting the role of multimodal fusion in improving robustness [16]. These advancements emphasize the need for resilient [8], multimodal AI systems in healthcare.

3 Methodology

3.1 Medical Corruption Benchmark

A. MediMeta-C Design: We introduce MediMeta-C, a corruption benchmark derived from the MediMeta dataset [27] that is designed to emulate distribution shifts encountered in real-world clinical imaging. Our benchmark encompasses 7 distinct corruption types, organized into four primary categories: *Noise Artifacts*, *Optical Distortions*, *Illumination Variations*, and *Quantization* or *Compression* errors depicting real-world medical imaging acquisition and preprocessing errors. To capture the variability depicting real-world corruption, each corruption type is implemented at five severity levels as depicted in Fig. 1. Unlike MedMNIST-C [5], which relies on low-resolution data and modality-specific corruptions, MediMeta-C employs diverse perturbations on high-resolution images to better reflect clinical variability. For example, brightness/contrast alterations induce pixel density shifts (Fig. 5C), while DCT analysis[1] reveals corrupted images exhibit amplified low-frequency content and suppressed high-frequency signals [28], a trend more pronounced in MediMeta-C than MedMNIST-C (Fig. 2). Latent feature divergence between clean and corrupted images, visualized via t-SNE (Fig. 3), further confirms the realistic simulation of corruptions in MediMeta-C.

---

[1] DCT frequency analysis [25] applies the Discrete Cosine Transform to convert an image's spatial data into cosine-based frequency components [21].

B. Common Medical Distortions: Specifically, Noise Artifacts—such as *Gaussian Noise* and *Impulse Noise*—can arise during medical image acquisition due to low-light conditions or sensor bit errors. Optical Distortions, including *Motion Blur* and *Zoom Blur*, often occur when there is patient movement or rapid changes in imaging focus. Illumination Variations, evidenced by shifts in *Brightness* and *Contrast*, are frequently encountered as a result of inconsistent exposure settings or variable ambient lighting during the scanning process. Quantization/Compression errors, like *Pixelation* and JPEG artifacts, may be introduced during image upsampling or through lossy compression techniques used in digital processing. Our benchmark encompasses these seven distinct corruption types to closely simulate the real-world challenges encountered in medical imaging acquisition and preprocessing.

C. Benchmarking Protocol: We establish our evaluation framework by leveraging both MediMeta-C and MedMNIST-C to assess the generalization capabilities of MVLMs. As illustrated in Fig. 4, clean samples from MediMeta and MedMNIST serve as in-distribution (*ID*) data representing instances the model has encountered during training while corrupted samples from corruption datasets correspond to Out-of-Distribution (*OOD*) shifts.

> **Constraint**
>
> It is critical to emphasize that our benchmark should be used solely for testing; models should be trained exclusively on clean datasets such as MedMNIST and MediMeta, and not on the corrupted versions provided in MediMeta-C.

This constraint guarantees that any observed performance degradation is attributable to distribution shifts rather than overfitting to specific corruptions. Comparative evaluation of MediMeta-C and MedMNIST-C underscores the benefits of a corruption benchmark that closely mimics real-world medical imaging distortions, thereby enhancing MVLM reliability. Overall, our MediMeta-C encompasses **175** (*i.e.*, $7 \times 5 \times 5$) distinct corruption sets—derived from 7 corruption types, each applied at 5 severity levels across 5 modality-specific datasets—using *testset* images from MediMeta to rigorously test MVLM generalization.

3.2 RobustMedCLIP

RobustMedCLIP (or RMC) enhances robustness against corruption benchmarks by incorporating few-shot fine-tuning into a BioMedCLIP pretrained MVLM. The goal is to efficiently adapt the model using a few clean samples from diverse modalities, achieving improved robustness against corruptions[2], while retaining the rich, generalizable semantics learned during large-scale pretraining. To achieve this, we update low-rank adapters within the query ($\mathcal{Q}$), key ($\mathcal{K}$), and value ($\mathcal{V}$) matrices of the visual encoder. The training objective focuses on optimizing the image encoder weights using only a limited set of annotated examples.

---

[2] Note that lower $\downarrow$ *mean* Corruption Error (mCE) indicates better robustness, while higher $\uparrow$ Accuracy reflects stronger generalization. Refer to Sect. 4 for details.

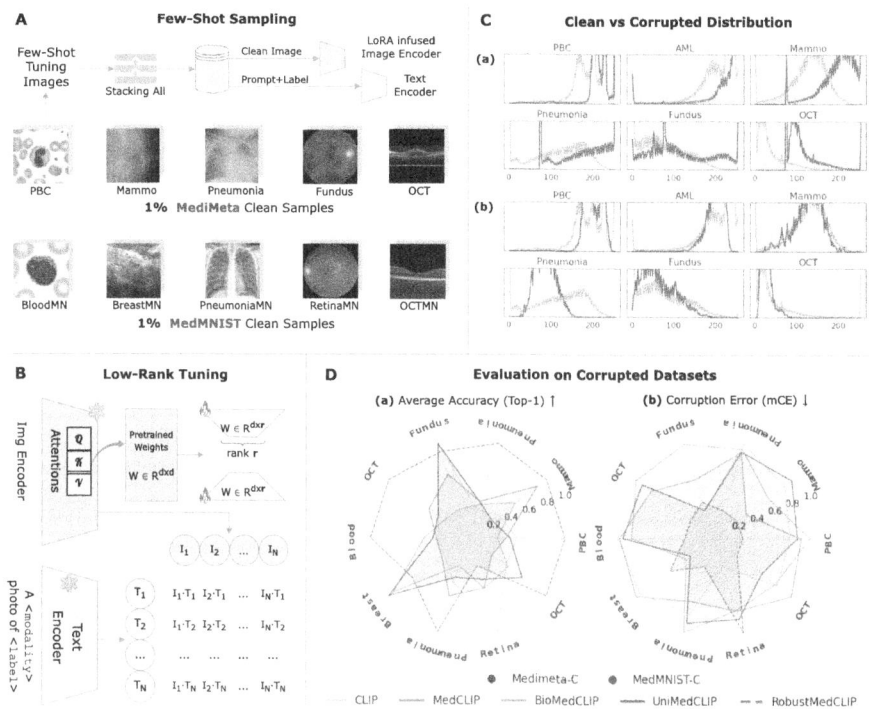

Fig. 5. A) Few-shot samples from each modality are drawn from the clean training set to adapt the LoRA-augmented image encoder of the pretrained BioMedCLIP. **B)** Low-rank attention matrices within the image encoder are updated using Eq. 2, enabling the model to learn from diverse in-distribution modalities while retaining pretrained knowledge. **C)** Pixel-level density distributions comparing Clean and Corrupted samples under (a) brightness and (b) contrast corruptions, highlighting input-level distributional shifts. **D)** (a) Top-1 Accuracy as a measure of *generalization*, and (b) *mean Corruption Error (mCE)* as a proxy for *robustness*, averaged over MediMeta-C and MedMNIST-C. All values are normalized for visual comparability across models.

Rationale behind RMC

We hypothesize that data-modality diversity is more critical than sheer volume, proposing that adapting a low-ranked image encoder with few-shot tuning across a broad yet representative range of clinical domains—*analogous to training on fewer but highly diverse institutions rather than a large dataset confined to a limited set of hospitals*—enhances robustness while preserving cross-modality generalization.

A. Few-Shot Fine-Tuning: Given a dataset $\mathbb{D} \supset \{(X_i, Y_i)\}_{i=1}^{N}$ consisting of medical image-text pairs (Fig. 5A), RMC fine-tunes on a limited subset of annotated examples using contrastively learned pretrained BioMedCLIP. This few-shot tuning allows the MVLM to adapt to unseen distribution shifts without overfitting the training distribution, thereby enhancing its robustness to diverse corruptions and improving generalization. The feature embeddings $\boldsymbol{f}_v$ and $\boldsymbol{f}_t$ for the image and text encoders are obtained as:

$$\boldsymbol{f}_v = \mathcal{F}_{\theta_v}(X_i), \quad \boldsymbol{f}_t = \mathcal{F}_{\theta_t}(Y_i') \quad \text{where} \quad Y_i' = \langle \text{Prompt} \rangle + Y_i, \tag{1}$$

here, $\mathcal{F}_{\theta_v}$ and $\mathcal{F}_{\theta_t}$ denote the image and text encoders, and $\langle \text{Prompt} \rangle$ is a modality-specific prefix (e.g., $\langle$A photo of a modality$(Y_i)\rangle$). $\mathbb{R}$MC employs cross-entropy between true labels Y_i and zero-shot predictions $\hat{Y}_i$ of pretrained MVLM (such as BioMedCLIP or MedCLIP). The fine-tuning loss $\mathcal{L}_{\text{FT}}$ that updates $\mathcal{F}_{\theta_v}$ is given as:

$$\mathcal{L}_{\text{FT}}(\theta_v) = -\sum_i Y_i \log \hat{Y}_i \quad \text{where} \quad \hat{Y}_i = \text{softmax}(S_{i,c}/\tau) = \frac{\exp(S_{i,c}/\tau)}{\sum_{c'} \exp(S_{i,c'}/\tau)}, \tag{2}$$

with $S_{i,c} = \cos(\boldsymbol{f}_v^i, \boldsymbol{f}_t^c) = \boldsymbol{f}_v^i \cdot \boldsymbol{f}_t^c/(\|\boldsymbol{f}_v^i\|_2 \cdot \|\boldsymbol{f}_t^c\|_2)$ representing the cosine similarity between $\boldsymbol{f}_v^i$ and $\boldsymbol{f}_t^c$ for class c, and τ being a temperature parameter.

B. Low-Rank Adapter Optimization: To avoid updating all model parameters during fine-tuning, $\mathbb{R}$MC employs *low-rank adaptation* (LoRA) [11] to efficiently update only a small subset of parameters in the transformer layers using $\mathcal{L}_{\text{FT}}$. Specifically, the query ($\mathcal{Q}$), key ($\mathcal{K}$), and value ($\mathcal{V}$) matrices are modified via low-rank decompositions as follows:

$$\mathcal{Q} = \mathcal{Q} + A_{\mathcal{Q}} B_{\mathcal{Q}}, \quad \mathcal{K} = \mathcal{K} + A_{\mathcal{K}} B_{\mathcal{K}}, \quad \mathcal{V} = \mathcal{V} + A_{\mathcal{V}} B_{\mathcal{V}}, \tag{3}$$

where $A_{\mathcal{Q}}, A_{\mathcal{K}}, A_{\mathcal{V}} \in \mathbb{R}^{d \times r}$ and $B_{\mathcal{Q}}, B_{\mathcal{K}}, B_{\mathcal{V}} \in \mathbb{R}^{r \times d}$ are low-rank matrices (with rank $r \ll d$). This strategy drastically reduces the number of trainable parameters, enabling efficient adaptation without incurring the heavy computational cost of full fine-tuning [12]. By restricting updates to the attention layers via LoRA (Fig. 5B), $\mathbb{R}$MC efficiently adapts domain-specific corruption patterns while preserving the generalizable representations acquired during pretraining.

C. Zero-Shot Inference: After fine-tuning, $\mathbb{R}$MC performs zero-shot classification by leveraging its robust multimodal representations. Given a test medical image X_{test} and a set of textual class descriptions $T = \{t_1, t_2, \ldots, t_c\}$ corresponding to c categories, the MVLM first encodes the inputs as:

$$\boldsymbol{f}_v = \mathcal{F}_{\theta_v}(X_{\text{test}}), \quad \boldsymbol{f}_t^i = \mathcal{F}_{\theta_t}(t_i) \quad \text{for } i = 1, \ldots, c. \tag{4}$$

The cosine similarity between the normalized image embedding $\tilde{\boldsymbol{f}}_v$ and each normalized text embedding $\tilde{\boldsymbol{f}}_t$ is computed as S_{v,t_i} using Eq. 2:

Finally, the model predicts the class corresponding to the highest similarity:

$$\hat{y} = \arg\max_i S_{v,t_i}. \tag{5}$$

This allows the model to assign labels in a zero-shot manner, without requiring any additional task-specific training. Moreover, by directly comparing the embeddings in a shared latent space, the MVLM effectively leverages the learned representations to generalize to unseen classes and corrupted conditions (Fig. 5D).

4   Experimentation

A. Robustness Metric: To evaluate MVLM performance under corrupted datasets, we adopt a robustness metric inspired by ImageNet-C. For a given MVLM model f and a corruption type c applied at severity levels $s = 1, \ldots, 5$, the Top-1 error is computed as

$$E_{s,c}^{f} = 1 - \text{Acc}_{s,c}^{f} \quad \text{where} \quad \text{Acc}_{s,c}^{f} \text{ is the Top-1 accuracy.} \qquad (6)$$

The **Corruption Error (CE)** for MVLM f on corruption c is then defined as

$$\text{CE}_{c}^{f} = \left(\sum_{s=1}^{5} E_{s,c}^{f} \right) / \left(\sum_{s=1}^{5} E_{s,c}^{\text{baseline}} \right), \qquad (7)$$

where the baseline is set to OpenAI CLIP with ViT-B/16. Finally, the **mean Corruption Error (mCE)** is calculated as the average of the CE values across all corruption types:

$$\text{mCE}^{f} = \frac{1}{|C|} \sum_{c \in C} \text{CE}_{c}^{f}, \qquad (8)$$

with C representing the set of corruptions. Moreover, for clean (In-Domain) samples, **Clean Error** is simply computed as $\left(E_{\text{clean}}^{f} \right) / \left(E_{\text{clean}}^{\text{baseline}} \right)$, where $E_{\text{clean}}^{f} = 1 - \text{Acc}_{\text{clean}}^{f}$ and $\text{Acc}_{\text{clean}}^{f}$ is the Top-1 accuracy on the clean dataset. This ensures that both the Clean Error and Corruption Error CE_{c} are computed in a comparable manner, making it easy to assess the relative robustness of a model across both clean and corrupted settings along with Top-1 Average Accuracy[3], providing a comprehensive measure of degradation under out-of-distribution corruption scenarios.

B. Implementation Setup: In our experiments, $\mathbb{R}$MC's few-shot fine-tuning was performed on both Vision Transformer (ViT) and ResNet (RN) backbones. For each backbone, four configurations–using few-shot 1%, 3%, 7%, and 10% of the train set for tuning–were evaluated, resulting in a total of eight variants. All results are reported on the 10% few-shot tuned $\mathbb{R}$MC, unless stated otherwise. We initialize the $\mathbb{R}$MC-ViT and $\mathbb{R}$MC-RN models using BioMedCLIP and MedCLIP pretrained weights, respectively. We optimize the vision encoder using LoRA rank $r = 16$ with the Adam optimizer across 20 epochs with a learning rate of 10^{-4} In computing the mCE (as in Eq. 8), the baseline model is set to OpenAI CLIP [23] consistently. Extended details are provided in **Appendix**.

C. Comparative MVLMs: We compare $\mathbb{R}$MedCLIP against several state-of-the-art MVLMs. **OpenAI CLIP (2021)** [23] is pretrained on 400 million natural imagetext pairs using standard augmentations, but not exposed to specific corruptions during training. **MedCLIP (2022)** [26] fine-tunes

---

[3] In addition to CE and mCE, we also employ **Average Accuracy** as a performance measure and is defined as: Avg. $\text{Acc}^{f} = \frac{1}{|C|} \sum_{c \in C} \left(\frac{1}{5} \sum_{s=1}^{5} \text{Acc}_{s,c}^{f} \right)$.

Table 2. Clean Error, Corruption Error **CE**, and mean CE **mCE** comparison for ViT-B/16 backbone MVLMs across Cell Microscopy, Breast Imaging, Chest X-ray, Fundoscopy, and Retinal OCT modalities. Here, **Clean** denotes Clean Error on "In-Distribution" samples, while the rest denote OOD corruptions. The **mCE** is the mean CE across all corruptions (See Eq. 8). **Bold** denotes best robustness while Underline denotes second-best. The Table that shows Accuracy metric is available in **Appendix**.

Cell Microscopy → Methods ↓	Clean	Gauss.	Impulse	Motion	Zoom	Bright.	Contrast	Pixelate	mCE
CLIP	100.0	100.0	100.0	100.0	100.0	100.0	100.0	100.0	100.0
MedCLIP	104.9	104.3	104.5	113.0	106.8	106.3	108.4	104.8	106.9
BioMedCLIP	111.2	111.2	114.0	114.4	110.3	113.3	112.7	111.1	112.4
UniMedCLIP	107.5	108.6	106.6	105.3	102.1	103.8	104.7	100.5	104.5
RMedCLIP	**24.3**	82.1	98.7	70.1	43.3	40.1	64.1	92.5	**70.1**
CLIP	100.0	100.0	100.0	100.0	100.0	100.0	100.0	100.0	100.0
MedCLIP	100.6	92.2	94.0	97.4	99.3	101.2	113.4	92.9	98.6
BioMedCLIP	86.9	89.4	92.7	84.4	86.8	87.8	105.8	83.1	90.0
UniMedCLIP	93.4	90.9	91.4	92.8	96.2	95.6	112.7	94.6	96.3
RMedCLIP	**33.7**	53.3	54.9	42.1	51.3	40.7	64.4	48.2	**50.7**

Breast Img. → Methods ↓	Clean	Gauss.	Impulse	Motion	Zoom	Bright.	Contrast	Pixelate	mCE
OpenAI CLIP	100.0	100.0	100.0	100.0	100.0	100.0	100.0	100.0	100.0
MedCLIP	78.1	79.9	78.6	67.3	70.0	75.9	74.3	72.4	74.1
BioMedCLIP	90.1	71.4	64.0	99.7	92.3	95.3	96.2	103.5	88.9
UniMedCLIP	102.6	107.5	101.1	100.7	100.5	100.4	112.6	110.1	104.7
RMedCLIP	**66.7**	70.0	66.2	65.3	65.4	65.4	74.9	70.2	**68.2**
OpenAI CLIP	100.0	100.0	100.0	100.0	100.0	100.0	100.0	100.0	100.0
MedCLIP	128.3	140.3	113.5	71.7	82.0	149.2	95.9	66.6	102.7
BioMedCLIP	79.2	75.5	58.4	83.0	56.0	89.8	61.0	49.3	67.6
UniMedCLIP	79.2	75.5	52.4	76.1	55.7	89.0	61.0	43.3	**64.7**
RMedCLIP	**75.5**	68.0	99.5	71.4	95.5	83.1	81.4	52.0	78.7

Chest X-ray → Methods ↓	Clean	Gauss.	Impulse	Motion	Zoom	Bright.	Contrast	Pixelate	mCE
OpenAI CLIP	100.0	100.0	100.0	100.0	100.0	100.0	100.0	100.0	100.0
MedCLIP	94.4	104.7	95.5	100.5	94.6	94.7	96.0	95.4	97.3
BioMedCLIP	100.0	100.7	94.0	100.0	99.8	99.9	99.0	95.6	98.4
UniMedCLIP	100.0	100.7	94.3	97.3	93.8	99.9	101.6	94.6	97.5
RMedCLIP	**62.6**	91.8	86.0	65.5	58.7	74.7	84.4	84.9	**78.0**
OpenAI CLIP	100.0	100.0	100.0	100.0	100.0	100.0	100.0	100.0	100.0
MedCLIP	45.4	89.8	82.2	109.2	84.4	47.4	113.2	101.7	89.7
BioMedCLIP	108.4	117.2	105.7	130.4	103.3	102.8	142.2	101.4	114.7
UniMedCLIP	142.5	119.1	106.1	122.0	81.9	138.6	121.7	59.4	107.0
RMedCLIP	**29.7**	112.6	105.6	44.0	23.3	26.6	65.6	49.2	**61.0**

(continued)

Table 2. (*continued*)

Fundoscopy → Methods ↓	Clean	Gauss.	Impulse	Motion	Zoom	Bright.	Contrast	Pixelate	mCE
OpenAI CLIP	100.0	100.0	100.0	100.0	100.0	100.0	100.0	100.0	**100.0**
MedCLIP	211.5	259.4	363.8	129.7	234.2	271.0	161.4	167.1	226.6
BioMedCLIP	364.0	369.7	375.4	375.4	372.6	365.6	370.1	377.0	372.3
UniMedCLIP	_97.1_	98.1	99.4	100.7	100.1	98.6	99.0	106.4	_100.3_
RMedCLIP	**95.0**	109.9	253.6	100.7	124.9	96.8	130.5	122.1	134.1
OpenAI CLIP	**100.0**	100.0	100.0	100.0	100.0	100.0	100.0	100.0	**100.0**
MedCLIP	_101.8_	146.1	127.5	141.0	127.4	113.2	88.8	114.6	122.7
BioMedCLIP	118.8	135.0	129.7	120.8	121.6	127.6	98.8	122.3	_122.3_
UniMedCLIP	118.5	137.2	128.7	126.4	128.8	119.2	112.9	134.1	126.8
RMedCLIP	126.4	143.5	138.2	135.6	139.1	122.5	114.1	142.7	133.7

Retinal OCT → Methods ↓	Clean	Gauss.	Impulse	Motion	Zoom	Bright.	Contrast	Pixelate	mCE
OpenAI CLIP	100.0	100.0	100.0	100.0	100.0	100.0	100.0	100.0	100.0
MedCLIP	_83.6_	97.9	97.8	95.8	95.7	83.0	92.7	96.4	_94.2_
BioMedCLIP	104.8	106.4	104.1	100.7	103.6	103.8	103.7	103.8	103.7
UniMedCLIP	99.5	104.6	98.9	100.1	98.6	97.1	99.2	101.2	99.9
RMedCLIP	**42.7**	49.6	71.3	60.1	75.7	65.1	64.8	96.8	**69.0**
OpenAI CLIP	100.0	100.0	100.0	100.0	100.0	100.0	100.0	100.0	100.0
MedCLIP	114.8	102.9	108.0	131.5	120.1	112.3	105.4	103.1	111.9
BioMedCLIP	100.5	96.3	100.5	102.1	98.4	100.2	94.7	96.6	98.4
UniMedCLIP	_78.1_	76.3	91.5	91.2	91.4	73.9	94.0	90.5	_87.0_
RMedCLIP	**72.2**	67.9	83.2	48.9	76.7	46.1	54.3	92.6	**67.1**

(Left margin vertical labels: MedMNIST-C MediMeta-C for first block; MedMNIST-C MediMeta-C for second block)

on medical imagetext pairs–typically chest X-rays [15] and retinal images–to improve diagnostic accuracy. **BioMedCLIP (2023)** [29] further refines CLIP for medicine using the PMC-15M [29] dataset—15M biomedical image-text pairs from PubMed Central [1] archive—but omits corruption-based training. **UniMedCLIP (2025)** [18] trains on MedMNIST [3], ROCO [24], and PMC-OA [20] datasets—ranging from multi-institutional imaging, radiology reports, to scientific articles—for cross-modal alignment but without any diversity exposure. These comparative MVLMs, though effective on clean data, as discussed in Sect. 5, suffer notable performance degradation under out-of-distribution conditions.

5 Results and Discussions

5.1 Main Results

A. Robustness of MVLMs: The experimental results in Table 2 reveal a variation in robustness across medical modalities. In Cell Microscopy, for example, although the baseline CLIP model consistently registers a clean error of

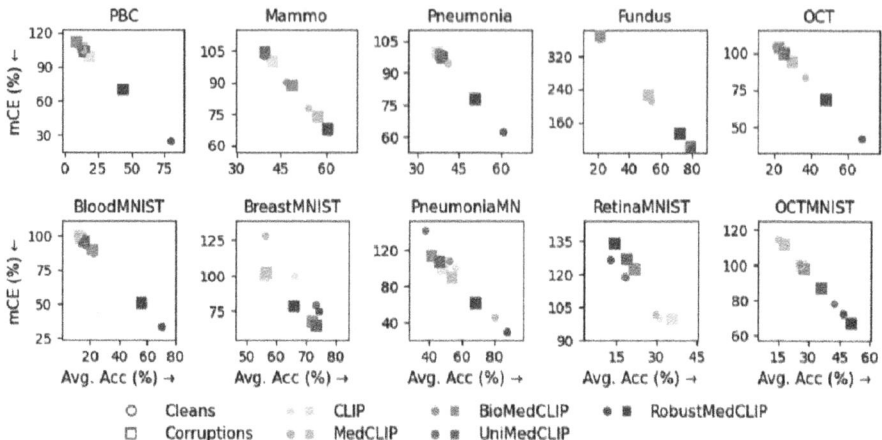

Fig. 6. Robustness vs. Accuracy trade-off across modalities and MVLM baselines. Most MVLMs exhibit consistently high mCE and lower average accuracy across five modalities and two benchmarks.

100%, subsequent models such as MedCLIP, BioMedCLIP, and UniMedCLIP exhibit moderate error inflation under corruptions. Notably, our ℝMC model shows a substantial reduction in clean error and a lower mCE, demonstrating that targeted robust adaptation can significantly mitigate the deleterious effects of visual distortions. In Breast Imaging, similar trends emerge; while the baseline and traditional MVLM variants suffer from pronounced error increases under corruption, our method consistently achieves lower mCE values, even when the absolute clean performance is slightly compromised. For modalities like Chest X-ray and Fundoscopy, the gap between clean and corrupted performance is less pronounced among models with higher intrinsic accuracy; however, the robustness of ℝMC remains superior, highlighting that improvements in clean accuracy alone do not guarantee robustness. These observations indicate that the *degradation observed under corrupted conditions is not simply a by-product of accuracy* enhancements. Rather, the ability of ℝMC to leverage few-shot fine-tuning and robust (*LoRA*) adaptation appears to directly counteract the effects of common image corruptions.

> **Not all MVLMs are consistently Robust but can certainly be!**
>
> While many MVLMs excel on clean data, their performance can deteriorate markedly under realistic corruption scenarios–a challenge that ℝMC's few-shot and low-rank tuning can help mitigate to some extent.

B. MVLMs across Different Modalities: Although models such as Med-CLIP, BioMedCLIP, and UniMedCLIP have been pretrained on various medical datasets, their performance across different modalities—Cell Microscopy, Fundoscopy, Breast Imaging, Chest X-ray, and Retinal OCT—varies considerably (Table 2). While baseline models maintain a clean error of 100%, the

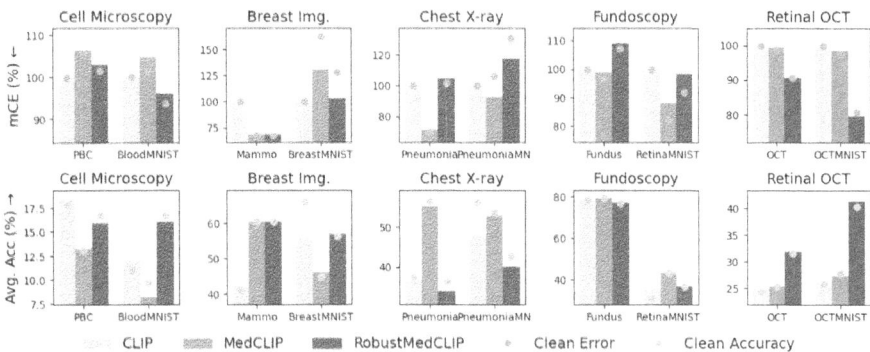

Fig. 7. mCE and Accuracy comparison of **ResNet-50-based MVLMs** (MedCLIP and our RMC) against the CLIP baseline across MediMeta-C and MedMNIST-C benchmarks. **MN** indicates the abbreviation for MNIST where applicable.

relative increase in error under corruptions (as measured by mCE) is highly modality-dependent. For example, in the Cell Microscopy setting, our RMC model achieves a dramatic reduction in clean error and mCE compared to other MVLMs, whereas in Breast Imaging, performance discrepancies are more pronounced. These results validate that the feature representations learned by current MVLMs are highly domain-specific, *failing to generalize uniformly across clinical imaging tasks*. Improvements in clean accuracy do not always translate into robustness, as even models with competitive performance on clean images suffer under corruption (Fig. 6). Thus, relying solely on MVLMs pretrained on *few-modality* imagetext pairs or on a single medical dataset is insufficient for clinical deployment. These observations underscore the critical need for diverse training data and robust adaptation strategies to achieve truly cross-modality generalization in MVLMs.

Existing MVLMs are Not Modality Generalizable

Existing MVLMs are inherently domain-specific; while few-shot robust adaptation enhances cross-modality robustness, large-scale training across diverse and numerous modalities is imperative for a truly generalizable MVLM.

5.2 Discussions and Analyses

A. Trade-Off Between Accuracy and Robustness: Despite progressive improvements in average accuracy from MedCLIP to more recent UniMedCLIP, the observed tradeoff in Fig. 6 reveals that corruption robustness has not kept pace. While some MVLMs achieve higher average accuracy, their resilience under OOD corruptions remains limited, highlighting a gap between clean-data success and robust generalization. Notably, MedCLIP maintains consistent results in one modality yet falters in others, reflecting a lack of universal cross-modal adaptability unlike RMC. This discrepancy suggests that simply enhancing average

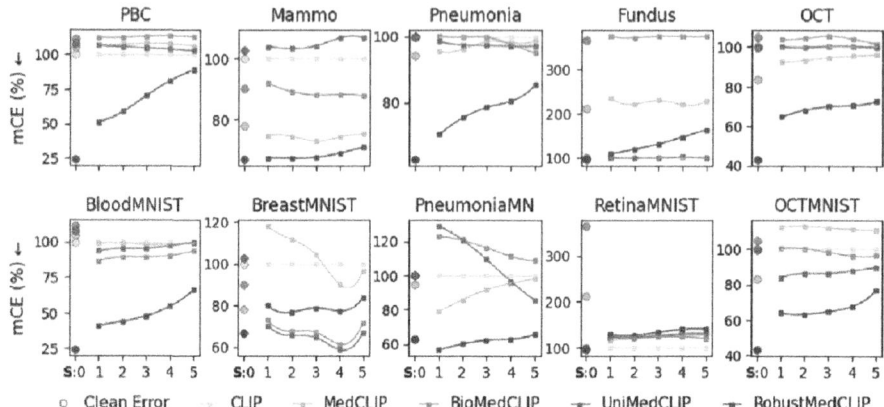

Fig. 8. Performance Degradation of Medical VLMs Across Five Corruption Severity Levels in terms of mCE. **S** means Severity Level while **S**:0 implies Clean Error.

accuracy does not guarantee improved corruption resistance. Instead, specialized strategies–such as domain-aware fine-tuning–appear essential for bridging the accuracyrobustness divide across diverse clinical imaging modalities. Robust adaptation remains essential for deployment.

B. Impact of Backbones on Robustness: ResNet-based MVLMs in Fig. 7 show limited gains in robustness compared to their ViT counterparts, as evidenced by the similar mCE bars across CLIP, MedCLIP, and ℝMC in multiple modalities. While MedCLIP occasionally reduces mCE slightly, it does not outperform CLIP consistently, suggesting that ResNet architectures alone do not guarantee stronger corruption resistance. In the lower row, MedCLIP likewise fails to achieve substantially higher accuracy than CLIP, indicating that improved backbone capacity does not automatically translate to enhanced performance. Notably, our ℝMC approach yields a higher average accuracy, surpassing both CLIP and MedCLIP in several modalities, yet still reflects only moderate gains in mCE. Overall, ResNet-based models remain less robust than ViT-based approaches.

C. Performance Against Severity Levels: Prior MVLMs exhibit systemic fragility under escalating corruption severity, with mCE increasing on average as distortions intensify (Fig. 8). These MVLMs struggle to retain discriminative features under artifacts. While having modality-agnostic design and *supposedly* broadly applicable, they fail to prioritize corruption-invariant features, leading to erratic performance in modalities prone to specific distortions (e.g., motion blur in OCT). Notably, the impact of severity varies by imaging modality—in Fundoscopy for instance—all models display relative resilience, suggesting anatomical context mitigates distortion effects. Our ℝMC achieves superior robustness on clean and mildly corrupted samples, attributed to few-shot adaptation that

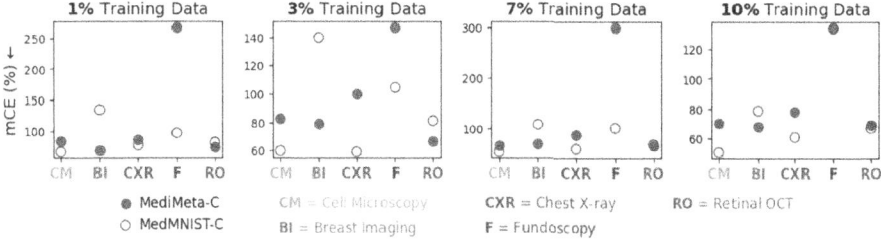

Fig. 9. Effect of Few-shot Samples on Fine-Tuning RMC. Performance of RMC across five modalities with varying percentages of clean training data. RMC model.

preserves feature integrity. At higher severities, RMC remains competitive, leveraging adapted few-shot representations to counter progressive degradation.

D. Ablation of Few-Shot Samplings: Figure 9 illustrates the few-shot performance of RMC across five medical imaging modalities with varying proportions of clean training data. While performance generally improves with increased data, gains are highly modality-dependent rather than strictly linear. Notably, modalities such as Fundoscopy maintain stable robustness regardless of data volume, suggesting insensitivity to sample size. In contrast, Chest X-ray and Retinal OCT exhibit sharp mCE reductions (e.g., 18% drop from 1% to 10% data), highlighting greater data efficiency. Breast Imaging and Cell Microscopy show more gradual improvements, likely due to intrinsic noise or task complexity. These results confirm that few-shot adaptation effectively mitigates corruption-induced degradation without compromising generalization, especially in resource-constrained clinical scenarios.

Discussions at a Glance

A. Increasing accuracy alone does not ensure robustness, especially under corruptions and across modalities.
B. Backbone choice influences performance, but ResNet-based MVLMs lag behind ViT in robustness.
C. Corruption severity critically degrades MVLMs, with modality-specific vulnerabilities emerging.
D. Few-shot fine-tuning improves robustness efficiently, especially in data-limited medical settings.

6   Conclusion

A. Summary: Our study demonstrates that enhancing robustness in Medical Vision-Language Models (MVLMs) requires a paradigm shift from maximizing clean accuracy to optimizing for resilience under distribution shifts. Our extensive evaluations, conducted using the comprehensive MediMeta-C and MedMNIST-C benchmarks, reveal that while baseline models such as MedCLIP,

BioMedCLIP, and UniMedCLIP achieve high accuracy on pristine datasets, they suffer significant increases in mean Corruption Error (mCE) when exposed to realistic corruptions. In contrast, our proposed RobustMedCLIP, which leverages few-shot fine-tuning with low-rank adaptation on a diverse set of clinical domains, achieves markedly lower clean errors and mCE. These results underscore that *data-modality diversity is paramount over dataset volume* for achieving robust cross-modality generalization. The analysis further indicates that variations in backbone architecture and corruption severity yield modality-specific performance gaps, highlighting the need for tailored adaptation strategies rather than relying solely on improvements in clean accuracy.

B. Future Directions: Future work should investigate integrating adaptive, parameter-efficient tuning mechanisms across a wider spectrum of OOD clinical domains to further enhance robustness. Expanding the evaluation framework to encompass additional corruption types and real-world clinical data will be crucial in developing MVLMs that are both accurate and robust in deployment.

Appendix

A. Additional Implementation Details: For fine-tuning, RMC-ViT is initialized with pretrained weights from BioMedCLIP with ViT-B/16, while RMC-ResNet (RN50) uses the MedCLIP RN50 variant. Few-shot tuning is performed using LoRA with a rank of $r = 16$, optimized with the Adam optimizer for 20 epochs at a learning rate of 10^{-4}. To evaluate robustness, the *mean* Corruption Error (*mCE*) is computed using OpenAI CLIP [23] with a ViT-B/16 backbone as the corruption robustness baseline, as defined in Eq. 8. This choice of baseline provides a standardized and model-agnostic point of reference, allowing for consistent comparisons of corruption robustness across both ViT and RN50-based MVLMs, including RMC (Table 3).

B. Computation and Parameter Scaling of RMC Variants: Table 6 presents parameter analysis of RMC variants trained on ViT and ResNet backbones. Notably, RMC-ViT achieves strong performance with only 1.02% of parameters fine-tuned via LoRA, maintaining competitive accuracy even with minimal sampling (e.g., 66.45% at 3% samples). As sample size increases, ViT shows marked gains, peaking at 80.05% accuracy with only a modest training time of 1.62 h. In contrast, RMC-RN exhibits limited accuracy gains despite higher parameter exposure (1.39%) and similar runtime, suggesting underutilization of representational capacity. Furthermore, RMC-ViT consistently outperforms its ResNet counterpart in both clean and corrupted settings, all while maintaining a stable computational footprint. This indicates that transformer-based MVLMs offer a more favorable robustness-efficiency trade-off, especially under few-shot constraints (Tables 4, 5 and Figs. 10, 11, 12, 13, 14 and 15).

Table 3. Clean Accuracy, Accuracy against Corruptions, and Average Accuracy (**A.Acc.**) comparison for ViT-B/16 backbone MVLMs across Cell Microscopy, Breast Imaging, Chest X-ray, Fundoscopy, and Retinal OCT modalities. Here, **Clean** denotes Top-1 Accuracy on clean "In-Distribution" samples, while **A.Acc.** is the average Accuracy across all corruptions (See Eq. 6 in main paper). **Bold** denotes best accuracy while <u>Underline</u> denotes second-best.

	Cell Microscopy → Methods ↓	Clean	Gauss.	Impulse	Motion	Zoom	Bright.	Contrast	Pixelate	A.Acc.
MedMNIST-CMediMeta-C	CLIP	<u>17.81</u>	17.58	17.96	20.09	17.20	19.30	18.84	17.94	<u>18.42</u>
	MedCLIP	13.75	14.02	14.25	9.68	11.54	14.26	12.02	13.99	12.82
	BioMedCLIP	8.60	8.32	6.49	8.60	8.68	8.55	8.53	8.80	8.28
	UniMedCLIP	11.61	10.46	12.56	15.89	15.45	16.23	14.99	17.56	14.74
	RMedCLIP	**80.05**	32.30	19.06	43.95	64.11	67.60	47.98	24.10	**42.73**
	CLIP	11.11	8.65	9.12	9.98	9.83	13.31	23.41	10.38	12.10
	MedCLIP	10.55	15.78	14.55	12.30	10.47	12.24	13.13	16.78	13.61
	BioMedCLIP	<u>22.71</u>	18.35	15.74	24.03	21.74	23.89	18.98	25.48	<u>21.17</u>
	UniMedCLIP	16.98	16.92	16.93	16.42	13.29	17.15	13.69	15.21	15.66
	RMedCLIP	**70.07**	51.29	50.11	62.09	53.78	64.69	50.69	56.81	**55.64**

	Breast Img. → Methods ↓	Clean	Gauss.	Impulse	Motion	Zoom	Bright.	Contrast	Pixelate	A.Acc.
MedMNIST-CMediMeta-C	CLIP	41.10	43.80	40.25	40.00	39.88	39.82	46.32	45.09	42.16
	MedCLIP	53.99	55.09	53.01	59.63	57.91	54.29	60.12	60.25	57.19
	BioMedCLIP	<u>46.93</u>	59.88	61.78	40.18	44.48	42.64	48.34	43.19	<u>48.64</u>
	UniMedCLIP	39.57	39.57	39.57	39.57	39.57	39.57	39.57	39.57	39.57
	RMedCLIP	**60.74**	60.67	60.43	60.80	60.67	60.61	59.82	61.47	**60.64**
	CLIP	66.03	64.36	48.59	64.62	51.67	69.74	55.90	37.82	56.10
	MedCLIP	56.41	50.00	41.67	74.62	60.38	54.87	57.69	58.59	56.83
	BioMedCLIP	73.08	73.08	70.00	70.64	72.95	72.82	73.08	69.36	<u>71.70</u>
	UniMedCLIP	<u>73.08</u>	73.08	73.08	73.08	73.08	73.08	73.08	73.08	**73.08**
	RMedCLIP	**74.36**	75.77	48.85	74.74	53.85	74.87	64.10	67.69	65.70

	Chest X-ray → Methods ↓	Clean	Gauss.	Impulse	Motion	Zoom	Bright.	Contrast	Pixelate	A.Acc.
MedMNIST-CMediMeta-C	CLIP	37.50	37.95	33.75	37.50	37.40	37.47	37.66	37.02	36.96
	MedCLIP	<u>41.03</u>	35.03	36.73	37.18	40.77	40.80	40.16	39.90	<u>38.65</u>
	BioMedCLIP	37.50	37.50	37.72	37.50	37.50	37.50	38.27	39.81	37.97
	UniMedCLIP	37.50	37.50	37.50	39.17	41.31	37.50	36.67	40.45	38.59
	RMedCLIP	**60.90**	43.01	43.01	59.07	63.24	53.27	47.40	46.54	**50.79**
	CLIP	56.25	47.47	41.09	52.85	41.15	55.10	59.62	38.91	48.03
	MedCLIP	<u>80.13</u>	52.82	51.57	48.49	50.32	78.72	54.29	37.88	<u>53.44</u>
	BioMedCLIP	52.56	38.43	37.72	38.53	39.20	53.85	42.56	38.04	41.19
	UniMedCLIP	37.66	37.44	37.50	42.50	51.83	37.76	50.83	63.69	45.93
	RMedCLIP	**87.02**	40.83	37.79	79.26	86.31	88.08	73.49	69.97	**67.96**

(continued)

Table 3. (*continued*)

	Fundoscopy → Methods ↓	Clean	Gauss.	Impulse	Motion	Zoom	Bright.	Contrast	Pixelate	A.Acc.
MediMeta-C	CLIP	78.28	78.62	78.94	78.94	78.78	78.38	78.81	79.03	**78.79**
	MedCLIP	54.06	44.56	23.38	72.69	50.31	41.41	65.81	64.97	51.88
	BioMedCLIP	20.94	20.97	20.94	20.94	20.94	20.94	21.59	20.94	21.04
	UniMedCLIP	78.91	79.03	79.06	78.78	78.75	78.69	79.03	77.69	78.72
	RMedCLIP	**79.38**	76.50	46.59	78.78	73.50	79.06	72.34	74.41	71.60
MedMNIST-C	CLIP	31.00	39.50	35.95	34.75	36.35	36.10	28.00	38.10	**35.54**
	MedCLIP	29.75	11.60	18.35	8.00	18.90	27.65	36.10	29.05	21.38
	BioMedCLIP	18.00	18.30	16.90	21.20	22.60	18.45	28.85	24.30	21.51
	UniMedCLIP	18.25	17.00	17.55	17.55	18.00	23.85	18.70	17.00	18.52
	RMedCLIP	12.75	13.20	11.50	11.50	11.45	21.70	17.85	11.65	14.12

	Retinal OCT → Methods ↓	Clean	Gauss.	Impulse	Motion	Zoom	Bright.	Contrast	Pixelate	A.Acc.
MediMeta-C	CLIP	24.30	26.26	24.98	24.84	24.58	23.02	24.70	25.94	24.90
	MedCLIP	36.70	27.84	26.60	27.98	27.80	36.08	30.16	28.60	29.29
	BioMedCLIP	20.70	21.52	21.90	24.34	21.88	20.10	21.90	23.16	22.11
	UniMedCLIP	24.70	22.84	25.84	24.76	25.66	25.24	25.34	25.08	24.97
	RMedCLIP	**67.70**	63.46	46.48	54.82	42.92	49.92	51.20	28.34	**48.16**
MedMNIST-C	CLIP	25.90	22.72	27.24	28.26	28.52	25.98	25.74	25.02	26.21
	MedCLIP	14.90	20.48	21.40	5.68	14.18	16.86	21.76	22.68	17.58
	BioMedCLIP	25.50	25.58	26.88	26.74	29.64	25.82	29.64	27.54	27.41
	UniMedCLIP	42.10	41.06	33.42	34.58	34.68	45.32	30.16	32.16	35.91
	RMedCLIP	**46.50**	47.52	39.44	64.94	45.20	65.90	59.68	30.54	**50.46**

Table 4. Dataset statistics for MediMeta [27] across five imaging modalities.

Modality ↓	Data Name	#Train/Val/Test	#Classes	Description	Class Labels
Cell Microscopy	PBC	11964/1709/3149	Multi-Class (8)	Blood cells	basophil, eosinophil, erythroblast, immature granulocyte, lymphocyte, monocyte, neutrophil, platelet
Breast Imaging	Mammo	1332/214/326	Binary (2)	Calcifications	malignant, benign
Chest X-ray	Pneumonia	4415/817/624	Multi-Class (3)	Lung infection	normal, bacteria, virus
Fundoscopy	Fundus	1920/640/640	Binary (2)	Eye diseases	abnormal, normal
Retinal OCT	OCT	91615/16694/1000	Multi-Class (4)	Retinal layers	cnv, normal, dme, drusen

Table 5. Dataset statistics for MedMNIST [3] across five imaging modalities.

Modality ↓	Data Name	#Train/Val/Test	#Classes	Description	Class Labels
Cell Microscopy	BloodMNIST	11959/1712/3421	Multi-Class (8)	Blood cells	basophil, eosinophil, erythroblast, granulocytes, lymphocyte, monocyte, neutrophil, platelet
Breast Imaging	BreastMNIST	546/78/156	Binary (2)	Breast tumors	malignant, benign
Chest X-ray	PneumoniaMNIST	4708/524/624	Binary (2)	Lung infection	normal, pneumonia
Fundoscopy	RetinaMNIST	1080/120/400	Multi-Class (5)	Eye diseases	0, 1, 2, 3, 4
Retinal OCT	OCTMNIST	97477/10832/1000	Multi-Class (4)	Retinal layers	choroidal neovascularization, diabetic macular edema, drusen, normal

Table 6. Performance comparison of few-shot RMC-ViT and RMC-ResNet variants on **clean** (MediMeta) and **corrupted** (MediMeta-C) datasets. Computation metrics include Training Time (in hours), Total Parameters, and the percentage of Trainable Parameters. Here, **M** denotes parameters in millions.

Cell Microscopy		MediMeta Cleans		MediMeta-C Corruptions		Computational Statistics		
RMC Variant	Few-Shots %	Avg.Acc. ↑	Error ↓	Avg.Acc. ↑	mCE ↓	Train Time(hrs)	Total Params	Trainable Params (%)
RMC-ViT	1	46.36	65.3	31.23	84.3	0.43	87M	1.02
	3	66.45	40.8	32.23	83.0	0.68	87M	1.02
	7	73.30	32.5	**44.83**	**67.5**	1.28	87M	1.02
	10	**80.05**	**24.3**	42.73	70.1	1.62	87M	1.02
RMC-ResNet	1	12.84	106	12.92	106.7	0.22	49M	1.39
	3	12.81	103.1	12.35	107.4	0.33	49M	1.39
	7	14.77	103.7	13.50	106.0	0.61	49M	1.39
	10	**16.67**	**101.4**	**15.93**	**103.0**	0.80	49M	1.39

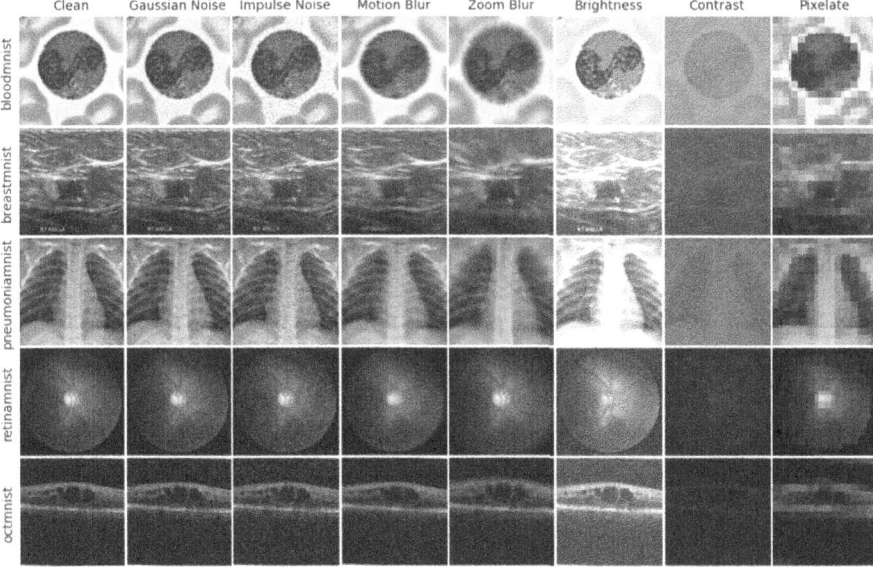

Fig. 10. Corrupted samples from MedMNIST-C [5] dataset. The y-axis shows dataset names by modality and the x-axis displays corruption types at a fixed severity level.

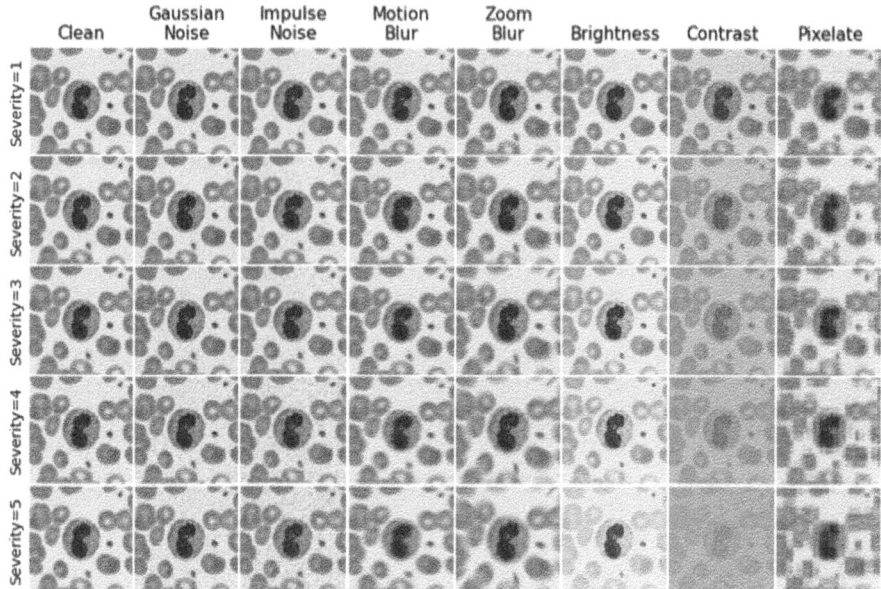

Fig. 11. Example images from cell microscopy modality of MediMeta-C – **PBC-C**, illustrating corruptions that mimic artifacts in blood smear microscopy and acute myeloid leukemia, including noise and blurring effects.

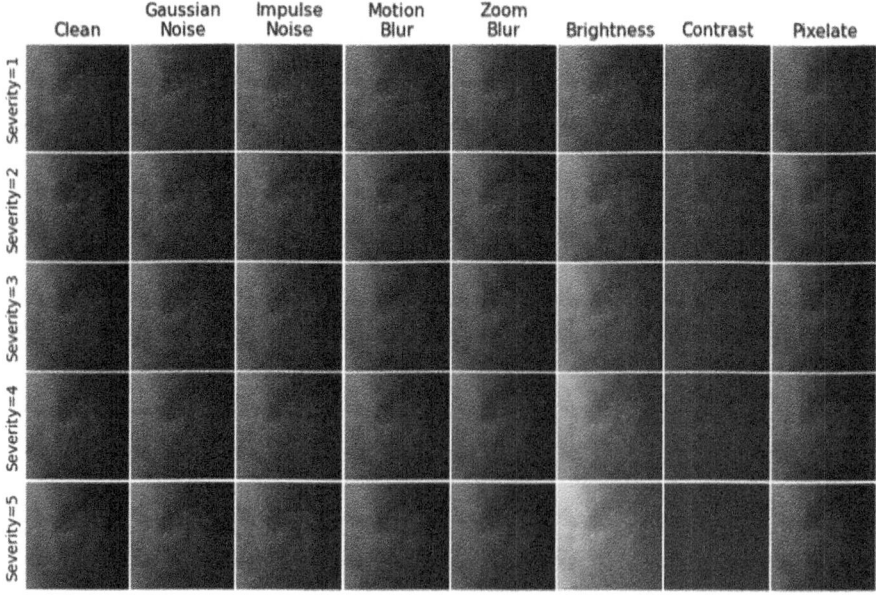

Fig. 12. Example images of Breast Imaging Scans including **MAMMO-C** from MediMeta-C, showcasing different corruption types. These corruptions simulate real-world degradation in mammography calcification scans.

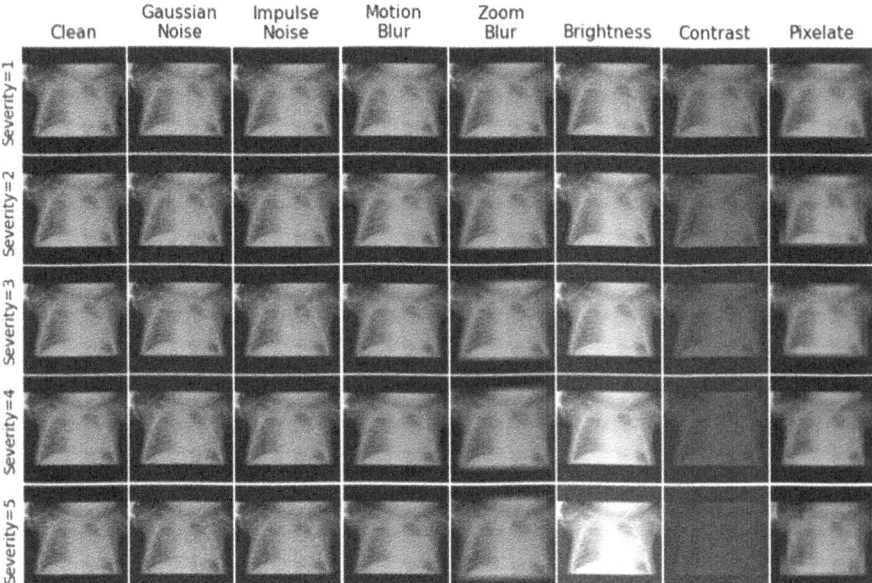

Fig. 13. Example images from **PNEUMONIA-C** in MediMeta-C, demonstrating corruption types commonly encountered in chest X-ray scans, such as motion blur and pixelation.

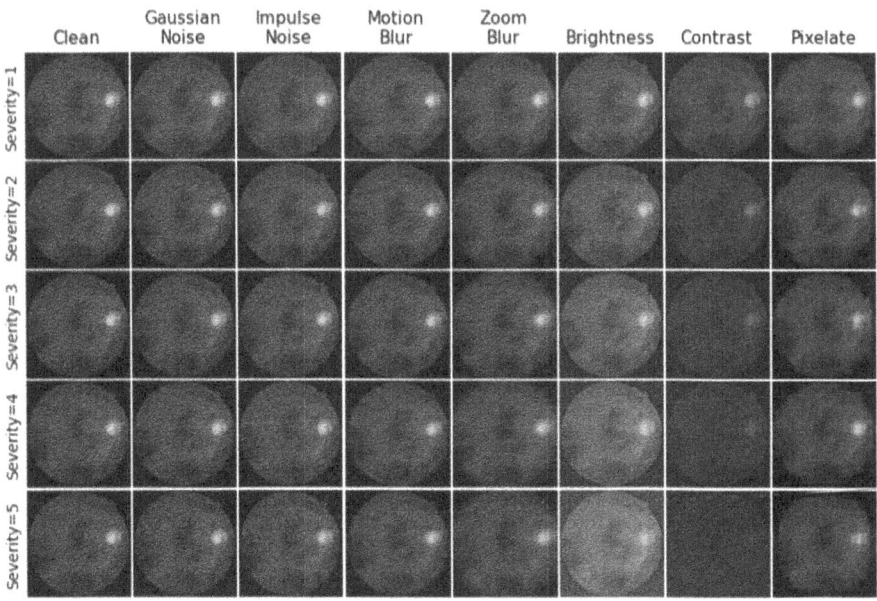

Fig. 14. Example images from **FUNDUS-C** in MediMeta-C, displaying distortions of Retinal Fundus scans that replicate issues in Fundoscopic examination, such as sensor noise and defocus blur.

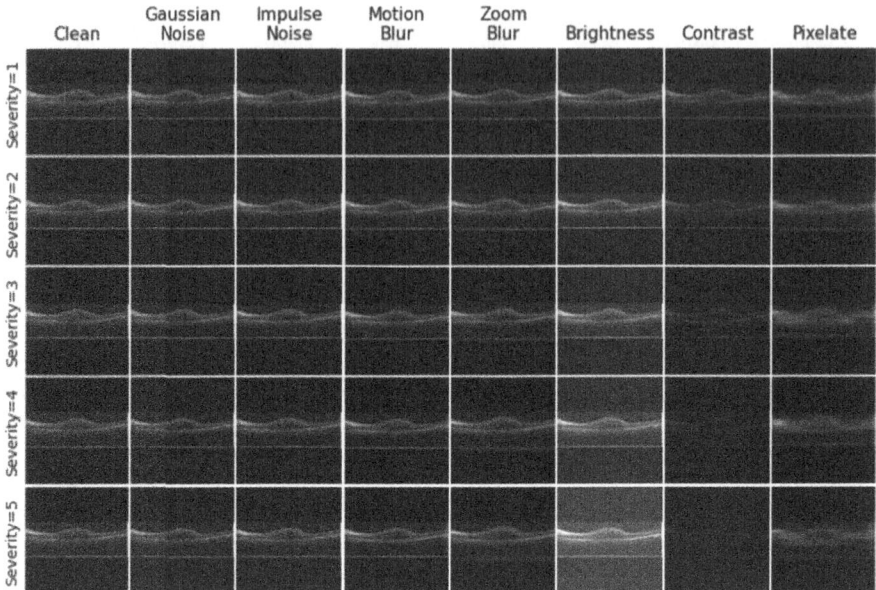

Fig. 15. Example images from **OCT-C** in MediMeta-C, displaying distortions of Retinal OCT scans that replicate issues in Optical Coherence Tomography (OCT) imaging, such as sensor noise and defocus blur.

References

1. Pubmed central. https://pmc.ncbi.nlm.nih.gov/. Accessed 05 Apr 2025
2. Chen, Q., et al.: A survey of medical vision-and-language applications and their techniques. arXiv preprint arXiv:2411.12195 (2024)
3. Chen, X., et al.: Medmnist: a collection of benchmarking datasets for biomedical image analysis. In: ICML Workshop on Computational Biology (2021)
4. Deanda, D., Masupalli, Y.P., Yang, J., Lee, Y., Cao, Z., Liang, G.: Benchmarking robustness of contrastive learning models for medical image-report retrieval. arXiv preprint arXiv:2501.09134 (2025)
5. Di Salvo, F., Doerrich, S., Ledig, C.: Medmnist-C: comprehensive benchmark and improved classifier robustness by simulating realistic image corruptions. arXiv preprint arXiv:2406.17536 (2024)
6. Hanif, A., Naseer, M., Khan, S., Khan, F.S.: On frequency domain adversarial vulnerabilities of volumetric medical image segmentation. In: 2025 IEEE 22nd International Symposium on Biomedical Imaging (ISBI), pp. 01–05. IEEE (2025)
7. Hanif, A., Naseer, M., Khan, S., Shah, M., Khan, F.S.: Frequency domain adversarial training for robust volumetric medical segmentation. In: International Conference on Medical Image Computing and Computer-Assisted Intervention, pp. 457–467. Springer, Cham (2023)
8. Hanif, A., et al.: Baple: backdoor attacks on medical foundational models using prompt learning. In: International Conference on Medical Image Computing and Computer-Assisted Intervention, pp. 443–453. Springer, Cham (2024)

9. Hayat, N., Geras, K.J., Shamout, F.E.: Medfuse: multi-modal fusion with clinical time-series data and chest x-ray images. arXiv preprint arXiv:2207.07027 (2022)

10. Hendrycks, D., Dietterich, T.: Benchmarking neural network robustness to common corruptions and perturbations. In: ICLR (2019)

11. Hu, E.J., et al.: Lora: low-rank adaptation of large language models. In: ICLR, vol. 1, no. 2, p. 3 (2022)

12. Imam, R., Gani, H., Huzaifa, M., Nandakumar, K.: Test-time low rank adaptation via confidence maximization for zero-shot generalization of vision-language models. arXiv preprint arXiv:2407.15913 (2024)

13. Imam, R., Hanif, A., Zhang, J., Dawoud, K.W., Kementchedjhieva, Y., Yaqub, M.: Noise is an efficient learner for zero-shot vision-language models. arXiv preprint arXiv:2502.06019 (2025)

14. Irvin, J., et al.: Chexpert: a large chest radiograph dataset with uncertainty labels and expert comparison. In: Proceedings of the AAAI Conference on Artificial Intelligence (2019)

15. Johnson, A.E., et al.: Mimic-cxr-jpg, a large publicly available database of labeled chest radiographs. arXiv preprint arXiv:1901.07042 (2019)

16. Khader, F., et al.: Multimodal deep learning for integrating chest radiographs and clinical parameters: a case for transformers. Radiology 230806 (2023)

17. Khan, W., Leem, S., See, K.B., Wong, J.K., Zhang, S., Fang, R.: A comprehensive survey of foundation models in medicine. IEEE Rev. Biomed. Eng. (2025)

18. Khattak, M.U., Kunhimon, S., Naseer, M., Khan, S., Khan, F.S.: Unimed-clip: towards a unified image-text pretraining paradigm for diverse medical imaging modalities (2024). arxiv:2412.10372

19. Khoshnevisan, F., Chi, M.: A scoping review of robustness concepts for machine learning in healthcare. J. Biomed. Inform. **135**, 104234 (2022)

20. Lin, W., et al.: PMC-clip: contrastive language-image pre-training using biomedical documents. In: International Conference on Medical Image Computing and Computer-Assisted Intervention, pp. 525–536. Springer, Cham (2023)

21. Maicas, G., Bradley, A.P., Nascimento, J.C., Reid, I., Carneiro, G.: Pre and post-hoc diagnosis and interpretation of malignancy from breast DCE-MRI. Med. Image Anal. **58**, 101562 (2019). https://doi.org/10.1016/j.media.2019.101562. https://www.sciencedirect.com/science/article/pii/S1361841518306893

22. Malik, H.S., et al.: On evaluating adversarial robustness of volumetric medical segmentation models. arXiv preprint arXiv:2406.08486 (2024)

23. Radford, A., et al.: Learning transferable visual models from natural language supervision. In: ICML (2021)

24. Rückert, J., et al.: Rocov2: radiology objects in context version 2, an updated multimodal image dataset. Sci. Data **11**(1), 688 (2024)

25. Shen, X., et al.: DCT-mask: discrete cosine transform mask representation for instance segmentation. In: Proceedings of the IEEE/CVF Conference on Computer Vision and Pattern Recognition, pp. 8720–8729 (2021)

26. Wang, Z., Wu, Z., Agarwal, D., Sun, J.: Medclip: contrastive learning from unpaired medical images and text (2022). arxiv:2210.10163

27. Woerner, S., Jaques, A., Baumgartner, C.F.: A comprehensive and easy-to-use multi-domain multi-task medical imaging meta-dataset (medimeta). arXiv preprint arXiv:2404.16000 (2024)

28. Xu, Y., Raj, A., Victor, J.D.: Systematic differences between perceptually relevant image statistics of brain MRI and natural images. Front. Neuroinform. **13**, 46 (2019)
29. Zhang, S., et al.: Biomedclip: a multimodal biomedical foundation model pretrained from fifteen million scientific image-text pairs (2025). arxiv:2303.00915
30. Zhao, Z., et al.: Clip in medical imaging: a survey. Med. Image Anal. 103551 (2025)

DiNO-Diffusion: Scaling Medical Diffusion Models via Self-Supervised Pre-Training

Guillermo Jimenez-Perez[1] , Pedro Osório[1($\boxtimes$)] , Josef Cersovsky[1] ,
Javier Montalt-Tordera[1] , Jens Hooge[1] , Steffen Vogler[2] ,
and Sadegh Mohammadi[1]

[1] DT&IT Pharma Decision Science - Computer Vision and Sound Analysis,
Bayer AG, Berlin, Germany
{guillermo.jimenezperez,pedro.osorio1}@bayer.com
[2] Diagnostic Imaging Data and AI, Bayer AG, Berlin, Germany

Abstract. Latent Diffusion models (LDMs) require large annotated datasets for training, limiting their applicability in medical imaging where datasets are typically smaller and sparsely annotated. We introduce DiNO-Diffusion, a self-supervised method for training LDMs that conditions the generation process on image embeddings extracted from DiNO, a pretrained vision transformer. By not relying on annotations, our training leverages over 868k unlabelled images from public chest X-Ray (CXR) datasets. DiNO-Diffusion shows comprehensive manifold coverage, with FID scores as low as 4.7, and emerging properties when evaluated in downstream tasks, allowing to generate semantically-diverse synthetic datasets even from small data pools, demonstrating up to 20% AUC increase in classification performance when used for data augmentation. Results suggest that DiNO-Diffusion could facilitate the creation of large datasets for flexible training of downstream AI models from limited amount of real data, while also holding potential for privacy preservation. Additionally, DiNO-Diffusion demonstrates zero-shot segmentation performance of up to 84.4% Dice score when evaluating lung lobe segmentation, evidencing good CXR image-anatomy alignment akin to textual descriptors on text-to-image LDMs. Finally, DiNO-Diffusion can be easily adapted to other medical imaging modalities or state-of-the-art diffusion models (DMs), allowing large-scale, multi-domain image generation pipelines for medical imaging.

Keywords: Diffusion Models · Self-supervision · Chest X-Ray · Medical Imaging · Synthetic Data

1 Introduction

Latent Diffusion models (LDMs) have recently emerged as robust and proficient foundational models in medical imaging, exhibiting substantial capabilities in image generation, image enhancement, reconstruction, and segmentation [1]. The field of synthetic image generation in particular has greatly shifted to

S. Ali et al. (Eds.): MIUA 2025, LNCS 15916, pp. 257–274, 2026.
https://doi.org/10.1007/978-3-031-98688-8_18

text-to-image LDMs, generating images that are nearly indistinguishable from real ones [2–6] and facilitating remarkable zero-shot performance in segmentation and classification tasks [7,8]. However, LDMs depend on the availability of large datasets containing images paired with corresponding descriptors (usually text) to guide the generation process, a requirement that presents a considerable obstacle in the medical domain [9]. Medical imaging datasets are typically small, contain free-form and inconsistent annotations including captions, binary labels or segmentations, and are generally prohibitively costly to compile and curate [9]. To address these challenges, some works have proposed pseudo-labeling with vision-language models (VLMs; [10]) or have trained lean mapping networks over frozen pretrained backbones to reduce the number of required annotated samples [11,12]. However, despite their promise, pseudo-labelling approaches find limited applicability in the medical field given a lack of high-quality medical imaging captioners [9]. In addition, while some authors have successfully trained mapping networks to bridge the gap between unimodal foundation models, they still require relatively large annotated datasets to be trained [9].

These limitations represent important roadblocks for medical LDMs. While the natural imaging literature focuses on saturating generation quality by improving the base architecture, optimization process or condition alignment [10,13,14], the medical imaging community navigates these hurdles by leveraging smaller or custom-annotated datasets [2–6]. Moreover, although mapping networks have found their footing in the diffusion literature with approaches such as ControlNet [12], these would still rely on large-scale medical LDMs trained with prohibitively extensive amounts of annotated images. In this context, applying a self-supervised approach to LDM training would be highly beneficial for medical image synthesis. Self-supervision enables models to learn from unlabelled data, providing exceptional results in multiple downstream tasks when used as image embedders [15–19].

With that in mind, we introduce DiNO-Diffusion, a novel self-supervised methodology for training medical LDMs at scale which conditions the image generation process on image-derived tokens extracted from a frozen DiNO model [15,16], as opposed to textual descriptors. DiNO-Diffusion allows independence from existing annotations, circumventing the limitations imposed by the scarcity and inconsistency of medical image labels. Moreover, it is agnostic to the choice of LDM architecture, medical imaging modality or optimization strategy. To test this, a model was trained on a large corpus of open-source CXR data found in the literature which do not share any common labeling or descriptor required to train regular LDMs (e.g., text captions), achieving low FID scores and high image quality. DiNO-Diffusion can generate medical images despite using DiNO embeddings, which are derived from natural images.

To test the alignment between DiNO embeddings and generated images, several downstream evaluation tasks were performed, comprising classification and segmentation, which addressed the model's ability to improve classification performance when adding synthetic data to a pool of real data or when fully replac-

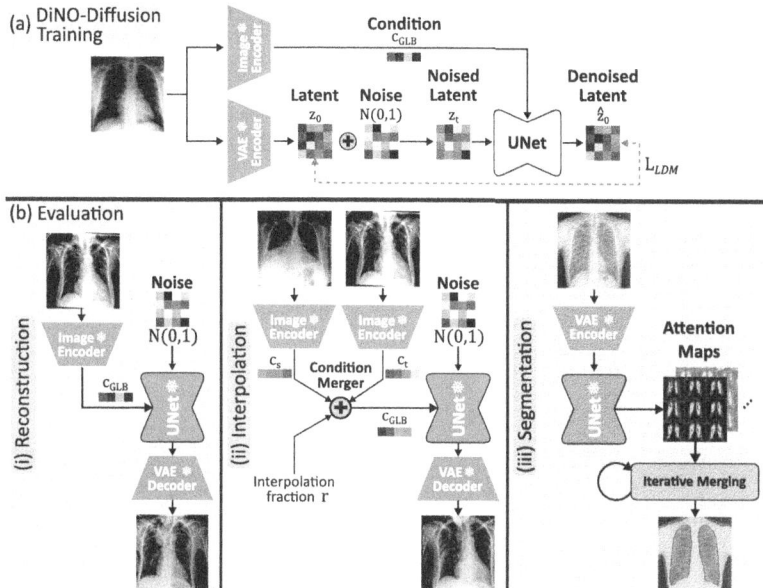

Fig. 1. DiNO-Diffusion's training (a) and evaluation (b) protocols. (a) the training image is both embedded into latents z_0 with a frozen (❄) VAE, and processed by a frozen image encoder to generate global tokens that act as condition c_{GLB}. Then, the latents are noised at timestep z_t and fed along the condition to the UNet, which denoises the latent $\hat{z}_0$. Then, the loss $L_{LDM}(z_0, \hat{z}_0)$ is computed. (b) the trained UNet is used to produce: (b-i) "reconstructions" of a given image; (b-ii) "interpolated" synthetic images from the embeddings of a source (c_s) and a target (c_t) real images at interpolation fraction r; or (b-iii) segmentations, by iteratively merging latent attention maps.

ing real with synthetic data; and assessing whether a self-supervised LDM can be used to create zero-shot segmentation masks for distinct anatomical structures.

In summary, our main findings are as follows: (1) DiNO-Diffusion allows training large LDMs given its independence from specific architectures, imaging modalities, available annotations, dataset sizes or optimization strategies. (2) DiNO's embeddings are descriptive enough for image generation despite not being trained on medical images. Using DiNO's global tokens seemed to bottleneck enough information to introduce semantic variability during DiNO-Diffusion's generation, thus avoiding replication of the input data. (3) DiNO-Diffusion was used to generate semantically-diverse synthetic datasets even from small data pools. These samples were used for data augmentation, improving classification performance on different data regimes. In addition, training on only synthetic data showed potential for mitigating privacy concerns. (4) DiNO-Diffusion can be leveraged for zero-shot medical image segmentation through iterative attention map merging. This demonstrates its ability to learn semantic coherence and its good alignment with anatomic structures. To our knowledge, this is the first application of zero-shot segmentation applied to medical LDMs.

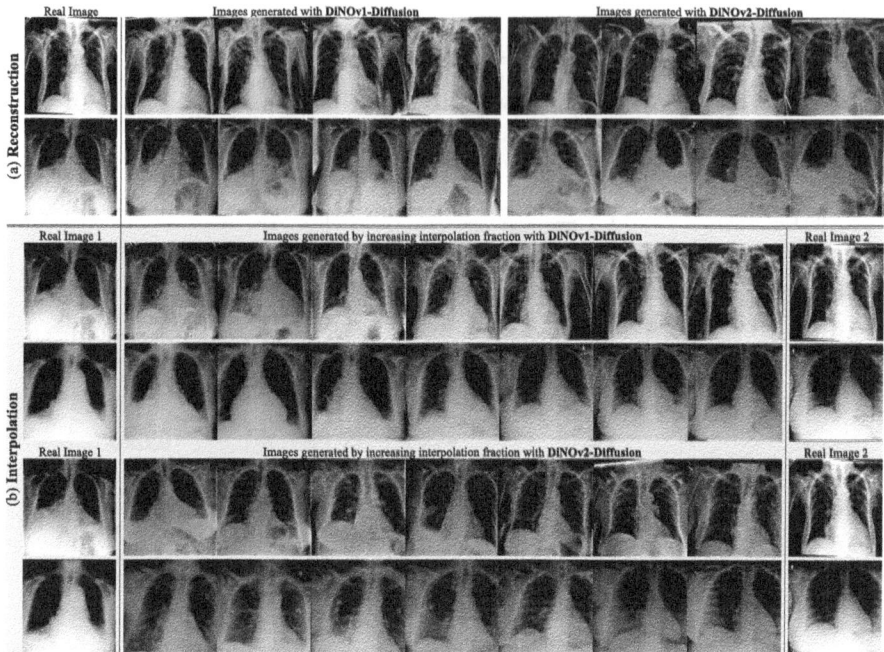

Fig. 2. Examples of generated images with DiNO-Diffusion. In the reconstruction experiment (a), each row represents randomly generated examples from two base images within MIMIC and for both DiNOv1- and DiNOv2-Diffusion, showing semantic variability. In the interpolation experiment (b), each row depicts two real images and the result from generating synthetic images by interpolating the embeddings incrementally for DiNOv1-Diffusion (b-top) and DiNOv2-Diffusion (b-bottom).

2   Methods

This Section explains the methodology employed for studying the self-supervised LDM. In Sect. 2.1, the datasets used for training and evaluation are described. In Sect. 2.2, the model's architecture and theoretical background is outlined. In Sect. 2.3, the designed mechanisms for self-supervised conditioning are detailed. In Sect. 2.4, the evaluation protocol employed to benchmark model performance is defined. Finally, in Sect. 2.5, the specific parameters used for model training and evaluation are enumerated. Figure 1 visually describes the training and evaluation pipeline.

2.1   Data

To explore DiNO-Diffusion's self-supervision capability, a large-scale dataset comprised of every openly accessible CXR dataset found in the literature [20–42][1]

---

[1] Thanks, among others, to the National Library of Medicine, National Institutes of Health, Bethesda, MD, USA.

was collected, reaching over 1.2M total images from 21 distinct data providers. Three different subsets were taken from this compound dataset for different purposes. Firstly, a subset comprising every dataset minus MIMIC-CXR [23] was selected for training the DiNO-Diffusion models. Their labels were discarded and label balancing was not performed, resulting in 868 394 samples with a variety of image sources, resolutions and patient characteristics. Secondly, MIMIC-CXR was used solely for evaluating the model via two classification tasks (see Sect. 2.4). MIMIC-CXR is composed of chest radiographs with free-text radiology reports, for which multi-label classification information is available. The MIMIC-CXR dataset was preprocessed to match similar literature [3] by discarding lateral views, by restricting the labels to those whose prevalence was of at least 4% (Atelectasis, Cardiomegaly, Consolidation, Edema, Pleural Effusion, Pneumonia and Pneumothorax), and by splitting its p10-p18 subsets for classifier training and leaving p19 as a held-out test set. Finally, the third subset for the segmentation task relied on three small datasets containing annotated masks: the JSRT ($N = 247$), Montgomery ($N = 138$) and Shenzhen ($N = 663$) datasets [26,31].

2.2 Generative Architecture Stable Diffusion

Latent Diffusion Models (LDMs) approach image generation as an iterative denoising process, transforming pure noise x_T into a defined image x_0 over T steps with a parameterized LDM $\epsilon_\theta(z_t, t, c)$, where c represents an optional condition. LDMs address the prohibitive computational demands of traditional diffusion models (DMs) by reducing the dimensionality of the input. LDMs currently find active development with ongoing research in different parameterised models, optimization strategies and dimensionality reduction pipelines.

This study adopts the Stable Diffusion (SD) framework (version 1, [43]) as its baseline. Despite being outperformed by more recent models and its output size limitation of 512×512 pixels, SD's lightweight architecture, open-source nature, and community adoption makes it ideal for our proof of concept. SD comprises a frozen *variational autoencoder* (VAE) and a trainable *conditional denoising UNet*.

The VAE consists of an encoder ($\mathcal{E}$) and a decoder ($\mathcal{D}$). The encoder compresses fixed-size images $x \in \mathbb{R}^{H \times W \times 3}$ into a latent $z = \mathcal{E}(x) \in \mathbb{R}^{(H/d) \times (W/d) \times k}$, where $k = 4$ is number of channels extracted by the VAE and $d = 8$ is the downsampling factor. The decoder maps latents back to the original image space $\hat{x} = \mathcal{D}(z)$. SD's VAE has been shown to generalize to medical data [3,44]. The UNet serves as the diffusion component and uses a ResNet architecture as its convolutional backbone, where the condition c is incorporated through attention mechanisms (see Sect. 2.3).

With this model, training with conditional information involves two phases: the *forward* and *reverse diffusion* processes. During the *forward* diffusion, an image x_0 (or its latent representation z_0) and condition c are chosen. A timestep t is randomly selected ($t \sim \mathcal{U}(1,...,T)$) so a noisy latent z_t is generated by mixing z_0 with noise $\epsilon \sim \mathcal{N}(0, 1)$, resulting in a *partially noised* latent. The *reverse* process uses the UNet to estimate the original noise ϵ from z_t, t and c.

The network is optimized using the Mean Squared Error (MSE) loss between the predicted and actual noise to adjust the weights of the UNet:

$$\mathcal{L}_{LDM} = \mathbb{E}_{z \sim \epsilon(x), c, \epsilon \sim \mathcal{N}(0,1), t} \left[||\epsilon - \epsilon_\theta(z_t, t, c)||_2^2 \right] \tag{1}$$

After training, image synthesis begins with sampling a noisy latent $z_T \sim \mathcal{N}(0, 1)$, progressively denoising it with condition c to obtain z_0 so that $\hat{z}_0 = \epsilon_\theta(z_{T:0}, c)$, and by using the VAE's decoder, so that $\hat{x} = \mathcal{D}(\hat{z}_0) = \mathcal{D}(\epsilon_\theta(z_{T:0}, c))$.

2.3   Self-Supervised Conditioning

LDMs condition image generation using a semantic tensor c to guide the diffusion process. This tensor is usually obtained from a frozen transformer model f_Φ that maps the label information into a tensor $c = f_\Phi(x) \in \mathcal{R}^{S \times N}$, where S is the token length (of variable size), N is the embedding dimension and x represents whichever input the embedder model requires (text, image, etc.). Although the current diffusion literature has mainly focused on using textual descriptors as their main conditioning strategy, other conditioning mechanisms have been employed [5,6,12].

In this work we explore conditioning using image-derived semantic descriptors. Specifically, a vision transformer trained with the DiNO method [15,45] was used to produce a semantic description of the image to be generated. Vision transformers split an image into small patches (usually $P = 14px^2$ or $P = 16px^2$) representing "visual words" and operate over them using a standard transformer architecture. The model outputs a tensor of tokens $c = f_\Phi(x) \in \mathcal{R}^{S \times N}$ comprising a class token $c_{CLS} \in \mathcal{R}^N$, sometimes a pooler token $c_{PLR} \in \mathcal{R}^N$, sometimes a predefined amount R of register tokens $c_{REG} \in \mathcal{R}^{R \times N}$ [46], and finally a series of L patch tokens $c_{LCL} \in \mathcal{R}^{L \times N}$, where $L = H/P_y * W/P_x$. Finally, the conditioning tensor outputted by the embedder was reduced to the available global information $c_{GLB} = [c_{CLS}, c_{PLR}, c_{REG}]$ before feeding it to the UNet, as upon initial exploration the patch tokens contained too much local information of the original image x and led to trivial models that learnt to reconstruct images from redundant information (see Supplementary Materials Appendix Section A). Figure 1-(a) visually describes the training pipeline.

Conditioning image generation on image embeddings offers flexibility on generation as long as a conditioning embedding exists. In this work, two simple generation strategies were explored, to evaluate the model's in-distribution and out-of-distribution performance, although more advanced approaches could be devised:

Reconstruction-Based Image Generation. The "reconstruction" strategy consists in synthesizing images $\hat{x} = \mathcal{D}(\epsilon_\theta(z_{T:0}, c))$ from the global information of an existing real example (x, y), where y is the image's label, $\hat{y} = y$ and

$f_\Phi(x)$ is the conditioning embedding as produced by DiNO. This reconstruction leverages DiNO-Diffusion's large-scale pretraining to produce semantic variations over the source image x. Exact replicas of x are prevented by design due to conditioning with the compressed information from DiNO's global embedding, causing a bottleneck. Figure 1 (b–i) depicts the reconstruction process.

Interpolation-Based Image Generation: The "interpolation" strategy uses the same image generation mechanism from above. The difference lies in the sampling method of the conditioning embedding c, which is interpolated from two images $(x_1, y_1), (x_2, y_2)$ so that $\hat{c} = lerp(f_\Phi(x_1), f_\Phi(x_2), r)$, where $r \in [0,1]$ is the interpolation fraction. This strategy attempts to generate synthetic images from less sampled regions of the real data manifold, located between existing samples, following approaches such as MixUp [47]. See Fig. 1 (b–ii) for a visual depiction of this strategy.

2.4   Evaluation

This section details four different evaluation protocols used for benchmarking DiNO-Diffusion:

Image Quality and Checkpoint Selection: The Fréchet Inception Distance (FID; [48]) was used to quantify generation quality at multiple checkpoints for both variants of DiNO-Diffusion. The FID scores computed for the data generated via the "reconstruction" strategy (see Sect. 2.3) were used as a proxy for overall model performance. Similarly to [3], FID scores were computed over a 5k subset of MIMIC-CXR's p19 dataset [23], and are reported every 2500 steps in Fig. 3. Also following the same work, the FID score was computed on the feature space of a pretrained domain-specific image encoder from TorchXrayVision [49] as opposed to the default Inception-V3 model, as the latter might not provide an accurate measure of image quality when dealing with medical image data. Finally, the optimal checkpoint for each DiNO-Diffusion model was the checkpoint with the lowest FID score.

Data Augmentation : This experiment explored DiNO-Diffusion's ability to enhance the sample size of a dataset by training a classification model on real and synthetic data using five-fold cross-validation and testing on a held-out test set (MIMIC's p19). For this purpose, MIMIC's training dataset (p10-p18) was subset into different data regimes with decreasing sample size $\mathcal{X}_n$, with $n \in \{10k, 5k, 1k, 500, 100, 50\}$ samples in the subset. Given that MIMIC has multi-label annotations, label balancing was performed by randomly selecting $n/card(\mathcal{L})$ elements of each label in the labelset $\mathcal{L}$ from $\mathcal{X}$ without replacement, ensuring sufficient representativity of all labels within the training set. Smaller subsets were also enforced to be contained into bigger ones, so that $\mathcal{X}_{\mathcal{N}_{i+1}} \in \mathcal{X}_{\mathcal{N}_i}$. With $\mathcal{X}_n$ defined, synthetic data was created to increase sample size by generating partially-synthetic datasets $\hat{\mathcal{X}}_n$ with real-to-synthetic ratios of 1:1, 1:5, 1:10 and 1:50 for the reconstruction- and interpolation-based synthesis (see Sect. 2.3). For the reconstruction experiments, ratios larger than 1:1 represent several semantic variations of a single source image (x, y), which aim at introducing realistic variance into the synthetic data while retaining the label-specific image features. The interpolation experiment addressed whether intermediate embeddings could still be decoded into an image that retains label-specific features from both elements in the pair. For this purpose, the sample pairs were enforced to have at least one label in common (see Sect. 2.3) without repetition. When not all the labels are in common between the pair, the labels of the interpolated example are set to the ones of the sample it is closest to, as defined by the interpolation fraction r. Finally, in the case of not having enough unique pairs for a given split, some pairings were repeated with different r.

Full Synthetic Training: This experiment explores whether test-set AUC drops when training a classifier solely on synthetic data, to address whether DiNO-Diffusion can serve as a privacy-preserving synthetic replacement for real data. The generation strategies, data regimes, real-to-synthetic ratios and 5-fold cross-validation settings from Sect. 2.4 were followed as evaluation strategy.

Zero-Shot Segmentation: This experiment investigates the model's ability to learn semantic coherence by generating segmentation masks from the internal representations generated during the DiNO-Diffusion's UNet forward pass. For this purpose, the zero-shot segmentation approach from DiffSeg [7] was followed, consisting of leveraging the self-attention weights from each transformer block of the UNet and iteratively merging them based on their Kullback-Leibler divergence. This methodology was applied both to DiNO-Diffusion and a vanilla natural image pretrained SD model [43] to generate lung lobe segmentation masks without further training. Using a combined dataset of 1,048 cases with ground truth annotations (See Sect. 2.1), candidate masks were evaluated by their Dice score and selected via non-maximum suppression. The relevant hyperparameters (merging threshold, timestep) as well as the best performing checkpoint were selected per model (see Supplementary Materials Appendix Section B). Refer to Fig. 1 (b-iii) for a visual depiction of the segmentation pipeline.

2.5 Experimental Setup

The models were trained by adapting HuggingFace Diffusers' script for training LDMs [50]. The LDMs were trained for 100 epochs ($\sim$ 140000 steps) using 4 H100 GPUs per model, an aggregated batch size of 512 ($bs = 64$, gradient accumulation of 2 steps), 8-bit Adam optimizer with constant $lr = 10^{-4}$ and 1000-step warmup and xformers' memory-efficient attention [51]. The specific versions of the DiNOv1 and DiNOv2 image encoder architectures used were "facebook/dino-vitb16" [15] and "timm/vit-base-patch14-reg4-dinov2"

Table 1. AUC scores (mean ± SD; 5-fold cross-validation) for (a) data augmentation experiments and (b) full synthetic trainings across DiNO-Diffusion variants, image synthesis strategies (reconstruction, interpolation), real-to-synthetic ratios (rs) and data regimes (N). The baseline (i.e., training with real data only) test performances are depicted at the top in light-blue. **Bold** values represent best performance improvement relative to the real-only baseline for each data regime, DiNO-Diffusion model and synthesis strategy. Asterisks (*) represent statistical significance ($p < 0.05$).

Strategy			rs ratio	$AUC_{N=50}$ ↓	$AUC_{N=100}$ ↓	$AUC_{N=500}$ ↓	$AUC_{N=1000}$ ↓	$AUC_{N=5000}$ ↓
			Real data 1:0 (real-only)	0.548 ± 0.013	0.566 ± 0.047	0.682 ± 0.011	0.715 ± 0.005	0.747 ± 0.006
(a) Data Augmentation	DiNOv1-Diffusion	Reconstruction	1:1	0.551 ± 0.037	0.602 ± 0.025	0.685 ± 0.012	**0.724 ± 0.002** *	0.756 ± 0.002 *
			1:5	0.564 ± 0.050	0.626 ± 0.016	**0.706 ± 0.010** *	0.725 ± 0.005	**0.756 ± 0.003** *
			1:10	0.608 ± 0.024 *	0.618 ± 0.030	0.701 ± 0.014	0.719 ± 0.007	0.745 ± 0.012
			1:50	**0.650 ± 0.020** *	**0.651 ± 0.013** *	0.698 ± 0.009	0.699 ± 0.012	0.735 ± 0.006
		Interpolation	1:1	0.540 ± 0.036	0.589 ± 0.033	0.676 ± 0.007	0.682 ± 0.011 *	0.686 ± 0.009 *
			1:5	0.579 ± 0.033	0.625 ± 0.011	0.696 ± 0.013	0.706 ± 0.007 *	0.703 ± 0.007 *
			1:10	0.589 ± 0.039 *	0.618 ± 0.018	**0.709 ± 0.009** *	0.709 ± 0.003	0.693 ± 0.018 *
			1:50	**0.632 ± 0.015** *	**0.644 ± 0.014** *	0.702 ± 0.013	**0.716 ± 0.013**	0.743 ± 0.004
	DiNOv2-Diffusion	Reconstruction	1:1	0.515 ± 0.026	0.566 ± 0.015	0.692 ± 0.022	0.716 ± 0.008	**0.747 ± 0.003**
			1:5	0.552 ± 0.036	0.608 ± 0.035	**0.705 ± 0.004** *	0.714 ± 0.006	0.744 ± 0.004
			1:10	0.611 ± 0.010 *	0.631 ± 0.029	0.705 ± 0.006 *	**0.717 ± 0.005**	0.745 ± 0.006
			1:50	**0.617 ± 0.018** *	**0.627 ± 0.016** *	0.700 ± 0.016	0.710 ± 0.005	0.744 ± 0.004
		Interpolation	1:1	0.574 ± 0.043	0.603 ± 0.049	**0.685 ± 0.009**	0.698 ± 0.007 *	0.681 ± 0.011 *
			1:5	0.580 ± 0.018 *	0.594 ± 0.053	0.657 ± 0.023	0.688 ± 0.011 *	0.710 ± 0.008 *
			1:10	0.608 ± 0.025 *	0.622 ± 0.026	0.681 ± 0.017	0.694 ± 0.005 *	0.689 ± 0.021 *
			1:50	**0.618 ± 0.020** *	**0.649 ± 0.016** *	0.690 ± 0.024	0.703 ± 0.008 *	0.702 ± 0.013 *
(b) Full Synthetic Training	DiNOv1-Diffusion	Reconstruction	1:1	0.546 ± 0.017	0.571 ± 0.046	0.667 ± 0.008 *	0.696 ± 0.010 *	0.730 ± 0.004 *
			1:5	0.574 ± 0.059	0.610 ± 0.029 *	**0.701 ± 0.007**	**0.724 ± 0.004** *	0.752 ± 0.005
			1:10	0.625 ± 0.020 *	0.631 ± 0.025 *	0.701 ± 0.010	0.722 ± 0.005	**0.753 ± 0.006**
			1:50	**0.655 ± 0.015** *	**0.645 ± 0.011** *	0.689 ± 0.018	0.709 ± 0.014	0.746 ± 0.006
		Interpolation	1:1	0.515 ± 0.029	0.491 ± 0.033	0.530 ± 0.035 *	0.546 ± 0.016 *	0.538 ± 0.020 *
			1:5	0.525 ± 0.015 *	0.576 ± 0.037	0.686 ± 0.011	0.695 ± 0.008 *	0.531 ± 0.009 *
			1:10	0.572 ± 0.023 *	0.574 ± 0.013	0.701 ± 0.005 *	0.706 ± 0.005 *	0.686 ± 0.005 *
			1:50	**0.635 ± 0.018** *	**0.644 ± 0.015** *	**0.705 ± 0.013** *	0.711 ± 0.011	0.736 ± 0.007
	DiNOv2-Diffusion	Reconstruction	1:1	0.509 ± 0.025 *	0.564 ± 0.044	0.646 ± 0.021 *	0.649 ± 0.005 *	0.711 ± 0.004 *
			1:5	0.523 ± 0.019 *	0.591 ± 0.048	0.684 ± 0.009	0.700 ± 0.007 *	0.728 ± 0.007 *
			1:10	0.574 ± 0.034	0.610 ± 0.021 *	0.687 ± 0.012	0.695 ± 0.011 *	0.730 ± 0.006 *
			1:50	**0.603 ± 0.033** *	**0.626 ± 0.015** *	**0.699 ± 0.014** *	0.708 ± 0.006	0.741 ± 0.006
		Interpolation	1:1	0.546 ± 0.045	0.567 ± 0.019	0.553 ± 0.035 *	0.558 ± 0.015 *	0.533 ± 0.024 *
			1:5	0.536 ± 0.030	0.593 ± 0.040	0.631 ± 0.029 *	0.669 ± 0.008 *	0.646 ± 0.016 *
			1:10	0.551 ± 0.030	0.602 ± 0.035	0.668 ± 0.017	0.660 ± 0.014 *	0.680 ± 0.017 *
			1:50	**0.610 ± 0.052** *	**0.625 ± 0.009** *	0.672 ± 0.018	0.677 ± 0.005 *	0.714 ± 0.016 *

[46], respectively. The webdataset library [52] was used for storing and streaming data directly from the bucket during all model trainings. The classification experiments were based on training HuggingFace's implementation of a "`densenet121`" for 150 max epochs using T4 GPUs with batch size 64, AdamW optimizer with $lr = 10^{-4}$ and weight decay of 10^{-5}, a LR reduction-on-plateau scheduler with patience 10 and early stopping after 25 epochs with no validation AUC improvement. For the checkpoint evaluation, a pretrained "`densenet121-res224-all`" [49] was employed as feature extractor. All images

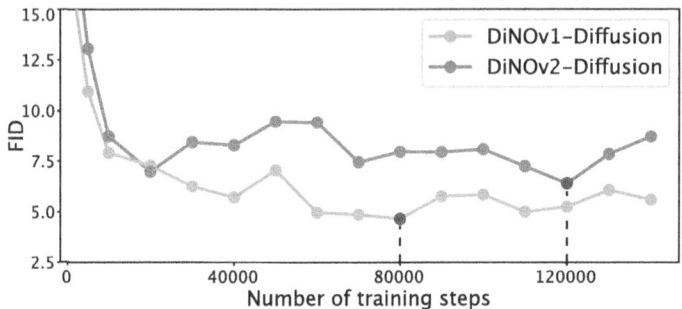

Fig. 3. FID scores over a MIMIC subset for DiNO-Diffusion every 2500 steps. Lower is better.

followed the same minimal preprocessing strategy before training or evaluation, similar to other works in the literature [3,49]. Dynamic intensity values (uint8, uint16) were rescaled to uint8. Images were center-cropped with a 1:1 aspect ratio, resized to 512×512 pixels and padded areas were removed. Minimal data augmentations were applied during all model trainings, including random sharpening and affine transformations (5% shearing, 5% translation, 90%–140% scaling).

3 Results

3.1 Image Quality anf Checkpoint Selection

The FID scores were calculated every 2500 steps over a subset of MIMIC's p19 dataset following [3]. Both the DiNOv1 and DiNOv2 models converged relatively late, reaching scores of 4.7 and 6.4 at 80k and 120k steps, respectively. The full FID scores for every checkpoint can be observed in Fig. 3. DiNOv1-Diffusion leads to lower FID scores when compared to DiNOv2-Diffusion. This is also evident by a slightly less saturated synthetic images generated with DiNOv2-Diffusion when compared to the source real images (see Fig. 2). Additional generated examples are provided as Supplementary Material in Appendix Fig. 1.

3.2 Data Augmentation

In this experiment, real and synthetic data were used in different proportions to train DenseNet-121 classification models. Table 1-a and Fig. 4-a provide the results of the cross-validation trainings. The 'reconstruction' workstream (see Sect. 2.3) depicts consistent improvements when used for data augmentation in all data regimes, with AUC increases up to approximately 20% in small-data regimes. In some larger-data regimes ($N \in [1000, 5000]$), the addition of large amounts of synthetic data slightly degraded performance, although never by a significant margin ($p > 0.05$). The'interpolation' workstream (see Sect. 2.3) also depicts improvements in smaller data regimes as compared to not using

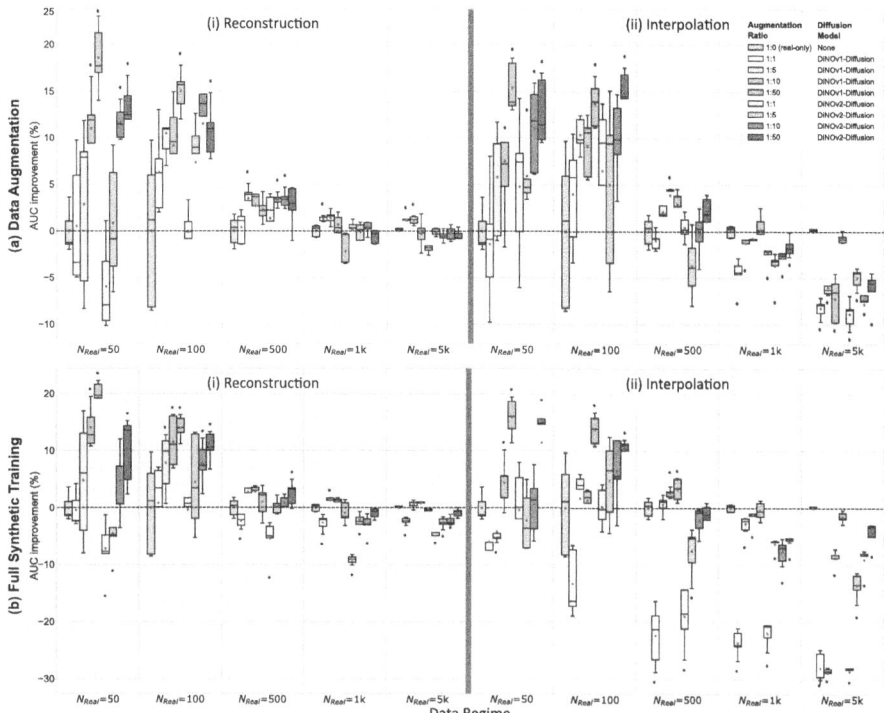

Fig. 4. Performance improvements for the Data Augmentation (a) and the Full Synthetic Training (b) experiments. The horizontal line represents a 0% improvement over the mean (red dot) classification performance when using real-data only (green bars) for each data regime and real-to-synthetic ratio (rs) independently. Values above the dotted line represent performance improvement. The vertical lines separate the different data regimes for easier comparison, where the performance of DiNOv1-Diffusion (yellow palette) and DiNOv2-Diffusion (blue palette) are jointly displayed. In (i), the results for the reconstruction experiment are explored, whereas (ii) depicts the results for the interpolation experiment. Asterisks (*) represent statistical significance to real baseline ($p < 0.05$). (Color figure online)

synthetic data, although it leads to a significant performance degradation in large-data regimes ($p < 0.05$). Also, DiNO-Diffusion using DiNOv1 yields larger performance improvements compared to when using DiNOv2. This is always true for both image synthesis strategies, except for the interpolation results on data regime $N_{real} = 100$, where the best test AUC is achieved with DiNOv2 for 1:50 rs ratio.

3.3 Full Synthetic Training

the test set results of the full synthetic trainings are shown in Table 1-b and Fig. 4-b. The data synthesised via the "reconstruction" strategy (see Sect. 2.3)

Table 2. Segmentation performance, measured by mean Dice scores (%). The displayed values are based on the hyperparameter configurations that led to best overall results.

Dataset	Stable Diffusion 1.5	DiNOv1-Diffusion	DiNOv2-Diffusion	Fully Supervised
Threshold	0.5	0.05	0.05	–
Timestep	300	300	300	–
Grid size	32x32	16x16	16x16	–
Shenzhen	80.7 ± 15.9	**84.2 ± 10.5**	82.3 ± 15.7	98.3 [53]
JSRT	80.9 ± 12.1	**88.4 ± 6.8**	84.7 ± 11.3	97.9[54]
Montgomery	77.3 ± 8.8	78.3 ± 8.6	**87.1 ± 3.4**	97.7[54]
Combined	80.3 ± 14.2	**84.4 ± 9.9**	83.6 ± 13.6	–

using DiNOv1-Diffusion provided good performance in almost all settings, where statistically significant performance decreases only existed for the lowest rs ratio in the largest three data regimes. For both "reconstruction" DiNO-Diffusion variants, training with sufficiently large rs ratios in small-data regimes ($N_{real} \in [50, 100, 500]$) led to significant performance improvements of up to 20%, mirroring the data augmentation results (see Sect. 2.4). However, for the "interpolation" based synthesis (see Sect. 2.3), this was only the case in the 1:50 ratio. Generally, the data synthesised via the "interpolation" strategy did not reliably train the classifier in splits larger than $N_{real} = 1k$ for DiNOv1-Diffusion and $N_{real} = 500$ for DiNOv2-Diffusion. Finally, DiNOv1-Diffusion yielded larger performance improvements and statistical significance when compared to DiNOv2-Diffusion.

3.4 Zero-Shot Segmentation

The performance of the zero-shot experiments are shown in Table 2. Both DiNOv1- and DiNOv2-Diffusion showed improvements of up to 10% Dice score when compared to a vanilla SD v1.5 model while also presenting lower variance. When addressing individual results, DiNOv1-Diffusion generated the best average Dice scores. Performance varied between datasets, with Montgomery [26] producing the lowest Dice scores for both vanilla SD and DiNOv1-Diffusion, but to the highest scores for the DiNOv2-based approach when comparing the overall best model. It should be noted that the best model checkpoint for segmentation was significantly earlier than the one found in Sect. 3.1. Moreover, the optimal parameters for DiffSeg were very similar for both self-supervised LDMs, while the optimal merging threshold was 10x larger for the base SD model. Finally, non-optimal combinations of parameters produced significant artifacts in the generated masks as shown in Fig. 5 (b). The Supplementary Material provides additional zero-shot segmentation examples in Appendix Fig. 3 and an additional segmentation performance evaluation across different model checkpoints in Appendix Fig. 4.

4   Discussion

Diffusion models are a cornerstone in modern foundation models, revolutionizing many tasks in Computer Vision. Their ability to generate high-quality images has caused a large scientific, economic and societal disruption, whose long-term repercussions are difficult to foresee [14]. However, despite their scientific and industrial utility, applying this technology in medical imaging is severely limited by key challenges such as a lack of large-scale labeled datasets including high-quality textual or non-textual descriptions [1]. Although this limitation might be temporary due to current trends in AI data acquisition and improved dataset interoperability [55], it is not clear whether the prevalent text-to-image generative recipe [43] is optimal for medical applications.

Some approaches employing LDMs in medical data exist. Chambon *et al.* [3] trained an SD architecture on the MIMIC-CXR dataset [23] with good synthesis fidelity, reporting low FID scores and high accuracy scores on several downstream tasks including classification, report generation and image retrieval. However, their approach is severely limited on the size of the development dataset (300k images) and the low quality of accompanying captions. In histopathology, multiple authors have proposed applying diffusion models for image generation [2,4]. For instance, Aversa *et al.*. relied on a custom-annotated dataset of large histopathology slides with segmentation masks representing different tissue subtypes within the slide and employed timestep unravelling to generate images larger than the typical $512\,px^2$. However, their approach heavily relied on a closed-source, custom-annotated dataset, and timestep unraveling might be impractical in other medical imaging modalities. In contrast, Xu *et al.*. [56] take a similar approach as the one proposed here, and train a diffusion model conditioned only on an image encoder's c_{CLS} for histopathology image synthesis. However, their method was partially supervised, as it relied on training additional label-specific DMs for c_{CLS} generation. Besides being compute intensive, their method fails to leverage the emerging data augmentation and segmentation capabilities that a self-supervision LDM training conveys. Finally, Pinaya *et al.* [6] trained an LDM on a large dataset of 31740 3D Brain MRI images from UK BioBank. However, despite the scale of this dataset, the fragmentation of clinical labels forced the authors to condition the DM with simplified clinical variables such as age, sex, ventricular volume, and brain volume.

DiNO-Diffusion addresses the data limitations in medical imaging by conditioning the image generation process on the images themselves. This allows training LDMs on unlabelled data, which is more abundant in the medical field. The resulting DiNO-Diffusion models demonstrated good manifold coverage, as indicated by low FID scores, and exhibited notable properties in several downstream tasks. Firstly, adding synthetic data using the "reconstruction" strategy improved performance across most configurations. However, performance gains diminished as more real data became available, which is to be expected. Secondly, the "interpolation" strategy degraded performance in higher data regimes. We hypothesize that, although the generated images qualitatively resemble plausible images (see Fig. 2-b), naïvely interpolating embeddings did not ensure that the interpolated

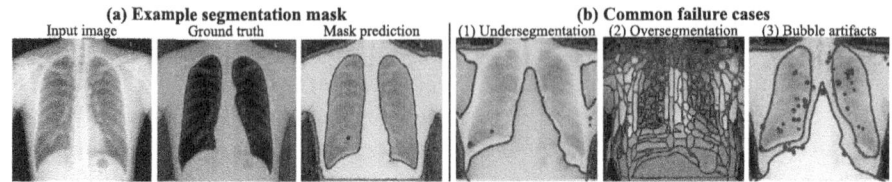

Fig. 5. (a) Example segmentation masks generated by the best DiNOv1-Diffusion model and (b) common failure cases. Failures are caused by sub-optimal hyperparameters: (1) incomplete segmentation, often observed in early checkpoints or high thresholds; (2) oversegmentation, usually due to low merge thresholds; (3) bubble-like artifacts, mostly observed in later checkpoints.

labels corresponded to the decoded image's features, thereby hurting classification performance. We leave to future work the exploration of more sophisticated interpolation strategies. Thirdly, full synthetic training demonstrated that synthetic data can replace real data while preserving privacy, and even improve performance in small-data regimes, when used in abundance. Finally, DiNO-Diffusion's zero-shot segmentation outperformed a vanilla SD architecture. This is remarkable given that the dataset used to train the vanilla SD model was several orders of magnitude larger. Despite DiNO-Diffusion's performance, conditioning the synthesis process on image embeddings has theoretical advantages and disadvantages. This type of conditioning relaxes the need for annotations, enabling the collection of larger datasets for model training, and has proven effective across various tasks. However, usage of an image-conditioned model is fundamentally different from text-based approaches, as image generation requires conditioning on an image. Still, this circular dependency between input and output could be advantageous in some use cases, such as data augmentation or privacy-preserving data sharing.

These advantages and disadvantages evidence room for improvement. Firstly, DiNOv1-Diffusion outperformed DiNOv2-Diffusion both quantitatively and qualitatively, despite the larger data pool used to train the DiNOv2 image encoder [16]. This suggests that using domain-specific encoders [17,19,49], or even a combination of different image encoders [13,14] could further improve these results. Secondly, DiNO-Diffusion would benefit from more recent diffusion architectures found in the literature [10,13,14]. Thirdly, generation based on other descriptors, such as text, could be enabled by using external networks to map the image embedding space to the text embedding [11,12]. Finally, the failure cases found in the zero-shot segmentation workstream require adapting the DiffSeg methodology to datasets with different characteristics, including image-level hyperparameter optimization, further attention-merging strategies, or using DiNO's attention maps to better locate anatomic structures.

In conclusion, while diffusion models have significantly impacted the Computer Vision community with broad scientific, economic, and societal implications, their application to medical imaging is constrained by data and annotation scarcity. Our DiNO-Diffusion approach addresses this problem by conditioning the image generation on the images themselves, eliminating the need for extensive annotations. The approach shows promising results in manifold coverage, data augmentation, privacy preservation and zero-shot segmentation. Finally, this work underscores the need for innovative solutions in medical imaging to fully leverage the potential of DMs in this space.

Acknowledgments. We would like to thank Marion Legler and Hendrik Esch for their support, constructive conversations and inspiration. All authors are employed by Bayer AG.

References

1. Kazerouni, A., et al.: Diffusion models in medical imaging: a comprehensive survey. Med. Image Anal. **88**, 102846 (2023). issn: 1361–8415. https://doi.org/10.1016/j.media.2023.102846
2. Osorio, P., et al.: Latent diffusion models with image-derived annotations for enhanced AI-assisted cancer diagnosis in histopathology. Diagnostics **14**(13) (2024). issn: 2075-4418. https://doi.org/10.3390/diagnostics14131442
3. Chambon, P., et al.: Roentgen: vision-language foundation model for chest x-ray generation. arXiv preprint arXiv:2211.12737 (2022)
4. Ye, J., et al.: Synthetic augmentation with large-scale unconditional pre-training. In: Greenspan, H., et al. (eds.) Medical Image Computing and Computer Assisted Intervention – MICCAI 2023, pp. 754–764. Springer, Cham (2023). isbn: 978-3-031-43895-0
5. Aversa, M., et al.: DiffInfinite: large mask-image synthesis via parallel random patch diffusion in histopathology. In: Oh, A., et al. (eds.) Advances in Neural Information Processing Systems, vol. 36, pp. 78126–78141. Curran Associates, Inc. (2023)
6. Pinaya, W.H.L., et al.: Brain imaging generation with latent diffusion models. In: Mukhopadhyay, A., et al. (eds.) Deep Generative Models, pp. 117–126. Springer, Cham (2022). isbn: 978-3-031-18576-2
7. Tian, J., et al.: Diffuse, attend and segment: unsupervised zero-shot segmentation using stable diffusion model. arXiv preprint arXiv:2308.12469 (2023)
8. Zhang, J., et al.: A tale of two features: stable diffusion complements DINO for zero-shot semantic correspondence. In: Oh, A., et al. (eds.) Advances in Neural Information Processing Systems, vol. 36, pp. 45533–45547. Curran Associates, Inc. (2023)
9. Beddiar, D.R., Oussalah, M., Seppänen, T.: Automatic captioning for medical imaging (MIC): a rapid review of literature. Artif. Intell. Rev. **56**(5), 4019–4076 (2023). issn: 1573-7462. https://doi.org/10.1007/s10462-022-10270-w
10. Betker, J., et al.: Improving image generation with better captions. Comput. Sci. **2**(3), 8 (2023). https://cdn.openai.com/papers/dall-e-3.pdf
11. Li, J., et al.: BLIP-2: bootstrapping language-image pre-training with frozen image encoders and large language models. In: Krause, A., et al. (eds.) Proceedings of the 40th International Conference on Machine Learning, vol. 202, pp. 19730–19742. Proceedings of Machine Learning Research. PMLR (2023)

12. Zhang, L., Rao, A., , M.: Adding conditional control to text-to-image diffusion models. In: Proceedings of the IEEE/CVF International Conference on Computer Vision (ICCV), pp. 3836–3847 (2023)
13. Esser, P., et al.: Scaling rectified flow transformers for high-resolution image synthesis. arXiv preprint arXiv:2403.03206 (2024)
14. Liu, Y., et al.: Sora: a review on background, technology, limitations, and opportunities of large vision models. arXiv preprint arXiv:2402.17177 (2024)
15. Caron, M., et al.: Emerging properties in self-supervised vision transformers. In: Proceedings of the IEEE/CVF International Conference on Computer Vision (ICCV), pp. 9650–9660 (2021)
16. Oquab, M., et al.: Dinov2: learning robust visual features without supervision. arXiv preprint arXiv:2304.07193 (2023)
17. Pérez-Garca, F., et al.: RAD-DINO: exploring scalable medical image encoders beyond text supervision. arXiv preprint arXiv:2401.10815 (2024)
18. Dippel, J., et al.: RudolfV: a foundation model by pathologists for pathologists. arXiv preprint arXiv:2401.04079 (2024)
19. Moutakanni, T., et al.: Advancing human-centric AI for robust X-ray analysis through holistic self-supervised learning. arXiv preprint arXiv:2405.01469 (2024)
20. de la Iglesia Vayá, M., et al.: BIMCV COVID-19+: a large annotated dataset of RX and CT images from COVID-19 patients with Extension Part I (2023). https://doi.org/10.21227/f3q6-0986
21. Irvin, J., et al.: CheXpert: a large chest radiograph dataset with uncertainty labels and expert comparison. In: Proceedings of the AAAI Conference on Artificial Intelligence, vol. 33, no. 01, pp. 590–597 (2019)
22. Goldberger, A.L., et al.: PhysioBank, PhysioToolkit, and PhysioNet. Circulation 101(23), e215–e220 (2000). https://doi.org/10.1161/01.CIR.101.23.e215. https://www.ahajournals.org/doi/pdf/10.1161/01. CIR.101.23.e215
23. Johnson, A..E.W., et al.: MIMIC-CXR, a de-identified publicly available database of chest radiographs with free-text reports. Sci. Data 6(1), 317 (2019). issn: 2052-4463. https://doi.org/10.1038/s41597-019-0322-0
24. Demner-Fushman, D., et al.: Preparing a collection of radiology examinations for distribution and retrieval. J. Am. Med. Inf. Assoc. 23(2), 304–310 (2015). issn: 1067-5027. https://doi.org/10.1093/jamia/ocv080. https://academic.oup.com/jamia/article-pdf/23/2/304/34147537/ocv080.pdf
25. Tabik, S., et al.: COVIDGR dataset and COVID-SDNet methodology for predicting COVID-19 based on chest X-ray images. IEEE J. Biomed. Health Inf. 24(12), 3595–3605 (2020). https://doi.org/10.1109/JBHI.2020.3037127
26. Jaeger, S., et al.: Automatic tuberculosis screening using chest radiographs. IEEE Trans. Med. Imaging 33(2), 233–245 (2014). https://doi.org/10.1109/TMI.2013.2284099
27. Candemir, S., et al.: Lung segmentation in chest radiographs using anatomical atlases with nonrigid registration. IEEE Trans. Med. Imaging 33(2), 577–590 (2014). https://doi.org/10.1109/TMI.2013.2290491
28. Bustos, A., et al.: PadChest: a large chest x-ray image dataset with multi-label annotated reports. Med. Image Anal. 66, 101797 (2020). issn: 1361-8415. https://doi.org/10.1016/j.media. 2020.101797
29. Cohen, J.P., et al.: Radiographic assessment of lung opacity score dataset. Version v1 (2021). https://doi.org/10.5281/zenodo.4634000
30. Reis, E.P., et al.: BRAX, Brazilian labeled chest x-ray dataset. Sci. Data 9(1), 487 (2022). issn: 2052-4463. https://doi.org/10.1038/s41597-022-01608-8

31. Shiraishi, J., et al.: Development of a digital image database for chest radiographs with and without a lung nodule. Am. J. Roentgenol. **174**(1), 71–74 (2000). PMID: 10628457. https://doi.org/10.2214/ajr.174.1.1740071

32. Kermany, D.S., et al.: Identifying medical diagnoses and treatable diseases by image-based deep learning. Cell **172**(5), 1122–1131.e9 (2018). issn: 0092-8674. https://doi.org/10.1016/j.cell.2018.02.010

33. Cohen, J.P., et al.: COVID-19 image data collection: prospective predictions are the future. arxiv arXiv:2006.11988 (2020)

34. Chowdhury, M.E.H., et al.: Can AI help in screening viral and COVID-19 pneumonia?. IEEE Access **8**, 132665–132676 (2020). https://doi.org/10.1109/ACCESS.2020.3010287

35. Rahman, T., et al.: Exploring the effect of image enhancement techniques on COVID-19 detection using chest X-ray images. Comput. Biol. Med. **132**, 104319 (2021). issn: 0010-4825. https://doi.org/10.1016/j.compbiomed.2021.104319

36. JF Healthcare. Object-CXR - Automatic detection of foreign objects on chest X-rays (2020)

37. Nguyen, H.Q., et al.: VinDr-CXR: an open dataset of chest X-rays with radiologist's annotations Sci. Data **9**(1), 429 (2022). 2052-4463. https://doi.org/10.1038/s41597-022-01498-w

38. Pham, H.H., et al.: PediCXR: an open, large-scale chest radiograph dataset for interpretation of common thoracic diseases in children. Sci. Data **10**(1), 240 (2023). issn: 2052-4463. https://doi.org/10.1038/s41597-023-02102-5

39. Zawacki, A., et al.: SIIM-ACR Pneumothorax Segmentation (2019)

40. Liu, Y., et al.: Rethinking computer-aided tuberculosis diagnosis. In: IEEE/CVF Conference on Computer Vision and Pattern Recognition, pp. 2646–2655 (2020)

41. Rahman, T., et al.: TB-CXRNet: tuberculosis and drug-resistant tuberculosis detection technique using chest X-ray images. Cogn. Comput. (2024). issn: 1866-9964. https://doi.org/10.1007/s12559-024-10259-3

42. Fedorov, A., et al.: NCI imaging data commons. Cancer Res. **81**(16), 4188–4193 (2021). issn: 0008-5472. https://doi.org/10.1158/0008-5472.CAN-21-0950. https://aacrjournals.org/cancerres/article-pdf/81/16/4188/3294013/4188.pdf

43. Rombach, R., et al.: High-resolution image synthesis with latent diffusion models. In: Proceedings of the IEEE/CVF Conference on Computer Vision and Pattern Recognition (CVPR), pp. 10684–10695 (2022)

44. Chambon, P.J.M., et al.: Adapting pretrained vision-language foundational models to medical imaging domains. In: NeurIPS 2022 Foundation Models for Decision Making Workshop, pp. 1–12 (2022)

45. Dosovitskiy, A., et al.: An image is worth 16x16 words: transformers for image recognition at scale. In: International Conference on Learning Representations, pp. 1–21 (2021)

46. Darcet, T., et al.: Vision transformers need registers. In: The Twelfth International Conference on Learning Representations, pp. 1–21 (2024)

47. Zhang, H., et al.: mixup: Beyond empirical risk minimization. In: International Conference on Learning Representations, pp. 1–13 (2018)

48. Heusel, M., et al.: GANs trained by a two time-scale update rule converge to a local nash equilibrium. In: Guyon, I., et al. (eds.) Advances in Neural Information Processing Systems, vol. 30, pp. 1–12. Curran Associates, Inc. (2017)

49. Cohen, J.P., et al.: TorchXRayVision: a library of chest X-ray datasets and models. In: Konukoglu, E., et al. (eds.) Proceedings of The 5th International Conference on Medical Imaging with Deep Learning, vol. 172, pp. 231–249. Proceedings of Machine Learning Research. PMLR (2022)

50. von Platen, P., et al.: Diffusers: state-of-the-art diffusion models (2022). https://github.com/huggingface/diffusers/blob/main/examples/text_to_image/train_text_to_image.py

51. Lefaudeux, B., et al. xFormers: A modular and hackable Transformer modelling library (2022). https://github.com/facebookresearch/xformers

52. WebDataset Contributors. WebDataset: A PyTorch I/O Dataset for Large- Scale Data (2021). https://github.com/webdataset/webdataset. Accessed 01 Jan 2024

53. Xu, X., et al.: Lung segmentation in chest X-ray image using multiinteraction feature fusion network. IET Image Process. **17**(14), 4129–4141 (2023). https://doi.org/10.1049/ipr2.12923. https://ietresearch.onlinelibrary.wiley.com/doi/pdf/10.1049/ipr2.12923

54. Liu, W., Luo, J., Yang, Y., et al.: Automatic lung segmentation in chest X-ray images using improved U-Net. Sci. Rep. **12**, 8649 (2022). https://doi.org/10.1038/s41598-022-12743-y

55. Akhtar, M., et al.: Croissant: a metadata format for ML-ready datasets. In: Proceedings of the Eighth Workshop on Data Management for End-to-End Machine Learning. DEEM '24, pp. 1–6. Association for Computing Machinery, Santiago (2024). isbn: 9798400706110. https://doi.org/10.1145/3650203.3663326

56. Xu, X., et al.: ViT-DAE: transformer-driven diffusion autoencoder for histopathology image analysis. In: Mukhopadhyay, A., et al. (eds.) Deep Generative Models, pp. 66–76. Springer, Cham (2024). ISBN: 978-3-031-53767-7

Knowledge-Driven Hypothesis Generation for Burn Diagnosis from Ultrasound with Vision-Language Model

Md Masudur Rahman[1]([✉]) [iD], Mohamed El Masry[2,3] [iD], Gayle Gordillo[2,4] [iD], and Juan P. Wachs[1] [iD]

[1] Edwardson School of Industrial Engineering, Purdue University, West Lafayette, IN 47907, USA
{rahman64,jpwachs}@purdue.edu
[2] McGowan Institute for Regenerative Medicine (MIRM), Pittsburgh, PA 15219, USA
moelmasry@pitt.edu, gordillogm@upmc.edu
[3] Department of Surgery, University of Pittsburgh School of Medicine, Pittsburgh, PA 15213, USA
[4] Department of Plastic Surgery, University of Pittsburgh School of Medicine, Pittsburgh, PA 15261, USA

Abstract. Although vision-language models (VLMs) have achieved strong results in general computer vision tasks, their effectiveness in medical imaging remains limited—primarily due to their insufficient reasoning capabilities. In this work, we introduce KODER, a novel knowledge-driven reasoning framework aimed at improving diagnostic accuracy for ultrasound-based burn assessment. KODER integrates pre-trained VLMs with first-order logic (FOL) reasoning to generate interpretable diagnostic hypotheses. By combining rich experimental descriptions and clinical insights into a unified prompt, the framework produces multiple diagnostic hypotheses and refines them through iterative consistency checks using an SMT solver. The validated hypotheses are then used to support both surgical decision-making and detailed burn depth classification. We evaluate our approach on a retrospective dataset collected from a U.S. burn center, where it achieves significant performance gains—reaching up to 93% accuracy in surgical classification and 87% in fine-grained burn depth prediction. Additionally, incorporating techniques such as chain-of-thought reasoning, self-consistency, and explicit explanation generation further boosts both interpretability and diagnostic reliability. Our experiments span multiple state-of-the-art VLMs, including GPT-4o, GPT-4 Turbo, and Gemini 1.5 and Gemini 2.0, confirming the generalizability of KODER across architectures.

Keywords: Vision-Language Models · Ultrasound Imaging · Burn Diagnosis · Hypothesis Generation · Chain-of-Thought Reasoning · Self-Consistency · First-Order Logic

© The Author(s), under exclusive license to Springer Nature Switzerland AG 2026
S. Ali et al. (Eds.): MIUA 2025, LNCS 15916, pp. 275–288, 2026.
https://doi.org/10.1007/978-3-031-98688-8_19

1   Introduction

Vision-language models (VLMs) have achieved significant success by integrating visual processing with natural language understanding, particularly in tasks where explicit reasoning is not a core requirement [1,5,7–10,12–14,17,21,22]. However, applying these models to complex medical scenarios—such as diagnosing burn severity from ultrasound scans—presents unique challenges. This difficulty arises from the fact that interpreting multimodal ultrasound data often involves a structured reasoning process rather than straightforward perception.

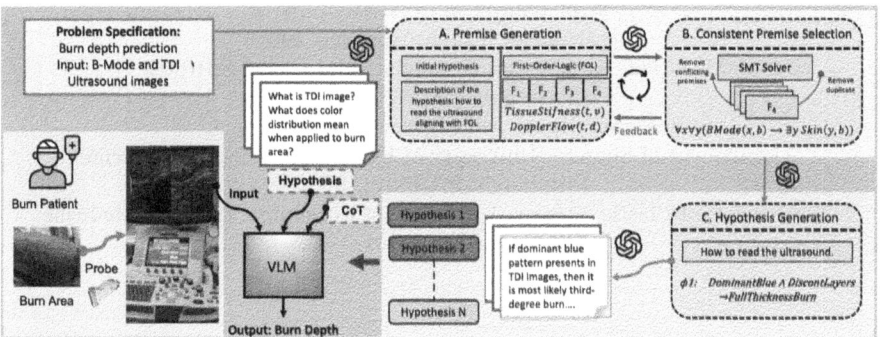

Fig. 1. Overview of KODER: **K**nowledge-**D**riven **R**easoning Framework.

These challenges become even more pronounced when working with novel imaging modalities and small, domain-specific datasets. VLMs are typically pretrained on massive, diverse datasets [13], but such data is rarely available in specialized clinical settings due to privacy concerns, proprietary limitations, or lack of standardization. This issue is particularly relevant in emerging areas like ultrasound-based burn care, where imaging protocols are still evolving and not widely adopted in practice [18]. As a result, training large, dedicated models for such tasks is often infeasible. To overcome these limitations, we propose a new framework that adapts existing, *general-purpose* VLMs to medical imaging tasks by incorporating structured reasoning.

Another critical limitation of large language models (LLMs) is their tendency to generate explanations that may be ambiguous, inconsistent, or lack clinical clarity [3,4,19,20]. This stems from the probabilistic nature of LLM outputs and can be problematic in high-stakes applications like medical diagnosis, where interpretability and reliability are essential [2,16]. For instance, ultrasound modalities such as Tissue Doppler Imaging (TDI) [6] and B-mode imaging capture nuanced features—including color-coded motion patterns and tissue structures—that require both image understanding and expert-level reasoning to interpret correctly.

To address this, we introduce **KODER** (**K**nowledge-**D**riven **R**easoning), a framework that combines the generative capabilities of LLMs with formal logical validation. As shown in Fig. 1, our method begins with a rich textual description of the imaging task, including details about modalities, scanning conditions, and patient context. The LLM uses this information to generate a diagnostic hypothesis along with a set of first-order logic (FOL) premises that encode the clinical rationale. These premises are then evaluated using an SMT (Satisfiability Modulo Theories) solver such as Z3 [11] to detect contradictions or ambiguities. This verification process enables iterative refinement of the hypothesis and logic until a consistent and clinically sound conclusion is reached.

We evaluate our framework on two downstream tasks: (i) binary classification to determine whether surgical intervention is needed, and (ii) a fine-grained, three-class burn depth prediction. Our experimental results on ultrasound datasets for burn diagnosis show that incorporating logically validated hypotheses leads to improved diagnostic accuracy. Across multiple state-of-the-art VLMs—including GPT-4o, GPT-4 Turbo, and Gemini 1.5 and Gemini 2.0—KODER consistently improves performance. For instance, GPT-4o combined with KODER achieves up to **93% accuracy** in surgical decision-making and **87%** in burn depth classification. Moreover, incorporating chain-of-thought reasoning and self-consistency further boosts both accuracy and interpretability, highlighting the effectiveness of structured, knowledge-guided diagnostic modeling.

In summary, our main contributions are:

– We introduce a novel framework that integrates vision-language models with formal logic to produce interpretable diagnostic hypotheses.
– We address the limitations of standard LLM/VLM outputs by validating generated content through logical consistency checks.
– We demonstrate the clinical utility of our approach through improved performance on real-world diagnostic tasks in burn care.

2   Methodology

2.1   KODER Framework

This section presents the **K**nowledge-**D**riven **R**easoning (KODER) framework, a method developed to formulate diagnostic hypotheses for predicting burn depth based on ultrasound imaging.

Problem Formulation and Input Description. The primary goal is to generate a global, dataset-level hypothesis for predicting burn depth based on ultrasound imaging. Instead of relying on raw image data, the method uses a detailed textual description that outlines both the imaging modalities and clinical rationale.

Let $\mathcal{T}$ denote the space of textual descriptions. We define $\mathcal{D}_{\text{exp}} \in \mathcal{T}$ as the *experimental setup description*, and $\mathcal{D}_{\text{clin}} \in \mathcal{T}$ as the *clinical context information*. For example, $\mathcal{D}_{\text{exp}}$ could be: "We employ Tissue Doppler Imaging (TDI) and B-mode ultrasound to predict burn depth. TDI provides color-coded velocity information, while B-mode offers structural imaging." Similarly, $\mathcal{D}_{\text{clin}}$ could be: "Clinical protocols indicate that dominant blue patterns in TDI images and discontinuous layers in B-mode images are correlated with full-thickness burns."

We define the *PromptBuilder* function to merge these two sources of information into a single prompt p:

$$p = \text{PromptBuilder}(\mathcal{D}_{\text{exp}}, \mathcal{D}_{\text{clin}}) = \mathcal{D}_{\text{exp}} \oplus \mathcal{D}_{\text{clin}},$$

where $\oplus$ represents concatenation, and PromptBuilder $\in \mathcal{T}$. This prompt provides the LLM with sufficient contextual knowledge for hypothesis generation.

Hypothesis and Premise Generation. Using the prompt p, the language model M_θ (parameterized by θ) generates both a natural language hypothesis h and a corresponding set of first-order logic (FOL) premises Φ. To promote diversity in the outputs, sampling parameters such as temperature τ and top-p nucleus sampling p_{top} are varied. Formally:

$$(h, \Phi) = M_\theta(p \mid \tau, p_{\text{top}}),$$

where h is a natural-language hypothesis, e.g., "If a dominant blue pattern is observed in TDI images and B-mode images show discontinuous layers, then the burn is likely full-thickness." Additionally, $\Phi = \{\phi_1, \phi_2, \ldots, \phi_K\}$ is a set of FOL statements encoding clinical rules. For instance:

$$\phi_1 : \quad (\text{DominantBlue} \wedge \text{DiscontLayers}) \rightarrow \text{FullThicknessBurn}.$$

Consistency Verification via SMT Solver. To verify the internal consistency of the logical premises Φ, a satisfiability modulo theories (SMT) solver (e.g., Z3 [11]) is used. The logical consistency is evaluated as:

$$\text{SMT}(\Phi) = \begin{cases} 1, & \text{if } \Phi \text{ is logically consistent,} \\ 0, & \text{otherwise.} \end{cases}$$

If $\text{SMT}(\Phi) = 0$, feedback is provided to the LLM to refine the hypothesis h or the logical set Φ. This process is repeated iteratively:

$$\Phi^{(\ell+1)} = \Gamma\Big(M_\theta\big(\text{RefinePrompt}(p, \Phi^{(\ell)})\big)\Big),$$

until the solver returns SAT (i.e., $\text{SMT}(\Phi) = 1$) or a maximum number of iterations m is reached. If no consistent set is found after m iterations, conflicting statements are discarded.

Final Hypothesis Generation. Once a consistent logical set Φ is established, the final diagnostic hypothesis is produced by integrating these validated FOL premises into a coherent natural language summary. An example output might be: "*Based on the dominant blue color patterns in TDI and the discontinuous layers observed in B-mode imaging, the burn is indicative of a full-thickness injury, suggesting that surgical intervention may be required.*"

2.2   Downstream Tasks

In the downstream tasks, we combine the diagnostic hypothesis with ultrasound image classification. Each ultrasound sample x_i is composed of a tuple:

$$x_i = \left(x_i^{\text{TDI}}, x_i^{\text{B}}\right),$$

where x_i^{TDI} and x_i^{B} represent the raw TDI and B-mode images, respectively. These images are first converted to RGB format and then concatenated horizontally, placing the B-mode image on the left and the TDI image on the right. This results in a composite image defined as:

$$z_i \in \mathbb{R}^{H \times W \times 3}.$$

The composite RGB image z_i is then used as input to the vision-language model (VLM) classifier.

For the **binary classification** task, which distinguishes between surgery and non-surgery cases (with labels $y_i \in \{0,1\}$), we define a classifier function:

$$g : \mathbb{R}^{H \times W \times 3} \to [0,1],$$

such that the probability of a positive label is given by:

$$P(y_i = 1 \mid z_i) = g(z_i).$$

To incorporate the hypothesis h, we use a logical support function $\mathcal{S}(h, \Phi, y)$, which measures how well the hypothesis supports a given decision y. The final prediction is computed as:

$$\hat{y}_i = \arg \max_{y \in \{0,1\}} \left\{ P(y \mid z_i) + \alpha \, \mathcal{S}(h, \Phi, y) \right\},$$

where α is a hyperparameter that balances the influence of the support function.

In the case of the **fine-grained burn depth classification** task, where classes $c \in \{1, 2, \ldots, N\}$ correspond to different burn depths (with $N = 3$ in our setting), we denote the class probabilities from a multi-class classifier as $P(c \mid z_i)$. The final prediction is then given by:

$$\hat{c}_i = \arg \max_{c \in \{1, 2, \ldots, N\}} \left\{ P(c \mid z_i) + \beta \, \mathcal{S}(h, \Phi, c) \right\},$$

where β is the associated balancing hyperparameter.

In our implementation of Logical Support Function, the VLM classifier is prompted with a query that integrates h along with the candidate class. For instance, to compute $\mathcal{S}(h, \Phi, y)$ for a candidate class y, the system may issue a prompt such as: *"Given the diagnostic hypothesis:* [h] *and the logical premises:* [Φ], *to what extent does this information support the diagnosis of* [y]?" The VLM's textual response is then mapped to a numerical score.

2.3 Classification with Hypothesis (Proposed Method)

In the proposed classification framework, the final diagnostic hypothesis h (and its corresponding reasoning, when applicable) is incorporated as a system prompt to guide the Vision-Language Model (VLM) classifier. We explore three different variants of this method:

1. **Hypothesis+VLM** In this variant, the VLM receives a prompt such as "What is the degree of burn depth?" or "Is this a surgery case or not?" The classification function is defined as:

$$f_{\text{VLM}} : \mathbb{R}^{H \times W \times 3} \times \mathcal{T} \to \mathcal{Y},$$

where $\mathcal{Y}$ is the label space, which could be $\{0, 1\}$ for binary classification or $\{1, 2, \ldots, N\}$ for multi-class classification. The final prediction is given by:

$$\hat{y}_i = f_{\text{VLM}}(z_i, h) = \arg\max_{y \in \mathcal{Y}} P(y \mid z_i, h).$$

2. **Hypothesis+VLM with Chain-of-Thought (CoT)** This variant enhances the model's reasoning capabilities by introducing a chain-of-thought (CoT) mechanism. A recursive reasoning process is used, defined as:

$$r^{(t)} = M_\theta\left(z_i, h, r^{(1)}, r^{(2)}, \ldots, r^{(t-1)}\right), \quad \text{for } t = 1, \ldots, T,$$

with $r^{(0)}$ initialized as an empty context. The complete chain-of-thought is represented as:

$$r = \{r^{(1)}, r^{(2)}, \ldots, r^{(T)}\}.$$

Each output $r^{(t)}$ is recursively included in the system prompt for subsequent iterations, progressively refining the prediction. The CoT-enhanced classification function is expressed as:

$$f_{\text{VLM}}^{\text{CoT}} : \mathbb{R}^{H \times W \times 3} \times \mathcal{T} \times \mathcal{R} \to \mathcal{Y},$$

where $\mathcal{R}$ is the space of chain-of-thought outputs. The final prediction is computed as:

$$\hat{y}_i = f_{\text{VLM}}^{\text{CoT}}(z_i, h, r) = \arg\max_{y \in \mathcal{Y}} P(y \mid z_i, h, r).$$

3. **Hypothesis+VLM with Chain-of-Thought and Self-Consistency** In the third variant, multiple candidate outputs are generated by varying sampling parameters such as temperature τ and top-p within the CoT framework. Let:

$$\{\hat{y}_i^{(1)}, \ldots, \hat{y}_i^{(K)}\}$$

denote the set of candidate predictions. The final output is obtained by aggregating these predictions, for example, using majority voting or weighted averaging:

$$\hat{y}_i = \text{Aggregate}\left(\{\hat{y}_i^{(k)}\}_{k=1}^{K}\right).$$

Across all these variants, the hypothesis h, and when applicable the chain-of-thought r, are integrated into the system prompt. This guides the VLM classifier toward producing more informed and interpretable predictions, further supported by the logical scoring function $\mathcal{S}(h, \Phi, \cdot)$.

3   Experiments

3.1   Dataset and Experiments Settings

Our study is based on a retrospective ultrasound dataset collected over one year at a U.S. burn center. The dataset consists of B-mode and Tissue Doppler Imaging (TDI) ultrasound scans [6] from 29 human subjects, each presenting with varying burn depths, including superficial, superficial partial-thickness (second-degree), deep partial-thickness (second-degree), and full-thickness (third-degree) burns. Ground truth labels for burn severity were obtained either through histological biopsy or, when unavailable, through expert clinical assessment and consensus from burn specialists. B-mode ultrasound was used to capture and quantify structural tissue features, while TDI provided dynamic assessments of tissue integrity. A visual example of the dataset is shown in Fig. 2. To ensure high imaging quality, we selected frames marked with green-labeled TDI quality indicators, which signal proper probe pressure. This initial filtering yielded 950 ultrasound frames across all patients.

To reduce redundancy from temporally adjacent frames, we applied uniform interval sampling within each video clip, minimizing the inclusion of visually repetitive frames. After this filtering, we curated a final dataset of 324 distinct ultrasound frames. Of these, 130 frames from 15 patients were reserved for evaluation, while the remaining data were used for training purposes, including chain-of-thought and n-shot prompting strategies.

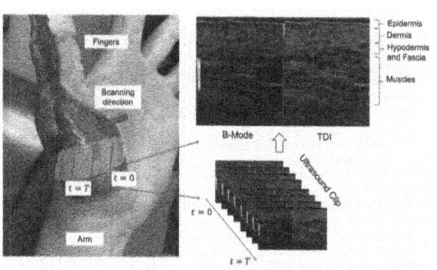

Fig. 2. An example from the burn dataset, showing B-mode and TDI ultrasound images captured from the wound site

Implementation Details. To generate diagnostic hypotheses within the KODER framework, we utilized OpenAI's `o3-mini-high` model, which is optimized for reasoning tasks. For the vision-language modeling component, we evaluated several state-of-the-art models, including OpenAI's `gpt-4o-2024-11-20`, `gpt-4o-mini-2024-07-18`, and `gpt-4-turbo-2024-04-09` [1], as well as Google's `gemini-2.0-flash` and `gemini-1.5-flash` [15].

To validate the first-order logic (FOL) premises, we employed the Z3 SMT solver [11] to ensure logical consistency. For Chain-of-Thought (CoT) reasoning [20], n-shot prompting was used, where each prompt included an ultrasound image, expert-provided explanation, and corresponding label to guide step-by-step reasoning. In the self-consistency experiments [19], we varied the VLM's temperature, top-p sampling values, and the order and number of CoT examples to analyze their impact on prediction stability. Final decisions were obtained using majority voting across outputs from multiple reasoning paths. For fine-grained burn depth classification, we implemented a two-step VLM querying process. In the first step, the model predicted whether a case was a third-degree burn. In the second step, remaining cases were classified as either second-degree deep or second-degree superficial. This hierarchical approach yielded better performance than a single-step three-way classification, as it reduced cognitive load by narrowing the decision space at each stage.

3.2   Results

Table 1 presents a comparative analysis of various VLMs with and without the KODER framework across two tasks: Surgical Decision-Making and Fine-Grained Burn Depth classification. Overall, KODER—particularly when combined with self-consistency—significantly enhances the diagnostic performance of all evaluated models.

The best results are achieved by **GPT-4o + KODER**, which obtains an accuracy of **93%** on Surgical Decision-Making and **87%** on Burn Depth classification. In contrast, the baseline GPT-4o model without KODER shows poor performance, with only 33% and 27% accuracy, respectively, highlighting the critical role of reasoning and logical refinement in achieving high diagnostic reliability.

Other models also benefit notably from the integration of KODER. For example, **Gemini 2.0 + KODER** reaches 87% accuracy for Surgical Decision-Making, though its performance on Burn Depth classification remains moderate at 60%. Similarly, **Gemini 1.5 + KODER** demonstrates meaningful gains, achieving 80% accuracy on Surgical Decision-Making and 67% on Burn Depth, significantly outperforming its base model which only scored 60% and 47% on the two tasks, respectively.

Table 1. Performance Comparison of KODER (with self-consistency) on Surgical Decision and Fine-Grained Burn Depth

VLM	Surgical Decision-Making				Fine-Grained Burn Depth			
	Accuracy	F-1	Prec	Recall	Accuracy	F-1	Prec	Recall
GPT4o+KODER	**93%**	**0.93**	**0.94**	**0.93**	**87%**	**0.87**	**0.87**	**0.87**
GPT4o	33%	0.17	0.11	0.33	27%	0.27	0.34	0.27
GPT4o-mini+KODER	80%	0.77	0.85	0.80	53%	0.42	0.35	0.53
GPT4o-mini	67%	0.67	0.69	0.67	73%	0.71	0.73	0.73
GPT4-Turbo+KODER	93%	0.93	0.94	0.93	53%	0.52	0.56	0.53
GPT4-Turbo	87%	0.87	0.87	0.87	60%	0.59	0.62	0.6
Gemini2.0+KODER	87%	0.86	0.89	0.86	60%	0.5	0.64	0.6
Gemini2.0	47%	0.41	0.79	0.47	47%	0.40	0.66	0.47
Gemini1.5+KODER	80%	0.79	0.85	0.8	67%	0.62	0.79	0.67
Gemini1.5	60%	0.5	0.42	0.6	47%	0.43	0.46	0.47

Across all configurations, the addition of KODER leads to consistent improvements in both precision and recall, indicating more reliable and balanced classification. Notably, even smaller or earlier-generation models such as gpt-4o-mini and gemini-1.5 show substantial boosts in performance when paired with the KODER reasoning framework.

These results confirm that the integration of structured hypothesis generation, logical consistency checking, and chain-of-thought prompting within KODER not only enhances interpretability but also improves clinical decision-making accuracy across VLM architectures.

Overall, these results highlight the effectiveness of KODER's domain-aware representations and its ability to generate knowledge-driven hypotheses that capture the subtle nuances present in clinical ultrasound data. This leads to notable improvements in predictive performance across all evaluated models. Among them, **GPT-4o with KODER** consistently outperforms other configurations, including Gemini 2.0 and smaller-scale models. In contrast, models such as GPT-4o Mini and GPT-4 Turbo demonstrate limited capability, particularly in the fine-grained burn classification task, where distinguishing subtle variations in burn severity is essential.

Even in a zero-shot setting, the KODER framework improves overall classification accuracy to 80%, demonstrating its robustness without requiring extensive in-context examples. When combined with Chain-of-Thought (CoT) prompting, **KODER+CoT** further increases accuracy to 87%, emphasizing the value of structured intermediate reasoning in clinical decision-making. Incorporating self-consistency into this pipeline boosts performance to 93%, illustrating that multiple reasoning passes can refine predictions and yield more dependable outcomes.

A breakdown of per-class accuracy reveals that the model achieves perfect classification for second-degree superficial burns. For second-degree deep burns, the model attains 88% accuracy, with 12% misclassified as third-degree. Third-degree burns are classified with 80% accuracy, with 20% misclassified as second-degree deep. These results indicate that the model excels at detecting superficial burns but encounters more difficulty distinguishing deeper injuries, likely due to overlapping imaging characteristics among these clinically similar categories.

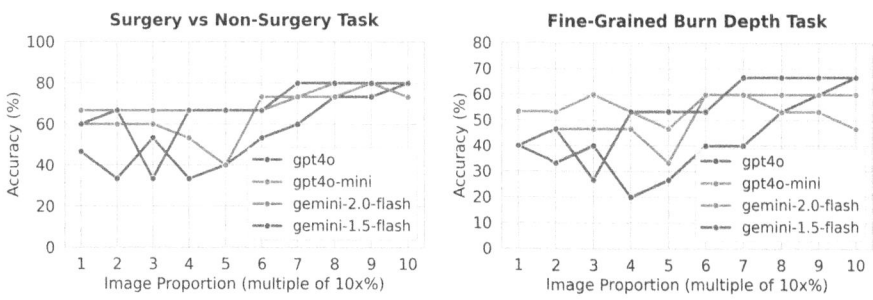

Fig. 3. Evaluation of KODER (4-shots CoT) with various image proportion

Effect of Image Proportion on Performance. To assess the robustness of KODER under varying data availability, we conducted experiments using increasing proportions of the image dataset (from right to left), ranging from 10% to 100% in 10% increments. Thus, for image proportions less than or equal to 50%, the input did not include B-mode information. The goal of this experiment was to evaluate how the amount of image input influences the performance of different VLMs when integrated with KODER.

Figure 3 shows the accuracy trends for the Surgery vs. Non-Surgery task (left) and Fine-Grained Burn Depth classification (right). Across both tasks, we observe that model (4-shots CoT) performance generally improves as more image data is included, although the rate and consistency of improvement vary across models.

In the **Surgery vs. Non-Surgery task**, gemini-1.5-flash demonstrates strong and stable performance, reaching its peak (approximately 80%) by the 6× image proportion and maintaining it thereafter. gpt4o-mini also performs consistently well across all data sizes. In contrast, gpt4o shows significant performance variability at lower image proportions but steadily improves with more data, eventually matching the top-performing models at the full dataset size. gemini-2.0-flash shows moderate improvements but fluctuates at lower proportions.

For the **Fine-Grained Burn Depth task**, the trends are more varied. gemini-1.5-flash again leads, achieving around 67% accuracy at the highest image proportion. gpt4o shows notable improvements as more images are used, especially after the 6× mark, suggesting that this model benefits from larger image contexts. gpt4o-mini and gemini-2.0-flash perform relatively well at low proportions but do not improve significantly with additional data, indicating a potential ceiling in their fine-grained classification ability under this setting.

These results suggest that while all models benefit from more image input, larger and more advanced models like gemini-1.5-flash and gpt4o scale better with increased visual context, particularly for tasks requiring fine-grained reasoning.

3.3 Ablation Study

Impact of Number CoT Shots. To better understand the contribution of in-context learning, we conducted an ablation study evaluating the performance of the KODER framework across different numbers of shots (0 to 4). Table 2 reports the classification accuracy for both Surgical Decision-Making and Fine-Grained Burn Depth tasks. Overall, we observe that increasing the number of in-context examples generally improves model performance. This trend is more pronounced in the binary Surgical Decision task, where several models (e.g., GPT-4o, Gemini2.0, and GPT-4 Turbo) reach their peak accuracy (87%) by the fourth shot. GPT-4o maintains a consistently high performance across all settings, highlighting its strong reasoning capabilities even in zero-shot conditions. Notably, GPT-4o-mini also benefits from one-shot prompting, achieving an 80% accuracy that surpasses its zero-shot performance.

Table 2. Evaluation with number of shots. Performance (%) of KODER framework on Surgical Decision-Making and Fine-Grained Burn Depth

KODER+	Shot-0	Shot-1	Shot-2	Shot-3	Shot-4
Surgical Decision					
GPT4o	**80**	80	**80**	**80**	**87**
Gemini2.0	67	67	**87**	80	80
GPT4o-mini	73	**80**	73	73	73
GPT4-Turbo	73	67	67	80	**87**
Burn Depth					
GPT4o	**67**	67	80	80	**87**
Gemini2.0	60	**73**	73	73	73
GPT4o-mini	60	47	60	60	60
GPT4-Turbo	40	33	33	47	53

For the more challenging Burn Depth classification task, improvements are more gradual but still significant. GPT-4o reaches 87% accuracy at shot-4, demonstrating the advantage of progressive reasoning refinement. Gemini2.0 shows a similar pattern, peaking at 73% from a lower zero-shot baseline of 60%. GPT-4 Turbo starts lower (40% in shot-0) but improves steadily with more examples, achieving 53% by shot-4. This suggests that while some models may struggle in zero-shot settings, they can benefit substantially from structured examples, especially in tasks requiring fine-grained differentiation.

Interestingly, performance gains plateau or slightly fluctuate for some models after two to three shots, implying diminishing returns beyond a certain point. This observation highlights the importance of balancing context complexity and example quantity in prompt design for clinical reasoning tasks.

Impact of Explanation Generation. Further, we evaluate GPT-4o's performance within the KODER framework under two hypothesis generation settings. In the *Label Only* setting, the model outputs only the predicted class label. This configuration achieves an accuracy of 87%, an F1-score of 0.86, a precision of 0.89, and a recall of 0.87. In contrast, the *Explain+Label* setting requires the model to generate an explanation followed by the class label. This more structured prompting yields improved results, reaching an accuracy of 93%, an F1-score of 0.93, a precision of 0.94, and a recall of 0.93. These findings suggest that explicit explanation generation supports more accurate predictions by prompting the model to engage in deeper reasoning before outputting a label.

Qualitative Analysis Figure 4 illustrates this effect with a representative example. In the sample case, the input imaging (left) corresponds to a second-degree deep (non-surgical) burn. The **GPT-4o+KODER** model (middle) correctly classifies the burn, producing a coherent explanation that highlights dermal layer involvement and preserved structural integrity—features consistent with a deep partial-thickness injury. In contrast, the base **GPT-4o**

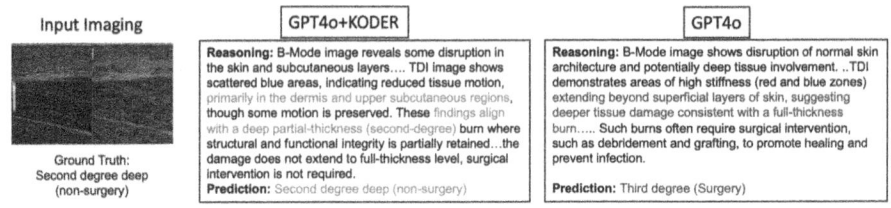

Fig. 4. In the sample results, the image input (left) reveals that GPT-4o (right) incorrectly identifies dermis layer damage as a third-degree burn rather than a second-degree deep burn. In comparison, the KODER framework (middle) demonstrates improved reasoning over the dermis layer, resulting in an accurate classification

model (right) overestimates the severity by interpreting the damage as consistent with full-thickness tissue involvement, leading to an incorrect classification of a third-degree (surgical) burn. This example reinforces the benefit of explanation-augmented reasoning in improving model reliability and interpretability in clinical tasks.

4   Conclusion

In this work, we introduced the KODER framework, a novel approach that combines domain-specific clinical knowledge with advanced reasoning techniques to improve ultrasound-based burn diagnosis. By incorporating structured reasoning through chain-of-thought prompting and enforcing consistency across multiple reasoning paths, KODER delivers substantial gains in diagnostic accuracy. For instance, in surgical decision-making, GPT-4o paired with KODER achieved up to 93% accuracy, while in fine-grained burn depth classification, it reached 87% accuracy. These results demonstrate that explicitly guiding the model to reason through its predictions leads to more accurate and interpretable outputs. KODER also showed strong performance across multiple VLMs, particularly under low-data settings, and adapted well across both binary and multi-class tasks. Overall, KODER represents a significant step toward robust, interpretable, and knowledge-guided diagnostic modeling in medical imaging applications.

Acknowledgments. This work was supported by the Office of the Assistant Secretary of Defense for Health Affairs under Award No. W81XWH-21-2-0030 and by NIH under Grant No. 5R21LM013711-02.

Disclosure of Interests. The authors have no competing interests to declare that are relevant to the content of this article.

References

1. Achiam, J., et al.: GPT-4 technical report. arXiv preprint arXiv:2303.08774 (2023)
2. Bombaro, K.M., et al.: What is the prevalence of hypertrophic scarring following burns? Burns **29**, 299–302 (2003)
3. Chen, X., Chi, R.A., Wang, X., Zhou, D.: Premise order matters in reasoning with large language models. In: Forty-First International Conference on Machine Learning (2024)
4. Gu, B., Desai, R.J., Lin, K.J., Yang, J.: Probabilistic medical predictions of large language models. NPJ Digit. Med. **7**(1), 367 (2024)
5. Guo, Y., et al.: Common vision-language attention for text-guided medical image segmentation of pneumonia. In: International Conference on Medical Image Computing and Computer-Assisted Intervention, pp. 192–201. Springer (2024)
6. Ho, C.Y., Solomon, S.D.: A clinician's guide to tissue doppler imaging. Circulation **113**, e396–e398 (2006)
7. Li, C., et al.: Llava-med: training a large language-and-vision assistant for biomedicine in one day. arXiv preprint arXiv:2306.00890 (2023)
8. Li, Q., et al.: Anatomical structure-guided medical vision-language pre-training. In: International Conference on Medical Image Computing and Computer-Assisted Intervention, pp. 80–90. Springer (2024)
9. Liu, H., Li, C., Li, Y., Lee, Y.J.: Improved baselines with visual instruction tuning. In: Proceedings of the IEEE/CVF Conference on Computer Vision and Pattern Recognition, pp. 26296–26306 (2024)
10. Liu, H., Li, C., Wu, Q., Lee, Y.J.: Visual instruction tuning. In: Thirty-Seventh Conference on Neural Information Processing Systems (2023)
11. de Moura, L.M., Bjørner, N.S.: Z3: an efficient SMT solver. In: International Conference on Tools and Algorithms for Construction and Analysis of Systems (2008)
12. Radford, A., et al.: Learning transferable visual models from natural language supervision. In: International Conference on Machine Learning, pp. 8748–8763 (2021)
13. Radford, A., Wu, J., Child, R., Luan, D., Amodei, D., Sutskever, I.: Language models are unsupervised multitask learners. OpenAI Blog **1**, 9 (2019)
14. Shakeri, F., et al.: Few-shot adaptation of medical vision-language models. In: International Conference on Medical Image Computing and Computer-Assisted Intervention, pp. 553–563. Springer (2024)
15. Gemini Team, et al.: Gemini: a family of highly capable multimodal models. arXiv preprint arXiv:2312.11805 (2023)
16. Thatcher, J.E., et al.: Imaging techniques for clinical burn assessment with a focus on multispectral imaging. Adv. Wound Care **5**, 360–378 (2016)
17. Touvron, H., et al.: Llama: open and efficient foundation language models. arXiv preprint arXiv:2302.13971 (2023)
18. Tuncer, H.B., Akın, M., Çakırca, M., Erkılıç, E., Yıldız, H.F., Yastı, A.Ç.: Do pre-burn center management algorithms work? Evaluation of pre-admission diagnosis and treatment adequacy of burn patients referred to a burn center. J. Burn Care Res. **45**(1), 180–189 (2024)
19. Wang, X., et al.: Self-consistency improves chain of thought reasoning in language models. In: The Eleventh International Conference on Learning Representations (2023)
20. Wei, J., et al.: Chain-of-thought prompting elicits reasoning in large language models. Adv. Neural. Inf. Process. Syst. **35**, 24824–24837 (2022)

21. Zhang, J., Wang, G., Kalra, M.K., Yan, P.: Disease-informed adaptation of vision-language models. IEEE Trans. Med. Imaging (2024)
22. Zhang, S., et al.: A multimodal biomedical foundation model trained from fifteen million image–text pairs. NEJM AI **2**(1) (2024). https://doi.org/10.1056/AIoa2400640

Multimodal Federated Learning with Missing Modalities Through Feature Imputation Network

Pranav Poudel[2,4], Aavash Chhetri[2], Prashnna Gyawali[3], Georgios Leontidis[1], and Binod Bhattarai[1(✉)]

[1] University of Aberdeen, Aberdeen, UK
binod.bhattarai@abdn.ac.uk
[2] NepAl Applied Mathematics and Informatics Institute for Research, Lalitpur, Nepal
[3] West Virginia University, Morgantown, USA
[4] Fogsphere (Redev.AI), London, UK

Abstract. Multimodal federated learning holds immense potential for collaboratively training models from multiple sources without sharing raw data, addressing both data scarcity and privacy concerns—two key challenges in healthcare. A major challenge in training multimodal federated models in healthcare is the presence of missing modalities due to multiple reasons, including variations in clinical practice, cost and accessibility constraints, retrospective data collection, privacy concerns, and occasional technical or human errors. Previous methods typically rely on publicly available real datasets or synthetic data to compensate for missing modalities. However, obtaining real datasets for every disease is impractical, and training generative models to synthesize missing modalities is computationally expensive and prone to errors due to the high dimensionality of medical data. In this paper, we propose a novel, lightweight, low-dimensional feature translator to reconstruct bottleneck features of the missing modalities. Our experiments on three different datasets (MIMIC-CXR, NIH Open-I, and CheXpert), in both homogeneous and heterogeneous settings consistently improve the performance of competitive baselines. The code and implementation details are available at: https://github.com/bhattarailab/FedFeatGen.

Keywords: Multimodal Learning · Federated Learning · Missing Modalities · Feature Generation

1 Introduction

Multimodal learning has emerged as a transformative field of research within medical machine learning. By combining information from diverse sources like imaging, omics, and pathology, multimodal AI holds the potential to transform the healthcare landscape [1]. Inspired by the human capacity to integrate multisensory information for more effective perception and interaction, these models

S. Ali et al. (Eds.): MIUA 2025, LNCS 15916, pp. 289–299, 2026.
https://doi.org/10.1007/978-3-031-98688-8_20

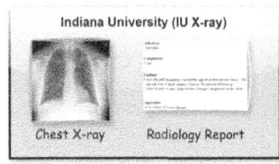 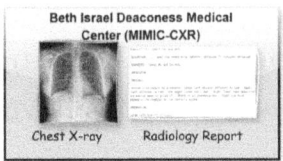 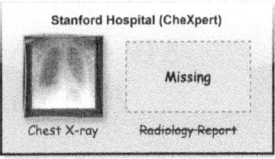

Fig. 1. This figure shows sample of data from three different datasets collected at three different institutions. In CheXpert, there are only X-ray scans available, while the two other benchmarks have both X-ray scans and radiology reports. This demonstrates an instance of missing modality in a real-world scenario.

leverage data from multiple modalities to construct a holistic representation of diseases, thereby significantly improving diagnostic accuracy [19,23]. However, effective training of such models typically requires substantial amounts of centralized data, which presents a major challenge, especially in healthcare settings, where data are often dispersed across multiple medical centers due to privacy concerns.

Multimodal federated learning is an important research topic due to its growing applications, and it offers an innovative approach for collaboratively training a shared model on heterogeneous healthcare data—such as X-rays, diagnostic reports, and time-series data—without sharing the raw data [8,21]. The main drawback of most prior work on multimodal federated learning is that it assumes the availability of complete modalities, overlooking the challenges posed by missing modalities [4,16,17]. In reality, as shown in Fig. 1, multimodal systems often encounter challenges related to missing or incomplete modalities across medical centers due to the unavailability of clinical equipment, variability in data acquisition procedures, or limitations in data storage capacity [21]. Naïve strategies such as zero-imputation and uniform filling are often used to handle missing modalities [13,26]. However, these approaches introduce bias into the global model, which adversely affects its performance and leads to suboptimal federated training. As a result, an increasing number of studies are aiming to fundamentally address the problem of missing modalities [21,24]. While research in the natural domain has been growing rapidly in recent years [3,13,20,25], there are still only a handful of studies in the medical domain [15,18], partly due to the lack of standardized benchmarks.

The existing literature in multimodal federated learning are broadly categorized into three groups: public data-based methods [15,25], class prototype-based methods [13], and architecture-focused methods [3,20]. The primary drawback of public data-based approaches is that model performance heavily depends on the quality and representativeness of the available public data. Class prototype-based methods rely on impractical assumptions, such as having distinct and independent class prototypes, thus limiting their applicability to multiclass classification tasks only. Meanwhile, architecture-focused methods typically require specialized designs, restricting their generalizability. Recently, generative model-based approaches [18] have also been explored, where missing reports are synthesized by pre-training generative models using data from available multimodal clients. Although this approach is conceptually simple and easy to implement, it demands significant data and computational resources for effective pre-training. Moreover, the data in healthcare are high-dimensional, such as Whole Slide Images (WSIs) have dimensions of 100,000, and reconstructing such high dimensional data incurs errors introducing un-necessary artifacts, which ultimately results in inferior performance [2].

To address the limitations of existing methods, we propose learning low-dimensional bottleneck features of the missing modalities. To this end, we propose to train a lightweight feature-generation model in a federated-manner that conditionally synthesizes abstract, high-level modality-specific feature representations based on available input modalities (e.g., image features conditioned on text or vice versa). Our approach brings several advantages compared to the previous methods. First, our method does not need to have access of publicly available real data. Also, the bottleneck features have low dimensionality, typically of a few hundred dimensions, which makes them easier to reconstruct with less error [2]. It is also lightweight, which is another advantage. To the best of our knowledge, this is the first work to compare the imputation of missing modalities at different level of input to offer a clear understanding of missing modality imputation strategies in federated scenarios where modality completeness cannot be guaranteed.

To validate our idea, we conducted experiments simulating real-world federated learning scenarios using standard medical imaging datasets (MIMIC-CXR [11], NIH Open-I [6], and CheXpert [10]). These experiments evaluate performance across configurations with varying ratios of multimodal and uni-modal clients (image-only or text-only), reflecting typical data heterogeneity. Our experimental results outperform naïve baselines as well as the most closely related generative method, and achieve performance competitive with methods based on publicly available datasets.

Our key contributions are:

- We propose a feature imputation method trained to handle missing modalities in multimodal federated learning.
- We present the first direct comparison and extensive evaluations of imputation strategies operating at the feature level versus the input (raw data) level in the context of federated learning.

2 Method

2.1 Problem Formulation

We consider a multimodal federated learning setting with C clients, each having its private dataset D_C with n_C samples. The ith data sample in D_C is represented by tuple $(\{X_m^{(i)}\}_{m=1}^{M_C}, Y^{(i)})$, where $Y^{(i)}$ and M_C represent the label set and the number of modalities in the Cth client respectively. Without loss of generalizability, we assume a scenario with two modalities: image (I) and text(T). All clients utilize the same global architecture, which consists of modality-specific encoders (f_e), concatenation-based fusion ($\oplus$), and a classifier head (f_c). Hence, we define the complete model as the set $\{f_e^I, f_e^T, \oplus, f_c\}$.

$$\underset{w}{\text{argmin }} L(\boldsymbol{w}) = \sum_{c=1}^{C} \frac{|D_c|}{|D|} \, l_c(\boldsymbol{w}, D_c) \quad (1)$$

$$\text{where, } l_c(\boldsymbol{w}, D_c) = \frac{1}{|D_c|} \sum_{(X_I^{(i)}, X_T^{(i)}, Y^{(i)}) \in D_c} \mathcal{L}(f_c(f_e^I(X_I^{(i)}) \oplus f_e^T(X_T^{(i)})), Y^{(i)}) \quad (2)$$

Here, D represents the combined dataset across all clients, while L denotes the local loss function at the client level for the model $\{f_e^I, f_e^T, f_c\}$ when applied to a data sample $(X_I^{(i)}, X_T^{(i)}, Y^{(i)})$. A widely used method for handling missing modalities is imputation sampled from a distribution. When a text sample is absent, the local loss function becomes:

$$\mathcal{L}(f_c(f_e^I(X_I^{(i)}) \oplus \psi), Y^{(i)}) \quad \text{where} \quad \psi \sim \begin{cases} 0 & \text{if zero-filling} \\ \mathcal{U}(0,1) & \text{if uniform sampling} \end{cases} \quad (3)$$

Naively optimizing Eq. 3 results in sub-optimal performance.

To mitigate such issues, we introduce the Feature Imputation Network(FIN), which approximates the missing modality feature based on the available modality. For modality-incomplete samples in unimodal clients, this network reconstructs the bottleneck features of the missing modality conditioned on the available one. Our overall method is illustrated in Fig. 2.

2.2   Feature Imputation Network (FIN)

The feature imputation network generates the feature vector of the missing modality from the available one. Let $z_I^{(i)} = f_e^I(X_I^{(i)})$ denote the latent feature representation extracted by the image encoder for the ith sample, and $z_T^{(i)} = f_e^T(X_T^{(i)})$ denote the latent text feature representation. We define imputation networks Φ_T and Φ_I such that Φ_T aims to approximate the text features from image features ($\Phi_T : z_I \mapsto \hat{z}_T$, where $\hat{z}_T \approx z_T$) and Φ_I aims to approximate image features from text features ($\Phi_I : z_T \mapsto \hat{z}_I$, where $\hat{z}_I \approx z_I$). At the start of each communication round, the server dispatches imputation networks (Φ_T, Φ_I) and a complete global model $\{f_e^I, f_e^T, \oplus, f_c\}$ to all clients. At multimodal clients, after training the model on local data for k steps, we proceed to train the imputation networks. Without loss of generality, let us assume we are training Φ_T to approximate text features. We first generate a pool of paired image-text feature vectors $P_c = \{(z_I^{(i)}, z_T^{(i)}) \mid (X_I^{(i)}, X_T^{(i)}, \cdot) \in D_c\}$. As shown in Fig. 2(b), this pool P_c is then used to train Φ_T by minimizing the Mean Squared Error (MSE) between the predicted text feature $\hat{z}_T^{(i)} = \Phi_T(z_I^{(i)})$ and the ground truth text feature $z_T^{(i)}$:

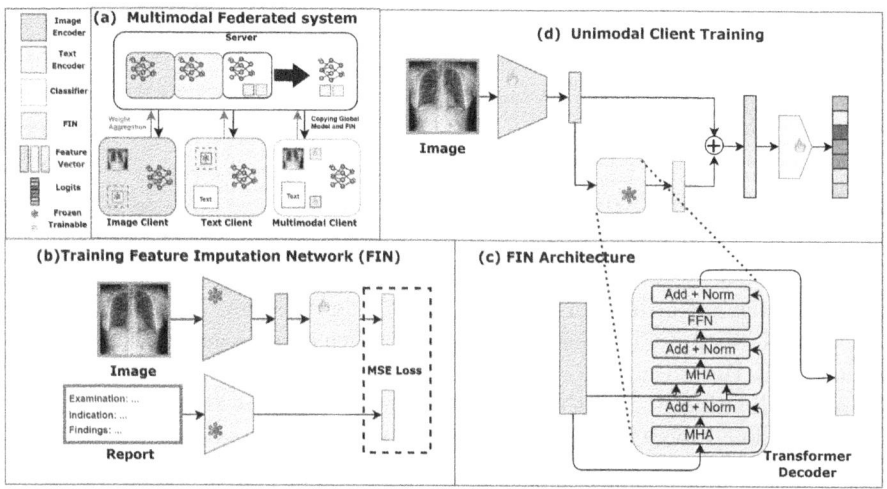

Fig. 2. Illustration of **Feature Imputation Network**-based Multimodal Federated Learning. (**a**) Multimodal Federated Learning system with different types of clients. (**b**) Training of the Feature Imputation Network in multimodal client. (**c**) Architecture of Feature Imputation Network (**d**) Unimodal image client training with the help of the Feature Imputation Network

$$\mathcal{L}(\Phi_T) = \frac{1}{|D_c|} \sum_{i=1}^{|D_c|} \|\Phi_T(z_I^{(i)}) - z_T^{(i)}\|_2^2 \tag{4}$$

After optimizing Φ_T (and symmetrically Φ_I) for k steps, both the updated main model and the updated imputation networks are uploaded to the server for aggregation. To complete the missing modalities, the unimodal clients receive both the model and the imputation network at the start of each round, and use the imputation network (e.g., Φ_T) purely for inference to generate features for missing modalities as shown in Fig. 2(d). The inferred features are concatenated with the bottleneck feature of the counterpart available modality and fed into the task-specific learnable network. And, the objectives for the multimodal learning in the clients with only image and text become Eqs. 5 and 6, respectively.

$$\mathcal{L}(f_c(f_e^I(X_I^{(i)}) \oplus \Phi_T(f_e^I(X_I^{(i)}))), Y^{(i)}) \tag{5}$$

$$\mathcal{L}(f_c(f_e^T(X_T^{(i)}) \oplus \Phi_I(f_e^T(X_T^{(i)}))), Y^{(i)}) \tag{6}$$

After optimizing for k steps, the model is uploaded to the server, where models from all clients and feature imputation networks from multimodal clients are aggregated. We have implemented a simple 6-layer Transformer decoder [22] with n = 4 heads and 1024 feed-forward dimensions as our feature imputation network. This choice is motivated by the demonstrated success of Transformers in numerous cross-modal tasks. We employ FedAvg [14] as the aggregation strategy in the server.

3   Experiments and Results

3.1   Datasets and Setups

Following [15], we utilize three publicly available datasets- MIMIC-CXR [11], NIH Open-I [6], and CheXpert [10]—to design two experimental setups: Homogeneous and Heterogeneous. Both setups consist of frontal chest X-rays and common validation and test sets derived from the official MIMIC-CXR splits, where the global model is validated and tested. In the homogeneous setup, 10 clients each contain training data from 810 patients, all sampled from MIMIC-CXR. Conversely, the heterogeneous setup consists of eightimage-only clients, each with data from 900 patients in CheXpert, and two multimodal clients, each containing data from 1,116 patients in NIH Open-I. This setup reflects real-world situations where data characteristics and label distributions vary across clients types. For simplicity, we denote client configurations using the format **I:T:M**, where I, T, and M represent the number of image-only, text-only clients, and the number of multimodal clients, respectively.

3.2   Implementation Details

We employ pre-trained ResNet-50 [9] and BERT-base [7] as the image and text encoders, respectively. Their outputs are transformed into 256-dimensional vectors and L2-normalized before fusion. We use a straightforward concatenation approach for multimodal fusion, followed by a linear layer for classification. The models are trained locally using Adam [12] with a learning rate of $1e^{-4}$ for three epochs per communication round, totaling 30 rounds. For evaluation, we measure macro AUC (the average area under the Receiver Operating Characteristic curve) on the multimodal test set, following the evaluation protocol outlined in [15]. The reported values represent the mean results from experiments conducted with three random seeds.

3.3   Baselines

We compare our method against two naïve but common approaches: Zero-filling and Uniform-filling, along with state-of-the-art methods that depend on generative models and public datasets. Zero-filling imputes the missing data using zero vectors, while Uniform-filling imputes the missing data with feature vectors sampled from uniform distributions.

R2Gen [5] is a generative model that generates radiology reports from X-ray images. We trained R2Gen in a federated manner and subsequently used it to generate missing reports from images. For a fair comparison, the original

ResNet-101 visual feature extractor was replaced with ResNet-50 to maintain consistency with our feature imputation approach.

CAR-MFL [15] It is a state-of-the-art method in multimodal federated learning with missing modalities. This method is not directly comparable to ours, as it relies on publicly available real datasets to fill the missing modality gap.

Table 1. AUC↑ Performance in Homogeneous and Heterogeneous setups in Unimodal Image Client Settings

Partition	Homogeneous			Heteregeneous
I:T:M	8:0:2	6:0:4	4:0:6	8:0:2
Zero-fillings	79.8	82.81	86.94	72.76
Uniform-fillings	80.6	84.83	87.79	71.16
R2Gen	77.32	83.1	86.83	67.32
Feature Imputation (Ours)	**86.16**	**87.61**	**89.31**	**77.94**

Table 2. AUC↑ Performance in Homogeneous Across Various Client Settings. An asterisk (*) indicates that the method is not directly comparable to other methods.

Partition	Homogeneous					
I:T:M	0:8:2	0:6:4	0:4:6	4:4:2	3:3:4	2:2:6
CAR-MFL*	89.22	90.12	90.06	88.93	89.62	89.94
Zero-fillings	86.18	86.8	88.21	80.3	84.57	87.09
Uniform-fillings	88.37	88.64	89.27	85.74	86.9	88.49
Feature Imputation (Ours)	**88.98**	**89.3**	**89.52**	**88.79**	**88.12**	**89.12**

3.4 Quantitative Results

Tables 1 and 2 present the performance of all baseline methods and our proposed approach across various client configurations in both experimental setups. As shown in Table 1, Feature Imputation method significantly outperforms all other imputation techniques in both homogeneous and heterogeneous settings, demonstrating its applicability to real-world, challenging scenarios. Remarkably, with only two multimodal clients (8:0:2), Feature Imputation achieves performance comparable to that of zero-filling in a six-client multimodal setting (4:0:6). This demonstrates that our method has a tremendous advantage even when only a few clients have data with complete modalities. Whereas, our competitor method severely fails to generalize in such a scenario as demonstrated by the performance gap of nearly 10%. Similarly, in Table 2, which details performance across various homogeneous client settings, our Feature Imputation method consistently surpasses the other baseline imputation techniques (Zero-fillings and Uniform-fillings). Notably, our approach achieves results highly competitive with the CAR-MFL method, even though CAR-MFL benefits from access to public datasets to fill modality gaps, a condition our method does not require, highlighting its practical applicability.

Predicting in the representation space rather than the input space simplifies the task and encourages the model to learn abstract, high-level, meaningful features [2]. Generative models make predictions in token space, which are prone to generating unnecessary or irrelevant tokens—especially when the model is trained on limited data. Consequently, both the feature extractor and the classification head are affected by noisy gradient updates, leading to degraded performance. In contrast, feature imputation methods operate directly in the representation space, reducing the likelihood of injecting irrelevant information. Moreover, these methods influence only the classification head during training, leaving the learned features of the missing modality encoders unaffected by gradient updates. This explains why even simple strategies like zero-filling or uniform-filling sometimes outperform generative models.

3.5 Qualitative Results

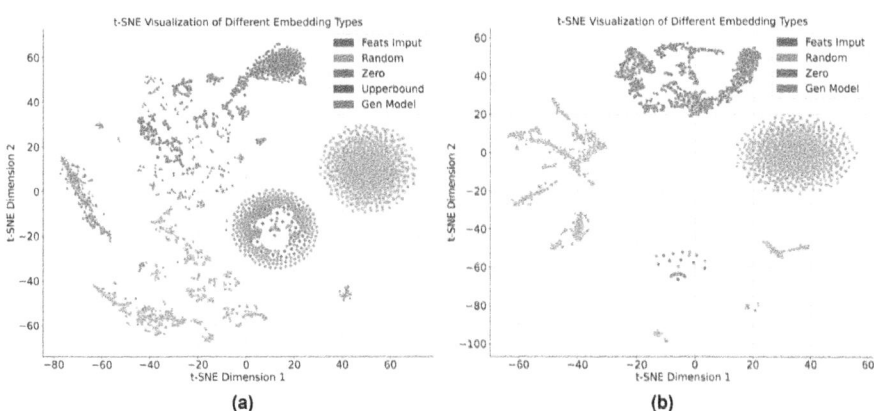

Fig. 3. t-SNE plot of feature vectors from the model trained in **(a)** the homogeneous setup and **(b)** the heterogeneous setup. In the Figure, **Upperbound** refers to the model trained in a federated manner with complete modalities. Feature vectors are generated using the validation data. (Color figure online)

Figure 3 displays a t-SNE visualization comparing different feature representations derived from the validation dataset, specifically within the 8:0:2 federated setting (8 image-only, 2 multimodal clients). This allows for a qualitative assessment of the embeddings generated by our Feature Imputation network (approximating text features from image features) against those resulting from baseline imputation techniques (zero/uniform filling, text encoder output of model trained in generated text report) and an ideal upper-bound model. The **upper-bound** is the scenario when all the clients have complete modalities. In the homogeneous setup, the representations generated by upper-bound model (represented by red dots) and our Feature Imputation network (represented by blue dots) exhibit notably similar structural characteristics, primarily forming one large cluster accompanied by smaller scattered clusters, with some degree of overlap between them. In contrast, embeddings from the generative model trained on raw generated data (purple) do not closely align with the structure of the upper-bound representations. Additionally, the zero-imputation ( ) and uniform vector imputation methods (orange), which produce embeddings from fixed distributions, result in dense clusters localized in single, confined regions.

3.6 Computational Complexity and Communication Cost

Table 3. Comparison of model components in terms of approximate parameter counts and FLOPs (Floating Point Operations Per Second). FLOPs were estimated using the `fvcore` library.

Model	Parameters	FLOPS
Generative Model (R2Gen)	59.74 M	94.059 G
Feature Imputation Network	6.324 M	6.318 M

Table 3 presents a comparison between the Feature Imputation Network and the Generative Model in terms of computational efficiency. We can see that the Feature Imputation Network reduces communication cost by nearly 10× per round and computational costs by approximately 1000× per inference.

4 Conclusion

We presented a feature imputation network designed to synthesize feature vectors for missing modalities using available data within a multimodal federated learning framework. Extensive experiments demonstrated that our approach significantly outperforms common baselines, including input-level generative models. Future research could explore extensions to more complex multimodal scenarios and investigate alternative architectures for the feature imputation network.

References

1. Acosta, J.N., Falcone, G.J., Rajpurkar, P., Topol, E.J.: Multimodal biomedical AI. Nat. Med. **28**(9), 1773–1784 (2022)
2. Assran, M., et al.: Self-supervised learning from images with a joint-embedding predictive architecture. In: Proceedings of the IEEE/CVF Conference on Computer Vision and Pattern Recognition, pp. 15619–15629 (2023)
3. Chen, J., Zhang, A.: FedMSplit: correlation-adaptive federated multi-task learning across multimodal split networks. In: Proceedings of the 28th ACM SIGKDD Conference on Knowledge Discovery and Data Mining, pp. 87–96 (2022)
4. Chen, J., Pan, R.: Medical report generation based on multimodal federated learning. Comput. Med. Imaging Graph. 102342 (2024)
5. Chen, Z., Song, Y., Chang, T.H., Wan, X.: Generating radiology reports via memory-driven transformer. In: Proceedings of the 2020 Conference on Empirical Methods in Natural Language Processing (2020)
6. Demner-Fushman, D., et al.: Preparing a collection of radiology examinations for distribution and retrieval. J. Am. Med. Inform. Assoc. **23**(2), 304–310 (2016)
7. Devlin, J., Chang, M.W., Lee, K., Toutanova, K.: BERT: pre-training of deep bidirectional transformers for language understanding. arXiv preprint arXiv:1810.04805 (2018)
8. Feng, T., et al.: FedMultimodal: a benchmark for multimodal federated learning. In: Proceedings of the 29th ACM SIGKDD Conference on Knowledge Discovery and Data Mining, pp. 4035–4045 (2023)
9. He, K., Zhang, X., Ren, S., Sun, J.: Deep residual learning for image recognition. In: Proceedings of the IEEE Conference on Computer Vision and Pattern Recognition, pp. 770–778 (2016)
10. Irvin, J., et al.: CheXpert: a large chest radiograph dataset with uncertainty labels and expert comparison. In: Proceedings of the AAAI Conference on Artificial Intelligence, vol. 33, pp. 590–597 (2019)
11. Johnson, A.E., et al.: MIMIC-CXR, a de-identified publicly available database of chest radiographs with free-text reports. Sci. Data **6**(1), 317 (2019)
12. Kingma, D.P., Ba, J.: Adam: a method for stochastic optimization. arXiv preprint arXiv:1412.6980 (2014)
13. Le, H.Q., Thwal, C.M., Qiao, Y., Tun, Y.L., Nguyen, M.N., Hong, C.S.: Cross-modal prototype based multimodal federated learning under severely missing modality. arXiv preprint arXiv:2401.13898 (2024)
14. McMahan, B., Moore, E., Ramage, D., Hampson, S., y Arcas, B.A.: Communication-efficient learning of deep networks from decentralized data. In: Artificial Intelligence and Statistics, pp. 1273–1282. PMLR (2017)
15. Poudel, P., Shrestha, P., Amgain, S., Shrestha, Y.R., Gyawali, P., Bhattarai, B.: CAR-MFL: cross-modal augmentation by retrieval for multimodal federated learning with missing modalities. In: International Conference on Medical Image Computing and Computer-Assisted Intervention, pp. 102–112. Springer (2024)
16. Qayyum, A., Ahmad, K., Ahsan, M.A., Al-Fuqaha, A., Qadir, J.: Collaborative federated learning for healthcare: Multi-modal Covid-19 diagnosis at the edge. IEEE Open J. Comput. Soc. **3**, 172–184 (2022)
17. Sachin, D., Annappa, B., Ambasange, S., Tony, A.E.: A multimodal contrastive federated learning for digital healthcare. SN Comput. Sci. **4**(5), 674 (2023)
18. Saha, P., Mishra, D., Wagner, F., Kamnitsas, K., Noble, J.A.: Examining modality incongruity in multimodal federated learning for medical vision and language-based disease detection. arXiv preprint arXiv:2402.05294 (2024)

19. Shrestha, P., Amgain, S., Khanal, B., Linte, C.A., Bhattarai, B.: Medical vision language pretraining: a survey. arXiv preprint arXiv:2312.06224 (2023)
20. Sun, G., Mendieta, M., Dutta, A., Li, X., Chen, C.: Towards multi-modal transformers in federated learning. In: European Conference on Computer Vision, pp. 229–246. Springer (2024)
21. Thrasher, J., et al.: Multimodal federated learning in healthcare: a review. arXiv preprint arXiv:2310.09650 (2023)
22. Vaswani, A., et al.: Attention is all you need. In: Advances in Neural Information Processing Systems **30** (2017)
23. Venugopalan, J., Tong, L., Hassanzadeh, H.R., Wang, M.D.: Multimodal deep learning models for early detection of Alzheimer's disease stage. Sci. Rep. **11**(1), 3254 (2021)
24. Wu, R., Wang, H., Chen, H.T., Carneiro, G.: Deep multimodal learning with missing modality: a survey. arXiv preprint arXiv:2409.07825 (2024)
25. Yu, Q., Liu, Y., Wang, Y., Xu, K., Liu, J.: Multimodal federated learning via contrastive representation ensemble. arXiv preprint arXiv:2302.08888 (2023)
26. Zheng, T., Li, A., Chen, Z., Wang, H., Luo, J.: AutoFed: heterogeneity-aware federated multimodal learning for robust autonomous driving. arXiv preprint arXiv:2302.08646 (2023)

Parameter-Efficient Multimodal Adaptation for Certified Robustness of Medical Vision-Language Models

Fahad Shamshad[1]([✉]), Noor Hussein[1,2], and Karthik Nandakumar[1,2][iD]

[1] Mohamed Bin Zayed University of Artificial Intelligence, Abu Dhabi, UAE
{fahad.shamshad,noor.hussein,karthik.nandakumar}@mbzuai.ac.ae
[2] Michigan State University, East Lansing, USA

Abstract. Medical vision-language models (Med-VLMs) have shown strong generalization in downstream tasks by leveraging large-scale image-text pretraining. However, their vulnerability to adversarial perturbations poses critical risks in safety-sensitive applications. While randomized smoothing provides certifiable guarantees against such perturbations, it requires the model to remain accurate under Gaussian noise—an assumption that fails in practice without specialized adaptation. Prior work, such as PromptSmooth, introduced text-only prompt tuning to improve robustness, but neglected visual adaptation and struggled under high noise levels. In this paper, we propose `PromptSmooth++`, a multimodal adaptation framework that enhances the certified robustness of frozen Med-VLMs under randomized smoothing. Our method introduces two complementary variants: (i) a few-shot strategy that jointly optimizes visual and textual prompts for noise-aware cross-modal alignment, and (ii) a zero-shot approach that performs test-time vision-side adaptation using lightweight Low-Rank Adapters (LoRA), optimized with a self-supervised entropy loss on noisy inputs. Extensive experiments across multiple Med-VLMs and multiple datasets spanning diverse medical modalities demonstrate that `PromptSmooth++` significantly improves certified accuracy over existing baselines while maintaining high clean performance and computational efficiency. Our results show that modality-aware prompting and vision-side adaptation are both essential for certifiably robust medical imaging systems. Code is available at https://github.com/fahadshamshad/multimodal-promptsmooth.

Keywords: Certified Robustness · Medical Vision-Language Models · Parameter-Efficient Adaptation · Randomized smoothing

1 Introduction

Medical Vision-Language Models (Med-VLMs) have emerged as powerful tools for a wide range of clinical imaging tasks by leveraging large-scale image-text pretraining [30,36,37]. Despite their success, they remain vulnerable to adversarial attacks, where subtle imperceptible perturbations in the input images can

S. Ali et al. (Eds.): MIUA 2025, LNCS 15916, pp. 300–315, 2026.
https://doi.org/10.1007/978-3-031-98688-8_21

alter predictions, posing risks to medical diagnoses [6,8,10]. Although empirical defense mechanisms have been explored, they often fail against stronger adaptive attacks [2], highlighting the need for certifiable defenses that provide provable robustness guarantees [23]. These *certifiable defenses* guarantee model's prediction accuracy for adversarial perturbations bounded by a *certified radius*, yet most of these approaches lack scalability to large medical foundation models or high-dimensional medical images [3,20].

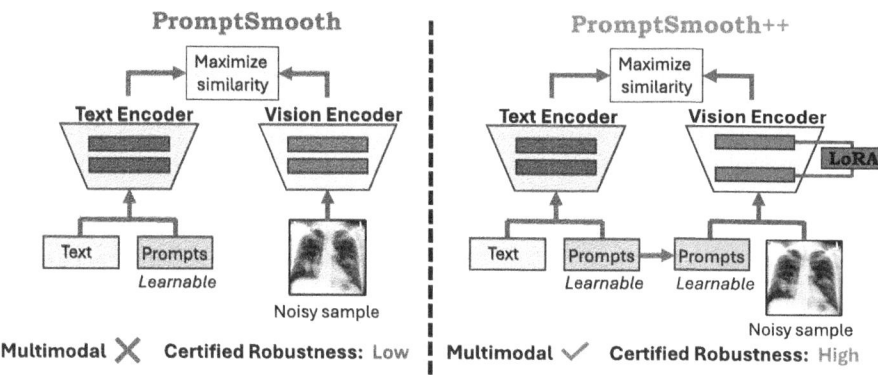

Fig. 1. Comparison between PromptSmooth [13] and our proposed PromptSmooth++. Unlike PromptSmooth, which optimizes prompts only for the text encoder, PromptSmooth++ extends the optimization to both text and vision encoders via multimodal prompting and further incorporates Low-Rank Adapters (LoRA) in the vision encoder for test-time adaptation, leading to significantly improved certified robustness under noise

To address these challenges, randomized smoothing (RS) [22] has gained prominence for its simplicity and theoretical guarantees. RS constructs a smoothed classifier that averages outputs of a base classifier under Gaussian perturbations. *The addition of Gaussian noise introduces a fundamental accuracy robustness trade-off, where higher noise variance improves certification guarantees but degrades clean accuracy* [23]. Existing approaches for optimizing this trade-off include: (1) noise-augmented training from scratch [5,25], (2) prepending custom-trained denoisers [28], and (3) leveraging pre-trained diffusion models as denoisers [4,21]. However, these methods encounter significant barriers in medical domains as they demand either extensive computational resources with privacy-sensitive medical datasets for model retraining, large-scale paired clean-noisy image collections for denoiser training, or prohibitively expensive diffusion model training.

A recent method, PromptSmooth [13], addresses these challenges by efficiently achieving certified robustness in pre-trained Med-VLMs. Instead of retraining the full model or introducing denoisers, PromptSmooth inserts a small number of learnable text prompts into the input and optimizes them on Gaussian-perturbed images while keeping the backbone frozen. Notably, PromptSmooth supports both few-shot and zero-shot settings via supervised prompt learning and test-time prompt tuning, respectively.

While effective, PromptSmooth exhibits two key limitations. *First*, in the few-shot setting, it optimizes prompts solely for the text encoder, neglecting the visual modality that is equally crucial in Med-VLMs. Since Med-VLMs rely on synergistic interactions between vision and language features, text-only adaptation hinders cross-modal alignment and limits the model's ability to learn noise-invariant representations. Given the inherently multimodal architecture of Med-VLMs, a robust prompting strategy must jointly optimize both textual and visual representations to fully leverage the model's capabilities for achieving superior certified robustness (see Fig. 1). *Second*, in the zero-shot setting, PromptSmooth adapts text prompts on-the-fly to noisy test samples. However, this adaptation becomes increasingly unstable at higher noise levels, where the perturbed images diverge significantly from the clean pretraining distribution. This distribution shift undermines the prompt optimization process during inference, leading to suboptimal feature extraction and degraded certified accuracy.

Contributions: To address the limitations of PromptSmooth, we propose `PromptSmooth++`, a multimodal prompt learning framework designed to enhance certified robustness in Med-VLMs. Our approach jointly optimizes visual and textual prompts, enabling stronger cross-modal alignment and the extraction of noise-invariant representations that improve classification performance under randomized smoothing. To handle distribution shifts in the zero-shot setting, we further integrate Low-Rank Adapters (LoRA) into the vision encoder, enabling lightweight, test-time adaptation to the Gaussian-perturbed inputs used during certification. These adapters learn compact, input-specific transformations with minimal overhead and are particularly effective at high noise levels, where deviations from the training distribution are most severe. Through extensive empirical evaluation across multiple Med-VLMs and diverse medical imaging datasets, we demonstrate that `PromptSmooth++` significantly outperforms existing smoothing-based approaches in terms of certified robustness. Specifically, our key contributions are:

– **Multimodal Prompt Learning for Robust Feature Alignment:** We jointly optimize both visual and textual prompts to improve cross-modal representation learning under noisy perturbations. Applied in the few-shot setting, this approach leverages a small number of labeled medical images to learn multimodal prompts, enabling the model to more effectively classify Gaussian-perturbed inputs and enhancing certified robustness.
– **LoRA-Based Vision Encoder Adaptation:** In the zero-shot setting, we introduce Low-Rank Adapters (LoRA) within the vision encoder, which are dynamically updated at test time to adapt the model to the noise distribution induced by randomized smoothing. This test-time adaptation is especially effective under high noise levels, where perturbed inputs significantly deviate from the training distribution of Med-VLMs, enabling improved certified robustness without requiring access to clean data or full model retraining.

– **Comprehensive Evaluation:** We conduct thorough experiments on representative state-of-the-art Med-VLMs and four downstream medical imaging datasets covering a range of modalities. Our results demonstrate that `PromptSmooth++` consistently outperforms existing baselines in terms of certified accuracy, validating its effectiveness across both few-shot and zero-shot settings.

2 Background and Related Work

Certified Robustness: In safety-critical domains such as medical AI, strong performance alone is not sufficient; models must also exhibit *robustness* to small, potentially adversarial perturbations in the input. Although empirical defenses aim to resist such perturbations through adversarial training or inference-time purification techniques, they often lack *provable guarantees* [1]. *Certified robustness* methods address this gap by providing formal guarantees that a model's prediction does not change when the input is perturbed within a certain bounded region [23].

Among certified robustness approaches, *Randomized Smoothing (RS)* [5] has emerged as one of the most scalable and theoretically grounded approaches for certifying robustness in high-dimensional models. The key idea is to construct a *smoothed classifier* by averaging predictions over multiple noisy versions of the input. Specifically, given a base classifier $h : \mathcal{X} \to \mathcal{Y}$, RS defines a new classifier g such that:

$$g(\mathbf{x}) = \arg\max_{y \in \mathcal{Y}} \mathbb{P}[h(\mathbf{x} + \boldsymbol{\eta}) = y],$$

where $\boldsymbol{\eta} \sim \mathcal{N}(0, \sigma^2 \mathbf{I})$ adds isotropic Gaussian noise to the input. Intuitively, if a particular class prediction dominates consistently under noise, then it is likely to be robust to small adversarial perturbations. RS quantifies this robustness via a *certified radius* R, guaranteeing that the model's prediction remains stable within an ℓ_2-ball of radius R around the input. Formally, if the predicted class y_A satisfies:

$$\underline{p_A} \geq \overline{p_B} \quad \text{for} \quad y_B = \arg\max_{y \neq y_A} \mathbb{P}[h(\mathbf{x} + \boldsymbol{\eta}) = y],$$

then the prediction is provably invariant to any perturbation $\|\mathbf{r}\|_2 < R$, where $R = \frac{\sigma}{2} \left(\Phi^{-1}(\underline{p_A}) - \Phi^{-1}(\overline{p_B}) \right)$, and Φ^{-1} is the inverse standard Gaussian cumulative distribution function (CDF). In practice, estimating $\underline{p_A}$ and $\overline{p_B}$ requires *Monte Carlo sampling* over multiple noisy inputs. A key challenge in RS lies in the *accuracyrobustness trade-off*: increasing the noise level σ expands the certified radius R but deteriorates clean accuracy by corrupting the input. As a result, recent work has sought to *improve model performance under noise*, enabling stronger certified guarantees without compromising accuracy.

Popular strategies include training models with noise [5,25], attaching denoising modules [28], or using generative models like diffusion networks to recover clean representations [4,21]. However, these methods are often impractical in medical contexts due to the need for full retraining, access to paired clean-noisy data, or high computational overhead. *In contrast, our approach leverages parameter-efficient tuning techniques, such as prompt learning and LoRA, to enhance the noise robustness of frozen Med-VLMs, offering a scalable and certifiable solution tailored to medical imaging.*

Medical VLMs: Medical VLMs, inspired by Contrastive Language-Image Pre-training (CLIP) [26,37], have emerged as powerful tools for medical imaging [37]. These models are trained on large-scale paired medical data to maximize similarity between semantically corresponding image-text pairs while minimizing it for mismatched pairs. Recent works have adapted this paradigm to diverse modalities, such as X-rays [12], histopathology [32], and multi-modal fusion [14], demonstrating their utility in diagnosis, retrieval, and report generation tasks. *However, despite their strong zero-shot generalization and cross-modal reasoning capabilities, the robustness of Med-VLMs under adversarial perturbations remains underexplored, particularly in safety-critical applications like disease detection, where certifiable guarantees are essential.*

Parameter-Efficient Adaptation in VLMs: Parameter-efficient adaptation techniques aim to fine-tune large vision-language models (VLMs) using a small number of learnable parameters, making them well-suited for data-scarce and often resource-constrained medical imaging domain [9,27,35]. Two prominent approaches are prompt learning [24] and Low-Rank Adaptation (LoRA) [11,15]. Prompt learning injects learnable tokens into the input space [39], allowing lightweight adaptation without modifying backbone weights [38,39]. Several methods improve its flexibility and generalization, including visual prompt tuning [7], multimodal ensembles [17], and test-time prompt tuning (TPT) [31], which adapts prompts dynamically during inference. LoRA, in contrast, inserts low-rank trainable matrices within transformer layers of vision encoder of VLM, enabling efficient tuning of the model's internal representations with minimal overhead. However, these approaches primarily target downstream performance and generalization, while overlooking robustness to input perturbations which is an essential requirement in high-stakes domains like healthcare. PromptSmooth [13] addresses this by adapting prompt learning for certified robustness, optimizing text prompts over Gaussian-perturbed images from randomized smoothing. While effective, it (1) neglects visual adaptation, limiting cross-modal robustness, and (2) becomes unstable under high noise levels in the zero-shot setting due to distribution shift. *In this work, we aim to handle these issues by jointly optimizing textual and visual prompts in the few-shot setting and introducing LoRA-based vision encoder adaptation at test time for improved robustness under strong perturbations.*

3   Methodology

Our goal is to improve the certified robustness of Med-VLMs against adversarial perturbations introduced by randomized smoothing, while preserving their

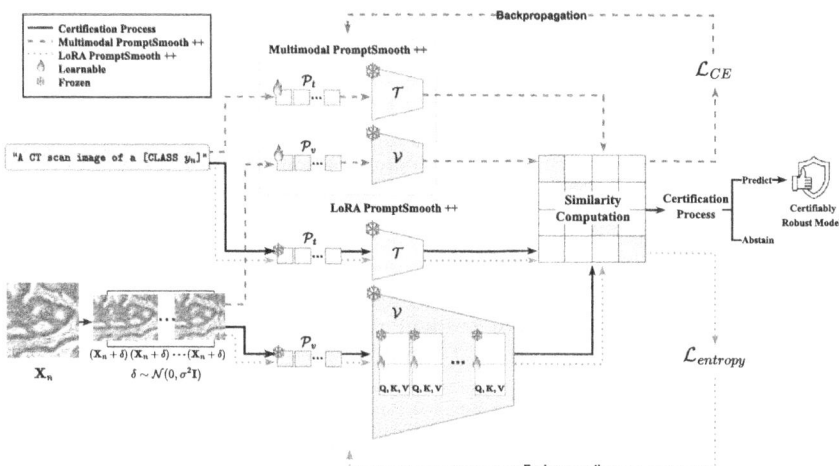

Fig. 2. Overview of the `PromptSmooth++` framework for certified robustness. Our method consists of two complementary components: *Multimodal PromptSmooth++* for the few-shot setting (left) and *LoRA PromptSmooth++* for the zero-shot setting (right). In the few-shot branch, learnable text and visual prompts are prepended to the input tokens of the text and vision encoders and optimized offline on noisy, labeled samples. In the zero-shot branch, Low-Rank Adapters are inserted into the Query (Q) and Value (V) projection layers of the self-attention modules in the vision encoder. These LoRA parameters are updated at test time using entropy minimization on Gaussian-perturbed views of the input. During certification, both components are combined: the model predicts over M noisy samples, and outputs a prediction with a certified radius or abstains. This design ensures robust cross-modal alignment and adaptation to unseen noisy distributions without retraining the Med-VLM backbone

strong zero-shot generalization in data-scarce medical imaging scenarios. To this end, we propose `PromptSmooth++`, a lightweight adaptation framework that builds on PromptSmooth by addressing two critical limitations: the lack of visual modality adaptation and instability during test-time tuning at high noise levels. Our approach integrates prompt learning and test-time tuning in a modality-aware and robustness-driven manner. We first formalize zero-shot inference in Med-VLMs and review the limitations of PromptSmooth, then present our two complementary variants of `PromptSmooth++` for few-shot and zero-shot settings.

3.1 Preliminaries: Zero-Shot Inference in Med-VLMs

Medical vision-language models (Med-VLMs) consist of a vision encoder $\mathcal{V}$ and a text encoder $\mathcal{T}$, both pretrained to align image-text pairs in a shared embedding space. Given an image $\mathbf{X} \in \mathbb{R}^{H \times W \times C}$ and a class label $y_i \in \mathcal{Y}$, we define a prompt template such as $\mathbf{t}(y_i) = $ "A CT scan of a [CLASS y_i]", which is encoded into a text feature $\mathbf{u}_i = \mathcal{T}(\mathbf{t}(y_i))$. The vision encoder maps $\mathbf{X}$ to an image embedding $\mathbf{v} = \mathcal{V}(\mathbf{X})$, and classification is performed via softmax over cosine similarities:

$$\mathbb{P}(y_i|\mathbf{X}) = \frac{\exp(\tau \cdot \mathrm{sim}(\mathbf{v}, \mathbf{u}_i))}{\sum_j \exp(\tau \cdot \mathrm{sim}(\mathbf{v}, \mathbf{u}_j))}, \quad \hat{y} = \arg\max_{y_i} \mathbb{P}(y_i|\mathbf{X}).$$

While effective for clean inputs, Med-VLMs suffer under Gaussian perturbations introduced by randomized smoothing. PromptSmooth [13] tackles this by learning text prompts that adapt the language encoder to noisy inputs. However, it suffers from two key limitations: (1) it neglects vision-side adaptation, resulting in suboptimal cross-modal alignment under noise, and (2) test-time prompt tuning becomes unstable at high noise levels due to the distribution shift between clean training data and Gaussian-perturbed test inputs.

3.2   PromptSmooth++

We propose `PromptSmooth++` to enhance certified robustness of Med-VLMs under different supervision settings. The first variant, *Multimodal PromptSmooth++*, is designed for the **few-shot setting**, where a small number of labeled examples are available. It jointly learns visual and textual prompts to improve cross-modal feature alignment under noise. The second variant, tailored for the **zero-shot setting**, introduces test-time vision-side adaptation using Low-Rank Adapters (LoRA) to effectively handle distribution shifts introduced by randomized smoothing without relying on labeled data. Next, as illustrated in Fig. 2, we first describe *Multimodal PromptSmooth++* for few-shot adaptation, followed by our test-time *LoRA PromptSmooth++* extension for zero-shot inference.

3.2.1   Multimodal PromptSmooth++

`PromptSmooth++` enhances certified robustness by introducing learnable prompts in both the visual and textual branches of pre-trained Med-VLMs. Inspired by prior work on multimodal prompting [17,18], we extend this idea to the certified setting under randomized smoothing, where robustness to Gaussian noise is paramount. Given a frozen Med-VLM comprising a vision encoder $\mathcal{V}$ and a language encoder $\mathcal{T}$, we inject learnable prompt tokens $\mathcal{P}_v$ and $\mathcal{P}_t$ into the input sequences of $\mathcal{V}$ and $\mathcal{T}$, respectively. Specifically, we append T learnable textual prompts $\mathcal{P}_t = \{\mathbf{p}_t^1, \mathbf{p}_t^2, \ldots, \mathbf{p}_t^T\}$ and V learnable visual prompts $\mathcal{P}_v = \{\mathbf{p}_v^1, \mathbf{p}_v^2, \ldots, \mathbf{p}_v^V\}$ to the input tokens of the language and vision encoders, respectively. The image encoder $\mathcal{V}$ processes visual tokens constructed as:

$$\tilde{\mathbf{X}} = \{\mathcal{P}_v, \mathbf{e}_{\mathrm{CLS}}, \mathbf{e}_1, \ldots, \mathbf{e}_P\},$$

where $\mathbf{e}_{\mathrm{CLS}}$ and $\{\mathbf{e}_1, \ldots, \mathbf{e}_P\}$ denote the classification and patch embeddings, respectively. The textual input for each class label y_i is formed as:

$$t(y_i) = \{\mathcal{P}_t, \text{``A CT scan image of a [CLASS } y_i]\text{''}\}.$$

Given a small labeled dataset $\{(\mathbf{X}_n, y_n)\}_{n=1}^{N}$ from a downstream medical imaging task, we optimize $\mathcal{P}_t$ and $\mathcal{P}_v$ using Gaussian-perturbed inputs. Specifically, we solve:

$$\mathcal{P}^* = \arg\min_{\mathcal{P}_t, \mathcal{P}_v} \mathbb{E}_{\delta \sim \mathcal{N}(0, \sigma^2 \mathbf{I})} \frac{1}{N} \sum_{n=1}^{N} \mathcal{L}(f_{\mathcal{P}}(\mathbf{X}_n + \delta), y_n), \quad (1)$$

where $f_{\mathcal{P}}$ is the zero-shot classifier augmented with multimodal prompts, and $\mathcal{L}$ is the standard cross-entropy loss. Following [39], prompt optimization is performed by minimizing the standard cross-entropy loss, with gradients back-propagated through the frozen text encoder $\mathcal{T}$ and vision encoder $\mathcal{V}$ to iteratively refine the textual $\mathcal{P}_t$ and visual $\mathcal{P}_v$ prompts, respectively. By keeping the Med-VLM backbone fixed, this optimization effectively enhances robustness of Med-VLM to Gaussian noise while preserving the model's zero-shot generalization, leading to improved certified robustness.

This multimodal strategy addresses a key limitation of PromptSmooth [13] by incorporating visual prompts alongside textual ones. This joint prompting enables stronger cross-modal alignment between the vision and language representations, allowing the model to better fuse noisy visual inputs with their corresponding semantic cues. As a result, the classifier becomes more robust to perturbations, particularly in settings where accurate alignment across modalities is essential for reliable prediction.

3.2.2 LoRA PromptSmooth++

In the zero-shot setting, where no labeled samples are available for downstream tasks, `PromptSmooth++` improves certified robustness by introducing test-time adaptation via Low-Rank Adaptation (LoRA) [15]. Unlike few-shot adaptation, this variant operates directly on the noisy inputs encountered during randomized smoothing, and updates only a small number of trainable parameters within the vision encoder at inference time.

Parameter-Efficient Adaptation Using LoRA: LoRA enables parameter-efficient tuning by approximating the gradient-based weight update of self-attention projections through low-rank matrices. Specifically, given the pre-trained query and value projection matrices $W_Q, W_V \in \mathbb{R}^{d \times k}$ in the self-attention layers of the vision encoder $\mathcal{V}$, where d is the input embedding dimension and k is the output dimension, LoRA introduces trainable low-rank matrices $A \in \mathbb{R}^{r \times k}$ and $B \in \mathbb{R}^{d \times r}$ with rank $r \ll \min(d, k)$. The combined update is parameterized as $\Delta W = BA$, and the full adapted weights become $W + \Delta W$. During adaptation, the original weights W_Q and W_V remain frozen, and only the LoRA parameters (A_Q, B_Q) and (A_V, B_V) are optimized. The modified forward pass through the l-th self-attention block is then given by:

$$\tilde{\mathbf{z}}_Q^l = W_Q^l \mathbf{x}_Q^l + \gamma \cdot (B_Q^l A_Q^l) \mathbf{x}_Q^l, \quad \tilde{\mathbf{z}}_V^l = W_V^l \mathbf{x}_V^l + \gamma \cdot (B_V^l A_V^l) \mathbf{x}_V^l,$$

where $\mathbf{x}_Q^l$ and $\mathbf{x}_V^l$ are the input features to the l-th attention block, and $\gamma = \frac{r}{\alpha}$ is a scaling factor controlled by the LoRA hyperparameter α.

LoRA-Based Test-Time Adaptation for Certified Robustness: To enable certified robustness in the zero-shot setting, we adapt the LoRA parameters Φ to the distribution of noisy inputs induced by randomized smoothing. Specifically, for a given test image $\mathbf{X}_t$, we consider perturbed versions $\mathbf{X}_t + \delta$, where $\delta \sim \mathcal{N}(0, \sigma^2 \mathbf{I})$. Since no ground-truth labels are available, we minimize the entropy of the model's output distribution on noisy inputs to promote confident predictions under perturbations. The optimization objective is given by:

$$\Phi^* = \arg \min_{\Phi} \mathbb{E}_{\delta \sim \mathcal{N}(0, \sigma^2 \mathbf{I})} \left[\mathcal{H}(f_\Phi(\mathbf{X}_t + \delta)) \right], \tag{2}$$

where f_Φ denotes the Med-VLM classifier with LoRA adaptation applied to the vision encoder, and $\mathcal{H}(p) = -\sum_{k=1}^{K} p_k \log p_k$ is the standard entropy over the softmax probabilities. By optimizing only the LoRA parameters at test time, this approach adapts the visual features to the local noisy neighborhood of the input without modifying the frozen backbone or requiring supervision. This mitigates the instability of prompt tuning observed in PromptSmooth's [13] zero-shot setting and leads to more reliable predictions for randomized smoothing. Crucially, LoRA PromptSmooth++ remains lightweight, test-time efficient, and scalable to various pre-trained Med-VLMs.

Finally, LoRA PromptSmooth++ can be applied on top of Multimodal PromptSmooth++ by using the learned few-shot prompts to initialize the text and visual branches, and then adapting LoRA parameters at test time. This hybrid configuration enables robust initialization with few-shot supervision while retaining flexibility for distribution shift during inference. We refer to this combined setup simply as `PromptSmooth++`.

4   Experiments

4.1   Experimental Setup

Implementation Details. `PromptSmooth++` is implemented in PyTorch and experiments are run on a single NVIDIA A100 GPU (40GB VRAM). All input images are resized to 224×224 and normalized to the $[0, 1]^3$ range using standard preprocessing. To interface with the text encoder, each class label is converted into a descriptive prompt (e.g., "Benign" $\rightarrow$ "A medical scan showing {Benign}"). In the **few-shot** setting, we use 16 labeled samples per class (16-shot), and train the multimodal prompts for 50 epochs using SGD with a learning rate of 0.002 and a batch size of 16. Prompt tokens are initialized following the CoOp-style context tuning strategy [39], using five randomly initialized embeddings. Prompt optimization is performed on Gaussian-perturbed images to align with the requirements of randomized smoothing. In the **zero-shot** setting, we apply test-time adaptation using LoRA-based updates to the vision encoder. LoRA weight matrices are initialized using Xavier initialization, with rank $R = 16$ and scaling factor $\alpha = 32$. Adaptation is performed only in the final transformer layers (layers 1012) of the vision encoder. For randomized smoothing, we follow standard protocol [5], estimating certified accuracy using $M = 10,000$ Monte Carlo samples and confidence level $\alpha = 0.001$.

Models and Datasets. We evaluate `PromptSmooth++` using two publicly available medical vision-language models (Med-VLMs): PLIP [12] and MedCLIP [34]. These models are pre-trained on large-scale medical image-text datasets, with PLIP primarily trained on histopathology images, and MedCLIP tailored for radiographic imaging. To assess both generalization and certified robustness, we evaluate across four downstream classification benchmarks spanning diverse medical modalities. PLIP is tested on two histopathology datasets: Kather-Colon [16] (9 classes) and SkinCancer [19] (16 classes). MedCLIP is assessed on two chest X-ray benchmarks: COVID-Xray [33] (2 classes) and RSNA Pneumonia [29] (3 classes). We use the official train-test splits provided with each dataset to ensure consistency and fair comparison.

Table 1. Certified accuracy (%) of PLIP on KatherColon and SkinCancer datasets under different noise levels (σ) and certified radii (r). The value in parentheses indicates the corresponding clean accuracy (%)

Method	Certified Accuracy at ℓ_2 radius (%)						
	0.1	0.25	0.5	0.75	1.0	1.25	1.5
KatherColon (9 Classes)							
Zero-shot PLIP (No PL)	$^{(56.6)}$49.4	$^{(56.6)}$38.2	$^{(28.9)}$20.8	$^{(28.9)}$17.6	$^{(11.0)}$11.0	$^{(11.0)}$11.0	$^{(11.0)}$11.0
Naive PL (CoOp) [39]	$^{(71.6)}$66.7	$^{(71.6)}$56.0	$^{(22.0)}$16.4	$^{(22.0)}$14.2	$^{(11.0)}$11.0	$^{(11.0)}$11.0	$^{(11.0)}$11.0
Denoised Smoothing [28]	$^{(55.0)}$48.2	$^{(55.0)}$39.2	$^{(45.2)}$31.0	$^{(45.2)}$25.6	$^{(26.2)}$17.4	$^{(26.2)}$16.2	$^{(26.2)}$14.6
Diffusion Smoothing [4]	$^{(58.0)}$57.0	$^{(53.0)}$49.0	$^{(53.0)}$41.0	$^{(53.0)}$34.0	$^{(53.0)}$26.0	$^{(53.0)}$22.0	$^{(53.0)}$16.0
Zero-shot PromptSmooth [13]	$^{(57.6)}$53.4	$^{(57.6)}$49.0	$^{(30.2)}$29.0	$^{(30.2)}$29.0	$^{(30.2)}$28.6	$^{(30.2)}$28.4	$^{(30.2)}$27.4
LoRA PromptSmooth++	$^{(59.2)}$56.0	$^{(59.0)}$53.8	$^{(38.8)}$34.2	$^{(34.0)}$31.6	$^{(34.0)}$30.8	$^{(34.0)}$29.8	$^{(34.0)}$28.6
Few-shot PromptSmooth [13]	$^{(81.2)}$78.2	$^{(81.2)}$67.6	$^{(75.6)}$52.2	$^{(75.6)}$35.6	$^{(50.4)}$26.4	$^{(50.4)}$22.2	$^{(50.4)}$17.6
Multimodal PromptSmooth++	$^{(85.8)}$81.20	$^{(85.8)}$72.2	$^{(76.4)}$55.8	$^{(76.4)}$42.0	$^{(59.2)}$34.8	$^{(59.2)}$28.6	$^{(48.8)}$26.4
PromptSmooth [13]	$^{(82.0)}$81.8	$^{(82.0)}$81.0	$^{(76.6)}$74.8	$^{(76.6)}$73.2	$^{(54.0)}$48.4	$^{(54.0)}$47.2	$^{(54.0)}$45.6
PromptSmooth++	$^{(86.2)}$83.0	$^{(85.8)}$82.6	$^{(76.6)}$76.0	$^{(76.4)}$74.0	$^{(59.2)}$50.8	$^{(59.2)}$49.2	$^{(59.2)}$47.8
SkinCancer (16 Classes)							
Zero-shot PLIP (No PL)	$^{(26.6)}$19.0	$^{(14.2)}$9.80	$^{(6.0)}$5.80	$^{(6.00)}$4.80	$^{(6.00)}$4.60	$^{(6.00)}$4.39	$^{(6.00)}$4.39
Naive PL (CoOp) [39]	$^{(67.2)}$57.8	$^{(67.2)}$43.8	$^{(34.2)}$16.6	$^{(34.2)}$7.00	$^{(6.20)}$6.20	$^{(6.20)}$6.20	$^{(6.20)}$6.20
Denoised Smoothing [28]	$^{(51.2)}$47.0	$^{(51.2)}$39.2	$^{(44.0)}$30.2	$^{(44.0)}$22.4	$^{(21.4)}$16.4	$^{(21.4)}$13.2	$^{(21.4)}$12.0
Diffusion Smoothing [4]	$^{(56.4)}$51.0	$^{(44.8)}$44.2	$^{(44.8)}$41.0	$^{(54.8)}$34.0	$^{(31.0)}$23.8	$^{(31.0)}$19.0	$^{(31.0)}$17.2
Zero-shot PromptSmooth	$^{(25.0)}$23.2	$^{(25)}$19.6	$^{(14.2)}$11.6	$^{(6.4)}$6.4	$^{(6.4)}$6.4	$^{(6 4)}$6.4	$^{(6.4)}$6.4
LoRA PromptSmooth++	$^{(29.0)}$26.2	$^{(28.4)}$26.0	$^{(20.0)}$16.2	$^{(11.4)}$8.0	$^{(11.4)}$8.0	$^{(11.4)}$7.8	$^{(11.4)}$7.8
Few-shot PromptSmooth	$^{(67.0)}$58.0	$^{(67.0)}$44.6	$^{(54.4)}$27.0	$^{(36.6)}$15.0	$^{(36.6)}$9.00	$^{(6.20)}$6.20	$^{(6.20)}$6.20
Multimodal PromptSmooth++	$^{(71.8)}$67.6	$^{(71.8)}$60.6	$^{(59.0)}$31.6	$^{(59.0)}$31.6	$^{(59.2)}$22.8	$^{(21.0)}$11.4	$^{(15.8)}$11.4
PromptSmooth	$^{(68.6)}$67.6	$^{(68.6)}$64.8	$^{(56.4)}$50.2	$^{(56.4)}$46.0	$^{(38.2)}$33.8	$^{(38.2)}$31.0	$^{(38.2)}$29.6
PromptSmooth++	$^{(73.2)}$71.4	$^{(73.2)}$65.6	$^{(61.8)}$52.0	$^{(61.8)}$48.2	$^{(44.0)}$34.8	$^{(44.0)}$34.2	$^{(40.2)}$29.6

Table 2. Certified accuracy (%) of MedCLIP on the COVID and RSNA Pneumonia datasets under varying Gaussian noise levels (σ)and certified radii (r). Clean accuracy is shown in parentheses. `PromptSmooth++` consistently outperforms prior methods across both datasets and all noise levels

Method	COVID				RSNA Pneumonia			
	0.1	0.25	0.5	0.75	0.1	0.25	0.5	0.75
Denoised Smoothing [28]	$^{(66.4)}$54.6	$^{(50.2)}$48.4	$^{(50.2)}$45.8	$^{(50.2)}$36.0	$^{(37.6)}$27.6	$^{(31.6)}$21.0	$^{(31.6)}$9.40	$^{(31.6)}$1.79
Diffusion Smoothing [4]	$^{(56.0)}$37.0	$^{(44.0)}$22.0	$^{(44.0)}$6.00	$^{(44.0)}$1.00	$^{(44.0)}$40.0	$^{(44.0)}$28.0	$^{(44.0)}$12.0	$^{(44.0)}$1.00
Zero-shot PromptSmooth [13]	$^{(62.4)}$62.0	$^{(62.4)}$60.6	$^{(50.2)}$50.0	$^{(50.2)}$49.8	$^{(37.0)}$35.4	$^{(37.0)}$33.4	$^{(33.4)}$33.8	$^{(33.4)}$33.2
LoRA PromptSmooth++	$^{(63.6)}$63.0	$^{(62.8)}$61.0	$^{(51.2)}$50.0	$^{(51.2)}$49.2	$^{(39.0)}$36.2	$^{(39.0)}$35.4	$^{(36.2)}$33.4	$^{(36.2)}$30.2
Few-shot PromptSmooth [13]	$^{(66.8)}$58.0	$^{(52.0)}$48.8	$^{(52.0)}$47.6	$^{(52)}$42.8	$^{(41.4)}$34.4	$^{(34.0)}$31.2	$^{(34.0)}$27.0	$^{(34.0)}$23.6
Multimodal PromptSmooth++	$^{(71.4)}$60.0	$^{(54.8)}$50.4	$^{(54.8)}$48.6	$^{(52.0)}$44.8	$^{(44.2)}$40.0	$^{(37.0)}$30.2	$^{(37.0)}$29.6	$^{(37.0)}$25.2
PromptSmooth [13]	$^{(69.4)}$69.0	$^{(69.4)}$68.4	$^{(53.0)}$52.8	$^{(53.0)}$52.6	$^{(42.4)}$40.8	$^{(42.4)}$35.8	$^{(34.6)}$33.4	$^{(34.6)}$32.0
PromptSmooth++	$^{(71.2)}$69.8	$^{(71.0)}$69.8	$^{(55.2)}$55.4	$^{(55.2)}$54.0	$^{(47.0)}$44.2	$^{(45.6)}$40.8	$^{(40.0)}$37.0	$^{(40.0)}$35.6

Baseline Methods. We compare `PromptSmooth++` against several representative baselines. **Denoised Smoothing** [28] enhances randomized smoothing using a separately trained denoiser, while **Diffusion Smoothing** [4] leverages pre-trained diffusion models for denoising prior to classification. As a basic reference, we include a **zero-shot Med-VLM** baseline without any prompt learning. **Naive Prompt Learning** [39], implemented in the style of CoOp, learns text prompts on clean data but does not account for noise. Finally, **PromptSmooth** [13] optimizes only textual prompts on noisy images to improve certified robustness.

Evaluation Metrics. We report both clean and certified accuracy. Certified accuracy is the proportion of test samples for which the model's prediction is provably stable within a certified radius r, as verified by CERTIFY [5]. Evaluations are conducted under four Gaussian noise levels: $\sigma \in \{0.1, 0.25, 0.5, 1.0\}$. To ensure consistency with prior work [4,13], we randomly sample 500 images from each test set and report the best certified radius for each input. All results are averaged over three runs following prior work [13].

4.2   Results and Discussion

Table 1 shows that `PromptSmooth++` achieves the best certified accuracy across all noise levels and radii on KatherColon dataset for PLIP model. Compared to zero-shot PromptSmooth, our zero-shot variant improves robustness notably at high radius (e.g., +2.2% at $r = 1.0$), while `Multimodal PromptSmooth++` outperforms its baseline by a wide margin (e.g., +8.4% at $r = 1.0$). The combined variant (`PromptSmooth++`) further boosts performance, outperforming all baselines including Denoised and Diffusion Smoothing. These results highlight the benefit of multimodal prompting and test-time LoRA adaptation in achieving scalable certified robustness without compromising clean accuracy. Similar trends are observed on SkinCancer, confirming the consistent benefits of multi-modal prompting and test-time LoRA adaptation across histopathology benchmarks.

Similarly, in Table 2, for the MedCLIP model n both the COVID and RSNA Pneumonia benchmarks, we observe that PromptSmooth++ consistently achieves the highest certified accuracies across all noise levels and radii. For instance, on COVID, it improves certified accuracy from 52.6% (PromptSmooth) to 54.0% at $r = 0.75$, while also improving clean accuracy. The few-shot variant (Multimodal PromptSmooth) further boosts robustness, especially at lower radii, achieving 60.0% certified accuracy at $r = 0.1$ compared to 58.0% for PromptSmooth. Similarly, on RSNA Pneumonia, PromptSmooth++ attains 35.6% at $r = 0.75$, outperforming all baselines including Diffusion and Denoised Smoothing. These gains validate the benefits of visual prompt tuning and test-time LoRA adaptation under distribution shift. Notably, LoRA PromptSmooth++ also improves over prior prompt-only methods, highlighting its adaptability in fully unsupervised settings.

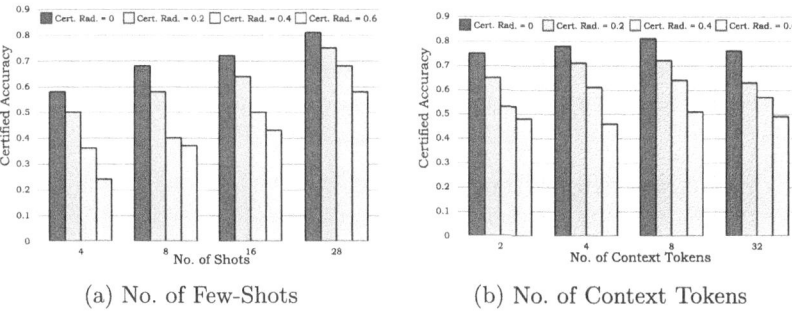

(a) No. of Few-Shots   (b) No. of Context Tokens

Fig. 3. Impact of changing the number of (a) shots and (b) context tokens in Multimodal PromptSmooth++

4.3   Ablations:

We conduct extensive ablation studies to analyze how different components of PromptSmooth++ affect the certified robustness performance. All ablations are performed on the samples from the official test set of KatherColon dataset with PLIP model.

Impact of Few-shot Examples: Figure 3 (left) shows the effect of varying the number of few-shot examples (shots) on certified accuracy across different ℓ_2 radii. We observe that increasing the number of shots generally improves certified robustness. Specifically, using 28 shots achieves the best performance, maintaining a certified accuracy of 0.7 even at a radius of about 0.4.

Effect of Context Length: Figure 3 (right) illustrates how the number of context tokens ($nctx$) influences the certification performance. Interestingly, we find that a moderate context length of 8 tokens achieves optimal performance across most radii, outperforming both smaller and larger context settings of 4 and 32 tokens, respectively. This suggests that while sufficient context is necessary for robust feature extraction, excessive context length may introduce noise in the certification process. The performance differences are particularly noticeable in the mid-range radii (0.2–0.6), where $nctx=8$ maintains higher certified accuracy compared to other settings. These findings indicate that carefully tuning the context length is crucial for balancing the model's ability to capture relevant features while maintaining robust certification guarantees.

LoRA Optimization Steps. In our default setting, we apply a single gradient update step to adapt LoRA parameters at test time for efficiency. To study the effect of additional adaptation, we increase the number of gradient steps and observe consistent improvements in certified accuracy. For instance, on the KatherColon dataset at radius $r = 0.5$, certified accuracy improves from **34.2%** (1 step) to **34.8%** (3 steps) and **35.2%** (5 steps), demonstrating more effective alignment with the noisy input distribution. Beyond 5 steps, however, performance gains saturate, with no significant increase in certified robustness. This comes at the cost of increased inference latency, suggesting a trade-off between robustness and speed that could be tuned based on application constraints.

5   Conclusion and Future Work

We introduced PromptSmooth++, a parameter-efficient framework for improving the certified robustness of medical vision-language models (Med-VLMs) under randomized smoothing. Our method addresses key limitations of prior prompt-based defenses by introducing two complementary strategies: (i) a few-shot multimodal prompting approach that jointly adapts both vision and language branches for improved cross-modal alignment under noise, and (ii) a zero-shot test-time adaptation technique that leverages Low-Rank Adapters (LoRA) to tune the vision encoder for distribution shifts without requiring supervision. Extensive evaluations across multiple Med-VLMs and datasets spanning diverse medical modalities demonstrate that PromptSmooth++ consistently improves certified accuracy while maintaining clean performance and computational efficiency. Our results highlight the importance of modality-aware adaptation and lightweight test-time tuning in building robust and generalizable medical AI systems.

In future work, we plan to extend PromptSmooth++ to handle domain shifts arising from hospital-specific data distributions and imaging protocols. We also aim to adapt the framework for temporal medical data, including videos and multi-frame modalities such as ultrasound or endoscopy, where robustness across frames is critical.

References

1. Apostolidis, K.D., Papakostas, G.A.: A survey on adversarial deep learning robustness in medical image analysis. Electronics **10**(17), 2132 (2021)
2. Athalye, A., Carlini, N., Wagner, D.: Obfuscated gradients give a false sense of security: circumventing defenses to adversarial examples. In: International Conference on Machine Learning, pp. 274–283. PMLR (2018)
3. Azad, B., et al.: Foundational models in medical imaging: a comprehensive survey and future vision. arXiv preprint arXiv:2310.18689 (2023)
4. Carlini, N., Tramer, F., Dvijotham, K.D., Rice, L., Sun, M., Kolter, J.Z.: (certified!!) adversarial robustness for free! arXiv preprint arXiv:2206.10550 (2022)
5. Cohen, J., Rosenfeld, E., Kolter, Z.: Certified adversarial robustness via randomized smoothing. In: International Conference on Machine Learning, pp. 1310–1320. PMLR (2019)
6. Finlayson, S.G., Bowers, J.D., Ito, J., Zittrain, J.L., Beam, A.L., Kohane, I.S.: Adversarial attacks on medical machine learning. Science **363**(6433), 1287–1289 (2019)
7. Gu, J., et al.: A systematic survey of prompt engineering on vision-language foundation models. arXiv preprint arXiv:2307.12980 (2023)
8. Han, T., et al.: Medical foundation models are susceptible to targeted misinformation attacks. arXiv preprint arXiv:2309.17007 (2023)
9. Han, Z., Gao, C., Liu, J., Zhang, J., Zhang, S.Q.: Parameter-efficient fine-tuning for large models: a comprehensive survey. arXiv preprint arXiv:2403.14608 (2024)
10. Hanif, A., et al.: Baple: backdoor attacks on medical foundational models using prompt learning. In: International Conference on Medical Image Computing and Computer-Assisted Intervention, pp. 443–453. Springer, Cham (2024)
11. Hu, E.J., et al.: Lora: low-rank adaptation of large language models. In: ICLR, vol. 1, no. 2, p. 3 (2022)
12. Huang, Z., Bianchi, F., Yuksekgonul, M., Montine, T.J., Zou, J.: A visual-language foundation model for pathology image analysis using medical twitter. Nat. Med. **29**(9), 2307–2316 (2023)
13. Hussein, N., Shamshad, F., Naseer, M., Nandakumar, K.: Promptsmooth: certifying robustness of medical vision-language models via prompt learning. In: International Conference on Medical Image Computing and Computer-Assisted Intervention, pp. 698–708. Springer, Cham (2024)
14. Ikezogwo, W., et al.: Quilt-1m: one million image-text pairs for histopathology. In: Advances in Neural Information Processing Systems, vol. 36 (2024)
15. Imam, R., Gani, H., Huzaifa, M., Nandakumar, K.: Test-time low rank adaptation via confidence maximization for zero-shot generalization of vision-language models. arXiv preprint arXiv:2407.15913 (2024)
16. Kather, J.N., et al.: Predicting survival from colorectal cancer histology slides using deep learning: a retrospective multicenter study. PLoS Med. **16**(1), e1002730 (2019)
17. Khattak, M.U., Rasheed, H., Maaz, M., Khan, S., Khan, F.S.: Maple: multi-modal prompt learning. In: Proceedings of the IEEE/CVF Conference on Computer Vision and Pattern Recognition, pp. 19113–19122 (2023)
18. Khattak, M.U., Wasim, S.T., Naseer, M., Khan, S., Yang, M.H., Khan, F.S.: Self-regulating prompts: foundational model adaptation without forgetting. In: Proceedings of the IEEE/CVF International Conference on Computer Vision, pp. 15190–15200 (2023)

19. Kriegsmann, K., et al.: Deep learning for the detection of anatomical tissue structures and neoplasms of the skin on scanned histopathological tissue sections. Front. Oncol. **12**, 1022967 (2022)
20. Kumari, A., Bhardwaj, D., Jindal, S., Gupta, S.: Trust, but verify: a survey of randomized smoothing techniques. arXiv preprint arXiv:2312.12608 (2023)
21. Laousy, O., Araujo, A., Chassagnon, G., Paragios, N., Revel, M.P., Vakalopoulou, M.: Certification of deep learning models for medical image segmentation. In: International Conference on Medical Image Computing and Computer-Assisted Intervention, pp. 611–621. Springer, Cham (2023)
22. Lecuyer, M., Atlidakis, V., Geambasu, R., Hsu, D., Jana, S.: Certified robustness to adversarial examples with differential privacy. In: 2019 IEEE Symposium on Security and Privacy (SP), pp. 656–672. IEEE (2019)
23. Li, L., Xie, T., Li, B.: SoK: certified robustness for deep neural networks. In: 2023 IEEE Symposium on Security and Privacy (SP), pp. 1289–1310. IEEE (2023)
24. Liu, P., Yuan, W., Fu, J., Jiang, Z., Hayashi, H., Neubig, G.: Pre-train, prompt, and predict: a systematic survey of prompting methods in natural language processing. ACM Comput. Surv. **55**(9), 1–35 (2023)
25. Qiu, K., Zhang, H., Wu, Z., Lin, S.: Exploring transferability for randomized smoothing. arXiv preprint arXiv:2312.09020 (2023)
26. Radford, A., et al.: Learning transferable visual models from natural language supervision. In: International Conference on Machine Learning, pp. 8748–8763. PMLR (2021)
27. Saadi, N., Saeed, N., Yaqub, M., Nandakumar, K.: Pemma: parameter-efficient multi-modal adaptation for medical image segmentation. In: International Conference on Medical Image Computing and Computer-Assisted Intervention, pp. 262–271. Springer, Cham (2024)
28. Salman, H., Sun, M., Yang, G., Kapoor, A., Kolter, J.Z.: Denoised smoothing: a provable defense for pretrained classifiers. In: Advances in Neural Information Processing Systems, vol. 33, pp. 21945–21957 (2020)
29. Shih, G., et al.: Augmenting the national institutes of health chest radiograph dataset with expert annotations of possible pneumonia. Radiol. Artif. Intell. **1**(1), e180041 (2019)
30. Shrestha, P., Amgain, S., Khanal, B., Linte, C.A., Bhattarai, B.: Medical vision language pretraining: a survey. arXiv preprint arXiv:2312.06224 (2023)
31. Shu, M., et al.: Test-time prompt tuning for zero-shot generalization in vision-language models. In: Advances in Neural Information Processing Systems, vol. 35, pp. 14274–14289 (2022)
32. Silva-Rodriguez, J., Chakor, H., Kobbi, R., Dolz, J., Ayed, I.B.: A foundation language-image model of the retina (flair): encoding expert knowledge in text supervision. arXiv preprint arXiv:2308.07898 (2023)
33. Tawsifur, R., et al.: Exploring the effect of image enhancement techniques on Covid-19 detection using chest X-ray images. Comput. Biol. Med. **132**, 104319 (2021)
34. Wang, Z., Wu, Z., Agarwal, D., Sun, J.: Medclip: contrastive learning from unpaired medical images and text. arXiv preprint arXiv:2210.10163 (2022)
35. Yu, B.X., et al.: Visual tuning. ACM Comput. Surv. **56**(12), 1–38 (2024)
36. Zhang, S., Metaxas, D.: On the challenges and perspectives of foundation models for medical image analysis. Med. Image Anal. **91**, 102996 (2024)
37. Zhao, Z., et al.: Clip in medical imaging: a comprehensive survey. arXiv preprint arXiv:2312.07353 (2023)

38. Zhong, Y., Xu, M., Liang, K., Chen, K., Wu, M.: Ariadne's thread: using text prompts to improve segmentation of infected areas from chest X-ray images. In: International Conference on Medical Image Computing and Computer-Assisted Intervention, pp. 724–733. Springer, Cham (2023)
39. Zhou, K., Yang, J., Loy, C.C., Liu, Z.: Learning to prompt for vision-language models. Int. J. Comput. Vis.. **130**(9), 2337–2348 (2022)

Author Index

The manufacturer's authorised representative in the EU is Springer
Nature Customer Service Centre GmbH, Europaplatz 3, 69115 Heidelberg,
Germany. If you have any concerns regarding our products, please
contact ProductSafety@springernature.com

Printed and bound by CPI Group (UK) Ltd, Croydon, CR0 4YY

28/04/2026

02098521-0003